ADVANCE PRAISE

"*Storming Bedlam* presents the history of psychiatry—including bio, social, democratic and demolition psychiatry, as Warren calls it—as a social and political problem. This sharp genealogy is a must read that does not fall into the binary of 'coercive psychiatry' versus 'bad/ good anti-psychiatry.' Instead, it paints a complex picture that analyzes the asylum as a site for critique and experimentation in relation to left movements and revolutions." —**Liat Ben-Moshe**, author of *Disability Incarcerated: Imprisonment and Disability in the United States and Canada* and *Decarcerating Disability: Deinstitutionalization and Prison Abolition*

"*Storming Bedlam* is a sweeping work of meticulous, thoughtful scholarship and a welcome addition to the canons of mad studies and critical histories of psychiatry. Navigating deftly and sensitively between psychiatry and anti-psychiatry, Sasha Warren interrogates this binary in its context of late-stage capitalism that defines madness, sanity, and care in terms of labor and surplus, dictating the parameters of our very lives. As Warren writes: 'We are on fire, and so is the Earth we stand on.' This deeply important book meets the urgent, burning times we inhabit with the unflinching 'weeping gaze of the clown.' *Storming Bedlam* is a book that inflames the imagination; may it provide fuel and sustenance to all seeking to dismantle oppressive technologies of harm and build a world rooted in true care and collective liberation."—**Leah Harris**, psychiatric survivor, activist, and independent journalist

"Sasha Warren's *Storming Bedlam: Madness, Utopia, and Revolt* is a thought-provoking book that challenges conventional narratives around psychiatry and anti-psychiatry by uncovering the radical and reactionary forces that have shaped this history. It is a bold and original work of scholarship that invites us to rethink the past, present, and future of psychiatric revolutions." — **Awais Aftab**, Clinical Assistant Professor of Psychiatry at Case Western Reserve University and editor of *Conversations in Critical Psychiatry*

* * *

T0274684

ISBN: 978-1-942173-89-2 | eBook ISBN: 9781-9-45335-05-1
Library of Congress Number: 2023950461
10 9 8 7 6 5 4 3 2 1

Common Notions
c/o Interference Archive
314 7th St.
Brooklyn, NY 11215

Common Notions
c/o Making Worlds Bookstore
210 S. 45th St.
Philadelphia, PA 19104

www.commonnotions.org
info@commonnotions.org

Discounted bulk quantities of our books are available for organizing, educational,
or fundraising purposes. Please contact Common Notions at the address above
for more information.

Cover design by Josh MacPhee
Layout design and typesetting by Suba Murugan
Printed by union labor in Canada on acid-free paper

STORMING BEDLAM

STORMING BEDLAM
MADNESS, UTOPIA, AND REVOLT

Sasha Warren

Brooklyn, NY
Philadelphia, PA

CONTENTS

DEDICATION

"To those who must go on, who can't go on, who go on."

ACKNOWLEDGMENTS

This book is the culmination of years of independent research, thinking, and struggling. I would never have been able to write this without the unconditional support and love of my partner and my closest friends. Nora Ulseth, you're always there for me no matter what. Our long walks, constant joking, and daily conversations about life, politics, disability, or the small pleasures of life stimulate me and give me a reason to want to get up in the morning. Michael Podgurski, Keegan Kiral, Felix Medina, and clara byczkowski have been my foundation for over a decade. Alie Kiral and Ohli have become just as beloved in half the time. Without the love, stability, and levity I've known from you all from growing up together in Chicago and since, I wouldn't be the person I am today. You all fill me up when I'm running on empty and don't hesitate to call me out when I'm in the wrong. Thank you to my family, to Luke, Leif, my parents, and everyone else who's stuck around through good times and bad.

Minneapolis is my home and the people and places I've come to know here have shown me nothing but kindness and care in my ventures, even when we went our separate ways. I thank the Mississippi River, the cliff overlook near Marshall Avenue, the swimming hole on the St. Croix near Afton, the brave geese at Woodlake Nature Center, the eagles swooping overhead, the woodpeckers in the tree outside my house, and Minnehaha Falls. I thank my dog, Goose, for all the love and even for your startling bark. So many people sustain me, make me laugh, join me on long walks in the woods (where I get us lost), sing and dance with me, and comfort me everyday: the Olson brothers (Jake, Todd, and Matt), Arianna Wegley, Dan Raskin, Joe, Jason, Tara, Jimmy Cooper, Traia, Haley, T, and many more. I have Cassandra Nagle, Robert Crane, and Tianna Crane to thank for welcoming me so warmly to this city I've come to see as my home and for allowing me to be a part of welcoming Harry and Juniper into the world. You all are like family to me.

I thank everyone who encouraged and supported me over the years as I stumbled around trying to find my footing living and working in the weird and sad world of mental health care and social services: Mattie Turner, Kelly Waterman, Matt, Isaiah, Eliot Joy, Liza Gorkova, Rosemary, Megan Moore, Tressa, Sara, E.S., R.W., anyone who's ever passed through at a Hearing Voices meeting, everyone at Cow Tipping Press, and so many more. I have to extend a very special thanks to both Taylor, for being my most consistent cheerleader, for taking time to encourage me and discuss politics with me, and for believing in me and my work through the years even when no one else knew about it or cared; and Lyn Corelle, for inspiring me with your own diverse projects, for always offering to help guide and assist me in my literary endeavors, and for being the first person I trusted to lay eyes on the present text.

I also have to thank all those I've come across over the years in seeking alternative approaches to mental health care. Caroline Mazel-Carlton, your work and the work of the Wildflower Alliance inspires and invigorates me. Seeing what you all have done in MA and attending the Hearing Voices training in St. Paul were profound experiences that helped me figure out what I needed to do. Liat Ben-Moshe, your book totally altered the way I thought about the historiography of institutions in this country and forced me to ask deeper questions than I was. Meeting with you in Chicago taught me so much and I will be forever grateful for your time and encouragement. Susana Caló, I was exuberant when you said you could write a preface because, when I discovered your work, I felt I had truly found the work of a kindred spirit and comrade like never before. Micah Ingle, Leah Harris, Livia Decandra, Celina Vilas-Boas, Zenobia Morrill, Vesper Moore, and everyone at IDHA, especially Jessie Roth: having such intelligent and kind national and international correspondents has made me more sensitive and helped to challenge many of the bad ideas I carried around with me. Mel Butler, you have become so much more to me than a brilliant collaborator, fellow Trieste enthusiast, and interlocutor on all things psychiatry as I now count you among my closest friends.

Finally, thank you to Common Notions, especially Malav Kanuga and Erika Biddle, for your help in preparing this text and for taking the risk in publishing my first book.

PREFACE

In the early 1970s, a four-meters-high blue papier-mâché horse, mounted on wheels and with long legs, was built following the instructions of patients of the Trieste asylum in Italy. Named Marco Cavallo, this horse contained in his belly countless letters, writings, and poetry telling of patient's dreams and hopes. It was named after a much-loved horse that had lived in the asylum carrying the laundry to the wards and had been saved from the slaughterhouse by the patients. Marco Cavallo was so large that it could not fit through the asylum doors on the day, in 1973, when it was taken outside the hospital. The walls had to be broken for it to pass through. It was with this great horse that doctors, patients, artists, and many citizens crossed together the city of Trieste, settling in the town square. In times when psychiatric hospitals were totally closed to the outside world, this gesture was highly symbolic. It was an act of liberation for those who suffered from life in the asylums, a celebration of patients' rights, placing emancipation at the center of care.

Scenes such as this and the movements that upheld them have been systematically excluded from mainstream psychiatric history. This is not just the case of democratic psychiatry, but institutional psychotherapy, social psychiatry, therapeutic communities, the Latin American antimanicomial movement, the medical civil rights movement, among many others. Moreover, the general intertwinement of psychiatry and wider social and political upheavals that characterized these movements have been either erased or pushed to the margins of dominant history. This neglect, along with the progressive dominance of the biomedical model of mental health, has impoverished the practice of psy-disciplines and delayed the much-needed radical transformation of responses to *mental ill-health* and to those suffering today.

Storming Bedlam disrupts this neglect and foregrounds radical attempts to transform psychiatry from within. In Warren's words: "psychiatry moves through the negative and is beholden to it," in an "enchaining and unchaining" movement that "begins at the moment it ends." From the utopian practices of the nineteenth century—which Warren notes were already produced and directed by the activity of patients, and where political visions of psychiatry inspired communist views of society—to the largely neglected psy-practices and political visions of social psychiatry, democratic psychiatry, or the Brazilian anti-asylum struggle, Warren draws an international constellation of progressive psychiatric practices, tracing points of contagion and movement. He frames them as reactions to political contexts and shows their revolutionary roots.

Central to these different practices is a view of illness that stems not from an individual and merely biologically perspective, but rather from the perspective of the material conditions to which it emerges as a response. Warren calls for a materialistic psychiatry against the pathologization of the difficult lives people live. Structural injustices' widely documented effects on health in poor, Indigenous, or racialized communities speaks clearly to the material and political nature of mental ill-health.

Moreover, where illness starts and health ends is a shifting line depending on context. For example, you need to be "mad" enough to be accepted as a survivor-researcher but sane enough for institutions to want to work with you. If you are just a little bit too mad then you are ill. In many aspects of our lives, sanity seems to be defined, often quite explicitly, as the capacity to accept and adjust to an unjust world. When facing these situations, I am often reminded of Jean Oury's notion of "normopathy," the illness whereby the norm is confused with reality, requiring the constant adoption of normative behaviors.

Today, we need to ask: what does it mean to be judged unfit, alienated, or mad in this world disordered by violence, racism, inequality, discrimination, exploitation, homelessness, and poverty? The beauty of Warren's work is that it implicitly conjures an idea of disalienation as therapy. Disalienation, not as an orderly or a-critical adjustment to our realities. On the contrary, as the process by which we can recognize that it is the world that is sick and that the sanest thing to do is to transform it. Such was Fanon's realization in the context of his work in Algeria for whom, as Warren explains, the "only hope for a psychiatry as desalienation is through the decolonizing revolution."

Sasha Warren is showing us that the revolution will be mad. But he refuses to do it on his own. Instead, he weaves many voices and experiences together in his writing and into his work at every turn. *Storming Bedlam* follows in the footsteps of the collective and militant research project *Of Unsound Mind*, a resource library and blog, a space for discussion of histories of psychiatry and its alternatives, that provided a unique portal into *collectively* rethinking the histories of madness, psychiatry, and care.

Storming Bedlam is an ammunition-book against the transformation of the mad into the insane and the capitalist into the sane. As Warren observes, "Normality may be built of stone or steel, but one day, it will crumble and rust. We are all disabled or on our way there; we all have a little bit of madness or will soon. We are united in the dynamism of our separations, our failures, and our shortcomings, limited only by our inability to appropriate them against a common nightmare."

Those who have struggled to find the words and the examples to convey that alternatives are always possible will cherish this book. After reading this book, if you find yourself asking "what now?"—you can start by lending the book to a friend. Because we will only be free together.

Susana Caló
December 2023

CHAPTER 1

THE WHITE RAT

I dream and cannot wake, and I am cast over the cliff and hang there
by two fingers that are danced and trampled on by the Giant Unreality.
—Janet Frame[1]

Since the end of the eighteenth century, every innovative generation of psychiatrists has set out to construct utopia in the midst of revolution, affirm humanity in war, wrench order from chaos. Every generation, in their disavowal of what this origin demands, eventually watched in dismay as their neat and orderly plans descended into nihilism and their beautiful constructions mutated into pale imitations of the paradise they proudly unveiled, if not custodial heaps for human refuse. In the scramble to maintain a shine on their ruins, they set the stage for the mechanical reproduction of drudgery and abandonment. The epic of psychiatry is the fever dream of restless utopians. Horrific monsters emerge from the shadows as the night falls on each grand, patricidal gesture like clockwork.

We have grown accustomed to reading about asylum psychiatry as the project of states seeking new, subtler means of social control. However, at its points of origin in France and England, psychiatry was among the most radical and promising of the reform movements that proliferated during the Industrial and French Revolutions. Unlike the reformers opening prisons or schools, its founders were motivated by a revolutionary approach to sociability that resembled nothing so closely as the socialist utopias of Robert Owen and Charles Fourier. In the early nineteenth century, psychiatrists in the moral treatment movement championed a therapeutic model that not only acted as if the mad person was human, but also that—in the best environmental and architectural conditions, immersed in a consciously and collectively organized social world, engaged in meaningful reproductive

I

labor in common—the asylum could prefigure a more perfect world for all. Some went even further still, arguing that the physician ought to put themselves on a level ground with the patients and abolish as far as possible the distinction between the professional healer and the receiver of care. In successive generations, the dream of utopia changed with the times, but its basic perimeters stayed the same. The radical movements of the twentieth and twenty-first centuries that went by the names Institutional Psychotherapy, Democratic Psychiatry, Therapeutic Communities, or Anti-Asylum Movements—the focus of the majority of the present book—were prefigured by the utopian movements of the nineteenth and can be understood as having tried to apply the lessons learned from their failures as far as possible in their own conditions. This book is an attempt at an immanent critique of the dream of utopia at the heart of the psychiatric project, its cycles of hope and despair, and the various attempts to consciously mold it into a socializing machine for liberation.

In order to do so, we must first draw, in a general outline, the maze of exhaustion that psychiatry, its apologists, and its critics find themselves lost in.

THE CHAINBREAKERS

Although its real origins are difficult to place, the mythic origins of modern psychiatry undoubtedly lay in the eighteenth century with the appearance of moral treatment. In 1876, the artist Tony Robert-Fleury depicted the most central of these mythic scenes with his *Pinel at the Salpêtriére* (often translated as *Pinel Freeing the Insane*), which memorializes what has become the central mythic event in modern psychiatric history when the young physician, Phillipe Pinel, recently assigned to the women-only Salpêtriére and animated by the spirit of the French Revolution, freed his patients from their chains in 1795. Left of center, you can see Pinel, one hand holding a cane, the other being kissed in supplication by an inmate of the Salpêtriére. The fully clothed benevolent doctors seem to arrive on the scene already endowed with the spirit of the Revolution and the Rights of Man, approaching the frenzied and half-naked madwomen with a mix of objective observation represented by the figure examining the woman's arm in the center and humanist recognition of the plight of the unfortunate.[2] While his peers had long succumbed to a therapeutic nihilism and chained the mad to walls to contain a threat—which, if not curable, could at least be kept at a comfortable distance from an already disorderly society—Pinel introduced an empirical approach to the study of madness, producing a systematic nosology that redrew the lines between types of madness by means of observation and rational deduction. The approach suggested that, with proper management and a humane central authority, patients could dramatically improve or even be cured of their mental alienation. In this story, Pinel serves as Atlas, singlehandedly carrying the weight of a new era of psychiatry regulated by the scientific spirit, humanism, and incipient medical norms on his republican shoulders.

The story is a great one, but it isn't exactly true. The original chain removal event took place at the men's Bicêtre hospital, where Pinel worked prior to transferring to the Salpêtriére and it happened in 1797, two years *after* he'd left, and was performed by the supervisor Jean-Baptiste Pussin. (Later, Pinel did supervise the removal of chains at the Salpêtriére, following his supervisor's example.) Nor was Pinel's, or rather Pussin's, act of removing chains the decisive break with tradition it has come to represent. When Pinel removed the chains of patients at the Salpêtriére, he did it with a select group under strict surveillance and replaced their chains with straitjackets. The nonrestraint movement found more success at Tuke's Quaker Retreat for the mad in England and became a requisite feature of every humanist and reformist psychiatry after: from the German neuropsychiatric or somatic turn beginning with Wilhelm Griesinger in Germany in the 1860s, closer to the time Robert-Fleury was painting, to the community psychiatry and deinstitutionalization movements between 1950–1980 in the US. Pinel was also far from the first to introduce the empirical or medical gaze into psychiatry or the moral principle of proper management: Thomas Willis, to name just one example, already connected psychological disturbance to the functions in "the Brain and Nervous Stock" in the seventeenth century,[3] while William Battie had already challenged the medical nihilism of John Monro at Bethlem when he suggested that madness was curable and ought to be cared for in well-managed environs at St. Luke's Hospital in 1751.[4]

But the strength of the Pinel story has always come from its mythic dimensions and what it suggests about the origins and purposes of the psychiatric field. In fact, Pinel's own contemporaries, specifically his family and students, already intuited the sentimental power of an emancipatory founding myth. His own son Scipion, just ten years after his death, falsely recounted the event to the Royal Academy of Medicine in 1836 as Pinel's heroic act of rebellion against the Committee of Public Safety guided by an interest in "his patients' right to personal freedom."[5] Compared to such retellings, Robert-Fleury's painting is among the more faithful depictions of the historic event within this narrative tradition, despite its inaccuracies. In the 1840s and '50s, republican Paris memorialized the invented gesture in a number of productions that claimed Pinel the liberator as one of their own (despite his ambivalent relationship to the Revolution[6]): from a painting by Charles Müller that hangs in the lobby of the Paris Academy of Medicine to streets named after him and busts of his head.[7] Of all these manifold productions, the most politically evocative of all was the unveiling of a statue of Pinel before the Salpêtrière by La Société Médico-Psychologique on July 13, 1885, "thus linking the breaking of the chains with the storming of the Bastille,"[8] drawing the psychiatric revolution definitively into the sphere of republican social transformations.

The partisans of neuropsychiatry were no less inspired in their appropriation of the past. A contemporary of Robert-Fleury, Pierre Aristide André Brouillet made a painting in 1887 called *A Clinical Lesson at the Salpêtrière* that mirrors select elements of the earlier image in a distilled and intensified form. Here, the objective observation of a woman's body in the same institution—this time by the new star of the Salpêtrière, Jean-Martin Charcot—is again the dominant theme, but the masculine observers have multiplied and the feminine object of study has been reduced to just one.[9] The scene is no longer set outside with its attendant distractions, but in an enclosed and controllable observation theater. Charcot is in a heroic position demanding the attention of his colleagues, but he is not the sole central figure. The central figure with which he shares the stage is not a person at all, but a reflex hammer and an electrotherapy device on a table, present to demonstrate that the institution's medical gaze has become increasingly quantitative, empirical, and scientific. Though they depict scenes set nearly a hundred years apart, both feature women displaying their agony through the same contorted gestures: behind the main figure in

Robert-Fleury's scene, a woman writhes on the ground in a classic but anachronistic hysterical pose better suited to this later era of Charcot than to Pinel's time.[10] It is in this context that Sigmund Freud, attending Charcot's lectures in 1885–1886 at the Salpêtrière, "which had witnessed so many horrors during the Revolution," could look upon the famous image of "citizen Pinel" and no doubt take pride in acts that framed his place of learning as "the scene of this most humane of all revolutions."[11] Robert-Fleury and his contemporaries, it seems, were not really interested in portraying a historical event at all; rather, they were projecting an ideal back onto the past that led naturally into the rational and humane present. The kernel of truth in Pinel's act has matured into a fully formed approach that naturally culminates with what already exists in the present. The past here serves above all to justify and exalt the contemporary world.

"Pinel the Chainbreaker" might be the most universal of psychiatric myths, but it's certainly not the only one. In England, they have the kind Tuke family, Quakers whose religious and humane sensibilities led them to open their own Retreat in York where the mad would learn to live like anybody else, without chains or fetters. In the US, we have the more ambiguous figure of Benjamin Rush (most of our national heroes require numerous qualifications and justifications, even from their most avid defenders), who is called the "founding father" of American psychiatry for writing the first US treatise on madness and caring for the mad in the first hospital wing designed for that purpose in the country. The appellation is doubly appropriate because Rush was also a red-blooded partisan of the Revolution, having served as a medic, and a signer of the Declaration of Independence. His reputation as a progressive thinker is somewhat marred by his passion for heroic medicine—like bloodletting or purging—and his tranquilizing inventions that look like nothing other than devices for torture. Vincenzo Chiarugi is much less known or written about outside of Italy, but he implemented elements of the moral treatment system prior to Pinel in 1780s Florence.[12] The original psychiatric breakthroughs of Phillipe Pinel, William Tuke, Benjamin Rush, or Vincenzo Chiarugi may have occurred at the turn of the nineteenth century, but their projects were mostly small and local; the systematization and implementation of their founding myths as a symbol for a rational system fell to the following generations who painted their predecessors' heroic deeds on their flags and banners. The influential American Psychiatric Institute uses Rush's face on their logo. It would not have been uncommon to see Robert-Fleury's image in an office or a library in an asylum, even as far away as the superintendent's office at the Central State Hospital in Indianapolis, which one can still visit as part of their museum tour. Even the patient newsletter of the New York State Lunatic Asylum in Utica, *The Opal*, adorned its cover with an image of Pinel beginning in 1851.

Why have these images, and the scenes they represent, proved to be so persistent in the history of psychiatry? What does positioning Pinel's removal of the chains as either the inaugural or paradigmatic event of modern psychiatry communicate about the history of the profession? It depends on your angle. It could suggest that it emerged as a force of humanitarian goodwill in a barbaric age. Over time, one can say, the heroic spark of Enlightenment has steadily grown brighter and now shines in the hearts and minds of the American Psychiatric Association (APA) and the National Institute of Mental Health (NIMH), which, despite the occasional scandal or two, are fundamentally oriented towards healing and liberating people from suffering. With more precision, it could allow one to tie medical paradigms to political transformations, positing causal circuits between, for instance, increasing administrative rationalizations with rationalizations in the categories of illness or systems of treatment. Finally, it could allow the inventors of modern epistemological approaches and therapeutic methods to trace their origins back to a seed planted in the soil of humble scientific inquiry. Regardless of interpretation, it's clear that psychiatry as a field cannot rid itself of the usage of symbols and organizing myths. Unlike other professions more exacting in their deployment, it produces and diffuses them constantly and vacillates between myths of a near opposite character. A myth of near total curability of the insane was supplanted by the nihilist myth that madness was the fruit of hereditary degeneration, the myth of the therapeutic function of removal into an asylum is today totally overshadowed by the myth of the mass transfer of the mad into prisons; the history of the field's pretensions and despair could be told in recounting the procession and subsequent deflation of totalizing myths. The core of this mythic longing is rootlessness: psychiatric camps—split by emphasis, organization, methods, objects, and understandings of the cause of insanity—live in the wake of their own Tower of Babel, unable to speak to one another clearly or without disdain. Such a situation evinces a profound lack of unity around the field's central justification or purpose.[13]

The roots of psychiatry's tortured conscience reach much further still, torn as it is between utopian dreams and bitter realities. Both its practitioners and its patients have presented its practice and legacy as a singular hope of redemption and balm in the face of civilization's ills, or negatively as the glue holding social disintegration at bay. The developmental or progressive ("whiggish") conception of medical history is the preferred interpretive schema for these true believers in psychiatry's universal mission. Its central apostle today is the historian Edward Shorter, who refers to the introduction of chlorpromazine (the first major antipsychotic) as a "revolution in psychiatry comparable to the introduction of penicillin in general medicine,"[14] but he's merely the newest scribe in a tradition including Albert Deutsch, Grigory Zilboorg, and others. Though each has their own favored method and tradition, they generally agree with Zilboorg's appraisal of psychiatry as a fundamentally humanist discipline: "The history of psychiatry," he tells us,"is essentially the history of humanism. . . . Every time the spirit of humanism has arisen, a new contribution to psychiatry has been made."[15] Progressivism suggests that psychiatrists today can symbolically and practically trace their practice directly back to Pinel's (or Tuke's, Kirkbride's, Freud's or any number of others') original act and that, over time, practices, diagnostic tools, and treatments that appeared in primitive form in his time have developed to become an altogether greater and more advanced whole. But the poetry of salvation, in a historic register or otherwise, is not merely the work of social reformers and professional historians: a profound optimism verging at times on revolutionary enthusiasm or religious revival has accompanied every great wave of psychiatric reform from the nineteenth century "cult of curability," whose proponents claimed the miraculous ability to cure all or almost all of the hopeless and mangled humanity under their control,[16] to the profound optimism of the somatic psychiatrists heralding the introduction of pathological anatomy in getting to the root of the proper classification and treatment of madness and the later discovery of the psychiatric "penicillin," Largactil.

Equally active are the revisionists who paint the legacy of psychiatry as one long, convoluted justification for state control or torture.

Thomas Szasz is doubtless the most infamous of the historians of suspicion. Naive tales of progress are only evidence that "we systematically delude ourselves by interpreting changing fashions in scapegoating as moral or scientific progress."[17] His major work dealing with psychiatric history, *The Manufacture of Madness*, consists of an extended analogy between the witch hunts and psychiatry, and an appendix that juxtaposes significant dates in their histories to the system of slavery, antisemitic legislation, and a number of other legally sanctioned forms of exclusion and persecution. The point is clear: the system in place for managing mental alienation is an abuse of enormous proportions, manufactured in the service of a Therapeutic State as a tool of social control.

But these two positions are not as far apart as they may appear at first glance: an enlightened break opening the door to progress often relies on a prehistory of horror and degradation; oftentimes, the difference between these narratives of horror or progress is whether or not the *telos*, the end point, has already been achieved in the present or lies in the future. Shorter can write his tale of glory because psychopharmaceuticals are already pervasive; Szasz's crusade to privatize the field—to make every encounter "voluntary" while leaving deviance to the police and prisons—has thankfully not come to pass. What's common between these two is the corrosive venom each has for the villains. Every writer and commentator on the history of psychiatry cannot help but note that what Andrew Scull calls "a culture of complaint"[18] has fermented in its guts since birth, making it the only medical field which has had its every step mirrored and countered by a shadowy doppelgänger, "antipsychiatry," an amalgam of various groups formed specifically to counter its scope and legitimacy. This term is usually used to refer to the long history of patient complaints extending back to the nineteenth century; to a movement from around the late 1960s through to the 1980s of psychiatrists, students, activists, and ex-patients who opposed parts or all of psychiatry; or to all of this together up through to the present.

Such formulations are too weak and limited. At worst, they limit a period of critique (even wholesale rejection) to specific time periods or only at the fringes, as if it wasn't present at all times and at the very heart of the discipline. Samuel Tuke reports that his family's Quaker Retreat for the mad—one of the earliest locations where moral treatment was practiced—was proposed after the death of a Friend at the hands of a superintendent in York.[19] Their moral humanist enthusiasm was built on the negative evaluation of the failures of medical psychiatry.[20] Pinel's reduction of restraint and John Conolly's implementation of a more complete system of nonrestraint at the Middlesex County Asylum at Hanwell in the 1840s would have been robbed of their symbolic power if they weren't inheriting "massive and gloomy mansions" that "were but prisons of the worst description."[21] More fundamentally, the great psychiatric revolutions (Pinel or Tuke's humanist moral treatment, the curability of the asylum, the discovery of antipsychotics) would not be deserving of the name had they not effected a sufficient break with the past. Psychiatry moves through the negative and is beholden to it. In other words, psychiatry is not countered by antipsychiatry as if by a foreign army marching on the backs of elephants over the mountain: it is founded in it and requires it for its dynamic permeation through the social world. But the negative spares none; in due time, the shepherds of men and architects of the great citadels of human reason would be characterized as rapacious villains and builders of prisons. Pinel's great unchaining is not just a mythic origin, it is a point on a circle—a revolution in the original sense of setting a practice in motion on an orbit suspended in space. Enchaining and unchaining are two overlapping scenes of a mad tragedy that begins where it ends.

A painting by the Canadian psychiatric patient William Kurelek called *The Maze* depicts this dilemma better than any founding myth. Kurelek painted *The Maze* in 1953 while interred at Maudsley Hospital in London, where Sir Aubrey Lewis (an optimist if there ever was one) was the senior psychiatrist. A skull lies immobile on the ground, facing away and cut in half with some pieces broken off. Within the skull, we see a number of scenes that don't flow from one into the next, but rather, are contained and juxtaposed violently against one another all at once. Horrible domestic scenes play out in the confinement of thin walls keeping the decay and rot and predation of the natural world at a precarious remove. In a lower segment, a gang of medical doctors stand in tight claustrophobic circles around a naked man in a test tube and poke and prod at him with pens and tools. Though the body is a framing device and some red ribbons evoking torn nerve fibers or veins hang here and there like drapery at a theater, the organic explains nothing on its own. It may appear that the scenes remain inaccessible to one another, but there are still similarities between the various scenes: a crow eating a lizard resembles the doctors prodding at the man; nature, war, domesticity, medicine, and art all exist side by side in this skull, which is furthermore permeable to the outside world, since the walls are open on our side. The irregular shape of the walls and heterogeneity of the figures and events exclude the possibility of linear progression, seeming rather to suggest that any movement between positions can only happen when one burrows into a new field only to pass, in a moment of crisis, typically a moment of extreme violence or degradation, into another. Reality—and more specifically, medicine—in this world is not the smooth development of an original idea towards perfection, but the irruption of contradictions that break with the norm and alter our perception of the image as a whole from moment to moment. The past does not run fluidly into the present, but bursts forward in particular moments of clarity and association. Where do these sudden transformations leave us? Look closely and you'll see small holes burrowed out from each segment, as if by a rat. We are looking, as the name makes clear, at a maze. Pick a direction and dig: move from the beating of a young boy to the colors and symbols of Ukrainian nationalism (Kurelek was of Ukrainian descent) to the dance of marionettes. Separate though they may be, the events belong to a single social and biological world such that everything past is present all at once, provided one knows where to look. There's no escape from artifice and decay, not even in the natural world: a ball is attended by automata; a man studies death by reference to a textbook rather than the skeleton in the room. Every burst into the new already contains the nucleus of a past deterioration and will end in a similar disappointment.

In his own interpretation of his work, Kurelek provides a succinct description of the "choice" faced by psychiatric patients in a section called "My Social Relations." Referring to the bottom center and left panels of the maze with a man lying in ditch, crows eating a lizard, and a group of doctors around a patient, he wrote: "Choice between A) the hospital, with its ordeal of the panel (I in the test tube), interpreted in two ways, 1) as a malevolent persecution, or 2) and a benevolent conspiracy: or B) the outside world – I continue to be the outcast, skirting the smooth level highway of life in the ditch behind the hedge, sensitive to being seen in the light."[22] And time just moves on: the following panels on life present existence as a museum of hopelessness and a conveyor belt towards destruction marked by the ticking clock. The white rat in the center, he says, "represents my spirit" and has "curled up in frustration from having run the passages so long without hope of escaping out of this maze of unhappy thoughts." Those of us concerned with the question of alienation look upon the history of psychiatry like the white rat, depleted and curled up into ourselves. Like the rat, we too are barely enticed by the possibilities that beckon from the outside world; like the man surveying the field, we are choked by bitter experiences, turning our eyes, tongues, and hearts into sharp burrs that we can't seem to shake. The best one can hope for, it seems, is to find some nook or corner where one can harbor the illusion of doing one good thing as long as possible before the inevitable realization that everything has already long fallen apart at the seams.

FROM THE POLITICS OF PSYCHIATRY TO PSYCHOPOLITICS

Psychiatry's mythic wanderings are not those of desert wayfarers in search of an oasis. There is no therapeutic desert waiting to be mapped and filled with institutions. To the psychiatrist's general dismay, their practices and forms of knowledge are tied forever to some of the greatest tumults of history: revolutions, wars, plagues, crises. The most efficacious way to temper the inherent instability of such a connection is to reduce these to "social factors" that alchemically mutate otherwise solid categories into liquids. Everyone will concede that madness enjoys some level of conceptual fluidity in everyday speech and culture. We call lots of things "crazy," many people or ideas "insane" or "psychotic." Politicians are narcissistic or psychopathic. On the granular level, one might cruelly refer to women one doesn't like as "borderline" or "hysterical." But in periods of insurrection, madness is less like a river with contained tributaries flowing out into culture or language and more like a torrential storm drenching entire populations and events. Satirical images of American Revolutionaries with syphilitic madness spreading the gospel of democracy and anarchy were designed and printed by the British during the war. The brief explosion of the Paris Commune birthed the figure of the *petroleuse*, the pyromaniac women who savagely burned the city and became a commonplace representation in the popular press virtually overnight.[23] It wasn't just the mudslingers in the popular press; the most respected psychiatrists also partook in political diagnostics. Pinel traded in this kind of discourse during the French Revolution, asking in his diagnostic writings, to what extent revolution either causes or cures insanity, or is itself the product of some sort of insanity.[24] The founding father of American psychiatry, Benjamin Rush, warned that the Revolution, a singular force of emancipation in the world, risked unleashing a "passion for liberty," which, if unchecked and unrestrained by reason or government, "constituted a form of insanity, which I shall take the liberty of distinguishing by the name of anarchia."[25] It seems that the barrier between sanity and madness, between the normal and the deviant, becomes thinner and more fluid as the social world is rapidly transformed and the bases for making such determinations are uprooted and destroyed.

The link between insanity and politics was integrated into psychiatric rhetoric in the question posed first in the nineteenth century and then in virtually every period of crisis: *does civilization cause insanity*? To the psychiatrists in the burgeoning city centers of Europe and the Americas, it seemed indisputable that the troublesome ranks of the insane were swelling, but why?[26] A romantic conservative thesis held that progress was demolishing the old world and its traditional virtues—gone was the good, old family, swept away by the winds of industry and all the evils it carries with it.[27] Various iterations of the civilization theory have been framed in terms of refinement and shock. Sir Andrew Halliday, for one, held that "[the] finer the organs of the mind have become by their greater development, or their better cultivation, if health is not made a part of the process, the more easily are they disordered."[28] It's only a short step from here to the nineteenth century's dominant racial theory of madness explaining why "savages" and slaves can only become mad following their induction into the sensitive universe of Western civilization, as Halliday's words themselves attest: "We seldom meet with insanity among the savage tribes of men."[29] "Civilization" is such a mighty word that it threatens to collapse under its own weight with connotations so broad as to mean nothing on its own. But that didn't stop it from becoming the central justification for the inherently therapeutic nature of early commitment. For if civilization's speed and intensity and the density and stress of city life were causing people to go mad, the first step was to swiftly and decisively remove the afflicted from this noxious environment, in order to sever their relations to anything and everything that posed a risk, radically scrubbing away all pathogenic residue to provide a clean slate for recovery. To ensure a quick rupture with the crazy-making speed of progress, commitment laws in France, Germany, the US, and elsewhere became increasingly lax in the mid-nineteenth century.[30] In their minds, little risk was involved for, once the patient was inevitably cured, they could be returned to their normal life post haste.

At the core of the civilization question is the idea that exciting factors of a certain intensity received by organs of variable sensitivity lie at the root of madness. The civilization thesis survived in modified forms, appearing repeatedly at times of great crisis: newly emancipated people at the end of the Civil War were presumed to be insane at exponentially higher rates because of their incapacity to deal with freedom;[31] the desultory effects of the apocalyptic wars of the twentieth century on the psyches of millions destabilized existing categories and gave us shell shock and eventually Post-Traumatic Stress Disorder (PTSD); in 2021, it's taken for granted that anxiety over climate change, political violence, and COVID-19 outbreaks have a disintegrative effect on global mental health. Positing a causal link between madness and events in the public sphere is the most constant gesture of the social psychiatric approach shared by both its proponents and critics, but it's also one of the most superficial. It does not yet tell us what is political about psychiatry or even madness *in themselves*, but only what political externalities they react to; in this causal relation, psychiatry does not yet reveal itself as psychopolitics, because politics remains an independent variable making occasional intrusions. We must also ask why psychiatry appears on the scene with revolutions or periods of rapid urbanization in settler-colonies as a necessary component of the new order. Why, in other words, has a systematic mental health program been a constitutive feature of liberal democracies and capitalist development since the Industrial and French Revolutions?

The most expressive image of the political analysis of psychiatry has been that of the state wielding psychiatric diagnoses or treatments as a political tool for shaping or controlling a populace. Enraptured as the world still is by Cold War fantasies, the Soviet category of "sluggish schizophrenia" and the incarceration and doping of political dissidents serve as archetypical examples of a state's appropriation of medicine to achieve explicitly political goals.[32] But what this example gains in terms of clarity, it lacks in terms of general applicability, as such clear-cut partisan appropriations of medical techniques have largely been undertaken by states in crisis or during the chaotic period of founding a settler-colony or dictatorship and were part of a general strategy of terror directed towards the population through the figure of the dissident.[33] In the French settler-colony in Algeria described by Frantz Fanon, *every* available institution and form of knowledge was mobilized to further entrench the invaders' mode of life and justify their invasion such that "[t]he colonized perceives the doctor, the engineer, the schoolteacher, the policeman, the rural constable, through the haze of an almost organic confusion."[34] But even here, Fanon's analysis has moved beyond a simple theory of instrumentalization. A generalization of the theory of instrumentalism has become a key tenet of groups in favor of the abolition of psychiatry who hold that the field is consciously maintained from elite, inaccessible back rooms as an organized weapon for a state with more or less clear underlying goals. The Madness Network News Collective, founded and run by ex-psychiatric patients in California, advanced this Szasz-influenced thesis in a particularly clear fashion in the Summer 1986 edition of their newsletter: "*We believe* that psychiatry is an oppressive, systematic method of social control, operating under the guise of medicine [that is] used by every form of government, regardless of political/economic system, to intimidate, control, monitor, and regulate society."[35] It's not hard to come up with examples of moments when psychiatrists characterized their work as a complex defense mechanism of society or of genetic purity, as in the widespread use of sterilization in mental institutions in the twentieth century or their justification of incarceration by emphasizing the future "danger" of patients.

Programmatic injunctions pertaining to the profession's role in the defense of society arise at the initial scene of every psychiatric plan and change. In 1751, Benjamin Franklin petitioned for a hospital to remove the increasing number of people "distempered in Mind" who were "a Terror to their Neighbors."[36] More recently, proponents of negative eugenics (sterilization, sequestration, euthanasia) frequently relied on warnings about the "unfitness" of the insane's degenerate genes, which persisted even through revelations of what devastating consequences this ardent defense of racial purity and public order brought about in Nazi Germany—though with dampened enthusiasm and less publicity.

Compelling though they are, it's not yet evident from these examples (and there are countless more) whether psychiatry has an inherent predisposition to political exploitation or domination any more than schools, engineering, or other medical fields (e.g., epidemiology) that take the population as an object of study and intervention do. The theories and critiques recounted above, with the notable exception of Fanon, usually treat psychiatry as a medical discipline organized and directed *in relation* to an independent body they call "society," which transmutes values into institutions and has or produces a number of problems that the state is tasked with solving. The critical analysis of psychiatry and politics has generally not been able to escape the parameters set out by the adherents of the civilization thesis: it's still a matter of teasing out the "effects" of political events, social facts, or cultural distinctions on psychiatry and vice versa. Since the 1960s, questioning the medical model has been the centerpiece and starting point of almost every critique of psychiatry, such that its seeming opposite, the theory of social causation, has consistently been associated with a left-leaning critique of institutional psychiatry. Unfortunately, it's not as simple as adopting one or another etiology, for the history of psychiatry suggests that a model that values social causes over organic ones doesn't de facto take the side of progressive initiatives but can just as easily serve the needs of those rallying for a renewed reverence of the trinity of social stability and moral rectitude: *back to the soothing comforts of the Family, State, and Church!* When the critic denounces psychiatry as a tool in the hands of a malevolent sovereign power, the apologist joins in with them to decry the "politicization" of the field. More troubling still, we must keep in mind that the great segregative clearinghouses—the penitentiary, the asylum, and the almshouse— appeared at a time of great clamor for change and were positioned as the avant-garde of social reform, not as exclusively medical institutions.

We have been told—not for the first time—that we are in a transitional phase between the domination of a biomedical reductionist model and something that might be called a "biopsychosocial" one. In 2011, the World Health Organization member states adopted the International Classification of Functioning, Disability and Health, or ICF, a tool for measuring a population's health and disability, which is based on the biopsychosocial model. For them, this entails viewing levels of disability as "outcomes of interactions between health conditions (diseases, disorders and injuries) and contextual factors."[37] Other national and international agencies have followed suit, especially in their research models. The federal NIMH[38] has adopted a model that divides areas of research into functional circuits, which interact with one another and subdivide individual units (for example, "fear" or "arousal") into their elements (molecular, cellular, behavioral, etc.). "Paradigm shifts" such as these would sound impressive were they not psychiatry's version of a major Hollywood franchise, appearing year after year with flashy aesthetics promising great change but retaining the same underlying structure. Viewed from afar, psychiatry is full of stories of an optimistic, apparently progressive push sliding into pessimism, custodialism, and abuse. From Pinel's revolution up to Vichy France's soft extermination of mental patients, the neuropsychiatric revolution in late-nineteenth-century Europe to the horrors of Nazi science, the hubris of colonial Christians "saving" people in China or South Africa by building custodial asylums, or the formulation of "reactive neuroses" following World War I to the rise of the mental health movement opening doors to the much-maligned psychiatrization of small differences. Each of these revolutions began with a negative evaluation of their predecessors and ended in failure. The great cathedrals of healing are periodically revealed to be nothing but cages painted in gold every few years by the next generation of reformers. Why should we believe that the rise of "holistic" diagnostic and research approaches would be any different? It appears that we are still in the position of the white rat, exhausted from running laps trying to determine the form and function of a branch of medicine that appears at once as "a malevolent persecution" and "a benevolent conspiracy." The difference between the two appears to be a simple matter of perspective and emphasis, or the selective mobilization of data revealing a salvational or hellish essence. One tips seamlessly into the other and it seems there's no way out.

Psychopolitics begins here: at the end of the maze of causes and effects, cornered and tired. "Scarcely one year has gone by, and everything has taken on a new countenance," wrote Pinel in reference to the French Revolution.[39] Benjamin Rush arrived at a similar observation from his experience in Philadelphia: "The revolution interested every inhabitant of the country of both sexes, and of every rank and age that was capable of reflection. An indifferent, or neutral spectator of the controversy, was scarcely to be found in any of the states."[40] One could certainly speak here of specific discrete causes in the Revolution (public beheadings, the shock of rapid change, the loss of property, etc.), but Pinel and Rush outline something more constitutive than the tender enticements of influence. The revolutions they describe are not the causes of a state of affairs; they alter the *medium* within which one articulates their movements, opening all future judgements to a mesh of criteria and demands unthinkable prior to their appearance together. In the context of a total transformation and the birth of a new state to regulate relations, in what empty field would such causes play out? From what neutral vantage point could an observer possibly view such an interaction? To speak here of cause or effect, or masters with their tools, takes too much for granted; it's already gone much too far. We can also begin to question here the progressivist or neutral posturing of the historians: when and under what conditions can someone adopt the posture of neutrality? Academics and experts may weigh the intellectual merits of one or another approach (social or organic? Political or scientific?), but what revolution and insurrection illuminates for those who live through them is the impossibility of nonparticipation, an insight that may press on the mind with more force under the duress of war, but which pertains just as well to peacetime. There are political determinations, but then there are events that define the social web within which any determinations at all occur. These transform the field on which any position at all is taken; to decline is already to stake a claim on the battlefield by naturalizing the existent.

Psychiatry was born in the bloody revolutions of the eighteenth and especially nineteenth century on that sliver of Earth in the dominion of ascendent capital condemning droves of newly fashioned proletarians to factories billowing hellfire and smoke spreading West in an anarchic advance, the attempted exterminations of native populations, and rising tensions in the slave industry. No space or institution was spared from polarization and disruption. Psychiatry took its first baby steps during the Revolutions—to the applause of learned men and philanthropists the world over—but didn't really get off the ground until the first decades of the nineteenth century. Prior to the 1820s in the US, the largest practices were based in the wealthier cities of long-settled states on the East Coast like Massachusetts and Virginia and they were primarily private, available mainly to people of means. So, what happened in the early nineteenth century? According to David Rothman's influential thesis in *The Discovery of the Asylum*, anxiety around population growth and urbanization is the key to the spread of psychiatric institutions. Rothman argues that throughout the eighteenth century, and particularly towards the end, the population continued to grow rapidly. But more importantly than simple population growth, after the Revolution, urban cores became densely populated, factories began to pop up all over the East Coast, and increasing enfranchisement of a broader swathe of the white male population gave us Andrew Jackson and the gospel of Western expansion with its bloodthirsty annihilation of the Native people who lived there. Rapid growth and expansion along with a general atmosphere of upheaval and violence induced immense swells of anxiety, particularly among social reformers, about the spread of crime and disorder arising from dislocations, mass migrations, and the overwhelming sense of transformation. The spirit of millennium was in the air and the social world appeared rife with chaos, crime, poverty, and lunacy.

Andrew Scull has, on more than one occasion, scrutinized Rothman's vagaries about this general anxiety thesis and his dependence on the meaninglessly broad category of "the Americans."[41] Scull rightly localizes this anxiety in the growth of capitalism and the disruption wrought in ever-increasing intensity across the continent and, soon enough, the world through privatization as its incessant growth compelled subsistence laborers to become wage workers dependent on market imperatives and irreparably reshaped the crust and waters of the Earth in its insatiable need to transform the living world into disposable material. Capital's propensity to scatter the familiar into the four winds didn't appear overnight and neither did the processes that catenate it to recurring series of social crises. Indeed, wherever it appeared, "[i]ncreased unemployment, higher prices, enclosures of peasant lands and related factors brought into being the problems of unemployment, vagrancy, and beggary."[42] Proletarianization—the severance of laborers from the means of subsistence such that they are compelled to sell their labor-power to survive—stretched the family and local community's capacity to provide for members excluded from the market, leading to a widespread demand for some mechanism of relief.

Already in the more developed urban centers of Europe of the fourteenth and fifteenth centuries and the Arab world in the eighth century, religious institutions and meager stockades proved themselves incapable of containing the common rabble, including the mad, a deficiency that rapidly accelerated wherever capitalist relations appeared. It's an odd fact that hospitals up until the nineteenth century were not exclusively, nor always even primarily, medical in character—despite major exceptions like the famous Bedlam—but were first and foremost places of segregation.[43] Massive clearinghouses for various outsiders corresponds to the earlier periods of the capitalist market, when the primary directives were to sort out the able-bodied (in this case, minded) laborer from the nonproductive, provide a bare means of subsistence for those excluded from exploitation, and to relieve the working class family of unsupportable excess. With the development of legal statutes and police regulations, the disorderly mad were generally included as a part of poor laws[44] or vagrancy statutes. No rigorous attempt was made to classify the mad or cater treatment to their needs. Thus, many early madhouses were privately owned and operated as glorified workhouses, exploiting free labor in exchange for removing individuals who were increasingly unmanageable for their families or the public. In the letter of the law, disorderly lunatics were scarcely distinguishable from rabid animals. In Tokyo during the Meiji Restoration, police regulations still "put the rules for the regulation of lunatics next to those about unrestrained and dangerous animals on the street, such as oxen, horses and mad dogs" until reforms in the successive decades.[45] For the lunatics who were not quite like "a brute or a wild beast,"[46] however, chaining was not deemed an unquestionably correct course and eclecticism in treatment was supreme, so to speak of a "great confinement" or rational plan at this juncture would be out of place. One might've passed a harmless madman on the street and taken little notice; or seen one through the window of a sketchy practitioner of physic bleeding them liberally by the light of a full moon after prescribing whatever new panacea was on offer that year, whether hellebore or the painful blows of a whip; or finally perhaps in the garden of the village church, being splashed with holy water and incantations.[47]

On account of their excessive depravities and deprivations, the dungeons and houses of segregation earned reputations far outsizing their spread or stature. The utopians, who rode to glory behind General Pinel with a broken chain around their necks, defined their mission in lurid contrast to these zones of disrepute and horror. The greatest rhetorician among them, W. A. F. Browne, superintendent of the Montrose Lunatic Asylum from 1834–1838 and Crichton Royal Hospital from 1838–1857, denounced these glorified "bastiles" as nothing but a massive "wretched and comfortless prison-house," where the lunatic was "left to linger out a lifetime of misery, without any rational attempt at treatment, without employment, without a glimpse of happiness, or a hope of liberation, he was terrified or starved into submission, lashed, laughed at, despised, forgotten."[48] One would be hard-pressed to find a similarly vicious indictment of one's forebears among even the so-called antipsychiatrists of the 1960s or '70s.

Confronted by people treated like animals in chains at a prison house, the utopians promised to "destroy every lingering remnant of the system from which they sprung, every trace of their existence and influence."[49] Freeing some of the insane wasn't enough, a whole technical ensemble was to be rendered inoperable: "I do arraign the whole system of error which they have sanctioned; I call for a verdict of guilty, and a sentence of total subversion, on the pernicious absurdities which continue to be practised in their name and authority."[50] It's not that the fanatical "crusade" (Browne's term) of the utopians was unleashed by ruptures in history. As Robert Castel argues in *The Regulation of Madness*, the adequate distance for this moral posture was opened by a fundamental event of the French Revolution that changed madness and psychiatry forever: the Constituent Assembly's 1790 abolishing of the *lettres du cachet*, royal letters that in many cases facilitated arbitrary imprisonment.[51] The end of arbitrary punishment left the revolutionaries with a lacuna in respect to the mad: with the celebrated Rights of Man, every citizen was to be considered sovereign, entitled to a set of at least nominal legal freedoms and protections. Confinement and punishment were to be preserved in a set of prescribed and rational procedures only set in motion after a clear transgression of the law. For example, a citizen only becomes a criminal and loses their rights and protections after breaking the law. But how then were they (and other liberal states) to deal with those troublesome members of the community who disturbed the public order, or with those who were for whatever reason deemed *unable* to manage their person or property and enter freely into contracts?

Despite the fact that the insane are numerically a smaller problem than criminals, vagrants, or the masses of the poor, they very quickly earn a special status in the laws of liberal democracies simply because they present the legal order with an existential paradox at their inception: here are adults who are neither criminal nor necessarily morally deplorable who nevertheless have no clear place in the commercial economy and pose a persistent challenge to public order. These asocial creatures deemed incapable of integrating themselves into the fictional universe of the contractual economy, whose affairs are never in order, and who threaten to break laws without thinking represent a persistent menace to the public peace. Even under the most flexible understanding of legal intent or responsibility, some of the mad will manage to circumvent it at every turn. To solve this dilemma, the modern states retained a residue of arbitrary—that is, discretionary and nonmechanical—authority in the form of *guardianship*, in essence equating the legal status of the lunatic with that of a child. To maintain a clear dividing line between the insane and criminals and demarcate the specific legal processes each must undergo to be imprisoned, it was necessary to create a legal "patient" status for the mad person and carefully prescribe roles for state actors in medical affairs.

BODIES LEAKING OVER A GREAT DIVIDE

The negative conditions of the first psychiatric revolution—moral treatment—have now come into view: the intensification of capital's corrosive migration through the social world and the liberal democratic revolutions' blood-soaked sweeps of royal authority split civil society between its need for self-regulation and protection from disintegration and its rejection of old methods of arbitration. Modern psychiatry *is* the twin appearance of a "new form of medicine and a new social relationship of guardianship"[52] to suture these holes in the social fabric, within which a complex matrix of administrative power took shape and grew over time. To borrow a phrase from Angela Mitropoulos, the administration of madness appears with the contract as the "hyphen between politics and economics, which is to say, the emergence of political-economy from moral economy, and the points of articulation between state and market."[53] Around the world, wherever liberalism appeared, so did similar divisions between the mad and the criminal, which set in motion similar medicolegal machines to administer the kind of compassion described by Castel:

> Compassion for the 'unfortunate' which forms the basis of the philanthropic attitude, for them makes up for the deficiencies of the law. Among those who lie outside the ambit of the law compassion establishes a new relationship, one which is no longer that of formal reciprocity but of regulated subordination—a relationship of guardianship. This is the matrix for every policy of assistance. Doubtless it is a relationship of domination, but one which still shares in the Utopia of a general rational exchange and imitates it even when one of the poles of reciprocity is missing.[54]

What counts above all is the functioning of this matrix; that is, the interlinked mechanisms, actors, and spaces that regulate the elusive movements of madness.

It's important to pause here to directly address the predominant presentation of contemporary conflicts in psychiatry in more detail and in consideration of its legal and political status. It is often taken for granted that psychiatry is split down the center into two warring camps separated by an abyssal rift: there are social/moral psychiatrists and there are biological/organicist psychiatrists. On the social side, one usually includes moral treatment, mental hygiene and prophylaxis (prevention of mental illness), social work, psychoanalysis, community care, outpatient clinics, therapeutic communities/milieu therapy, and occupational therapy; on the biological side, we can place university clinics and laboratories, pathological anatomy (opening up corpses), hereditary theories of degeneration, genetics, neural imaging, psycho-pharmaceuticals, and biomarkers. Edward Shorter, a fervent apologist and partisan of biopsychiatry, spells it out in typically simplistic fashion: "Psychiatry has always been torn between two visions of mental illness. One vision stressed the neurosciences, with their interest in brain chemistry, brain anatomy, and medication, seeing the origin of psychic distress in the biology of the cerebral cortex. The other vision stresses the psychosocial side of patients' lives, attributing their symptoms to social problems or past personal stresses to which people may adjust imperfectly."[55]

The history of the field has been reinscribed into this binary to assure the victory of one's chosen approach: Robert Whitaker of the Mad in America project reads the moral treatment movement as a fundamentally humanist project of recognizing "'brethren' who were suffering and needing comfort,"[56] while an apologist for medical psychiatry like Gerald Grob reads it as the introduction of medicine and empirical methods borrowed from the natural sciences into the field.[57] For those on the biological side, the partisans of social psychiatry at best merely add layers to the patient's profile and, at worst, are the vindictive puppets of a broader antiscience agenda with roots in political extremism and new age religious movements. For many critics on the social side, progressive medicalization represents a grave danger to social deviants,[58] political radicals, and even the "normal,"[59] while the bolder among them characterize biopsychiatry as nothing but a veil drawn over a mechanism of social control.

Some great works have been written on both sides of this supposed binary and there is truth in some of it. However, when I look at the binary in itself, in its overwrought straining to arrange biological or social "factors" into convincing effigies of a historical subject on one side or another of a juridical scale (as if the mysteries of human suffering through history and the art of therapeutics were a question of arithmetic), I can't help but feel like Camille in Georg Büchner's play *Danton's Death*: "Let someone whittle a marionette where the strings pulling it are plainly visible and whose joints crack at every step in iambic pentameter: what a character, what consistency! Let someone take a little bit of feeling, an aphorism, a concept, and clothe it in a coat and pants, give it hands and feet, color its face and let the thing torment itself through three acts until it finally marries or shoots itself: an ideal! . . . Take people out of the theater and put them on the street: oh, miserable reality!"[60] It's amazing how easily that which is ostensibly most familiar to us—our bodies, our relations—become phantoms invested with attributes and character, compared to whom we become mere incidental extras. To move out of the theater and back into the miserable street, we must acknowledge that everything we do as humans is biologically substantiated. Extravagant fantasies and thought experiments aside, take away the organic and we are not at all. Everything we do and have ever done is done by the body; spirit might not be a bone,[61] but it sure needs them. One may feel as though the body doesn't exist until it cries out in pain or fails to perform to our expectations, but we are our body even when we take little note of its extension in space. To not pay much attention to one's feet is one way of having feet (a frame of mind available only to those who have feet, in fact), not a real abstraction from it. Things would be much simpler if we could conclude from this that because we all have bodies, and we cannot experience or imagine anything at all without them, that we find here a common language for overcoming any confusion around the roots of our malaise. But here's the problem: if we encounter one another as embodied organic beings with no possibility of escape, the form of our embodiment and our consciousness of that form are social in character.

The social character of the biological can be grasped through two central concepts: normalization and objectivity. The question of the norm and its relation to health and disease is the central theme of Georges Canguilhem's 1941 book *The Normal and the Pathological*. For Canguilhem, health refers to an adaptive "regulatory flywheel of the possibilities of reaction."[62] If disease is that which disturbs and makes one aware of one's own body, then to be in good health means to live in such a way that one produces one's own values in overcoming and surviving danger. Canguilhem criticizes the physiologists and biologists who tried to discover norms that could designate the bounds of health and illness in a general or socially average way beyond their real expressions in a milieu. In the most extreme cases, health is reduced to inactivity, to the "silence of the organs,"[63] and disease, referring solely to the deviation from a norm, can exist independently of any sense of discomfort, harm, or pain. In contrast, Canguilhem holds that "there is no objective pathology," because the baseline of stabilization and the means of achieving it will differ across ecological-social milieus. "Structures or behaviors," he continues, "can be objectively described but they cannot be called 'pathological' on the strength of some purely objective criterion."[64]

Because there is no transcendental value standing above all the rest, Canguilhem maintains that the criteria with which we establish something's objective status as normal or pathological predetermines the character of the result we are seeking. If we are seeking normal weight, it will appear to be the average weight, for example, because two conditions have already been set in advance: 1) a normal state can be ascertained through quantitative measurement and the law of averages and 2) what is most common to a population is normal, good, natural, etc. Any norm arrived at in a lab or through strictly ontological deductions comes up short against the fact that norms are found in concrete milieus. A monk and a wrestler's weight may differ in the extreme, but they are both "normal" in their respective milieus. He writes: "The concept of norm is an original concept which . . . cannot be reduced to an objective concept determinable by scientific methods. Strictly speaking then, there is no biological science of the normal. There is a science of biological situations and conditions called normal. That science is physiology."[65]

Normalization names those processes or acts that orient what is towards what ought to be, towards the norm. There is a danger here of interpreting this move as a lapse into a kind of medical relativism, where "health" is simply what the majority agrees to, but what Canguilhem means to make clear is that determinations of the *normal*, which is not always healthy (after all, eternal ease and comfort is, on average, abnormal), cannot be considered outside of the real method of capture in which its parameters are already laid out. Abnormality, unlike the varieties of sickness, is arrived at through deduction from the definition of the normal or through deviation from the statistical average, not necessarily through an experience of dis-ease. It's not necessary to take on Canguilhem's vitalism to take heed that an *objective normal/abnormal* binary is inseparable from the form of its application, i.e., from its position within an ontology, its technical capture, and the social value attributed to it.

Drawing leaves through a camera obscura; freezing the scene through photography; making frog legs twitch under currents of electricity; rewriting the language of heat, muscle contraction, and blood pressure through the technical mediums of thermometers, kymographs, and the sphygmograph; mapping the neural pathways of the brain and dividing its vast territories into visible layers in PET, MRI, EEG, and the more general fMRI imaging—such are some of the highpoints of scientific visualization and technical mediation in the quest for objective knowledge.[66] Thinking with Canguilhem, is it not bizarre that the scientist claims to make increasingly precise determinations pertaining to the nature of the normal by means of an abnormal relationship to the world? We do not normally set aside a leaf and contemplate its image with complex technical apparatuses for hours at a time, nor do most people set aside the corpses of animals to test various influences on them in one's room. Does this feverish, never-ending search for capturing the object from every possible vantage point and level of abstraction not indicate a deeply ingrained need to erase the self in the image of objectivity? This is what Lorraine Daston and Peter Galison argue, positing that this drive to self-annulment has roots in a profound fear: "fear that the world is too labyrinthine to be threaded by reason; fear that the senses are too feeble and the intellect too frail; fear that the memory fades, even between adjacent steps of a mathematical demonstration; fear that authority and convention blind; fear that God may keep secrets or demons deceive."[67] But where is this nature they desperately need to "let speak for itself," and where does it appear outside of the means we have to observe it? To the one who simply "observes nature:" from what position relative to nature do you do this observing? When we realize that nature does not speak to us because *we are nature,* we can see that, in truth, our technical interventions can only modify our own discourse and introduce discontinuities and breaks in speech with ourselves. None of this yet implies that these representations are *determined* by a social form, but rather that the social form and technological mediums constitute the condition of possibility for any such representations along with the ways in which these representations are disseminated and used.

While the concept of "social psychiatry" is an obscure one that requires further elucidation, the tradition of "biological psychiatry," both conceptually and practically, has not adequately grappled with these fundamental paradoxes. The Brazilian novelist Joaquim Maria Machado de Assis perfectly described the tragicomic figure of the bio-psychiatrist in his 1881 story "The Alienist," an impressive feat given that psychiatry had made almost no mark on his country and was still in its infancy at the time. The story follows the eminent Dr. Simão Bacamarte, "the son of landed gentry, and the greatest physician in Brazil, Portugal, and the two Spains"[68] who moves to the town of Itaguaí from Portugal to devote himself to the study of science and master the art of healing. Soon enough, he marries Dona Evarista, having deduced from her promising "physiological and anatomical attributes" that she'd surely provide him with worthy offspring. When this fails to materialize, seemingly due to Dona Evarista's refusal to heed the doctor's dietary advice, Bacamarte throws himself back into his studies. At that point, in his review of science's "lesser nooks and crannies,"[69] he realizes that Brazil had no great alienists or national experts on the subject, a role he could surely fill. Without much scruple or struggle, he convinces the town council to proffer funds for the construction of a small asylum he names "Casa Verde," on account of its green shutters. After slapping a common humanist sentiment on the fence, he opens the doors to great interest from the townsfolk.

Like Emil Flechsig, a central figure of the German clinical psychiatry movement in the 1880s, Bacamarte professes not to care too much about the therapeutic aspect of his work: "Charity" he says, "certainly enters into my way of thinking, but only as seasoning—like salt you may say." What he really set out to do was to arrive at a more perfect classification, the true causes, the degrees, and—just imagine!—a universal panacea for madness. This, he reasons, is of greater benefit than helping one or two people anyways, and if it brings him a bit of fame and glory on the side, all the better. In order to fully devote himself to this project, he brings on two administrators and some younger staff to handle the worldly affairs. With this administrative machine in motion, Bacamarte's hunger for knowledge could be fed with more constancy, but it also leads to strange discoveries about the nature of madness: after observing and classifying all the patients into divisions and subdivisions, an idea thrusts itself upon him with the force of a divine revelation: "Madness, the object of my studies, was, until now, considered a mere island in an ocean of reason; I am beginning to suspect that it is a continent."[70] As with any revelation, everything falls into place quite quickly from that point on as Bacamarte sets about institutionalizing everyone who evinces even the slightest hint of eccentricity in their gait. Bad with money? Asylum for you! Engaging in common superstition? You must be mad! For the townspeople, a humanist revolution had descended into a general state of terror. They respond with their own counterrevolution against this "Bastille of human reason."[71] Bacamarte received these rebels on his doorstep with confusion; "science is a serious matter," he reassures them, "I do not answer to anyone for my professional actions, save to God and the great masters of science."[72]

Casa Verde survives this first test, but soon after, the barber's new revolutionary government stages a successful coup and visits once again. To his surprise, Bacamarte is neither jailed nor exiled, but told that his asylum is a venerated public institution and will remain. He asks, no doubt as the French revolutionaries asked, "can a government take it upon itself to abolish madness? Certainly not. And if governments cannot abolish madness, are they better qualified to detect and identify it? Again no—it is a matter for science."[73] Nothing could stop him now and the "harvest of men proved unstoppable."[74] But then, suddenly, it dawns upon Bacamarte that he must be wrong. The sheer mass of people locked up as insane convinces him of the inadequacy of the standard view of abnormal mental health as a disturbance of psychic equilibrium, since most people, it turned out, were abnormal in some way. What was truly abnormal, more pathological than pathology, was perfection. Here he faces a new problem: among the most perfect specimens in town, none combined the trueness of heart with the soundness of mind that makes a lunatic. None except one: Bacamarte himself. He closes the doors behind him and devotes his life to studying his own lunacy, dying before discovering the cure for his illness.

The term "biopsychiatrist," as I use it, refers to a person who acts *as if* they have effaced their own person and relations from their work as much as possible. Although they sequester and remove others from society, a Bacamarte first and foremost cloisters themself. Paul Emil Flechsig, the director of the Clinical Institute of Psychiatry and Neurology in Leipzig, set his mind to obtaining and opening up corpses in hopes of finding the source of madness in some fleshy region of the brain and finally acquiring a "calculation of the human soul"[75] at the expense of his patients' well-being and happiness. His patient Dan-iel Paul Schreber accused him of "soul murder" in conspiracy with a predatory God who didn't know a thing about human beings and "dealt only with corpses."[76] Schreber was right. Flechsig serves as an extreme example of the German university psychiatry of the 1860s–1880s, be-gun by Wilhelm Griesinger, whose proponents sought to distinguish themselves from the day-to-day drudgery and imprecision of asylum psychiatry by centralizing their research on the brain as an "immense reflex apparatus"[77] and the true seat of mental illness. It may well be the case that few psychiatrists claim a similar level of purity from the pedestrianism of worldly life, but precisely on account of their hubris, the Germans stand in here as our Bacamartes made flesh. What ties them together to the scores of geneticists, chemists, and neurologists who came in their wake is their incessant need to remove all trace of self, like the criminal who scours the crime scene for shoe marks and fingerprints.

How, on the other hand, can we define social psychiatry? Max-well Jones, the Scottish psychiatrist who coined the term "therapeutic community" out of his communal experiments with soldiers during World War II, writes that it's an "elastic" concept that must "include all social, biological, educational, and philosophical considerations which may come to empower psychiatry to win its striving towards a society which functions with greater equilibrium and with few psychological casualties."[78] Social psychiatry has at least one major advantage over scientistic Bacamartism: society is not a light you turn off when you enter the lab. Scientism is an aesthetic, which tellingly can only ex-press its own powers in social or political terms. Hence, when Edward Shorter explains the revolutionary import of Griesinger's battle cry that all mental illnesses are really illnesses of the nerves and brain, he can only think to compare it to Lenin's *What Is to Be Done?*[79] In the final pages of his epic apology for medical psychiatry, the final word on the biological model's "smashing success" is that patients undergo a unique catharsis around whitecoats because they *feel* more at ease when talking to a doctor.

Every psychiatrist knows their actions are essentially social in the back of their head, for otherwise there would be no regularity between their appearances or the spaces they inhabit whatsoever. The concrete walls of the psychiatric ward or the plain white or wallpapered walls of the outpatient clinic, much like the forensic psychiatrist's suit and tie or the laboratory worker's white coat, betray a devotion to the aesthetic trappings of scientism. What else could it signify? What do white walls have to do with a genetic anomaly? None of this has any bearing whatsoever on their daily operation besides imparting a social meaning through the arrangement of inert objects. And what of their tone of voice or their body language? If diagnosis is purely "medical," how is this information communicated? In a conversation or over a technical device like email? How is research organized and communicated? Who is funding all this? I know Bacamarte would prefer not to think about such trifles, but this much is unavoidable: medical activities—medicalization, pathologization, research, treatment, experimentation—are *social* activities (otherwise they would not signify an action involving more than one person), medical spaces are social spaces, and medical aesthetics are socially valued, all of which is conditioned upon determinate economic and political circuits. Social psychiatry usually names this conscious understanding that all therapeutics happen in a plenum—of spaces, environmental conditions, human subjects, cultures, and discourses—and involves thinking how these might be successfully rearranged. These deserve attention not because the social psychiatrist particularly likes these domains, but because they continue to work on the subject even when ignored. When the medically inclined pride themselves on not taking these very seriously or leaving them to others, it's not that they disappear, as their magic reasoning seems to suggest, they are just that much more impoverished, boring, disconnected, and arbitrary. "Biopsychiatrist" is all too often the name for a social psychiatrist who represses consciousness of their position in a matrix of relations and the conditions of their existence and power.

The predominance of the question of diagnosis and the etiology (the question of the cause or origin of mental illness) underlying it in public debates around psychiatry for decades, over and above all other questions, is a useful yardstick to measure how central scientistic aesthetics have become as a form of social power. This debate is due in part to professional failure to unite around a common theory and the connected embarrassment of having to walk back overhasty claims about the explanatory power of previous ones. Anne Harrington's *Mind Fixers* is a rather sad procession of the unfortunate gamblers of human fortune who bet it all on head bumps or serotonin levels or—like Thomas Insel, former head of the US federal mental health research agency, the National Institute of Mental Health (NIMH)—on "the neuroscience and genetics of mental disorders" before ending up broke without having "moved the needle in reducing suicide, reducing hospitalizations, improving recovery for the tens of millions of people who have mental illness."[80] Though these Don Quixotes show little sign of slowing their intergenerational war on windmills, Insel's confession ought to make us question why we are so singularly interested in *where* madness comes from or *why* it exists at the expense of interrogating the form of discourse that demands such an explanation and the administrative machine that puts it into motion.

Since Thomas Szasz published *The Myth of Mental Illness*, which reduces the concept of mental illness to a euphemistic metaphor for problems of living, critiques of psychiatry have devoted a disproportionate amount of time to disproving the material basis for psychiatric diagnoses, as if it were the keystone holding the whole construction together. Naturally, psychiatrists practicing with a sound theory of origin and action of a therapy act with the peace of mind and confidence that their actions are better contained within a local economy of direct reciprocal exchanges denied to those working in the dusk of the scientific spirit who tend to lash out wildly, lost as they are in a therapeutic wilderness.

Still, optimism of spirit and confidence of action are not solely reliant on the possession of a proven etiology. Pinel—like the other purveyors of moral treatment and the bulk of social psychiatrists after him—relied on a dynamic theory of causation that wasn't concerned with arriving at the absolute origin: "It is a bad choice" he warns, "to take mental alienation as the specific subject for research, as this opens one up to vague discussions about the seat of the understanding and the nature of its various faults, and nothing is more obscure or more impenetrable than this;" instead, one would do well to "to a study of the distinctive varieties of derangement as shown by outward signs."[81] He assumed that stimuli (from the environment or treatment) had a definite effect on the feelings of the patient, which in turn transformed the illness, but, like the phenomenological psychiatrists of the twentieth century, Pinel was above all concerned with these signs as they appeared on the surface, and devoted little time the deeper truth hidden below. Similarly, Emil Kraepelin—a German psychiatrist working at the crest of the university-based movement that sought the truth of madness in corrupted brains—did not make any serious attempt to penetrate past the crystalline chassis of madness. He contented himself with organizing cases based on observable action and prognosis (anticipated outcome). If anatomy was not to yield some clear lesion or anomaly then the proper course of action for the scientific mind was to focus on what was visible and, even better, quantifiable: repeating patterns of behavior, regular changes over time, reaction times, memory, attention span, cognitive testing.[82] Though Pinel and Kraepelin both laid their principal emphasis on the act of watching, Kraepelin abstracted the external signs into quantifiable data in the service of deforesting the dense thicket of psychiatric diagnostics to replace it with a proper garden, which, when properly tended to, would be easily understood and teachable to students. We inherited the basic distinction of Kraepelin's system between manic-depressive psychosis (with a comparatively good prognosis, given early treatment) and "dementia praecox," or, later, schizophrenia (with a comparatively bad one).

Kraepelin and Pinel understood, in their own ways, that the strategic relation of the psychiatrist to the patient does not principally derive its power from the capacity to define the "truth" beyond observable reality, but in the former being situated and authorized to deal with mental illness, defined clinically *and* legally. Just as "most prisoners walk into prison because they know they will be dragged or beaten into prison if they do not walk,"[83] we can say that most of the psychiatrically committed walk into hospitals because they know they will be restrained and dragged in if they don't walk. Often, this power *has not* required the psychiatrist to know the exact source of the ailment they treat nor exactly how their methods act upon the mind; what matters is that the machine is running. A whole system, a tightly interwoven mesh of relays and discourses is in place to transform the psychiatrist's judgment into effective action: a working theory and classificatory system to organize the clientele and separate them from other objects of care or punishment (taxonomy or nosology); institutional spaces (the asylum is historically the most pervasive, but also clinics, group homes, psychiatric wards, etc.); juridical codes defining the status of the mad (generally analogized to animals or children); prescribed roles for legal actors (police, judges, forensic experts); a chain of bureaucrats to sort out matters of insurance, finance, and property in cases of institutionalization or guardianship; and approved mechanisms of surveillance and reporting to translate individual complaints into the state's administrative codes. There are as many points of contact as there are spaces of encounter and discourses of legitimation in the social world. One or more of these elements can be disturbed or totally revolutionized without fundamentally changing the general connection between the parts. For example, at various points throughout its existence, as we've already seen, a theory of "social causation" prevailed over a biological one without changing the matrix that defines modern psychiatry, and the same can be said for some of the legal alterations to the patient's status throughout the twentieth century.

There is no psychiatrist-patient encounter set apart from a broader circuit of relations: patient–apartment–work–family–cop–partner–school–neighbor–psychologist–state–guardian–probate–judge–psychiatrist–hospital. And to be clear: our biology itself is shared and leaks throughout this chain at every step. Our bodies are permeable, open, they leak, bleed, consume, excrete; our bodies flow out into a common world, and are open to outside influence, as the COVID-19 pandemic has made so excruciatingly clear. A patient of the Utica Asylum put it beautifully in *The Opal* in 1852: "Like fermentation in the chemical world, [humanity's] atomic adhesions are in constant enlargement and in silent operation, seeking out relations, and forming relations of unsurpassed beauty and comfort, because in conformity with nature and adapted to its condition, means and end."[84] Attempts to neutralize this network by relegating every actor and space in the chain external to the domain of the psychiatrist onto the order of natural history ("we're just responding to the demands of the family . . ." or "that's a matter for the police . . . I just deal with the patient once they arrive here") expose this posture as a naively religious one. In denial of the profane world and its complications extrinsic to the holy circuitry of neural or endocrine highways of the One in isolation, they declare a monastic fealty to an object of study over and above the matrix that makes its study possible or their conclusions efficacious in any real encounter. Like Bacamarte, in their practice of isolation from the world, the biopsychiatrist's objects of contemplation increasingly become images of their own creation held in captivity. Like any creature's gnawing itch to escape when trapped in a small cage, their very rejection of the world fuels the rapacious imperialism of their designs. In revenge for exile, they begin mapping patterns of life onto isolated features of the body treated as the universal in their repeated resuscitations of phrenology's rotting corpse.

We've seen it all before. When the millennium failed to appear in the second half of the third century, the desert fathers followed Anthony the Great into the wilderness, fleeing human company in a grand gesture of denial. But solitude is not a place. Beset by memory in the lawless abode of temptation, even isolation appears to be just another way to be with others. Macarius the Great takes this to its conclusion: "[Macarius] said to the brothers at Scetis when he dismissed the assembly, 'Flee, my brothers.' One of the old men asked him, 'Where could we flee to beyond this desert?' He put his finger on his lips and said, 'Flee that.'"[85] Denial of the social is the act of fleeing beyond infinitely receding horizons of sociality. If psychiatry still takes refuge in the desert of scientism—speaking in tongues of prolix jargon—it's because a paradise of healing *did* materialize, but not as a Promethean forge of liberated humans, nor even as a solemn resting place of broken souls, but sank so low as to appear as nothing more than a mundane prison. Burdened by the unbearable weight of their failure, the next generation abandoned their project and ran away to the labs, relinquishing responsibility for the armies of the living dead. At least they hung a sign at the door of the asylum on their way out. It read: "abandon every hope, who enter here."[86]

PSYCHIATRY: UTOPIAN OR MATERIALIST

"The promised land was in sight; it was not reached,"[87] said W. A. F. Browne about the "total revolution" signaled by Pinel's gesture. Once the light of Utopia is glimpsed, even briefly, it's enough to change everything. Some spend their life trying to open the floodgates and let the light shine through; others curse the light as a mirage superimposed over the possible for sending them on errant paths. The latter erect temples and take refuge in solitary postures. Even if Pinel and Rush were not quite revolutionaries, the chain-breaking gestures of moral treatment, not unlike Luther's nailing of the Theses, reverberated in ways they never intended, concentrating around their gestures a collective desire for something new.

What is vital to grasp in the spread of capitalist industry and exchange is not merely the accumulation of wealth nor even the destruction of traditional communal patterns with the loss of the commons and proletarianization, but the way complex manufacture and industry revolutionizes the social form of labor. Manufacturing is not simply the cumulative effort of a certain quantity of laborers, Karl Marx explains, because their combination comprises "the creation of a new productive power, which is intrinsically a collective one"[88] in which the laborer "strips off the fetters of his individuality, and develops the capabilities of his species."[89] By rationally producing in a common form, each worker is joined to a social body endowed with productive and social capacities substantially different from what an individual or a series of individuals could possibly produce. If cooperation can still appear as an arithmetical increase tipping over at a certain point into a qualitative difference in intensity, the implementation of the division of labor on an industrial scale cut much deeper still in its "suppression of a whole world of productive drives and inclinations."[90] Division of labor according to the despotic rationality of an overseer mutilates the individual, cutting the body up into the smallest functional units until "[u]nfitted by nature to make anything independently, the manufacturing worker develops his productive activity only as an appendage of that workshop."[91] Labor torn asunder left behind a protean form as an adaptive potential teeming with energy like a nebula collapsing in on its own weight and becoming a sun.

Around the same time, the great pedagogic movements appeared, which suggested that everyone was teachable, "even" the blind and deaf.[92] As David Rothman wrote about the American reformers: "[They] stripped away the years from adults and turned everyone into children."[93] Even the most alienated social categories were dragged in from the outskirts and recast as civilization's children to be brought up and taught. In these broad transformations that turned the mad person into a patient and railed against arbitrary punishment now associated with the despised royals, all the while revealing the malleability and raw power of reshaping social bodies in production and education, Pinel and the moral entrepreneurs were less like so many Hercules in their labors and more like men ready and well-positioned to step into an opening made by revolution—an opening that showed humanity's form to be of hard plastic.

As industrial capitalism pivots to an intensive mode of exploitation with increasingly rationalized and regulated machinery, the most coveted laborer becomes one who can maximize their bodily efficiency in the factory. Over time, this concentrates industrial labor markets around a socially average ideal type of laborer, such that any could be easily replaced by another in case of loss (e.g., injury or death). Though capitalism always maintains a pool of surplus labor (the "reserve army of labor") to mobilize during shortages or depress the wages of skilled labor, the disabled and mad increasingly become part of a permanent surplus of those "who were apparently most resistant to the monotony, routine, and regularity of industrialized labor."[94] In line with the pedagogic and political revolutions of the day, moral treatment rested on the assumption that everyone, including the mad, was treatable, adaptable, ultimately social. But it went much further than the disciplinary regime of the factory or contemporary reforms in schools or prisons, which sought merely to train or reform an incomplete individual. Mad people didn't just have a screw loose; they were assumed to be completely alienated from their social milieu and their own sensations. As John Haslam of Bethlem in England put it in 1798, "[m]adness being the opposite to reason and good sense, as light is to darkness, straight to crooked," there was no such thing as degrees of madness because "a person cannot correctly be said to be in his senses and out of his senses at the same time."[95] Haslam's binary can only lead to the asymmetrical power struggle typical to psychiatry: the disciplinary authority strives to instill a pattern of reason totally foreign to the mad person, who can thus only experience treatment as an assault. Moral treatment begins by exploding this binary and opening it up to the possibility of reciprocal exchange. To do so means radically rearranging all facets of treatment. Thus, Browne criticizes those who replace the entirety of therapy with a synecdoche when they reduce the moral treatment system to one sphere of influence or another:

> All recent writers on insanity have spoken loudly in praise of moral treatment. But they have spoken vaguely of its nature. Each of them

attaches a different meaning to the word. Employment is the panacea of one; amusement is the specific of another; classification is
advocated by a third. The authors to whom I have alluded have mistaken parts, unexceptionable, it is true, but still merely parts of the
system for the whole. Every arrangement, beyond these for the regulation of the animal functions, from the situation, the architecture
and furniture of the buildings intended for the insane to the direct
appeals made to the affections by means of kindness, discipline, and
social intercourse, ought to be embraced by an effective system of
moral treatment.[96]

Moral treatment refers to the restructuring of the total situation in
service of the production of collectivities capable of appropriating their
social activity such that the "mysteries which lead theory to mysticism
find their rational solution in human practice and in the comprehen-
sion of this practice."[97] Utopian psychiatry sought not to reform the
person or heal them of their afflictions, but centrally to resocialize
human beings from within the ranks of the abandoned and the lost.
What does such a total program of disalienation include? In ideal conditions, a moral treatment system would utilize and have power over:
1) the physical environment, 2) management of daily affairs and relations, 3) labor. To reintegrate the alienated back into human affairs,
nothing should be considered extrinsic—ventilation requires just as
much attention as the day's schedule and sleeping arrangements.

Browne's description of the perfect asylum is among the clearest
and most comprehensive visions of utopian psychiatry:

Conceive a spacious building resembling the palace of a peer, airy,
and elevated, and elegant, surrounded by extensive and swelling
grounds and gardens. The interior is fitted up with galleries, and
workshops, and music-rooms. The sun and the air are allowed to
enter at every window, the view of the shrubberies and fields, and
groups of labourers, is unobstructed by shutters or bars; all is clean,
quiet, and attractive. The inmates all seem to be actuated by the
common impulse of enjoyment, all are busy, and delighted by being
so. The house and all around appears a hive of industry. When you
pass the lodge, it is as if you had entered the precincts of some vast
emporium of manufacture; labour is divided, so that it may be easy
and well performed, and so apportioned, that it may suit the tastes
and powers of each labourer. You meet the gardener, the common

agriculturist, the mower, the weeder, all intent on their several occupations, and loud in their merriment. The flowers are tended, and trained, and watered by one, the humbler task of preparing the vegetables for table, is committed to another. Some of the inhabitants act as domestic servants, some as artisans, some rise to the rank of overseers. The bakehouse, the laundry, the kitchen, are all well supplied with indefatigable workers. In one part of the edifice are companies of straw-plaiters, basket-makers, knitters, spinners, among the women; in another, weavers, tailors, saddlers, and shoemakers, among the men. For those who are ignorant of these gentle crafts, but are strong and steady, there are loads to carry, water to draw, wood to cut, and for those who are both ignorant and weakly, there is oakum to tease and yarn to wind. The curious thing is, that all are anxious to be engaged, toil incessantly, and in general without any other recompense than being kept from disagreeable thoughts and the pains of illness. They literally work in order to please themselves, and having once experienced the possibility of doing this, and of earning peace, self-applause, and the approbation of all around, sound sleep, and it may be some small remuneration, a difficulty is found in restraining their eagerness, and moderating their exertions. There is in this community no compulsion, no chains, no whips, no corporal chastisement, simply because these are proved to be less effectual means of carrying any point than persuasion, emulation, and the desire of obtaining gratification. But there are gradations of employment. You may visit rooms where there are ladies reading, or at the harp or piano, or flowering muslin, or engaged in some of those thousand ornamental productions in which female taste and ingenuity are displayed. You will encounter them going to church or to market, or returning from walking, riding, and driving in the country. You will see them ministering at the bedside of some sick companion. Another wing contains those gentlemen who can engage in intellectual pursuits, or in the amusements and accomplishments of the station to which they belong. The billiard room will, in all probability, present an animated scene. Adjoining apartments are used as newsrooms, the politicians will be there. You will pass those who are fond of reading, drawing, music, scattered through handsome suits of rooms, furnished chastely, but beautifully, and looking down upon such fair and fertile scenes as harmonize with the tranquillity [sic] which reigns within, and tend to conjure up images of beauty and serenity in the mind which are akin to happiness. But these persons have pursuits, their time is not wholly occupied in the agreeable trifling of conning a debate or gaining so many points. One acts as an amanuensis, another is engaged in landscape painting, a third devolves to himself a course of historical reading and submits to examination on the subject of his studies, a fourth seeks consolation from binding the books which he does not read. In short, all are so busy as to overlook, or all are so contented as to forget their misery.[98]

If it's true that in communism "society regulates the general production and thus makes it possible for me to do one thing today and another tomorrow, to hunt in the morning, fish in the afternoon, rear cattle in the evening, criticise after dinner, just as I have a mind, without ever becoming hunter, fisherman, herdsman or critic,"[99] then in the perfect asylum, one ought to be able to do just the same. Because it orients itself to fundamental matters of human social life and the social body's conditions of reproduction, in its fullest dimensions, by "moving into the sphere of explicit, intentional, and self-governing social action a process that has up to that point been left to improvisation, anarchy, and obscurity,"[100] psychiatry less resembles other reformist and philanthropic movements of the nineteenth century which sought merely to improve conditions in some corner or other of society, and appears to exist within the traditions of utopian socialism in the works of Charles Fourier, Robert Owen, and Henri de Saint-Simon.

Indeed, given that the socialists shared psychiatry's goal of changing humanity by transforming its environment and social form, it should come as no surprise that they looked to psychiatry for inspiration. Robert Owen, founder of utopian communes in Scotland and Indiana, often compared the nineteenth-century world of industry to a great madhouse that caused lunacy: "The organised, absurd, unjust, and most ignorant system contrived to punish man by man, is, at this day, one of the strongest evidences of the extent of irrationality, or rather, to speak correctly and truly, of downright insanity, to which the laws of men lead; and the daily incarcerations and murders, private and public, and wars between nations, are unmistakable declarations to the world, of the low state of intellect and the total absence of right reason, among the people of all nations, climes, and colours."[101] It's only natural, then, that when he described a more perfectly arranged society, he looked to the asylums of moral treatment:

The time approaches when it will be discovered that the speediest mode to terminate the innumerable diseases—physical, mental, and moral—created by the irrational laws invented and introduced by men during their irrational state of existence in progress towards rationality, will be to govern or treat all society as the most advanced physicians govern and treat their patients in the best arranged lunatic hospitals, in which forbearance and kindness, and full allowance for every paroxysm of the peculiar disease of each, govern the conduct of all who have the care of these unfortunates—unfortunate generally made to become so through the irrationality and injustice of the present most irrational system of society.[102]

All shared the ideal of consciously producing society as "a therapeutic community modeled on the outside world, yet operating according to hygienic principles."[103] Moral treatment, and modern psychiatry, begins with the idea that even the most deranged among us retain mental powers that can be improved. Such people are alienated "rather than destroyed."[104] The discovery of the power of the asylum to act on the mind coincided with the discovery that "[w]ithin their walls, humanity shines in unborrowed lustre . . . amid the dark pathways of life's desolateness."[105] To be an "alienist," as psychiatrists used to call themselves, was to devote oneself to the disalienation of persons.

Alienation is not a state of total detachment, for this is impossible, but is instead a "relation of relationlessness," in Rahel Jaeggi's words.[106] To be mad is to socially relate to the world *as if separated from it*. Here, the utopian psychiatrist is but one step removed from the socialist position that everyone living in capitalism is alienated from the concrete social activity that reproduces the world and from the products of their labor. "Asylumia," as the patients behind *The Opal* referred to it, was supposed to be isolated from the risks and agitations of an irrational society, but at the same time, it was the grounds for their socialization: "It cut them off from society, but it brought them out of their self-containment, from their confinement within their own bounds, from their inaccessible otherness; it brought them back to the open, multidimensional space of coexistence."[107] Ralph Remmington of *The Opal* waxed at length on this contradiction at the heart of moral treatment. He begins his piece, "A Crazy Man's Commonsense" with reference to the mixed-race anti-Catholic preacher from Guyana,

James Sayer Orr, called "the Angel Gabriel" for his tendency to attract crowds with a trumpet, by reaffirming the social exclusion of mad-men like him, writing "[y]our bounden duty behoves, to place us as a class by ourselves."[108] The piece is infused with hyperbolic admonitions about the danger of the "irresponsible tinder words of mad men" arising from "our poor crazy brains." Censured and feared, rightfully, as their "sphere is not in the world," Remmington kindly extends the olive branch to leaders of mobs and the disorderly with the perhaps unwanted consolation that "it is only by us that he is appreciated." In fact, it is specifically "unwitting recklessness" and its concomitant dangers that earns one a place "in our castle of defense." It is here that the excluded, dangerous madman is bold enough to suggest that Asylumia has perhaps a more rational notion of freedom than the world that excludes it: "Liberty is not an individual thing, but a social affair. The earth is not the terra firma of an individual, but of society at large. Were only one person existent, all things would be free to that one person; he would embody in his personal action the absolute idea of individual liberty. The actual idea is social liberty, freedom of dependent natures. . . . The freedom is made mutual." If prison is a "machine for the social production of guilt,"[109] and therefore an individualizing machine, Asylumia is designed to be a machine for the production of self-conscious therapeutic communities, communes where the social form and its demands are no longer taken for granted but taken up as a problem for collective production and "made mutual." For what is disalienation besides appropriating that which *seems* alien, which *seems* to stand outside and against you, but is actually a product of one's own continuous activity?

Patient control of treatment and peer support has been a recurring rallying cry of ex-patient radical psychiatry and antipsychiatry groups since the 1960s. This demand will get its due attention in a later chapter, but what's striking about moral treatment is that, in a very real sense, the utopian psychiatry of the nineteenth century was produced and directed by the real activity of patients. Of course, some or even most of the superintendents[110] were anxious to maintain clear lines of hierarchy and distinctions between doctor and patient and between lower staff and higher staff, but perhaps this anxiety is rooted in inherent destabilizing qualities of their method. If the physician wanted to tailor treatment to the patients, it was necessary to "live among them;

he must be their domestic associate; he ought to join in their pursuits and pastimes; he ought to engage them in converse during the day, and listen to their soliloquies in the retirement of their cells; he must watch, analyze, grapple with insanity among the insane, and seek for his weapons of aggression in the constitution and dispositions of each individual, and not in general rules or universal specifics."[111] Moral treatment's therapeutic commune made a paradoxical demand: the healer must utilize everything at hand in the service of health, but, in order to do so, they must actually be *in* and *of* the same social world as the mad. In this practice of immersion and letting the world they arranged play out, the psychiatrist must give up at least some of their professional distinctiveness. At its theoretically perfect implementation, would this not entail the self-annulment of the psychiatrist as a distinct actor?

More often than not, moral treatment was described, as most forms of social psychiatry would be after, as the form of therapeutics that takes stock of all existent facts that can be known in the service of consciously organizing the best possible conditions for therapy. This means they sought whenever possible to "[incorporate] rather than . . . obliterate the patients' individual or social differences."[112] In much the same way, Maxwell Jones explains that what distinguished the therapeutic community (the spiritual successor of moral treatment) in the middle of the twentieth century from other treatment modalities was "the way in which the institution's total resources, staff, patients, and their relatives, are self-consciously pooled in furthering treatment."[113] Precisely through this incorporation of difference, the division between an individual's need and the social need—or between individual desire and the social life it emerges within—is continually reduced. The auto-production and coming-to-self-consciousness of the counter-societies, Gladys Swain and Marcel Gauchet have argued, rejected all laws from the outside, attempting to resolve the tension between freedom and conformity through their conscious social decisions and mechanisms for reflection. This is why Foville could compare the asylum to Charles Fourier's great socialist communes: "The insane assembled in an asylum should, we have said, to a certain extent realize a Utopia of the phalanstery, unrealizable anywhere else, in which the work of each individual serves to contribute to the welfare of all."[114] It's how, in 1848, a disciple of Jean-Étienne Dominique Esquirol, the student of and direct sucessesor to Pinel's moral treatment in France, could describe moral treatment as a form of "communism" against "individualism:" "Social individuality must disappear and blend into the common life. . . . The very principles of communism are the ones applied to the governance of the insane."[115] At the maximal point of integration, moral treatment, or the therapeutic community, can be described as a psychiatric model organized and reproduced *by the patients*, a category which includes the attendants and the psychiatrist once it becomes the communal social form itself.

Strong as these tendencies are, there is no doubt that the asylum was designed to pivot around a central figure with a plan. The central paradoxes of utopian psychiatry are similar to those that plagued utopian socialism, which only partly resolved the problem of William Kurelek's two conspiracies: stuck between "a malevolent persecution" and "a benevolent conspiracy," they opted for the latter in the mistaken belief that disalienation can be legislated from above by throwing the mad "into doctrinaire experiments [that seek] to achieve . . . salvation behind society's back, in private fashion, within . . . limited conditions of existence, and hence necessarily suffer a shipwreck."[116] Not unlike the socialized factory described by Marx, it is the patients and attendants who do the actual work of reproducing the therapeutic commune, a reality obscured by the principle of centralization and hidden manipulation:

> The productive forces . . . developed [by] social labour . . . appear as the productive forces of capitalism. . . . Collective unity in co-operation, combination in the division of labour, the use of the forces of nature and the sciences, of the products of labour, as machinery – all these confront the individual workers as something alien, objective, ready-made, existing without their intervention, and frequently even hostile to them. They all appear quite simply as the prevailing forms of the instruments of labour. As objects they are independent of the workers whom they dominate. Though the workshop is to a degree the product of the workers' combination, its entire intelligence and will seem to be incorporated in the capitalist or his understrappers, and the workers find themselves confronted by the functions of the capital that lives in the capitalist.[117]

So even as moral treatment in the end consists in the *patients'* practical activity and reproductive labor, Samuel Tuke describes moral treatment as instilling what Spinoza described as "a dominion within a dominion"[118]: the overseers control the environment and manage personal relations so as to discover "[by] what means the power of the patient to control the disorder, is strengthened and assisted."[119] Proper configurations emanate from the one who knows best down to those who don't yet know anything at all in the great chain of order mirroring in near perfection the hierarchies of nature and society. "One of the essential features in every well run hospice" according to Pinel, "is having a general centre of authority who makes decisions with no appeal, aimed at keeping order amongst the staff, exercising correct restraint over turbulent or very agitated patients, and determining whether a patient is suitable for the interview requested by one of his friends or close relatives. This overall authority must lie with the superintendent."[120] Psychiatric utopias always teetered on the edge of a tyrannical nightmare.

Tied as they were to the state and philanthropists for their continued operation, none of the utopian psychiatrists of the mid-nineteenth century proved capable of following through with their therapeutic task of disalienation. Fearful of losing the centralized power they believed was at the root of their broad range of demiurgic powers, they, and especially their successors towards the end of the nineteenth century, opted to betray the central tenets of moral treatment over taking up a real political position against worsening conditions as states around the world overutilized their segregative function without providing adequate means to keep up with the massive increase in inhabitants. General misery was the result: by the end of the century, only a fool would have still characterized the overburdened snake pits as utopias. The shining cities of the mad where the alienated *disalienated themselves* under the prudent guidance of shepherds became the homes of tyrants with their infernal machines for intensifying alienation. The death of the asylum, its transformation into a graveyard for the living dead, was a traumatic wound for those who lived through it, patients and high-minded professionals alike. Who among the patients—piled densely into hallways like so many cattle eating meager gruel, lacking any control or choice in daily activity—could possibly see the experience as one of appropriating their social conditions for the sake of healing, or even as a program of discipline to produce productive workers at the edges of the economy? What was the use of such a place, this giant unreality, besides the efficient removal of the "Dead weight of Society?"[121]

Since then, there have been many times when thoughtful and delicate models and codes of ethics drawn up by caring minds and offered to the public—or, just as often, to politicians—in hopes of a paradigm shift have been readily absorbed into the segregative function of mental institutions or ended up in the hands of wardens and cops. The introduction of psychiatric frameworks in corrections has only served to euphemize the violence of punishment, as in when veritable trauma-factories like prisons have unironically imported the language of "trauma-informed care," or has even paradoxically concentrated such violence in a monstrous hybrid like the psychiatric ward of a maximum-security prison examined by Lorna Rhodes in *Total Confinement: Madness and Reason in the Maximum Security Prison*. In the 1970s, one of the central demands of the antipsychiatry and psychiatric survivor movement was that any mental health care practice must integrate the experience and expertise of the patient or sufferer. This has roots in the disability movement's demand for "nothing about us without us." At various times and places, this is—in itself—a radical political demand that fundamentally challenges the way knowledge is formed and practice is legitimated. But the incorporation of mental health service users does not in itself guarantee fundamental or radical transformations: increasingly, clinical and institutional workplaces employ peer-support specialists, researchers of all stripes have made strides to incorporate accounts from patients and service users in their studies (however superficially), and some psychiatrists and social workers have no qualms referring patients to peer-run alternative support groups, like a Hearing Voices Group, so long as it doesn't disrupt their own work. What does this suggest? First, that no model and language is universally applicable and will not have the same effect in every locality or with every group of people under such a massive umbrella as "psychiatric patients." Second, it signals that we must be wary of the risk of confusing the production of novel ethical principles (like the centrality of peer voices or the modification of language) or prefigurative models for a transformation of the social matrix through which power flows. This matrix can withstand a breakage with a single link (a certain language, a particular practice, a specific law), while still maintaining the general relations (of guardianship, of imprisonment) in general stability.

At this point, we can place the radical projects in their correct place. Surely, we could say that what tied radical experiments together was an explicit relationship to negativity, an antagonistic relationship to their field worthy of the name "antipsychiatry." But antipsychiatry is common to all of psychiatry as a component of its rejuvenating gesture of clearing the ground for new foundations. An acolyte like Edward Shorter is just as antipsychiatric as Thomas Szasz in that both can only define their positive objectives in terms of their negative relations to other forms of psychiatry. The way it's used as a handwaving pejorative is akin to Martin Luther's *Against the Robbing and Murderous Hordes of Peasants*. Just as there was nothing in the words of Thomas Müntzer that couldn't be interpreted from the holy word, there is nothing in what is called "antipsychiatry" foreign to the basic principles and history of psychiatry. Just as Luthor raged against an insurrectionary interpretation of scripture, the establishment psychiatrist's fury towards the antipsychiatry of the other is first and foremost against seeing the fundamental principles and ethical project of their own field turned against them, being put to use in political projects they oppose. By beginning with the fact that the asylum or the clinic is not an island, but a point in a social matrix, the radicals recognized that the development of a therapeutic commune entailed, by necessity, an engagement with negativity and the opening up of contradictions in the heart of the social fabric. This does indeed bring about a special relationship to negativity, for theirs is an imminent movement that does not limit the negative to *somewhere else* away from where they stood, but recognizing it and working with it as something internal to their practice.

The projects, movements, and figures I cover in this book—particularly Democratic Psychiatry, the Luta Antimanicomial (anti-Asylum struggle in Brazil), and Institutional Psychotherapy—are often placed in the camp of the utopians: the sociologist Nick Crossley said they created "working Utopias"[122]; Franco Basaglia talked of the "utopia of reality."[123] In a similar register, it is said of figures like Félix Guattari or Nise da Silveira that they treated the hospital as a political laboratory. What I want to argue, however, is that it is establishment psychiatry that creates "an ideal to which reality [will] have to adjust itself"[124] and delimits its space of action to a discrete laboratory. Radical projects are better referred to as *critical-utopian* forms of psychiatry, or, if you like, *materialist psychiatry*.[125] What ties them together is not their opposition to psychiatry, but rather their attempts to take psychiatry to its limits within their particular contexts. In their pursuits, they recognized further limits that, for reasons of time, funding, or some other factor, would be left for others to interrogate. This by no means suggests a progression. In the following chapters, I will argue that the openings created by utopian psychiatry and moral treatment—the conscious production and use of space and language, the power of collective work, the appropriation of history and all that is alien in the service of the therapeutic community—were the starting point for all radical projects in psychiatry and show how only the so-called radicals followed these through to their conclusions, even when it meant abolishing professional distinctions and hierarchies, breaking ties with professional associations, breaking the law, or coming into direct conflict with the authorities.

At a certain point, those who earnestly attempt to create therapeutic environments or communities realize that this pursuit is necessarily curtailed. Not because of this or that theoretical mistake or "good intentions gone bad," but because the imperatives of capitalism set discrete limits on the aspirations of the healer. In moments of crisis, the healer must make a choice: follow the comfortable path with institutional and financial security, even if it means watching a vital refuge become a cesspool of despair; or, fight against everything that tends to limit or degrade one's capacity to care. Psychiatry becomes materialist with the realization that the transformation of social conditions for communal healing consists in joining all those who struggle for freedom and health around the world. At the point of crisis, it either orients itself towards its own productive destruction or allows itself to become the next benevolent terror.

Notes

1. Janet Frame, *Faces in the Water* (North Sydney: Vintage Books, 2008), epub.

2. For a feminist reading on this painting, see Elaine Showalter, *The Female Malady: Women, Madness and English Culture, 1830–1980* (New York: Penguin Books, 1985), 3.

3. Thomas Willis, *Two Discourses Concerning the Soul of Brutes* (London: Thomas Dring & John Leigh, 1683).

4. William Battie, *A Treatise on Madness* (London: J. Whiston and B. White, 1758).

5. Dora B. Weiner, "'Le geste de Pinel': The History of a Psychiatric Myth," in *Discovering the History of Psychiatry*, ed. Roy Porter and Mark S. Micale (New York: Oxford University Press, 1994), 233.

6. Laure Murat, *The Man Who Thought He Was Napoleon: Toward a Political History of Madness* (Chicago: University of Chicago Press, 2014), 37.

7. Weiner, "'Le geste de Pinel,'" 240–242.

8. Weiner, "'Le geste de Pinel,'" 243.

9. Showalter, *The Female Malady*, 149.

10. Sander L. Gilman, "The Image of the Hysteric," in Sander L. Gilman, Helen King, Roy Porter, G. S. Rousseau, and Elaine Showalter, *Hysteria Beyond Freud* (Berkeley: University of California Press, 1993), 345–347.

11. Elizabeth Fee and Theodore M. Brown, "Freeing the Insane," *American Journal of Public Health* 96, no. 10 (October 2006): 1743, https://ajph.aphapublications.org/doi/10.2105/AJPH.2006.095448.

12. Of all the eighteenth-century reformers, Chiarugi is the most neglected in English-language literature. George Mora is one who has worked to introduce him to the anglophone world. See George Mora, "Vincenzo Chiarugi (1759–1820) and his Psychiatric Reform in Florence in the Late 18th Century," *Journal of the History of Medicine and Allied Sciences* 14, no. 10 (October 1959): 424–433, https://doi.org/10.1093/jhmas/XIV.10.424.

13. On this lack of unifying myths, see Patrick Vandermeersch, "'Les mythes d'origine' in the History of Psychiatry," *Discovering the History of Psychiatry*, ed. Roy Porter and Mark S. Micale (New York: Oxford University Press, 1994), 219–221.

14. Edward Shorter, *A History of Psychiatry: From the Era of the Asylum to the Age of Prozac* (New York City: John Wiley & Sons, 1997), 255.

15. Quoted in Roy Porter and Mark S. Micale (eds.), "Introduction: Reflections of Psychiatry and Its History," in *Discovering the History of Psychiatry* (New York: Oxford University Press, 1994), 7.

16. Albert Deutsch, *The Mentally Ill in America: A History of Their Care and Treatment from Colonial Times* (New York: Columbia University Press, 1949), 134. Deutsch dates the peak of this curability optimism to around 1820–1850. Some doctors, like George Burrows, believed they could cure over 90 percent of their patients.

17. Thomas Szasz, *Manufacture of Madness* (Syracuse: Syracuse University Press, 1970), xii.

18. Andrew Scull, "A Culture of Complaint: Psychiatry and its Critics," in *Psychiatry and Its Discontents* (Oakland: University of California Press, 2019), 54.

19. Samuel Tuke, *Description of the Retreat, an Institution near York for Insane Persons of the Society of Friends Containing an Account of its Origins and Progress, the Modes of Treatment and a Statement of Cases* (1813), The Retreat Archive, Wellcome Collection, https://wellcomecollection.org/works/dcy3yd8x.

20. See Chapter 4 of Tuke's *Description of the Retreat*.

21. John Conolly, *The Treatment of the Insane Without Mechanical Restraints* (London: Smith, Elder & Co., 1856), 5.

22. "The Maze. Artist: William Kurelek (1927–1977)," Bethlem Museum of the Mind, https://museumofthemind.org.uk/learning/the-maze/.

23. Murat, *The Man Who Thought*, 212.

24. Murat, *The Man Who Thought*, 37 and 51.

25. Benjamin Rush, *Medical Inquiries and Observations*, Vol. 1 (Philadelphia: J. Conrad and Co., 1805), 293.

26. George Rosen, *Madness in Society: Chapters in the Historical Sociology of Mental Illness* (Chicago: University of Chicago Press, 1968), 175.

27. Robert Castel, *The Regulation of Madness: The Origins of Incarceration in France* (Berkeley: University of California Press, 1988), 98.

28. Quoted in Rosen, *Madness in Society*, 183.

29. Quoted in Showalter, *The Female Malady*, 24.

30. For the US, see David Rothman, *The Discovery of the Asylum* (New York: Aldine de Gruyter, 1990), 143. For France, see Castel, *The Regulation of Madness*, 73. For Germany, see Eric Engstrom, *Clinical Psychiatry in Imperial Germany: A History of Psychiatric Practice* (Ithaca: Cornell University Press, 2003), 21–22.

31. Mab Segrest, *Administrations of Lunacy: Racism and the Haunting of American Psychiatry at the Milledgeville Asylum* (New York: The New Press, 2020), 165–167.

32. Robert Whitaker, *Mad in America: Bad Science, Bad Medicine, and the Enduring Mistreatment of the Mentally Ill* (New York: Basic Books, 2002), 215–217.

33. Nancy Hollander, *Love in a Time of Hate: Liberation Psychology in Latin America* (New Brunswick: Rutgers University Press, 1997), 102–107.

34. Frantz Fanon, *A Dying Colonialism*, trans. Haakon Chevalier (New York: Grove Press, 1965), 121.

35. Madness Network News Collective, "Working Draft to Abolish Psychiatry," *Madness Network News* 8, no. 3 (Summer 1986): 3.

36. Deutsch, *The Mentally Ill*, 59.

37. World Health Organization, *Towards a Common Language for Functioning, Disability and Health* (Geneva: World Health Organization, 2002), 9.

38. National Institute of Mental Health, "Research Domain Criteria (RDoC)," https://www.nimh.nih.gov/research/research-funded-by-nimh/rdoc.

39. Murat, *The Man Who Thought*, 37.

40. Rush, *Medical Inquiries*, 279.

41. Andrew Scull, *Social Order/Mental Disorder: Anglo-American Psychiatry in Historical Perspective* (Berkeley: University of California Press, 1989), 36.

42. Rosen, *Madness in Society*, 159.

43. Scull, *Psychiatry and Its Discontents*, 39–40; Klaus Doerner, *Madmen and the Bourgeoisie: A Social History of Insanity and Psychiatry* (Oxford: Basil Blackwell, 1981), 15.

44. Gerald N. Grob, *The Mad Among Us: A History of the Care of America's Mentally Ill* (New York: The Free Press, 1994), 7.

45. Akihito Suzuki, "The State, Family, and the Insane in Japan, 1900–1945," in *The Confinement of the Insane International Perspectives, 1800–1965* (Cambridge: Cambridge University Press, 2009), 198.

46. Deutsch, *The Mentally Ill in America*, 41. For more, see David Wright, "Getting Out of the Asylum: Understanding the Confinement of the Insane in the Nineteenth Century," *Social History of Medicine* 10, no. 1, (April 1997): 140.

47. Deutsch, *The Mentally Ill in America*, 26–30.

48. W. A. F. Browne, *The Asylum as Utopia: W. A. F. Browne and the Mid-Nineteenth Century Consolidation of Psychiatry*, ed. Andrew Scull (London: Routledge, 2014), 101.

49. Browne, *The Asylum as Utopia*, 99.

50. Browne, *The Asylum as Utopia*, 133.

51. Castel, *The Regulation of Madness*, 2.

52. Castel, *The Regulation of Madness*, 3.

53. Angela Mitropoulos, *Contract and Contagion: From Biopolitics to Oikonomia* (Wivenhoe: Minor Compositions, 2012), 32.

54. Mitropoulos, *Contract and Contagion*, 37.

55. Shorter, *A History of Psychiatry*, 26.

56. Whitaker, *Mad in America*, 287.

57. Grob, *The Mad Among Us*, 26.

58. Peter Conrad, *The Medicalization of Society: On the Transformation of Human Conditions into Treatable Disorders* (Baltimore: Johns Hopkins University Press, 2007).

59. Allen Frances, *Saving Normal: An Insider's Revolt Against Out-Of-Control Psychiatric Diagnosis, DSM-5, Big Pharma, and the Medicalization of Ordinary Life* (New York: William Morrow, 2013).

60. Georg Büchner, "Danton's Death," in *Complete Works and Letters*, ed. Walter Hinderer and Henry J. Schmidt (New York: Continuum, 1986), 85–86.

61. G. W. F. Hegel, *Phenomenology of Spirit*, trans. A.V. Miller (Oxford: Oxford University Press, 1977), 208.

62. Georges Canguilhem, *The Normal and the Pathological*, trans. Carolyn R. Fawcett (New York: Zone Books, 1991), 198.

63. Canguilhem, *The Normal and the Pathological*, 91.

64. Canguilhem, *The Normal and the Pathological*, 226.

65. Canguilhem, *The Normal and the Pathological*, 228.

66. On the long search for objectivity, see: Lorraine Daston and Peter Galison, *Objectivity* (New York: Zone Books, 2007) along with Nikolas Rose, "If Mental Disorders Exist, How Shall We Know Them?" and "Are Mental Disorders 'Brain Disorders?'" in *Our Psychiatric Future* (Cambridge: Polity, 2019).

67. Daston and Galison, *Objectivity*, 372.

68. Joaquim Maria Machado de Assis, "The Alienist," in *26 Short Stories* (New York: Liveright Publishing Corporation, 2018), 46.

69. Machado, "The Alienist," 47.

70. Machado, "The Alienist," 56.

71. Machado, "The Alienist," 69.

72. Machado, "The Alienist," 71.

73. Machado, "The Alienist," 78.

74. Machado, "The Alienist," 81.

75. Quoted in Martin Stingelin, "*Die Berechnung Der Menschlichen Seele*," *Wunderblock: Eine Geschichte Der Modernen Seele*, ed. Jean Clair (Deisenhofen: KUNSTFORUM International, 1989), 297–308. My translation.

76. Daniel Paul Schreber, *Memoirs of My Nervous Illness* (New York: New York Review of Books, 2000), 62.

77. Wilhelm Griesinger, *Mental Pathology and Therapeutics*, trans. C. Lockhart Robertson and James Rutherford (London: The New Sydenham Society, 1867), 23–24.

78. Maxwell Jones, *Social Psychiatry in Practice: The Idea of the Therapeutic Community* (Middlesex: Penguin Books, 1968), 30.

79. Shorter, *A History of Psychiatry*, 76.

80. Quoted in Anne Harrington, *Mind Fixers: Psychiatry's Troubled Search for the Biology of Mental Illness* (New York: W.W. Norton & Company, 2020), epub.

81. Philippe Pinel, *Medico-Philosophical Treatise on Mental Alienation*, trans. Gordon Hickish, David Healy, and Louis C. Charland (West Sussex: John Wiley & Sons, 2008), xxv.

82. Engstrom, *Clinical Psychiatry in Imperial Germany*, 131.

83. Robert Cover, "Violence and the Word," *The Yale Law Journal* 95 (1986): 1607, http://digitalcommons.law.yale.edu/fss_papers/2708.

84. Anonymous, "On the Claims of the Insane to the Respect and Interest of Society," *The Opal* 2, no. 8 (1852): 240. Courtesy of the Oskar Diethelm Library, DeWitt Institute for the History of Psychiatry, Weill Cornell Medical College.

85. *The Sayings of the Desert Fathers: The Alphabetical Collection* (Kalamazoo: Cistercian Publication, 1975), 42.

86. Dante Alighieri, *The Divine Comedy*, trans. Allen Mandelbaum (New York: Alfred A. Knopf & Everyman's Library, 1995), 68.

87. Browne, *The Asylum as Utopia*, 139.

88. Karl Marx, *Capital. A Critique of Political Economy. Volume 1. Book One: The Process of Production of Capital*, trans. Ben Fowkes and David Fernbach (London: Penguin Books, 1990), 443.

89. Marx, *Capital, Vol. 1*, 447.
90. Marx, *Capital, Vol. 1*, 481.
91. Marx, *Capital, Vol. 1*, 482.
92. Marcel Gauchet and Gladys Swain, *Madness and Democracy: The Modern Psychiatric Universe* (Princeton: Princeton University Press, 1999), 127.
93. Rothman, *The Discovery of the Asylum*, 76.
94. Andrew Scull, *Decarceration: Community Treatment and the Deviant—A Radical View* (Englewood Cliffs: Prentice-Hall, 1977), 26.
95. John Haslam, *Observations on Insanity* (London: F. and C. Rivington, 1798), 15, https://gutenberg.readingroo.ms/3/7/0/5/37057/37057-h/37057-h.htm.
96. Browne, *The Asylum as Utopia*, 156.
97. Karl Marx, "Theses on Feuerbach," *Marx & Engels Collected Works, Volume 5: Marx and Engels 1845–47* (London: Lawrence & Wishart, 2010), 5.
98. Browne, *The Asylum as Utopia*, 229–231.
99. Karl Marx and Frederick Engels, "The German Ideology," in *Marx & Engels Collected Works, Volume 5: Marx and Engels 1845–47* (London: Lawrence & Wishart, 2010), 47.
100. Gauchet and Swain, *Madness and Democracy*, 66.
101. Robert Owen, *The Revolution in the Mind and Practice of the Human Race; Or, the Coming Change From Irrationality to Rationality* (London: Effingham Wilson, 1849), 115.
102. Owen, *The Revolution in the Mind and Practice of the Human Race*, 115.
103. Nancy Tomes, *A Generous Confidence: Thomas Story Kirkbride and the Art of Asylum-Keeping, 1840–1883* (Cambridge: Cambridge University Press, 1984), 131.
104. Tuke, *Description of the Retreat*, 137.
105. Anonymous, "On the Claims of the Insane," 240.
106. Rahel Jaeggi, *Alienation* (New York: Columbia University Press, 2014), 1.
107. Gauchet and Swain, *Madness and Democracy*, 101.
108. Ralph Remmington, "A Crazy Man's Common Sense," *The Opal* 4, no. 9 (1854): 269. Courtesy of the Oskar Diethelm Library, DeWitt Institute for the History of Psychiatry, Weill Cornell Medical College.
109. Quoted in Andrew Scull, *Social Order/Mental Disorder*, 93.
110. Nancy Tomes discusses Thomas Story Kirkbride's anxiety to maintain control in *A Generous Confidence*, 72 and 179.
111. Browne, *The Asylum as Utopia*, 181.
112. Tomes, *A Generous Confidence*, 193. See also Browne, *The Asylum as Utopia*, 155.
113. Jones, *Social Psychiatry in Practice*, 85.
114. Quoted in Castel, *The Regulation of Madness*, 211.
115. Gauchet and Swain, *Madness and Democracy*, 83.
116. Karl Marx, "The Eighteenth Brumaire of Louis Bonaparte," *Marx & Engels Collected Works, Volume 11: Marx and Engels 1851–53* (London: Lawrence & Wishart, 2010), 110–111.
117. Quoted in Marcello Musto, "Revisiting Marx's Concept of Alienation," *Socialism and Democracy* 24, no. 3, (2010): 98.
118. Spinoza, *A Spinoza Reader: The Ethics and Other Works*, 152.
119. Tuke, *Description of the Retreat*, 138.
120. Pinel, *Medico-Philosophical Treatise on Mental Alienation*, 95.
121. Anonymous, "Thoughts as They Arise," *The Opal* 2, no. 4 (1852), 119. Courtesy of the Oskar Diethelm Library, DeWitt Institute for the History of Psychiatry, Weill Cornell Medical College.
122. Nick Crossley, *Contesting Psychiatry: Social Movements in Mental Health* (London: Routledge, 2006), 107.
123. Franco Basaglia, *L'utopia della realtà* (Milan: Piccola biblioteca Einaudi, 2005).
124. Marx and Engels, "The German Ideology," 49.
125. Gilles Deleuze and Félix Guattari, *Anti-Oedipus: Capitalism and Schizophrenia*, trans. Robert Hurley, Mark Seem, and Helen R. Lane (Minneapolis: University of Minnesota Press, 1983), 22.

CHAPTER 2

BAREFOOT THERAPEUTICS

The dreary asylum on the hill is the quintessential image of psychiatry in popular culture. If you know nothing at all about psychiatry, you at least know the asylum. You know that only the most unfortunate souls end up there. You can picture its foreboding castle-like exterior. You can feel its malevolent aura. You can hear the screams and electric shocks down the hallway. As a theme, asylums conjure up more associations and images of what it means to be insane than couches, drugs, and checklists combined. As physical structures, they dominated (and often still dominate) the landscape and were effectively the center of smaller towns' economic life and collective fantasy. In this chapter, I'll be focusing on the internal social world of the asylum, the physical arrangement of space, and individuals who tried to modify these to create a different way of being with one another from within.

A phantasmagoria of horrors seems to have always haunted the places the mad have congregated. Dracula himself, after all, chose the asylum's dark corridors as his hunting grounds in Bram Stoker's 1897 tale. In his depiction of a young aristocrat's downfall, A Rake's Progress, the eighteenth-century social commentator and satirist William Hogarth could imagine no worse fate for his character, Tom Rakewell, at the end of an allegorical fall from grace than being surrounded by nude madmen in chains. Gawked at by aristocratic ladies, with an agitated look on his face, we are made to understand that Rakewell paid dearly for his failures. "ABODES OF HORROR have frequently been described, and castles, filled with spectres and chimeras, conjured up by the magic spell of genius to harrow the soul, and absorb the wondering mind"[1] begins Mary Wollstonecraft's 1798 novel about a woman being locked up in an asylum by her husband, *Maria: Or, The Wrongs of Woman*. "But," she continues, "formed of such stuff as dreams are made of, what were they to the mansion of despair." Indeed, gothic tropes of the evil mysteries lurking behind the madhouse walls have long been taken up by social reformers and in commentaries on social issues as a symbol of arbitrary power, rotten conditions, or the irrationality of other institutions (marriage, the prison, the economy). Because of these various associations, it's not always possible to ascertain what is intended as basic fact and what is allegory in works documenting life in the asylum. Even so, the documentary exposé has proved to be as enduring as any genre. Right around the period of Pinel's reforms, in 1794, Francisco Goya painted *Yard with Lunatics*, realistically portraying a group of inmates in an enclosure of the Zaragoza asylum in Spain. Some are chained to walls, others stare blankly ahead at nothing, or perhaps watching the nude patients wrestle with each other while an attendant strikes them in the center. Though a bright light clearly shines outside, it fails to penetrate, and the enclosure stays enveloped in shadow.

The psychiatrists who rose to prominence in the first half of the nineteenth century entirely agreed with this depiction, enthusiastically trading in horror tropes about the hospitals for the mad. This is how John Conolly described the mental hospitals that preceded moral treatment and non-restraint in 1856:

> These were but prisons of the worst description. Small openings in the walls, unglazed, or whether glazed or not, guarded with strong iron bars; narrow corridors, dark cells, desolate courts, where no tree, nor shrub, nor flower, nor blade of grass grew; solitariness, or companionship so indiscriminate as to be worse than solitude; terrible attendants, armed with whips, sometimes (in France) accompanied by savage dogs, and free to impose manacles, and chains, and stripes, at their own brutal will; uncleanliness, semi-starvation, the garotte, and unpunished murders: these were the characteristics of such buildings throughout Europe. There were, I need scarcely add, no gardens for exercise and recreation, and health, such as surround all our new asylums; no amusements, no cheerful occupations, no books to read, no newspapers or pictures, no evening entertainments, no excursions, no animating change or variety of any kind, no scientific medical treatment, no religious consolation.[2]

It was in large part by mobilizing around the image of the general hospital and jails as zones of torture and abandonment that nineteenth century reformers succeeded in accelerating the growth of the asylum form: Dorothea Dix, an activist nurse in the US, and Esquirol in France convinced legislatures to set aside funds and land for asylums after delivering detailed reports on the unhygienic and cruel enclosures in which the mad were held.[3] Improving the living conditions had to be a top priority for any therapeutic model claiming to take advantage of any and all influences, as Pinel already made clear in his 1809 treatise: "The internal lay-out and amenities of the premises are of such great importance in a psychiatric hospice that we must hope to see one day the inauguration of a new kind of establishment especially designed for this purpose and worthy of a powerful and enlightened nation. But will the architect yet again model his buildings on the places where ferocious animals are confined? Does the mentally ill patient not also need clean and healthy air to breathe?"[4] His question would have to wait to be answered by the next generation, when some devoted themselves to the question of physical space and social organization with surgical precision.

Preeminent among the architects of healing was Thomas Story Kirkbride. His *On the Construction, Organization, and General Arrangements of Hospitals for the Insane* (1854) was the definitive text of asylum construction in the nineteenth century. The principles it outlined had already been officially adopted in 1851, at the first conference held by the Association of Medical Superintendents of American Institutions for the Insane (AMSAII), the first professional medical association in the US (of which Kirkbride was the secretary. United behind him and his designs, the utopian psychiatrists of moral therapy plotted the demise of the gothic dungeon that took the name "madhouse."

The Kirkbride Plan, as it was called, took everything into account, beginning with the ideal land plot for an asylum all the way down to the best type of urinal or dust flue for varying conditions. Its most distinctive feature is the large central administrative tower with kitchens, the superintendent's office, a library, and chapel.[5] From here, the building fans out into long wings outfitted with dining rooms and parlors, with rooms regularly spaced out throughout, segregated into east and west by sex and into compartments by the temperament and status of the patient. The patient was to begin in the farthest section and move towards the front doors to symbolize their progression towards freedom. Plentiful windows welcomed sunlight from any angle it might hit, also allowing the entrance of a cool breeze in the warmer months. If one looked outside, one would've seen an idyllic, peaceful country scene extending into the horizon, far from the hustle and bustle of the inner city. A great deal of attention was paid to heating and ventilation to ensure the most hygienic conditions and avoid foul odors. By perfecting the spaces they moved through, the best possible conditions were ensured for a holistic reform of the person and their world, making cure all but inevitable in the eyes of the doctors.

To their creators, these were architectural marvels, designed to normalize movements and activities in a rational whole and prepare patients for the outside world by simultaneously mimicking and perfecting it. Though the greater amount of detail was devoted to construction, this rationalization was extended to the organization of the community as well, especially the relationship between the different institutional occupations and patient-laborers. For Kirkbride and his friends, regimented and disciplined labor was therapeutic in itself since "it composes the restless and excited, promotes a good appetite and a comfortable digestion, and gives sound and refreshing sleep to many who would without it pass wakeful nights."[6] A well-ordered asylum was a hard-working asylum. In addition to opportunities for work, some asylums could boast of a wide range of artistic and cultural activities on offer—like painting studios, organized sports, patient-edited journals like *The Opal*, or even excursions. Taken together, activities that stimulate the body and mind for the purposes of distraction, improving coordination, achieving concrete goals, or increasing one's sense of strength and well-being—including work and recreational activities—are referred to at various points in psychiatric history as "Occupational Therapy." With this in mind, the planning of the asylum environment can be more precisely seen as a structural part of a more general organization of a social form dedicated to healing and reason.

As I discussed in Chapter 1, the founders of the asylum system believed that the social world of contemporary civilization—that is, city life—was among the primary causes of insanity. The road to health then obviously required quick and decisive removal, a policy which justified lax civil commitment laws and the construction of self-contained asylums. With the benefit of hindsight, we often forget that, at least for a brief period in the middle of the nineteenth century, the asylum of the moral treatment system enjoyed widespread approval, though exactly how widespread is hard to say. If one finds it difficult to accept that the psychiatrists of this era genuinely desired the approval and comfort of their patients and their social circles—something I believe is true for plenty in the tradition of moral treatment, however mistakenly they may have pursued it—they themselves provide a number of additional reasons why they might seek to obtain it anyways. Kirkbride explains that it's not only vital for the patients that the asylum have "a cheerful and comfortable appearance, [which avoids] every thing repulsive and prison-like," but also for their friends who "cannot fail to see that neither labor nor expense is spared to promote the happiness of the patients, and they are thus led to have a generous confidence in those to whose care their friends have been entrusted, and a readiness to give a steady support to a liberal course of treatment."[7] This plan seems to have worked, as family commitments went from being rare to being a common route for institutional treatment, in no small part due to the perceived successes of moral treatment.[8] In Edgar Allan Poe's 1845 short story "The System of Doctor Tarr and Professor Fether," the narrator thinks to make a short detour to visit a private asylum in France practicing a "system of soothing," clearly an allusion to moral treatment. Poe's story captures the ambivalence of the asylum under moral treatment: when the narrator arrives, he is actually welcomed to dinner, without his knowing, by a group of patients who had recently staged a revolt and locked up the staff. Despite some eccentricities, the narrator doesn't suspect anything is amiss even as the leader of the lunatics explains that *they* were the sane staff and the staff were the lunatics they had to repress, that is, until chaos erupts as the "real" staff stage a counter-rebellion and take back control. That the relationship between staff and patient rested on an insurgent violence barely simmering below the surface reveals Poe's general pessimism about the possibility of a harmonious community in an institutional setting, but, to take a step back, could we even imagine seeing a character in a novel or film in the twenty-first century who decides to take a sojourn to a psychiatric ward or an outpatient clinic just to check it out? That we're left wondering who the actual patients were speaks to the attempted leveling between patients and staff in this system, and further, the fact that the encounter occurs at all betrays a much deeper level of comfort and transparency than exists today when no one is left wondering who the patient in a psychiatric hospital is, first and foremost because their invisibility is a mark of their excluded status.

By the 1870s, the 250 person cap for the ideal asylum set by Kirkbride was already far surpassed across the board and suddenly, the same vitriol and disgust formerly weaponized by the superintendents was turned against them as former patients like Elizabeth Ware Packard in Illinois, Ebenezer Haskell in Pennsylvania (at Kirkbride's asylum, no less), Louisa Lowe in England, and so many more released text after text exposing the asylum as a space of arbitrary brutality and irrationality. By the end of the century, Poe's image of the asylum as a pressure cooker looked less like subtext than common knowledge. At multiple points up to now, I've described the descent of the asylum as a transformation into a prison, but prisons in the nineteenth century, as Carla Yanni makes clear, were not considered simple dumping grounds but were host to their own expansive and idealist visions about how to influence behavior through space.[9] It's more accurate to say that, at a certain level of concentration, the institutional specificities in the reformist architectures of prisons and asylums start to blur together and converge back into the primordial custodial poorhouse. The corridors of Kirkbride asylums once tread by patients on the progressive path to liberation were filled to the brim with beds. The sunlight streaming in from the windows cast the shadow of iron bars on the stale interior. The ascent to recovery symbolized by the long winding hallways became a hellish circle to nowhere. Patient labor was pervasive, but the idea that it was helping anyone was just window-dressing; its main purpose was to ensure that the institution could crawl once more into the next miserable day. Amusing or pleasant activities came to a halt or were offered by legal necessity under strict surveillance. Why did this happen?

It can't be said that these realities were completely alien to the designs of the reformers. No one was stabbed in the back. Their great principles and practices were not betrayed to make way for a reign of terror. Kirkbride and his "brethren" advocated and emphasized discipline, removal from society, and regimented labor as reformatory. Though they may have harbored dreams about creating a harmonious and dynamic community, its specific organizational form was more often than not modeled on the typical patriarchal family, which is hardly a natural unit, but arises within specific economic circuits. I say circuits, because, as Wilhelm Reich explains, there is a certain circularity to its form: it is the product of its economic conditions under capitalism as a basic unit of enterprise while performing the social-political functions of extending guardianship ("protecting" and withholding civil rights) over women and children and acting as an educational apparatus for the dominant moral and sexual mores.[10] It's no surprise then that the early feminist critiques of the asylum, like Elizabeth Packard's 1868 *The Prisoner's Hidden Life* and 1874 *Modern Persecution*, not only likened being committed to being under the tutelage of a tyrannical patriarch, but identified the asylum as a strategic node in a patriarchal web of power: "That class of men who wish to rule woman, seem intent on destroying her reason, to secure her subjection. If they cannot really put out this light in her, which so much annoys them, they will credit this work as done, by falsely accusing her of insanity, and when once branded by Dr. McFarland's diploma of 'hopelessly insane,' they fondly think they can keep her under their feet. And this has actually been done in many instances, by the help of the Illinois Insane Asylum."[11]

This authoritarianism extended across the whole structure of the Kirkbride Plan: the patients were supposed to move from the farthest wings (where the worst were kept) up towards the central tower, as if through purgatory. This embedded a pattern of discipline into something as basic as the sleeping arrangements. But, thanks to economic constraints, even this was rigged since the wealthy patients could simply purchase better units and more space.[12] Basic inequality persisted in the new egalitarian system simply because the asylum, from the beginning, was teetering on the edge of its own economic dissolution. It was able to survive for a while on charitable contributions, serviceable state funding, and private boarders in its heyday, but once the optimistic bubble of the cult of curability definitively popped, chronic cases piled up just as the money stopped flowing in. Everything went to hell. Economistic claims that a well-funded asylum would save more money in the end by repairing workers to "add directly to the wealth of the State, [or] at least support their families"[13] looked increasingly unrealistic as the "incurables" became the face of the institution.

Security, which the Kirkbride Plan strained so hard to conceal, became the asylum's organizing principle. True economy consisted in ridding the public spheres of these dependents as quickly and cheaply as possible. Under quantitative intensification, whatever therapeutic qualities may have been built into the structure tipped over into segregation for its own sake, drudgery, and brutality such that the secondary considerations of hierarchy and security they were at such pains to conceal became the order of the day. Most of these spaces never improved. It suffices to look at the images of Albert Maisel's 1946 *Life Magazine* series "Bedlam" to see that asylums described by the great exposés of the mid-to-late twentieth century look and sound almost exactly like those described at the end of the nineteenth.

THE EXPERIENCE OF THE TOTAL INSTITUTION

It was in the shell of this failed asylum that the Canadian sociologist Erving Goffman performed his famous ethnographic studies at St. Elizabeths Hospital, one of the United States' only federal asylums, which he published in *Asylums: Essays on the Condition of the Social Situation of Mental Patients and Other Inmates* (1961). His book offers some useful tools for thinking about the primacy of sociality in the context of the asylum, even in the worst possible conditions. Significantly, Goffman was not exclusively studying the asylum, but rather the "total institution," conceived as any space set out apart from the outside world where inmates or lodgers are immersed into a social field with its own separate codes, laws, norms, and expectations. This included prisons, military barracks, and concentration camps. In the essay "On the Characteristics of Total Institutions," Goffman explains that the asylum sets out to "untrain" the incoming patient, in a bid to institute a break in their life to ensure a tranquil acquiescence to treatment, or simply to break them and ameliorate their more excessive behaviors for the benefit of the staff and society at large. Upon arrival, personal belongings are taken and stored, clothes are removed, their hair may be cut, and their personal boundaries are immediately unsettled when they find out that the staff has access to the most intimate regions of their body and can, at their own discretion, exert force and violence when deemed necessary. In this way, the patient is "shaped and coded into an object that can be fed into the administrative machinery of the establishment, to be worked on smoothly by routine operations."[14]

Any amusements cease to be meaningful as everything is subsumed into the stupid logic of distraction. Anything to pass the time. In these somber rituals of mortification, the remaining shards of intimacy still available from the shattering of moral treatment were swept under the rug. Anything else would be too painful. Out of necessity, the staff destroy themselves in the process: they become paranoid (is the patient trying to take advantage of me?), produce collective fantasies about their real role and why they must commit acts of enormous cruelty (locking them in there is part of the treatment . . . their screams are a symptom of a disease)—and become cold and insensitive as what was once basic and obvious becomes alien and strange. Guilt-ridden and wounded, they rush to integrate their minds and bodies into the cold embrace of an institutional machine to prevent the formation of a self-image as executioner or prison guard.

But, for all that, are the inmates transformed into mere robots mechanically acting out the performances expected of them? Not at all. Desire does not disappear; it is displaced and dispersed across a new social field. If cigarettes, alcohol, or treats are offered as rewards or in the black market, new activities arise oriented around these small pleasures (gambling, for example). Sexual relations are pursued in secret or in exchange for material privileges. Slang and linguistic shorthand are coined to facilitate underground economic or social exchanges. While the staff may be invested in trying to break the patient, to discipline them, or to inscribe them in a treatment program, a whole range of countermeasures are available: they can pretend to participate in therapy or activities to have more social interactions or pursue a romantic interest, they can pretend to take medicines and parrot the language of the psychiatrist, and they can even sabotage infrastructure or organize a small protest against bad conditions or simply run away. The psychiatric inmate is not fated to become the model patient and adopt the language of their doctors; they can just as well withdraw into isolation in a corner, lash out in violence to maintain personal integrity, or carve out a niche existence with enough pleasures. It was actually in the asylum's interest to keep a vestige of the outside, at least as an image, to use as leverage and an incentive for good behavior.[15] One of the shortcomings of Goffman's presentation is that it tended to isolate the psychiatric hospital more than was actually possible. There may have been attempts to close it off to the outside world, but with staff, visitors, and new patients, outside influences were flowing in constantly. The institution is not so much an alien planet as an island. In other words, the mad doctors could never remove people from the social world; all they could do was transplant them from one milieu into another.

We can treat Goffman's account here as a description of the typical social life of an asylum organized around segregation and concentration. To anticipate what's about to come by using a term popular with the French group I want to discuss, one could describe this mode of life using Jean-Paul Sartre's concept of "seriality:" a life lived according to a formal, rigid schema, "a ritualization of the quotidian, a regular and terminal hierarchization of responsibility."[16] As low as they'd fallen, a group of dissident psychiatrists, psychoanalysts, and communists in central Europe, shaken by wartime experiences, nevertheless believed they could return to the task of shaping the space and structure of the mental institution into places of refuge worthy of the name "asylum." They, like Kirkbride, subscribed to the notion that the spatial arrangement produced a world, but, having seen what became of the earlier citadels of healing, they set up "mechanisms to fight, every day, against all that could turn the whole collective toward a concentrationist or segregationist structure."[17] In time, this group would call their approach "Institutional Psychotherapy."

What is it to offer asylum? Asylum is refuge, a space of rest, but also a place of transit, somewhere to move within and through on the way to something better. Institutional Psychotherapists were those who, without remorse or sentimentality, had the resolution to amputate those institutional limbs and tissue of the asylum succumbing to rigor mortis. François Tosquelles was central to this movement. Tosquelles was born into an anarcho-syndicalist family in Reus, Spain in 1912. During the Spanish Civil War, he was part of a group that founded POUM, an anti-Stalinist Marxist party. Camille Robcis argues that it was Tosquelles' exposure to Catalan anarchist movements and anti-Stalinist groups' tendency to decentralization that convinced him of the need to promote self-management over authoritarian modes of organization.[18] He became interested in psychiatry at a time when Catalonia was implementing an early form of decentralized psychiatry. His early experience with practicing on the move served him well during the war when he treated partisans' traumatic reactions to battle within just a few kilometers of the frontline. Likely by virtue of necessity, he worked in the main with nonprofessionals—lawyers, painters, and sex workers.[19] Always a master of bricolage ready to make use of whatever was around him, Tosquelles found that the lack of professionalism actually inculcated a spirit of innovation, collectivism, and mutual reliance that freed their practice from its hypostatized patterns of thought. After the war, Francisco Franco's regime put out a death sentence on Tosquelles, who was forced to flee to France along with many other Spanish republican, anarchist, and communist comrades. Like hundreds of thousands of other undesirables from across the border, Tosquelles ended up in captivity. In the Septfonds concentration camp, he once again practiced psychiatry under extraordinary conditions with nothing guaranteed, no training programs, surrounded by disease and suicide. The organization of plays and group therapy sessions helped, in their small ways, to ward off despair. From then on, Tosquelles intimately understood the deleterious effects of living in confined spaces defined and organized by rigid categories. In this way, he became one of the first psychiatrists to draw a direct line between the organizational principles and physical space of the mental institution and the prison to the concentrationist and segregationist model of the concentration camp. Particularly after the horrors of the Shoah would become more widely known, this mode of comparison would be frequently and successfully mobilized in campaigns for deinstitutionalization.

In 1940, French Resistance soldiers facilitated the successful escape of the detainees at Septfonds. Free, but unable to return home, Tosquelles accepted the invitation of Paul Balvet, then director of the remote Saint-Alban psychiatric hospital to come work with him. Soon after, and especially after Balvet left and was replaced by the communist Lucien Bonnafé, Tosquelles and company welcomed Jewish refugees and resistance fighters like Georges Canguilhem and Paul Eluard, oftentimes signing false admission forms, if necessary.[20] In the convergence of communists, poets, and refugees the movement later named Institutional Psychotherapy was born. Tosquelles wrote about it that "[a] good citizen is incapable of doing psychiatry. Psychiatry includes an anti-culture, a culture with a different point of view."[21] The position of this new rebellious milieu, whose members had survived war and camp life, was that it was not the psychiatric patient considered in isolation who ought to be the object of therapeutic intervention, but the hospital they moved through and all the factors that converged to make it into a medical prison.

The hospital was sick, they said. It had a social life but it was impoverished and dehumanizing. It claimed to offer shelter and refuge from the outside world, but it took the form of a prison, or even a camp. If the asylum was to become a real refuge, then its role must be to "disoccupy" and "disalienate" the person, not replace one alienation for another. In their effort to heal this space, they mobilized disparate discourses and histories: Marxist political and social theory; Freudian insights into mental alienation; theories of psychiatric architecture and semiotics; and a variety of local, rural knowledges about communal life, agriculture, and more. It was a time of great theoretical and practical exchange across disciplines with similar goals—including Maud Mannoni, who also applied a Lacanian approach in her work with mentally ill children, and Fernand Deligny, the nonviolent guerilla who lived with nonverbal autistic children in the mountains in search of new ways of communicating—were fellow travelers of these renegade psychiatrists. Jean Oury, who worked at Saint-Alban in the 1940s, opened a second, private clinic under the same premises along with Félix Guattari in 1953 called La Borde. Guattari later became the most famous member of the Institutional Psychotherapy group after publishing the book *Anti-Oedipus* with Gilles Deleuze, which, for many, captured the excitement and imagination of the movements of '68.

PUTTING PSYCHIATRY ON ITS FEET

The first necessary task was to change the way space is organized with an eye to the opportunities for social life in the institution, for this, in turn, meant changing the way space organizes people. Psychiatry had to become a "geopsychiatry" in which space was conceived as a therapeutic agent. In theory, geopsychiatry is not far from the principles of moral treatment as described by Thomas Kirkbride or W. A. F. Browne. The latter also advised that psychiatry is just as much about healing the space and attendants as the patients: "[y]our first attempt . . . ought to be to cure your keepers; you need not proceed to your patients until you have done so."[22] The theory of environmental determinism led many of them to the belief that the space through which the patient moved was *the* decisive element. David Rothman ably summarized this common position: "[c]reate a different kind of environment, which methodically corrected the deficiencies of the community, and a cure for the insane was at hand."[23] This point is, characteristically, taken to its most consistent theoretical conclusion by Browne:

> The association of lunatics requires to be skillfully managed. But when classes have been formed in conformance to the mutual wants, and wishes, and dispositions of the parties, the system is at once beautiful and self-operating. There is no need of keepers to direct, and chide, and caution. Their presence is required to regulate the machine, but its motions are spontaneous. The little kindnesses of co-operation and assistance go forward, the weaver plies his shuttle as vigorously, and the dance and song conclude the day as regularly as if a whip or a comfit were displayed. It is a mistake to suppose that, as a general rule, these bands should consist of patients of similar dispositions.[24]

If properly organized, the psychiatrist and their effects ought to disappear into the milieu, where the real process of healing happens and the highest level of organization appears. They are mere tinkerers of healing-machines, for which they dedicate all their frail effort once they hear its rhythmic whirring. Institutional Psychotherapy was likewise not the first movement to combine Freudian insights into mind with a Marxist orientation—the rogue German psychoanalyst Wilhelm Reich had already written *The Mass Psychology of Fascism* that connected the economic unit of the patriarchal family in capitalism to mass neuroses and the desire for fascism—but they seized, in this small, neglected hospital in France, the chance to apply the idea that the goal of psychiatry was to confront social and mental alienation through the organization of space and social life more thoroughly than Kirkbride was able, because they were willing to pursue this goal *against* the bottom line or professional stature rather than in subservience to them.

Unlike the radical psychiatric traditions in the US, the French were deeply rooted in psychoanalysis, and especially the work of Jacques Lacan.[25] Lacan provided a useful common language outside of the vulgar materialisms of the various biological discourses in psychiatry, holding instead that "the unconscious is structured like a language." Institutional Psychotherapy consists largely in spatializing this idea: if the unconscious is structured like a language, then that language is mapped onto space. Thus, the institution is also structured like a language, or, as Jean Oury put it, it is structured like "phonemes"[26] with different spaces seeming to repeat patterns of signification that could be broken down and remade. By walking its corridors, one discovers a strict symmetry between the regular patterns of one's physical movements and their psychic investments and conflicts. In arresting this movement out of economistic necessity, psychiatry became tragically invested in pretending knowledge was tied to the notion of isolated control. Jean Oury described the desire to intern madness within walls and books by comparing it to entomology: "In the end, nosologies are only frameworks for imprisoning madmen. They are put in books, like a butterfly collection. A psychiatry book is the same thing: what the butterflies are like, in what room; to preserve them you drop them in formaldehyde, to observe them you put them in rooms with portholes."[27] This comparison is particularly apt for it's not that the butterfly pinned into a book or inundated with chemicals isn't real, but that it's not the same butterfly on display there as the one flying over your head and out the window. The expressive capacity of the butterfly has been reduced to just one: displayability. To some extent, geopsychiatry is supposed to make good on moral treatment's promise of freedom, or "the power of gratifying every innocent propensity, every justifiable desire, of pursuing every object which is calculated to inspire present pleasure, or conduce to the ultimate re-establishment of reason"[28] without accepting the presupposed moral parameters expressed by the words "justifiable" or "innocent." Patients were enlisted to literally tear down walls created to hem them in, and doors were unlocked.[29] Townspeople were invited into the hospital, and the patients left their confinement on the hill to go into town. What mattered were not the specific spaces themselves, but, as Tosquelles said, "to be able to go from one part to another, from one's quarters to the kitchen, from the kitchen to the cemetery even."[30] Common space, or space in general, was defined by constantly shifting patterns of movement—routes and pathways—rather than defined physical boundaries. Some of the staff and doctors began living at the hospital with the patients with their families, eating the same meals, and participating in the same activities. This created a situation in which everyone was materially invested in improving the living conditions of the space, where a superintendent could no longer say "I'll have the dining room cleaned later" because it didn't really matter to him. Increasingly, patients and staff worked side by side. This role refusal and breakdown of boundaries was not an addition to a biological treatment but was the necessary condition for therapy itself. Maud Mannoni elaborates: "The gulf between the world of the 'sick' and the world of the healthy is one which we have introduced as protection against our own fear. Experience shows us that a therapeutic approach is possible only if we become part of the 'sick' man's world."[31] Beyond that, the collective spirit of work was a saving grace in a time when the Vichy government allowed over 40,000 patients to die of malnutrition or cold; since Saint-Alban's productive output was much higher, since they did not embrace the sacrificial logic of soft eugenics that turned away from starvation, and because the doctors had no qualms about flubbing records to receive extra rations or trading with villagers, no patients died there in this way.[32] The space of the hospital became permeable and open, its boundaries were fluid. It was no longer the isolated island described by Goffman, with its paranoid directive to keep all contagions, that is, human beings, contained and segregated.

Everything had to be put into motion; the world was to reinvent itself anew every day. What had to be avoided was the comfort and passivity of distinct roles and positions. For Tosquelles, "[w]hat counts is not the head, but the feet. Knowing where you put your feet. It is the feet that are the great readers of the world, of geography."[33] His experience of being a migrant and a refugee is doubtless tied to this attitude. He said that "[t]he human is a creature that goes from one space to another, she cannot stay all the time in the same space. . . . That's to say that the human is always a pilgrim, a creature who goes elsewhere"[34] and affirmed that geopsychiatry was a "species of migrant work."[35] There was a joke at La Borde that it was actually the doctors who were the most chronic cases: they never left, while the patients were just passing through.[36] The rediscovery of motion brought with it the rediscovery of Occupational Therapy—the arts, collective projects, the trades, festivals, and parties. The patient club, in which political power was invested, was one of the major innovations. Patients were asked to make significant decisions for the hospital and could contest decisions made by the staff. A patient bar was opened, dances were organized regularly, along with films and dinners. Isolation, cliques, and "egocentrism" were to be combated with festivals, parties, and the reorganization of roles to shake things up and create new connections and associations.

In their hands, the meeting, a space where groups are consolidated and rules are made known, was made into a machine for challenging what was going unsaid, as Tosquelles explains: "Nothing should ever be obvious, everything is subject to discussion. Everybody must be consulted, everybody can decide. Not just for the sake of democracy, but in order to facilitate the progressive conquest of speech, to learn mutual respect. The patients must be able to have a say on the conditions of their stay and their care, their rights of exchanges, expression, and circulation."[37] Maud Mannoni came to the same conclusion at a "Special" school: "[t]o prevent an institution from closing in on itself," she wrote, "each of its members must be guaranteed the chance of projecting to the future. The participation of everyone in scientific work is in itself therapeutic."[38] Beyond providing a forum for exchange, Guattari notes that the meeting also served a cathartic function. In his experience in the Daily Activities Committee, one of many meeting spaces created every day, he notes that "[t]his daily meeting eliminated the dross to focus on what remained." In reference to the arguments and fights that would frequently break out, he said he was "absolutely sure that this was the mainspring of the patients' local resocialization."[39] At La Borde, they formalized decentralization and instituted a complex grid for redistributing roles and the division of labor on a regular basis to produce new social arrangements and "frame the deregulation."[40] This ensured that nurses would wash dishes, doctors would farm, staff members would perform routine medical tasks, and residents would lead art classes. Guattari emphasized in his work that, thanks to this arrangement, the same person could be a patient at one time, a nurse at another, and the analyst at another. This constant changing and shifting was meant to break people free of the seriality imposed by other institutions, so that they could, in Guattari's words "reappropriate the meaning of their existence in an ethical and no longer technocratic way."[41] Naturally, it was a difficult pill to swallow when a doctor was asked to clear the dinner table, but, if they can survive the ordeal and the "panic of being torn apart,"[42] the doctor advances towards a closer understanding of the group dynamics and fantasies circulating in the daily reproduction of their spaces, so typically taken for granted.

LINES OF COMMUNICATION, PATHS OF DESIRE

In the average mental hospital, desire officially flows in one direction: the only desire with any acknowledged reality is that of the superintendent, the guard, or the nurse. Desire is permitted to exist, or be represented, as the expression of force. "Fatally," said Tosquelles, "the guards, leaders, bosses, the doctors, or psychiatrists only make everyone a prisoner of their own particular psychopathology, their character."[43] Unlike the traditional asylum, desire in Institutional Psychotherapy was not taken to be some personal longing "hidden in the recesses of the mind or in stereotyped complexes," but something which "exists and functions on the same level as social reality"[44]; in other words, as something emerging through common factors among the milieus at La Borde and Saint-Alban.

The urge to move, to develop relations with the world, new associations, to try out new tasks or set out exploring a novel sexual, romantic, or friendly relationship do not disappear in the mental institution; but by being denied, by forcing the patient to quash their wants and enthusiasms and often even their physical movements, they are stuffed into niche-hidden corners finding expression through frustration, anger, aggression, and despair. The movement of desire facilitates, in turn, the development of new minor languages, lingos, and slangs. One of the organs of communication at Saint-Alban was *Trait-d'union*, a newsletter run by and for residents. This publication differed from a typical asylum newsletter, since the latter were often edited and therefore limited by staff who oftentimes recruited only those patients who were already sympathetic to the institution's operations. In my study of patient publications at Minnesota's institutions, I commonly came across articles in which the author expressed the hope that, by writing, the staff would consider them more competent and therefore potentially worthy of an earlier release. But because the psyche is, according to Guattari, "the resultant of multiple and heterogenous components," it was necessary to step outside the circle drawn around verbal enunciation in the standard dual psychoanalytic encounter and take seriously "nonverbal means of communication, relations of architectural space, ethological behaviors, economic status, social relations at all levels, and, still more fundamentally, ethical and aesthetic aspirations."[45] While still in Spain, Tosquelles had studied muscular tonus. He compared the psychiatric encounter to a game of football: what is important is to pay attention to the positions of the players, their postures, their attitudes and conflicts, and their muscular tones and reactions.[46] What we are dealing with here are mediums of communication parallel, and imminent, to the privileged verbal form involving the enunciation of words, a reckoning with a whole range of possible communications and investments in what Tosquelles called a "transferential constellation."[47] One can describe Institutional Psychotherapy as the style of treatment that disperses the standard psychoanalytic arrangement point by point. The encounter between two people, in verbal language, often in a private, closed room is opened up to groups in common, moving through fluid space using irregular, incommensurable mediums of communication, i.e., gestures, visual cues, touch, activity, or something else.

Any "analysis" taking place in this paradigm, any treatment being pursued, does not flow downwards from the analyst to the patient in a vertical way, but neither does it pass from one patient to another in a horizontal way. It cuts across many lines at once in an irregular fashion. Guattari coined the concept "transversality" to describe communicative movements within therapeutic encounters, which he opposes to the psychoanalytic notion of "transference" wherein a patient's feelings from outside the binary therapeutic relationship are "transferred" into the present—onto the analyst, for example. The libidinal energy channeled through the encounter could be put to great use or present a grave danger, but it was presumed to exist between two. What becomes of the transferential relation within the group? In the traditional asylum, institutional languages were officially structured vertically with messages flowing from the top down to the bottom. Of course, at every level, horizontal slangs cut across these messages leading to enclaves where minor languages were formed: the doctors chit chat about how lazy this or that nurse is, about how much they hate that patient who's so difficult; the nurses talk about what "really needs to get done," and which no one else understands; the patients talk about what you need to say to avoid shock treatment or which nurse is more likely to give you privileges if you're nice to them. A bureaucratic language of order messages and a flat language of coping. In the concept of transversality, Guattari offered an alternative to traditional psychiatric hierarchies, but also to isolated forms of self-management, anticipating exclusively patient-led projects in the decades that followed. Transversality can be said to describe the ways in which diagonal lines of communication or social encounters cut across and through vertically and horizontally arranged ones, "when there is maximum communication among different levels and, above all, in different meanings."[48] "The analyst is no longer the mirror; rather, it's the group,"[49] writes Gary Genosko. Transversality is certainly about power, but not about divesting it from one place to invest it into another. It's true that a kind of power flows downwards from the directives of the superintendents, but other kinds flow in and through the relations between nurses and from the patients themselves, who together, oftentimes without their own awareness, are the actors who materially reproduce the institution. Transversal communication is not about inventing power, it is about bringing it into one's hands and feet, letting it flow more freely, from unexpected positions, more consciously, and with more intention.

Institutional Psychotherapy is not as simple as "unleashing" a well of preexisting desires nor seeking to fulfill a series of lacks but consists in cultivating a network. This is how fellow traveler Fernand Deligny conceived it in his pedagogical forays into the mountains, namely as a "mode of being."[50] Deligny was something of an outsider, even in this eclectic group. After working as a special education teacher at an asylum in the early 1940s, he helped create an organization designed to keep young people out of mental institutions called La Grande Cordée [The Great Cord], which ran a drop-in center for some time out of an abandoned theater in Paris.[51] In the 1950s, he began running residential programs near the Cévennes Mountains—and at La Borde as of 1966, after financial issues—with nonverbal autistic children. Communication is premised on a number of commons: a common means of expression, a common form of life, a common experience, etc. Those of us who speak are accustomed to taking communication for granted and, in the process, we tend to become insensitive to the existence of other modes of expression.

A common life among the speaking and the nonspeaking is not so much premised on the latter acquiring new means of communication, but on the former resisting the pull of the familiar: "we were in search of a mode of being that allowed them to exist even if that meant changing our own mode, and we did not take into account any particular conceptions of mankind, whatever these might be, and not at all because we wanted to replace these conceptions with others; mankind mattered little to us; we were in search of a practice that would exclude from the outset interpretations referring to some code; we did not take the children's ways of being as scrambled, coded messages addressed to us."[52] Within the communicative web being woven through the network's activity, Deligny at times may have played the spider, but "the same goes for the ten or twelve others whose presence weaves our network."[53] What weaves itself into being in this arachnid network is a "primordial communism" Deligny likens to the canvas of a work of art, to the physical movements coded as gestures, to the lines that form letters, to fossils. "The work of art lies in the canvas," he insists, "[w]here else could it lie? Inside heads, ideas, inside hearts, or somewhere else?"[54] Far away from some simulated "primitivism" imagined as a regression on a line, the network weaves the communicable into itself through its own activity, in search of surface components (the canvas, the stone, the line) that make the common structures we already use visible and something to be shared.

NISE DA SILVEIRA AND THE "UNITY OF THINGS"

If it's true that communication networks tend to arise *like* a work of art, it's also true that they can arise *as* a work of art. Opinions differed as to the usefulness of art in psychiatry, but arguments tended to revolve around whether beautiful art had a calming or agitating effect on patients, e.g., whether something like a landscape painting was a gentle encouragement towards recovery or an odious reminder of the chaos of the outside world. Even if most of the utopian psychiatrists of the nineteenth century agreed on either the physical-therapeutic or diversionary value of art production, this was generally so because they kept the patient busy, as did any other hands-on occupation. Genuine interest in the work of the patient itself was much rarer. This, even though art is constantly being produced in the asylum: it's scratched into the walls, scrawled on napkins, or inscribed into the skin. Any psychiatric project centered around art is therefore simply taking note and making use of something that already happens with or without their involvement.

Works had been referenced by psychiatrists here and there, but the earliest collection of such art was possibly W. A. F. Browne's at Crichton, beginning in 1839. Browne encouraged art production as a therapeutic activity and even organized an exhibition of works in 1841.[55] Over eighty years later, German psychiatrist Hans Prinzhorn wrote a systematic study of "psychotic art" in 1922 and collected over 5,000 pieces that are in the Prinzhorn Collection in Heidelberg today, which continues to grow and display pieces by psychiatric patients. Surrealists saw latent genius expressed through the waking dreams of delirium, elevating mad art to a purer sphere of inspired production. Jean Dubuffet, through his encounters with it at Saint-Alban and at a number of institutions first in Switzerland and then around the world, coined the term "art brut," or "raw art" to describe the productions of those without any training in the arts. In the US, we generally use the unfortunate term "outsider art." These masculine art circles in Europe tended to view the artwork as either evidence of an untamed, primitive creative force or an expression of an inner pathology. We have to go to Brazil to examine how artistic activity can be put into common without superimposing a stereotypical codification of meaning by analyzing the work of the inimitable psychiatrist Nise da Silveira, the first woman to graduate from the Faculdade de Medicina da Bahia in 1926. According to the Brazilian author Graciliano Ramos, it was, for her, "not enough to be woman and Northeastern, doctor and psychiatrist; but [she also had to be an] early antipsychiatrist and communist in the fascist State."[56] She was not the first to introduce art therapy into Brazil—it has enjoyed a great deal of popularity since Osório César began collecting work in the 1920s[57]—but she grasped at something more elemental with a greater degree of experimentation.

In the 1930s, Silveira began working at the Centro Psiquiátrico Nacional Pedro II in the neighborhood of Engenho de Dentro in Rio— Brazil's first asylum, founded in 1841—in the period of the fascist

Vargas government. Marlon Miguel characterizes early Brazilian psychiatry as being split between a progressive vanguard and a "heavy, exclusionary, violent, and carceral"[58] mode. Like the United States, the former slave state of Brazil governed its subjects through race, resulting in uneven and differentiated lines of force. These are particularly visible in Brazil, where psychiatrists' seizure of total control over the asylum system from religious authorities coincided with the abolition of slavery. Even prior to abolition, slave owners would free slaves suspected of being insane and leave them to wander the streets, so that they would not be financially liable for their care when they were arrested and sent to the asylum.[59] With the abolition of slavery and the declaration of the republic in 1889, the asylum served an essential pressure-release function in the construction of a new fragile civil society by operating as a point where the legal meaning of citizenship remained more flexible. In other words, the production of the legal category of the mentally ill ward, with their own special rights and guarantees, opened a legal space that rationalized the continued exclusion of newly freed slaves. This helps to explain why, throughout its history, Brazilian psychiatry has overwhelmingly hospitalized Black people, as the psychiatric patient Lima Barreto remembered from his time in an asylum: "All is black," he wrote, noting the "dark pigment of most of the ill. . . . Black is the most trenchant, most arresting color."[60] Playing the role of a social stabilizer following legal abolition and administering a population coming increasingly from former plantations marked Brazilian psychiatry early on with a modified ideology of a slave state with its necessary dehumanization, the continuity of violent repression, and the centralization of forced work as a form of healing (especially agricultural labor).[61]

The problem of the "mental disturbances of Black people" was a common theme in psychiatric discourse from the beginning up until the dictatorship period, when eugenics became attached to the state's project of purging the social body of ever-feared communists, who were linked to this notion of inherent degeneracy, and whitening the population through external immigration controls and internal population management. The language of inheritable degeneration and disease and the strong link being drawn between localizable biological factors and pathology in the twentieth century contributed to the widespread popularity of aggressive physical treatments like the lobotomy technique of the Portuguese psychiatrist António Egas Moniz, along with electroshock and insulin shock later on. Already, in this early period, Silveira defied the logic of this violent regime by forming simple human relationships with her patients. She describes at one point how—despite her colleagues telling her that schizophrenic patients have no affect or internal life—she formed a friendly relationship with a patient with this diagnosis even though the latter did not verbally communicate. In 1936, a nurse found Marxist literature among Silveira's things and turned her into the state. While she was serving her year-and-a-half sentence, the patient found out who had given her up and beat the nurse up very badly. This was "an affective reaction," Silveira said, "[t]he schizophrenic is not indifferent."[62]

After eight years in exile, she returned to the hospital Pedro II in 1944 and set out to form an entirely new psychiatric practice within this urban prison. She arrived at a moment when electroconvulsive therapy was being introduced onto the wards and describes seeing it applied for the first time: "We stood over the bed of a patient who was there to have electric shocks," she said, "[t]he psychiatrist pressed the button and the man started to seize. When the other patient was ready to receive a shock, the doctor said to me, 'Press the button.' I said, 'I won't!' And that's where the rebel began."[63] Beyond being revolted by the raw brutality of these acts, Silveira also questioned their philosophical underpinnings: what concept of the body was being operated on here? To her, reliance on such practices betrayed a faith in a mechanistic model of the human body with roots in Descartes' assertion that the body was a mere automaton mirrored in her time by various branches of phrenology which sought the final cause of human behaviors in localizable regions of the brain. In her open letters to the seventeenth-century philosopher Baruch de Spinoza, she reflected on an early exposure to Cartesian mechanical thought that stayed with her throughout her life: "Only man is capable of thinking. Only man possesses reason. If the body of man and the body of animals are quite similar machines . . . fundamental differences separate them. Descartes concludes by saying that animals do not only have less reason than men, but they have no reason at all. If they scream or wiggle, it is only the effect of movements that take place in the machine of their bodies." She continues in another: "I read this famous speech in my father's library when I was very young. I was outraged. I would never admit that my beloved dogs Top and Jiqui were incapable of thinking and feeling. Between the three of us, understanding and affection walked hand in hand in a deep relationship."[64] For Silveira, the mechanical view of the body was directly connected to the use of force and the denigration of "lower functioning" animals and people. She recalls being revolted by this attitude and the callous brutality visited upon weaker beings while in school: "I remember as if it were today a practical physiology class which had the mechanism of the circulation as its theme. A frog was stretched and had its four limbs nailed (crucified) to a cork board, and its chest was crudely opened so that we could see its tiny beating heart. The frog was popeyed and seemed to ask us: why such cruelty? It was for nothing. Nobody learned anything in that stupid class."[65] She turned sharply away from the Cartesian school that framed the mental patient as a "sick machine" and towards concepts that opened doors to communication and simple relationships. During her eight years of exile, she studied Spinoza who revealed "the unity of things" to her through his monist conception of the universe in which everything is interrelated and has the capacity to affect everything else. She became especially fond of Carl Gustav Jung's exploration of the collective unconscious, which allowed her to comprehend small gestures and visual productions as expressions of primordial communicative acts. A third influence was the work of the French madman and playwright Antonin Artaud, who, perhaps more forcefully than most, declared the fundamental right of the insane to find expression in insanity.

What was Silveira seeking in Jung that she couldn't find in Freud? She felt that Freudian psychoanalysis, in her time, had joined psychiatry in the demand to translate all manner of expression into verbal or written language. Analysts were too quick—too anxious to ease their own discomfort—to interpret the seemingly incoherent enunciations, dreams, visual materials, or acted behaviors back into their own linguistic symbolisms in their clinical cases. Inspired by Jung, she turned to images to find ways to communicate with those apparently outside the order of symbolic reason: "The psychiatrist sets his mind on the word and wants to translate everything into words; nobody is trying to belittle the words, but there are many other ways of communicating . . . So we set out to study the images."[66] Spinoza, Jung, and Artaud gave Silveira the philosophical tools to consider how the image on its own had concrete effects on those who perceived it and that this alone, without translation, was a sufficient medium of communicating and relating: "There are schools that study the images, but understand that the painted images serve only as means to develop verbal expression, that is considered to be by them the only valid language. . . . For us, the image is valid in its own value, it speaks by itself, and eloquently."[67] Like the Institutional Psychotherapists, "Nise used to say that the hospital collaborated with the disease and believed that occupational therapy had an important role to perform in changing that environment."[68] So, in 1946, she opened the Seção de Terapêutica Ocupacional e Reabilitação [Occupational Therapy and Rehabilitation Ward] to offer a broad range of activities: "functional (gardening, bookbinding, sewing, cobbling), expressive (painting, modeling, music), recreational (games, parties, cinema) or cultural—related to teaching and studying."[69] Of these, the painting atelier she set up with the help of visual artist Almir da Silva Mavignier, who was working as a day laborer, proved the most important.

Silveira struggled to maintain her artistic circle within the hospital for a few years before seeking wider recognition in the Brazilian art scene, which likely saved her practice. The long relationship between psychiatry and the art world is highly ambivalent, so we cannot unconditionally sing the praises of art therapy and artistic production alone. In Europe, the art of the mad "was posited as radically other and marked by externality, while at times used to refresh and expand the formal vocabulary of modernist art."[70] Often enough, this involved placing the artwork of the mad on the same plane as that of children, Indigenous people, and all those considered to be "pre-social," "uninhibited" by civilization, as if they somehow stood outside the social relations that make up their contemporary worlds. Hence, they call it "Outsider Art" or *art brut* [raw art.] The Nazis were also very interested in the artwork of the insane and displayed it to interested audiences alongside art by Jewish and avant-garde artists under the banner of "degenerate art" in cities around Germany. More often, mad artworks are excitedly and proudly displayed by a staff that "can't believe" what the mentally ill and disabled are capable of. And there is hardly an institution or ward today that wouldn't espouse the value of art therapy as a mechanism for calming patients. Distracting someone with painting is better than lashing out, they might say.

Silveira had an ambiguous relationship to the art world. For one exhibition, she wrote about the nine artists on display:

> Before seeking to understand them, it is concluded that they have blunted affectivity and their intelligence is in ruins. They would thus very well inhabit the building-prisons called hospitals, given shelter and food. . . . Come and see them wandering in the walled-in courtyard, such ghosts...This situation is due to having arbitrarily admitted that our mentally ill have extinguished all human needs other than sleeping, eating, and at most working in rudimentary jobs. . . . The current exhibition could be a message of appeal. . . addressed to everyone who came here and intimately participated in the enchantment of forms and colors created by human beings enclosed in the sad places that are the hospitals for the mentally ill.[71]

This explicitly frames the presentation of these works as a way to win the public over to the project of transforming mental institutions. Central to Silveira's perspective was that it could simultaneously be true that the mentally ill were artists like any other and also that the production of art was a therapeutic activity. The work they produced, over time and with careful study, began to reveal those psychic processes the artist was struggling with and the others that they already possessed that could aid them. When she noticed that a patient's art appeared more chaotic and unorganized, with more violently scraped lines and terrible figures, she might ask a monitor to simply stand by their side, silently, to be a witness and a support in their struggle.[72] In 1952, she opened the Museum of Images of the Unconscious in Rio de Janeiro, which is still open in 2024 and is the largest museum of its kind, containing over 350,000 works.

Primitivism has little to do with the primordial forms of sharing space Silveira and Deligny sought after, as neither imagine a spectrum of time or progress, but were instead on the lookout for what, in our daily activities, already ties us together and allows us to enact plans, to send messages, to live in shared space with shared communicable and intuitive norms. We might contrast Spinoza's thinking about falsity to a standard psychiatric one, since this is an interpretive function of the understanding. Traditionally, delusion is considered negatively as simple nonreason; it is that which is incommensurable with reality. False ideas are nontrue ideas. Spinoza explains that a false idea, or, in our case, a delusion, is not untruth, but inadequate truth. Inadequate according to what? Since "[t]he order and connections of ideas is the same of the order and connections of things,"[73] it can't be according to some transcendental standard of truth, but rather an imminent, relational one. A falsity is a positive fact, insofar as it is an expression of a concrete relationship to the world. No idea, he reminds us again and again, is formed separately from the body and mind being affected by something else in the world, thus the products of the imagination are always true in themselves (*as* objects of the imagination). Indeed, this is the primary way we all come to know the world. For Spinoza, the imagination, falsity, or so-called delusion should not be judged according to a simple criterion of reality/unreality, but rather must be thought in relation to the ways in which we form ideas through being affected by things. All ideas, insofar as they express a manner of being bodily or mentally affected, express a kind of truth. A delusion is not wrong, not misguided nor lost; what is being expressed and acted upon is an idea born of this world with an effect on the people and things around you and is, in that sense, real and true. At the same time, diverse contacts with other people and things in the world brings the imagination closer to those "common notions," those simple elements common to all that allow us to form ideas. Through these common notions, our ideas can be better integrated into a common social world, allowing our ideas to be shared more fully and disposed increasingly toward joy and the fulfillment of manifold unknown capacities.

Silveira's notion of visual communication was far from a static paradigm about extracting truth claims from those who don't speak; rather, she held that by continuously honing creative and communicative capacities in a common space, clients would become increasingly adept at expressing themselves and understanding others through the visual field. She welcomed but also reached far beyond the standard notion of the occupations as distraction:

> Labor therapy, praxis therapy, ergo therapy . . . It was about keeping the patient active without having specific psychological benefits in mind. . . . Naturally the idea of putting patients to work, or giving them a bit of leisure, would be wonderful for a philanthropically minded [person]. But I'm not a philanthropically minded lady. I am

drawn to the abyss. Although I am aware that the abyss is so deep that I am simply walking around the edge. I thought of using activities as ways to express the patient's internal issues. And offering them or utilizing activities that might somehow address those issues, compensating or diverting.[74]

This is why she hated the "horrible term" Americans gave it, "Occupational Therapy."[75] The point wasn't to simply be occupied, but to foster reparative drives in a communal activity, which was slow work, as she admitted: "Many will probably feel that such a process of return to consciousness is far too slow. The repetitious variations on the same theme may seem tiresome." She entreats us, however, not to forget:

> that it is a long journey indeed to the deepest underground regions and back and a hard one too, under quite unfavorable circumstances. Psychiatric hospitals do not provide adequate conditions for such journeys. The oppressive environment, the bustle of the ward: these things promote aggression instead. And what does traditional psychiatry have to offer? It amputates and smothers the traditional forces of the unconscious with massive use of drugs and shock therapy. But the unconscious emerges once again and the patient returns to the hospital again and again. More drugs! And the record sheets proclaim: blunted affectivity, deterioration, insanity.[76]

One needs "perseverance, patience, and an environment free of any coercion so that relationships of friendship and understanding can be created."[77] That is a fundamental condition of healing, and it takes time.

The trilogy of films *Imagens do inconsciente* [*Images from the Unconscious*], directed by Leon Hirszman and written by Silveira in 1986, dramatizes this slow work and the form this production took. In each, we hear the story of a patient who first arrived in various states of disrepair and quietude—Fernando Diniz, Adelina Gomez, and Carlos Pertuis—who gradually became more invested in their artistic work, despite the drab surroundings of the hospital. Prior to any interpretation or reading, what was of primary importance was to establish contact with the patient through artistic activity, on the basis of simple movements and actions: "I did not examine the paintings of the patients who frequented our atelier sitting in my office," she notes; "I saw them paint. I saw their frowns, I saw the impetus that moved their hands."[78] Silveira believed that human beings are often more capable than we think, that "[i]n any individual, even in the shabbiest beggar discharged from a psychiatric hospital, there are creative drives, self-curing forces, waiting for support, love, and human warmth."[79] Far from the regression diagnosed by her colleagues and the art critics, Silveira saw in the mad person's artistic propensity for geometrical shapes and abstractions like mandalas—in a synthesis of Spinoza and Jung—strategies for organizing reality by subjecting its chaotic phenomena to the strict rules of mathematics, thus warding off the very disintegration her contemporaries saw in it. Such strategies, if they might be called "internal," were not indifferent to the events of the world but a part of them. The role of the healer, then, must be facilitating the affection of joy, for "[it] is joy that heals, it is the lack of prejudice that heals."[80] A sweet gesture, like the subtle affirmation of a gentle hand on a shoulder, can represent the promise of safety and be a catalyst for creative reactions.[81]

To sum up the major points: the image is itself communicative, and not necessarily linguistically; second, the patient is given the space and the means to explore and discover what in their environment and psychic world may aid them in their pursuit of truth, comfort, and happiness with constant support; and third, expression and perception through artistic practice in a common space (in this case in the visual field), with all the gestural movement that entails, is enough to constitute a real social form. This social form is not impoverished; it is not "lacking language," at least not any more than primarily verbal communicators are lacking in touch, smell, and visual relations with the world. Despite its immense importance for Nise da Silveira's practice, I would surmise that the visual field is not the essential element: if she had opened up a floral arrangement clinic, however odd that would be, the same arguments could be made for olfactory productions, simply because "all activities are expressive. The point is to know how to observe an individual performing them. The way he holds a hammer or a saw, how he works with a loom or even cuts the thread to sew can tell us a lot."[82] Her aim was to "[coordinate] intimately hand and eye, sentiment and thinking, body and psyche."[83] With this aim in sight, it is entirely natural that Silveira introduced cats and dogs for the patients to take care of as "co-therapists." This was no humorous simile: after a patient adopted a dog who would hang around the painting workshop she noticed that the "dog, in particular, has qualities that make it very capable of becoming a stable point of reference in the outside world. It would never cause frustration, it gives unconditional affection without asking anything in return, it brings warmth and joy to the cold hospital environment."[84] Insofar as the animals had imminent therapeutic effects in the orientation of self to group and group to world, they were in fact therapists.

What matters is the sociality and communication opened up by a practice, not this or that treatment, no matter how calming or pleasurable, and these in turn, as the school of Institutional Psychotherapy teach us, cannot be conceived separately from institutional organization. Everyone knows—besides maybe those poor souls who blunt their own understanding by speaking of "blunted affect"—that a prisoner would rather do theater or paint than sit in isolation all day, but, if they are locked up somewhere, this doesn't say anything profound. Nise da Silveira expressed this better when she said that "hardly ever will a treatment be efficient if the patient does not have someone by his side representing a point of support in which he makes an affective investment."[85] Art can be valorized anywhere, as an aesthetic object or pleasurable activity, but to follow through to the end the notion that greater social cohesion and robust lines of communication can emerge through artistic practice would mean placing institutional constraints and treatments in question, something the vast majority of psychiatric hospitals, prisons, and group homes are unwilling to do. Like the Institutional Psychotherapy group, Silveira began to see the psychiatric hospital's organization as a sick place that made the people who stayed there sicker: "[t]he hospital is reinforcing the pathology, because it does not help at all in re-establishing connections between the patient and their milieu, from which they are being separated because of the pathology. . . . The Hospital becomes an extremely efficient apparatus for the chronification of disease."[86] This is why, after ten years of struggle, in 1956, she opened the Casa das Palmeiras [Palms House] in Rio de Janeiro, an outpatient facility where visitors could pursue an artistic practice outside of the confined spaces of both the home and the hospital without the expectations of the former or the constraints of the latter. The Casa, which is still open in 2024, acts as a bridge—a place of support both open to the bustle of the street and sheltered from it—to disrupt the admission, discharge, readmission cycle.

WHITHER ASYLUMNIA?

There is a common myth that the age of mental institutions is past, that deinstitutionalization happened, and now all that remains are the ominous haunted relics of a bygone era. Unfortunately, this is far from true. Besides the numerous hospital wards, many long-term residential psychiatric facilities are in operation, some of which are in the very same old psychiatric hospitals many assume were closed. Many changed their name to "residential treatment center" or "security hospital," euphemisms cleverly designed to mask their persistence past the era of dehospitalization. The network of nursing homes and group homes also serve many of the same functions as the psychiatric hospital, while psychiatric wards have been opened in maximum security prisons. We have certainly witnessed a shake up, but one which is perhaps better characterized as a recalibration of the matrix than a total transformation of paradigm. As long as a single institution exists as the possible outcome of a psychiatric case, its effects are still a regulator in every psychiatric encounter—as a looming threat instilling the fear of commitment, or as the end of a spectrum invented by the institutional landscape itself for encouraging or disciplining the slightly mad by reminding them they are much better off than "those sorts," for now at least. Residents recall that in Chicago in the 1950s and '60s, "bad behavior came to a halt with a stern warning: 'Be careful, or you're going to Dunning [the mental institution].' The prospect sent shivers down the spines of youngsters, who regarded it as the most dreaded place imaginable."[87] Across an ocean, the word "'Leros' [referring to the mental hospital there] remains, in Greece, a term for what cannot be described, cannot be conceived: a kind of concentration camp or, even, a death camp."[88] Around the world, the names of mental institutions, or the names of their locations, function as threats or warnings whose disciplining effect is actually magnified by the remoteness and singularity that makes them unimaginable.

Is there any possibility for institutional restructuring today? Were the French thinkers correct in thinking that we need institutions to experiment with broad social and group transformations? They felt that the movements that would soon arise in Italy, the United States, and later in Brazil and elsewhere that called for the negation or destruction of the institution were misguided, because they were losing in this way a space that could be appropriated and transformed to offer true refuge and transform our relations with one another. Guattari summarized this optimistic attitude when he wrote that "the mental institution could become, if permanently rearranged . . . a very elaborate instrument for the enrichment of individual and collective subjectivity and for the reconfiguration of existential territories concerning—all at once—the body, the self, living space, relations with others[.]"[89] They were treated as spaces in which to build a new life in common. Let's review some of the salient features the rearrangements required with some help from psychiatrist Jean Claude Polack: the elevation of patients to client status with rights and an autonomous social life; the constant reshuffling and questioning of professional roles to "prevent the identification of carers with their status;" the generalization of the analytic and therapeutic capacity of everyone involved; the valorization and exploration of nonstandard mediums of communication; and the permanent problematization of a sane, normal subject as a model to adjust to.[90]

As other critical psychiatry movements came to connect and share with Institutional Psychotherapy, the latter repeatedly came under fire for conservatively holding onto aggressive techniques (electroshock therapy, for example) and traditional hierarchies. Was their optimism in their ability to transform institutions shortsighted? Was it a way to hold onto some vestige of power and prestige, however small? "Can an institution be militant?"[91] Nise da Silveira, though she belongs to a different tradition and likely never met these French thinkers, arguably put the idea of Institutional Psychotherapy into practice more thoroughly than they managed, but at the expense of broader transformations of the hospital. She was effectively partitioned into a separate space and remarked in the 1980s that she felt the hospital had become even worse with time.[92] By the 1970s, the founders of the institutional movements themselves also began to doubt how transferable their models were. Guattari considered the reformed "Secteur" psychiatry of that time to be so overbearingly technocratic and functionalist that it strangled every innovation while it was still in its infancy. In an interview, Tosquelles said simply that Institutional Psychotherapy "died with pills."[93] Polack remarked that Saint-Alban went into decline following the death of Tosquelles while La Borde began to change once Guattari passed, and further wondered whether institutional experiments were essentially tied to a confluence of events (the war and camp experiences above all). For all the talk of intensities, milieus, and escaping egocentrism, this reflection forces us to ask whether movements such as these are only possible within an institution when attached to a charismatic individual, usually a well-spoken and well-known man. On the other hand, the effects of the transformations, however much they softened with time, did not die with the founders. These effects are unquantifiable and hard to track, but contemporaries in Brazil, France, and around the world repeatedly return to Silveira, Deligny, and Guattari to seek out new ways to reconfigure pedagogical and therapeutic relationships. Is something like the "Secteur" policy of France an outgrowth of these movements or a co-optation? What about the "service-client" consumer model? The rise of art therapy? With these questions, we've already reached the limit of the question of the institution's internal form, and are approaching—as Silveira did with the Casa das Palmeiras—the question of the institution and psychiatry's roles in a broader social terrain.

Notes

1. Mary Wollstonecraft, *Mary, A Fiction and Maria: Or, The Wrongs of Woman* (Ontario: Broadview Editions, 2012), 161.
2. John Conolly, *The Treatment of the Insane without Mechanical Restraints* (London: Smith, Elder & Co., 1856), 4–5.
3. Andrew Scull, *Psychiatry and its Discontents* (Oakland: University of California Press, 2019), 44. Scull notes that Italy and Germany generally lagged in construction.
4. Philippe Pinel, *Medico-Philosophical Treatise on Mental Alienation*, trans. Gordon Hickish, David Healy, and Louis C. Charland (West Sussex: John Wiley & Sons, 2008), xxiii.
5. Thomas Story Kirkbride, *On the Construction, Organization, and General Arrangements of Hospitals for the Insane* (Philadelphia, 1854), 12, https://ia903402.us.archive.org/16/items/onconstructionorookirk/onconstructionorookirk.pdf.
6. Kirkbride, *On the Construction, Organization, and General Arrangements of Hospitals for the Insane*, 62.
7. Kirkbride, *On the Construction, Organization, and General Arrangements of Hospitals for the Insane*, 11–12.
8. Nancy Tomes, *A Generous Confidence: Thomas Story Kirkbride and the Art of Asylum-Keeping, 1840–1883* (Cambridge: Cambridge University Press, 1984), 124–125.
9. Carla Yanni, *The Architecture of Madness: Insane Asylums in the United States* (Minneapolis: University of Minnesota Press, 2007), 45–49.

10. Wilhelm Reich, *The Sexual Revolution: Toward a Self-Governing Character Structure*, trans. Therese Pol (New York: Farrar, Straus and Giroux, 1969), 71–74.

11. Elizabeth Packard, *The Prisoner's Hidden Life: Insane Asylums Unveiled* (Chicago: Self-published, 1868), 125. It's important to note that Packard's critique was against "unjust" usage of patriarchal authority and the stigma of insanity. She was in favor of the "proper" patriarchal power and treatment of the insane.

12. Kirkbride, *On the Construction, Organization, and General Arrangements of Hospitals for the Insane*, 5.

13. Kirkbride, *On the Construction, Organization, and General Arrangements of Hospitals for the Insane*, 2.

14. Erving Goffman, *Asylums: Essays on the Social Situation of Mental Patients and Other Inmates* (New York: Anchor Books, 1961), 16.

15. Goffman, *Asylums*, 13.

16. Félix Guattari, *Chaosophy: Texts and Interviews 1972–1977*, trans. David L. Sweet, Jarred Becker, and Taylor Adkins (Los Angeles: Semiotext(e), 2009), 181.

17. Jean Oury, quoted in Camille Robcis, *Disalienation: Politics, Philosophy, and Radical Psychiatry in Postwar France* (Chicago: The University of Chicago Press, 2021), 2.

18. Robcis, *Disalienation*, 19.

19. Angela Melitopoulos, "Ways of Meaning: Machinic Animism and the Revolutionary Practice of Geo-Psychiatry," PhD diss., Goldsmiths College, University of London, 2016, 126, https://research.gold.ac.uk/id/eprint/19684/1/VIS_thesis_Melitopoulo-sA_2016.pdf.

20. Martine Deyres, dir., *Our Lucky Hours*, Alleyras, France: Lightdox, 2019. Vimeo, https://vimeo.com/ondemand/ourluckyhours.

21. Melitopoulos, "Ways of Meaning," 125.

22. W. A. F. Browne, *The Asylum as Utopia: W. A. F. Browne and the Mid-Nineteenth Century Consolidation of Psychiatry*, ed. Andrew Scull (London: Routledge, 2014), 152.

23. David Rothman, *The Discovery of the Asylum* (New York: Aldine de Gruyter, 1990), 133.

24. Browne, *The Asylum as Utopia*, 203.

25. Sherry Turkle, "French Anti-psychiatry," in *Critical Psychiatry: The Politics of Mental Health*, ed. David Ingelby (New York: Pantheon, 1980), 151. Maud Mannoni notes this as well in the Appendix to *The Child, His "Illness," and the Others* (London: Maresfield Library, 1967), 226. Here, Mannoni says that Institutional Psychotherapy can be distinguished from Anglophone social psychology on account of their attention to the unconscious.

26. François Dosse, *Gilles Deleuze & Félix Guattari: Intersecting Lives* (New York: Columbia University Press, 2010), 61–62.

27. Félix Guattari, *Psychoanalysis and Transversality: Texts and Interviews 1955–1971*, trans. Ames Hodges (Los Angeles and New York: Semiotext(e), 2015), 27.

28. Browne, *The Asylum as Utopia*, 204.

29. Deyres, *Our Lucky Hours*.

30. Melitopoulos, "Ways of Meaning," 141.

31. Mannoni, *The Child, His "Illness," and the Others*, 242.

32. Robcis, *Disalienation*, 1 and 33.

33. Melitopoulos, "Ways of Meaning," 109.

34. Melitopoulos, "Ways of Meaning," 51.

35. Quoted in Gary Genosko (ed.), "Introduction," in *Deleuze and Guattari: Critical Assessments of Leading Philosophers, Volume II: Guattari* (London: Routledge, 2001), 484.

36. Guattari, *Psychoanalysis and Transversality*, 31.

37. Robcis, *Disalienation*, 46.

38. Mannoni, *The Child, His "Illness," and the Others*, 240.

39. Dosse, *Gilles Deleuze & Félix Guattari*, 55.

40. In Susana Cálo, "The Grid," *Technoscience*, April 23, 2016, https://www.anthropo-cene-curriculum.org/contribution/the-grid.

41. Guattari, *Chaosophy*, 180.

42. Genosko, "The Acceleration of Transversality in the Middle," in *Deleuze and Guattari: Critical Assessments of Leading Philosophers, Volume II: Guattari*, 853.
43. Melitopoulos, "Ways of Meaning," 142.
44. Hannah Levin and Mark Seem, "Revolution and Desire: An Interview with Felix Guattari," *State and Mind: People Look at Psychology* 7, no. 1 (Summer/Fall 1978): 53–57. Courtesy of the Oskar Diethelm Library, DeWitt Institute for the History of Psychiatry, Weill Cornell Medical College.
45. Guattari, *Chaosophy*, 191.
46. Melitopoulos, "Ways of Meaning," 51.
47. Quoted in Robcis, *Disalienation*, 46.
48. Guattari, *Transversality and Psychoanalysis*, 113.
49. Genosko, "Introduction," in *Deleuze and Guattari: Critical Assessments*, 88.
50. Fernand Deligny, *The Arachnean and Other Texts*, trans. Drew S. Burk and Catherine Porter (Minneapolis: Univocal, 2015), 33.
51. Leon Hilton, "Mapping the Wander Lines: The Quiet Revelations of Fernand Deligny," *LA Review of Books*, July 2, 2015, https://lareviewofbooks.org/article/mapping-the-wander-lines-the-quiet-revelations-of-fernand-deligny/.
52. Deligny, *The Arachnean*, 79.
53. Deligny, *The Arachnean*, 53.
54. Deligny, *The Arachnean*, 89.
55. Maureen Patricia Park, "Art in Madness: Dr. W. A. F. Browne (1805–1885), Moral Treatment and Patient Art at Crichton Royal Institution, Dumfries, With Special Reference to his Medical Superintendence, 1839–1857," Master's thesis, University of Glasgow, 2007, 241, https://theses.gla.ac.uk/71009/1/10390566.pdf.
56. Marcela Costa, "Icepick to Paintbrush: Nise da Silveira's Psychiatry," *Synapsis*, 2018, https://medicalhealthhumanities.com/2018/02/06/icepick-to-paintbrush-nise-da-silveiras-psychiatry/.
57. Osório César's *A expressão artística dos alienados* [*The Artistic Expression of the Alienated*], published in 1929, was the first book on psychiatry and art in Brazil and was a major influence on Silveira.
58. Marlon Miguel, "Psychiatric Power: Exclusion and Segregation in the Brazilian Mental Health System," in *Democracy and Brazil: Collapse and Regression*, ed. Jorge Chaloub, Bernando Bianchi, Patricia Rangel, and Frieder Otto Wolf (London: Routledge, 2020), 251.
59. Manuella Meyer, *Reasoning against Madness: Psychiatry and the State in Rio de Janeiro, 1830–1944* (Rochester: University of Rochester Press, 2017), 83.
60. Quoted in Meyer, *Reasoning against Madness*, 83.
61. Manuella Meyer, "'Work Conquers All': Psychiatry, Agricultural Labor, and the Juliano Moreira Colony in Rio de Janeiro, Brazil (1890–1958)," *Palgrave Communications* 5, no. 99 (September 2019), https://doi.org/10.1057/s41599-019-0305-y.
62. Kaira M. Cabañas, *Learning from Madness: Brazilian Modernism and Global Contemporary Art* (Chicago: University of Chicago Press, 2018), 81.
63. Felipe Sales Magaldi, "Psyche Meets Matter: Body and Personhood in the Medical-Scientific Project of Nise da Silveira," *História, Ciências, Saúde–Manguinhos* 25, no. 1 (2018): 6, https://pdfs.semanticscholar.org/8036/67d6340a2c159b5532ec9d3b532cda671b86.pdf.
64. Nise da Silveira, *Nise da Silveira—A Revolução Pelo Afeto* [The Revolution by Affection] (Rio de Janeiro: Studio M'Baraká, 2021), 193–194, https://www.mbaraka.com.br/nise.
65. da Silveira, *Nise da Silveira*, 194.
66. da Silveira, *Nise da Silveira*, 190.
67. Vitor Pordeus, "Nise da Silveira: Brazilian Pioneer in Art and Transcultural Psychiatry," 5–6, draft paper, https://www.academia.edu/34364588/Nise_da_Silveira_Brazilian_Pioneer_in_Art_and_Transcultural_Psychiatry.

68. Eliane Dias de Castro and Elizabeth Maria Freire de Araújo Lima, "Resistance, Innovation and Clinical Practice in Nise da Silveira's Thoughts and Actions," *Interface* [*Botucatu*], Selected Edition (2007): 3.

69. da Silveira, *Nise da Silveira*, 196.

70. Kaira M. Cabañas, *Learning from Madness: Brazilian Modernism and Global Contemporary Art* (Chicago: University of Chicago Press, 2018), 58.

71. Cabañas, *Learning from Madness*, 78–79.

72. Leon Hirszman, dir. and Nise da Silveira, writer. *Imagens do inconsciente: Em busca do espaço cotidiano.* Rio de Jenairo: Embrafilme and Leon Hirszman Produções Cinematográficas, 1986, DVD.

73. Spinoza, *A Spinoza Reader: The Ethics and Other Works*, 119.

74. Leon Hirszman, dir. and Nise da Silveira, writer, *Imagens do inconsciente: Postfácio*, Rio de Jenairo: Embrafilme and Leon Hirszman Produções Cinematográficas, 1987, DVD.

75. Hirszman and da Silveira, *Imagens do inconsciente*.

76. Hirszman and da Silveira, *Imagens do inconsciente*.

77. da Silveira, *Nise da Silveira*, 194.

78. da Silveira, *Nise da Silveira*, 190.

79. Hirszman and da Silveira, *Imagens do inconsciente*.

80. da Silveira, *Nise da Silveira*, 194.

81. Dias and Freire, "Resistance, Innovation," 9.

82. Castro and Lima, "Resistance, Innovation," 6.

83. Castro and Lima, "Resistance, Innovation," 10.

84. da Silveira, *Nise da Silveira*, 193–194.

85. Castro and Lima, "Resistance, Innovation," 9.

86. In Marlon, "Psychiatric Power," 255.

87. Robert Loerzel, "The Story of Dunning, A 'Tomb for the Living,'" WBEZ Chicago, April 30, 2013, https://www.wbez.org/stories/the-story-of-dunning-a-tomb-for-the-living/6d-71dc74-bb21-4a25-8980-c2d7a5670b06.

88. Theodoros Megaloeconomou, "Franco Basaglia's Influence on the Greek Mental Health System," in *Basaglia's International Legacy: from Asylum to Community*, ed. Tom Burns and John Foot (Oxford: Oxford University Press, 2020), 167.

89. Guattari, *Chaosophy*, 194.

90. Jean Claude Polack, "Analysis, between Psycho and Schizo," *The Guattari Effect*, ed. Eric Alliez and Andrew Goffey (London: Continuum, 2011), 59.

91. Susana Caló, "Can an Institution be Militant?," *Metabolic Rifts: A Reader* (Lisbon and Berlin: Atlas Projectos, 2019), 115–131.

92. Hirszman and da Silveira, *Imagens do inconsciente*.

93. Melitopoulos, "Ways of Meaning," 146.

CHAPTER 3

DEMOLITION PSYCHIATRY

THE WORK OF THE NEGATIVE

"It all began with a 'no,'"[1] said Franca Ongaro Basaglia about the Democratic Psychiatry movement that, in the period between 1960 and 1980, declared war on contemporary psychiatry in Italy and would go on to close the hospitals. What manner of subject can enunciate such an explosive "no?"

The trajectory of Democratic Psychiatry is usually recounted in parallel with the life of one of its leading figures, the Venetian psychiatrist Franco Basaglia. Refusal seems to have been in his bones: in 1944, at nineteen, the young medical student was arrested in Venice during the Nazi occupation for writing antifascist graffiti with known subversives and stuck in the rank prison's group cell where he remained for the next six months. As John Foot recounts, an uprising broke out in April 1945 that led to an extended standoff between political prisoners with some of the guards against Nazis and fascists who attempted to siege the prison.[2] Having successfully fended them off, their mutiny turned into a prison break, and Basaglia found himself free again amongst his comrades. "An armed insurrection followed right across the city,"[3] which the Nazis fled two days later. Even here, at the beginning, "no" appears as a crowd's refusal—a plural, fluid "no" that circulates through the insurrection.

Despite the disruptions of war and prison, he was able to finish his medical studies in Padua in 1949 before moving on to study psychiatry and philosophy throughout the 1950s. Italy may have been host to one of the earliest experiments with moral treatment—those of

Vincenzo Chiarugi in Florence in the 1780s (years before Pinel)—but, in the twentieth century, it was considered one of the most stagnant and backward systems in all of Europe. By midcentury, its legal apparatus was among the most bluntly coercive, still organized around a 1904 law that centered society's right to sequester the dangerous "*alienati*" ["the alienated" or "mad"] and granted absolute power over them to the director of asylums.[4] Throughout Basaglia's decade at the university psychiatric clinic, Italian psychiatry was split into two static camps that supported, in their mutual feedback loops, an unalterable complacency. There were the university clinics where researchers were well paid to study wealthy clients and churn out the same old biomedical objectifications formed and formulated in a vacuum; and then there were the asylums. Patients entered the crowded hells called asylums and never came out.

Before he left, Basaglia already showed interest in challenging the biomedical orthodoxy that buttressed both camps. Without a vibrant native radical tradition to draw from or plug into, Basaglia first turned to German phenomenology—Karl Jaspers and Edmund Husserl, but especially Ludwig Binswanger—and grounded his thinking in the concrete experiences of people. Although he never denounced or denied the biological in psychiatry, Binswanger's sensitivity to the "encounter" led Basaglia to reject models that required the production of passive objects in the sciences: "Biological psychiatry looks for a relationship between a subject (the psychiatrist) and an object (the patient). In opposition to this stance, Binswanger, who regards the gnoseological split between subject and object as the 'cancer of all psychologies and philosophies,' proposes the idea of an 'encounter' between the psychiatrist and the patient, where both subjectivities could be called into question. Binswanger's encounter takes place between two subjects."[5] Checklists of symptoms are of little use here, and a whole new set of questions arises: how does this human before me describe what they see, feel, hear, hate, or love? How do I receive that information? How do they orient themselves in space (clinical, institutional, or otherwise) in relation to me and my actions? To forefront the encounter is to ensure thought stays attentive to how one's subjectivity emerges from relationships with others. If such relations presuppose how one becomes what they are, then one ought to ask: what type of person emerges from isolated laboratory study and internment?

Dissatisfied with the complacency of his profession, Basaglia chose not to pursue the more comfortable university career and was instead given a directorship at the asylum in Gorizia, a town on the border between Italy and Yugoslavia where he would surely be damned to marginality and drudgery with few prospects and even fewer expectations beyond keeping the place barely functional. In 1961, he stepped inside the asylum in Gorizia for the first time and experienced an emotional revulsion in body and mind: "it took me straight back to the war and the prison. It didn't smell of shit, but there was the symbolic smell of shit. I was convinced that that institution was completely absurd, that its function was only to pay the psychiatrists who worked there. In the face of this absurd, disgraceful logic of the asylum—we said 'no.'"[6]

The asylum's patients sat around, many were nude, others were chained to walls, abandoned in a space that received as much daily care as they did, which is to say it was chaotic, filthy, and ruinous. One of the nurses recalled later that "the patients were so used to seeing them as torturers that they would cower whenever they approached."[7] Faced with such abject suffering and destitution, the phenomenological understanding of the person falls painfully short. Against the more common interpretation that the objectification of a psychiatric diagnosis or internment puts you at a great distance from others, Basaglia and Franca Ongaro Basaglia held that the problem with the institution is that it colonized one's subjective horizons and became more or less equivalent to the world. With no room to move, and no distance to distinguish oneself from others, one is forced into the state of *alienità* [alienation], that defines psychosis as a collapse of the distinction between self and reality.

As Franca Ongaro Basaglia wrote: "Where can one trace, in this total invasion and expropriation by the institution, the distance between the 'I' and the 'self,' the interval between the 'I' and the body necessary for the subject, if these bodies are possessed by the institution, if they are the very body of the institution?"[8] What, in other words, does the understanding of a concrete experience offer when one's suffering is overdetermined by institutional violence and decay? In this space, according to Franco Basaglia, "neither analyses of Oedipal complexes, nor theories about our being-in-the-world have saved patients from the lethal passivity and alienation of their condition."[9] It would have been "an insult to reality" to offer "a phenomenological

analysis of the-being-in-restraint or of the-being-together-in-segre-
gation."[10] Sound theoretical interpretation was destined to fail when
there was no space between doctor-subjects, patient-objects, and the
environment they were placed in. Worse, to do so risked objectifying
an *outcome* of institutionalization, wrapping it up in the trappings of
scientism, and representing it as the pretext for an exclusion that pre-
supposes it.

The typical psychiatric diagnosis facilitates this violent reality
by flattening the complex social processes that lead from a life's
assortment of problems to asylum and by tying behavior to objectified, organic causes: "[t]he mental patient is an outcast, but in our
present society, he can never oppose those who exclude him, since
all his actions are circumscribed, defined and finally, dismissed, by
his illness."[11] Democratic Psychiatry, more than any other movement in psychiatry at the time, insisted on the relationship between
class, marginality, and madness. To them, it was obvious that there
are two psychiatries: one for the rich and one for the poor. Look
around, they said; the asylum is full of poor people, deviants, pet-
ty criminals, the disabled. In short, everyone from the margins of
society. Comparing the relative privilege of the average client of
psychoanalysis—the YARVIS (young, attractive, rich, verbal, intelligent, and sophisticated)—to the abjectness of the inhabitants of
the asylum in Italy is a major cause behind the general dismissal of
Freud in Italy, in contrast with his huge influence in other radical
psychiatric movements. Class analysis of the asylum inmates suggested that the violence of the institution was only the most recent
coercion in their patients' lives. In addition to: the capitalist imperative that says work or die, produce or starve; the police officer who
picks them up like refuse when they don't contain their outbursts
and breakdowns; and finally, the psychiatrist who treats them like
a disease enveloped with skin. These are stages the patients have
already lived through as objects of violence before arriving at the
front door of the hospital.

If there is such a thing as a "mental illness," how could we know
it under these conditions? How could we possibly study it "objectively" when our present relations are conditioned on capitalism and its
contradictions that lead some to prosper and many to starve and suffer? Or when our horizon of potential is completely saturated with

institutional norms for cruelties and pressures, for all to abjure into the safety of solipsism? Capital, like nature, abhors vacuums. Psychiatry was a fortress formed around its own self-image that tended to sequester whatever came into its ambit because, as Franca Ongaro and Franco Basaglia wrote, "instead of dealing with people with mental disorders in the society in which they live, [psychiatry] has gradually constructed an ideal image of man, in order to guarantee the scientific validity of the castle of disease, which imprisoned the symptoms."[12] As a counter-offensive to this progressive ossification, they put the psychiatric illness "in brackets," or suspended judgment on it, a maneuver borrowed from Edmund Husserl. "It is not that we put the illness aside," Basaglia wrote:

> but rather that we believe that in order to have a relationship with an individual, it is necessary to establish it independent of the label by which the person has been defined. I have a relationship with someone not because of the diagnosis, but because of who she is. In the moment that I say, 'this person is a schizophrenic' . . . I will begin to behave toward her in a unique way, that is, knowing full well that schizophrenia implies an illness for which nothing can be done. My relationship will be that of someone who only expects 'schizophrenicity' from the individual. . . . This is why it is so very necessary to draw closer to her, bracketing the illness, because the diagnostic label has taken on the weight of a moral judgment that passes for the reality of the illness itself.[13]

Even antipsychiatry's assertions that madness was purely the result of social processes were still operating "within the logic of positivism" since they objectified their object and viewed it as a tangible thing that could be observed in isolation from the world rather than as a dynamic process born of contradictions in social processes or of contradictions within the body itself.[14] To suspend the diagnosis is to deny every "mental anatomy" that objectifies a "dead mind"[15] in order to foreground the person, the urgency of their needs, and the fact that madness is experienced as a public, that is, political, problem. It is an elegant way to avoid that inexhaustible vicious circle of nosological claims and counter claims and cut straight to the task at hand: the destruction of the psychiatric hospital.

A MOVEMENT DESIGNED TO SELF-DESTRUCT

At first, they proceeded much the way other humanistic psychiatric projects did. Mirroring especially the therapeutic community model developed by Maxwell Jones with ex-soldiers at Mill Hill School, Henderson Hospital, and more famously later in Dingleton, Scotland, but also Institutional Psychotherapy in France, Franco Basaglia and his team removed restraints, opened doors, threw away the straitjackets and did all the things a humanist psychiatrist was supposed to do. Jones' therapeutic community—a consistent reference point for Democratic Psychiatry—is the apotheosis of social psychiatry in the institutional setting; it is the rediscovery of moral treatment tailored to the postwar era.

By his own account, Jones was unmoved by the organicism of his psychiatric training, and, while never recalcitrant, he became increasingly alienated by the distance placed between caregivers and the cared for, finding the suspension of ordinary courtesies disturbing: "to see a young woman patient in a lecture theatre exposed physically to 200 students without being forewarned didn't thrill me—I thought it was insensitive, the lack of privacy, everything about it was so callous. And I never made friends with any of the lecturers. I resented their aloofness and lack of warmth."[16] When working in a one-hundred-bed psychosomatic unit for patients with effort syndrome, a thought occurred to him: since everyone is experiencing similar things, why not just meet all together for therapy? A simple idea, yes, but sometimes the simplest ideas pursued in earnest bring about the greatest changes.

Over the course of his twelve years at Belmont (later Henderson Hospital), from 1947 to 1959, Maxwell Jones perfected the liberal model of social psychiatry, the therapeutic community, by adhering to this basic collectivizing impulse and distilling it down into its simplest formulation: the therapeutic community is a collective subject which self-consciously pools "the institution's total resources, staff, patients, and their relatives . . . in furthering treatment."[17] In practice, this results in cascading alterations. If everyone is in some way involved in molding the form of therapy, everyone's activity, no matter how high up, is subject to discussion and scrutiny according to standards developed in a public space, if not necessarily in common. Everyone becomes responsible for what they bring to the community, including those in power. For example, Jones cites an incident when nurses' fantasies about patients' presumed sexual lives was coloring their rejection of co-ed meetings in the hospital.[18] Fantasies like these—along with attitudes, assumptions, body languages—are taken up explicitly in a daily meeting that "exposes the staff to some of the social forces which make up this shared life,"[19] further increasing the leveling effect by forcing them to account for hitherto unchallenged activities and attitudes before people they weren't used to being accountable to. Normally, when the patient arrives at the hospital at the end of a protracted struggle with reality, they are asked to contort their way of living for long-sedimented hospital norms they must discover and adapt to without acknowledgement. Therapeutic communities shine a bright light on the "therapeutic culture," break it down and put it in motion, so that each has a role in this enculturation process.[20] Like moral treatment, the therapeutic community is an art of bricolage, implying first of all a flexibility and openness to what's available, including negative phenomena so that "the life of the hospital becomes a sort of living laboratory where crises, instead of being seen as troublesome and unnecessary, can be turned to good effect as learning situations."[21]

Democratic Psychiatry looked to the therapeutic community model (and later, Institutional Psychotherapy) not as a goal, but as an opening to new problems in an ongoing process. Humanizing measures were valued solely to the extent that they revealed contradictions at the heart of the field. As Franca Ongaro and Franco Basaglia wrote in their preface to the Italian edition of *Social Psychiatry in Practice*: "The classic therapeutic community, set up after 1949 by Maxwell Jones, is based on some key elements: freedom of expression, the destruction of authoritarian relationships, an understanding of the real world, permissiveness, democratization—these are all crucial aspects of the unmasking of asylum structures, which are founded on authoritarian structures, violence, the objectivization of the ill patient, the absence of communication."[22] They paid the patients standard wages for any labor, exposing the sham that was and is "occupational therapy" as a friendly name for unpaid or subminimally compensated labor. As at Saint-Alban in France, a patient club was empowered to make administrative decisions, open a cafe, a theater, and much more, and began publishing their thoughts and criticisms openly in *Il Picchio*, their own independent publication in 1962. With no recourse to restraints, doctors and nurses could not sit around and relax all day, for now everyone was called to be present and solve problems creatively. Out of "no" —that first refusal to participate in acts of coercion justified as therapy—was born new ways of being in common space, of solving problems with one another.

Democratic Psychiatry's partisans borrowed concepts, recycled theories, imported methods—none of that pertains to what defines their movement. The singularity of the Italian strategy consists in the fact that they, like the Roman hero Mucius Scaevola, did not retract their hands from the fire in the fearless pursuit of the negative as a motivating force. Social psychiatry was to be critiqued not because of some theoretical shortcoming or practical misstep that could be remedied by patching up contradictions with tighter logic, but because its adherents proved themselves incapable of following those contradictions down the paths they laid before them. Having stopped short, argues Giovanni Jervis in the mid-1980s, social psychiatry will only embody those same contradictions in a new form:

> Social psychiatry and interpersonal psychiatry have examined both the sociocultural context in which the patient is defined as patient and the 'therapeutic' relationship as a system of psychological interactions. Psychiatry itself, that is, psychiatric practice, has become the object of psychiatry. But here, too, the psychiatrist has merely raised the level of inquiry: by including himself, in his relationship with the patient, as part of the subject matter of his own discipline, he has confirmed the basic validity of that discipline. The psychiatrist continues to accept his social mandate, although he acknowledges that it is based on a convention.[23]

Psychiatry's role in the social matrix is contradictory; first in its relation to the social forces it answers to—as in when the concrete needs of patients are no longer satisfied by the economic surplus made available to them or when the maintenance of a healing environment contradicts the exorbitant demands made by the family—and then, in relation to itself in its dual mandate to protect society and heal the wounded. Changes in its material form disrupt multiple points of that social chain at once, which is why all reformist movements eventually converge at a point where the traditional patient-healer relation demands its own sublation.

In its broadest, most sincere social form, psychiatry "has laid all the necessary foundations for its own destruction, but has been unable to face the consequences,"[24] Jervis writes. Examples from the nineteenth-century moral treatment and nonrestraint movements suggest that barbarism tends to enter through the doors one refuses to shut. A controversy arose around John Conolly, the foremost militant in the fight for nonrestraint, and the fact that, in his rejection of mechanical restraint, he could not let go of solitary confinement, even coming to believe it had restorative calming effects on the agitated. Pursuit of this belief led him to create the famous padded room, so strongly associated with psychiatric hospitals, where patients could ride out their fury without the possibility of smashing their skulls against the walls.[25] Leslie Topp's analysis of the nonrestraint movement's debates shows that its participants were well aware of the contradictions they fell into in their definition of "nonrestraint." "The dilemma of seclusion was the dilemma of the asylum in microcosm," writes Topp, insofar as the "removal of restraints from the limbs of its inmates served to call attention to the forms of restraint represented by the patient's locked room, and by the enclosing walls of the institution itself."[26] From the first proposal that patients ought not to be tied up, one arrives back at the central contradictions of psychiatry: "The whole purpose of the asylum—embodied in its very name—was to offer retreat, retirement and removal from the stresses and irritants of life in the world. But that sense of distance and enclosure could easily tip over into a suspicion of imprisonment, invisibility, and abuse. At the pivotal moment in asylum history represented by the introduction of nonrestraint, the single room behind the locked door—the cell—became a microcosm of this dilemma of symbolism—and also the site of new, very real and highly controversial practices."[27]

It is awareness of this historical tug-of-war between cruelty and liberality that led the Gorizian group to reject both an aggressive, exclusionary model *and* the integrationist tendency towards the "premature closure or crystallization of change into new immobile institutions, even if these may be more modern, efficient, 'democratic,' 'communitarian,'" believing instead that the "renewal of psychiatric structures can only proceed by continual crises and self-criticism, or by a dialectical supersession of stages."[28] Topp quotes Thomas Wakley, founder and editor of the medical journal *The Lancet*, who oversaw a literary debate about the merits of nonrestraint in England in the 1840s: "The term 'nonrestraint,' we may remark, is not literally correct; for, when the system is most rigidly carried out, the patient is confined to the asylum, and in many cases to his room. But this confinement is not felt like fetters; it is less degrading, irritating, and exasperating, than ligatures on the limbs. The restraint is little more severe than the voluntary confinement of servants to the house, or of workmen to their daily task."[29] This practically makes Jervis' point for him: the initial refusal led to an unavoidable awareness of the carceral nature of internment itself. Where Conolly faltered, Democratic Psychiatry said *yes, we must destroy the asylum.* But this confinement is only worse than the "free" confinement of servants or wage-laborers by degree, one might retort. *True,* they would say, *then let us also continue the fight against all so-called 'voluntary' confinement!*

If psychiatry always corresponds and answers to forces outside of itself, a truly social psychiatry must open itself up to the world, regardless of what must be demolished along the way. No technical intervention could be responsive enough to sever this circuit. The word "correspond" is vital here, because psychiatry is never a simple cover over a more *real* reality defined in economic or political terms; its contradictions return to the incommensurability of *cura* [therapy, healing] and *custodia* [guardianship] in the social encounter between patient and caregiver. Therefore, though it may be enticing to say that psychiatry is a tool for a specific class or that it "fits in perfectly with the dominant social structure," this would ultimately resolve the tension at the core of the practice, paradoxically foreclosing its real political potential. Jervis explains that "[t]he dangers here are assuming that power (indeed, the question may be posed even more specifically, i.e., capitalist power) constitutes a homogeneous system, devoid of contradictions, identifiable as 'capital' or the rational plans of a neocapitalist elite, and further to claim, concomitantly, that psychiatric organizations are structured and changed, without contradictions, in accordance with the dominant political designs."[30] Only by seeing the psychiatric relation as a contradiction within a contradiction can we grasp that it maintains an all-too-often anachronistic and tense relationship with political and economic power. Psychopolitics takes place in the interstices of a network swallowing all. Like an occlusive sound made by the air forced through a passage closing in on itself, it articulates us by stopping us at opportune times, turning us inside out, letting us become another through confronting what is other in ourselves.

After three years of pushing liberalizing initiatives as far they could realistically go, the group at Gorizia publicly announced that the therapeutic community fought for with blood, sweat, and tears there and in Scotland, England, and France was a mere starting point. At the first conference for Social Psychiatry in London in 1964, precisely when the Western world turned to community psychiatry and the therapeutic community as humanist alternatives, Franco Basaglia stated outright that the therapeutic community he and other participants had struggled to establish were gilded cages, a more effective reinforcement of the alienating and disempowering relation inherent to the field. He immediately confronted the social psychiatrists, so fond of imagining themselves as the new humanist Pinels descending to save their patients, assembled there for the very first time, with a quote from the Surrealist Manifesto about the "looney bin:" "Tomorrow morning, at visiting time, when without any lexicon you try to communicate with these men, you will be able to remember and recognise that, in comparison with them, you are superior in only one way: force."[31] Even the most social therapeutic intervention "means preventing the patient from becoming conscious of being excluded, and moving from the narrow sphere of persecution by family, friends, and hospital to the global level, where he is conscious of being excluded by a society in which he is superfluous. [The therapeutic intervention] acts to soften the reaction of the excluded towards those that exclude them."[32] Benevolence from above is productive, in the end, of a friendlier passivity: "[the patients] sit quietly by and they wait for someone to tell them what to do next, to decide for them because they no longer know how to appeal to their own efforts, their own responsibilities, their own freedom. As long as they accept liberty as a gift from the doctor they remain submissively dominated."[33] What was needed was not a more perfect model or more tender conception of mental alienation, but a total relinquishment of the desire for resolution. Without an ideal set out before them, the tensions between unequal actors engaged in concrete acts of destruction only illuminated further contradictions, further proving that the import of models geared towards "seeing the whole person" or "recovery" tended instead to hide them away behind pleasant abstractions for the comfort of social technicians.

On the practical level, daily assemblies became spaces in which anyone—patients, nurses, doctors, even townspeople, volunteers, and visitors—could participate. Like the daily meeting of Jones' therapeutic community, the meeting served the dual function of exposing the real problems encountered on the wards—mean words exchanged, frustrations with the sleeping arrangements, the lack of activities on offer—and encouraging increasing involvement in facing them from all sides. But if the daily meeting in the therapeutic community contented itself with demystification and the birth of a minimal patient government, those held at Gorizia were not expected to arrive at group consensus nor even to facilitate smooth lines of communication earned through compromises that were guaranteed to reinforce the asylum hierarchies. Refusing institutional compromise and the illusion of peace it represented, the meetings became "unsafe" places where unreason, protest, and incoherent expressions were heard and considered.[34] Over time, the long-repressed chaotic rage settled down and they became a space in which common languages were developed while new alliances and goals formed in the interstices.

Peppe Dell'Acqua, one of the successors of Basaglia as the director of mental health in Trieste, and Silvia D'Autilia describe a similar process of demolition-construction at a later period of the movement:

> We started moving furniture. The rooms in the wards, then opened, though wide and bright, would keep on rendering misery, emptiness and melancholia. Following the opening [of the doors] and the more and more diverse frequenting, the stiff order, which furniture would help to guarantee inside the closed wards, was completely undermined. Furniture had then become just witness of the stillness and of the lack of care for the people, which that order had long concealed. Burning hopes and great expectations were in the air, so close to be felt. And then we kept on moving furniture, to change everything right then![35]

Each break, every destructive act, opened up a crack in the fabric of reality out of which the impossible could emerge: "When you point out contradictions you are opening up a crack. For example, when we demonstrate that psychiatric institutions only exist as an apparatus of social control, the State is forced to create something else to replace it. From the time when the contradiction first explodes into consciousness to the time when it is inevitably covered up, there is a moment, a chance for people to realize that the health system does not correspond to their needs because society itself is not organized to meet those needs."[36] Some cracks were more literal than others, as for instance, in cases when patients and staff collectively engaged in the joyous act of smashing the hospital walls or fences. Bruno Astrologhi, a patient at the time, reported that "[h]appiness can be defined as breaking down the walls of the madhouse with a hammer. I had blisters on my hands, but it was intensely satisfying."[37]

The asylum's walls were only the most obvious form of securitization. Democratic Psychiatry aimed towards the abolition of all restraints along with burdensome checks on patients' whereabouts. Aggressive treatments like ECT and insulin coma therapy were suspended. While drugs were available, they were not to be administered as a treatment in themselves. Activities were made voluntary; "those which did nothing to fulfill the patient's needs were dropped, and the emphasis was on those which helped the patient to become a social being once more."[38] Among the latter activities, one can include artistic workshops and theater, outings, holiday trips, and parties.

By 1968, at the height of their success as a therapeutic community, the group concluded that they'd reached the limit of possible conflict in Gorizia and left for new ventures in Parma, Arezzo, Cividale, and Perugia. Unified in general strategy, each location of the "Gorizian diaspora" (as John Foot calls it) was marked by varying emphases and theoretical divergences. In Cividale, Giorgio Antonucci and Edelweiss Cotti subscribed to an antipsychiatric position that closely resembled Thomas Szasz's in the US, which categorically denied the existence of mental illness and rejected all language perceived to be psychiatric. There, they occupied a hospital for three days and generally moved much faster to shut down existing services than the Gorizian group. Challenges arose in Parma to shut down not just the asylum, but nursing homes, special schools, and all segregative institutions and to work towards immediate integration despite any conflicts this created. The group in Perugia moved to make their operations more public and set up community centers to replace the hospital. In Reggio Emilia, Giovanni Jervis and others placed the emphasis on preventing people from entering the hospital at all; their strategy consisted in finding potential patients early and setting them up with support in apartments to avoid imminent institutionalization. A wide range of tactics—occupations, mass visitations to hospitals, professional walkouts, patient-worker and professional strikes—were developed and borrowed from place to place around the country. During the Italian Hot Autumn marked by strike waves and student participation in radical struggles in 1968–69, cross-pollination was frequent and encouraged, with many student radicals becoming volunteers and participants in the anti-asylum struggle while tactics and theories were developed in conversation. As Franco Basaglia put it, speaking to an audience in Brazil in 1979, "When we say no to the asylum, we say no to the misery of the world and we join all the people in the world fighting for a situation of emancipation. Right now, we are not just a psychodrama society, nor a social psychiatry society. We are united people struggling for a real freedom in the world."[39] Democratic Psychiatry was resolutely and centrally political in character: strikes, occupations, riots, and anticolonial wars around the world were conceived of as part of the same general tendency to develop new communal forms through concrete struggles within and against the existing social fabric.

Psychiatry's function in relation to capitalism is far from static. Moral treatment in its heyday was able to pride itself on its integrative and disciplinary functions for the market, believing itself capable of curing the ill and returning them to the productive sphere. Historically, this optimism responds to the early period of a freefall from the liberal contract society's euphoric fantasy that "it is sufficient to free the conditions for access to employment in order to resolve in principle"[40] the social ills stemming from poverty and vagabondage. This was, as we know, far from true, premised as it was on the liberal illusion that social dysfunctions are categorically distinct from economic ones. When it is recognized that pauperism and misery are necessary byproducts of capital accumulation—that social disorder is unsolvable through formal legal intervention—then it becomes necessary to at least prevent those with no productive value from disrupting it. Psychiatry steps in here to technically mitigate the paradoxes of an economic system that produces misery and chaos by removing the problem to a space outside of direct production.

At this point, it becomes possible to say, as Giovanni Jervis does, that "[t]he patient in a mental hospital cannot be compared with a producer of goods and services who is still a part of a system that demands from him the 'free' alienation of his labor power; he is alienated as a person in an institution and is useless to the system insofar as, once hospitalized against his will, his presence in the institution thereafter contributes to the maintenance of social stability only indirectly."[41] The mental patient is the waste product, the dross, that requires removal for free circulation—like trash on the freeway. This has been widely recognized by critics of psychiatry, but all too often the analysis stops short of seeing how psychiatry works to resolve social conflicts inherent to capitalism by focusing entirely on its segregative function, and thus, it offers the hasty recommendation to integrate the mental patient or disabled person into the market as an end in itself.

One major point of departure for Democratic Psychiatry lies in the insistence on a continuity of exclusion and exploitation between the "mad" and the "normal." In the official program of Democratic Psychiatry, they vowed to "continue to fight against exclusion, by analysing and rejecting its sources in the social structure (the social relations of production) and in the superstructures (norms and values) of our society. This struggle can be carried on only by combining all the forces and movements which, sharing these analyses, act concretely to transform the social order."[42] Destroying the hospital becomes a necessity "not because it is archaic, repressive and segregative, but because it is a structure whose persistence guarantees social stability and inequality."[43] Yves-Luc Conreuer, a representative of the Belgian Group of Information on Asylums (GIA) at the 1977 Conference of the European Network of Alternatives to Psychiatry, summarized this approach in the powerful "Statement from the Psychiatrized":

> We reject the demand by certain psychiatrized people to be exploited like everyone else. It is not a matter of having more rights in hospitals but of destroying the asylum and the logic of the asylum which has spread throughout our society. Hence, we must struggle. Whoever does not struggle dies, and whoever does not die is buried alive, in prisons, in rehabilitation centers, in kindergartens and over-populated schools, in psychiatric hostels and hospitals.[44]

If liberty is the "most obvious" discovery of psychiatry,[45] an honest appraisal of the institutional field must concede first that psychiatry is far from the only means available for sequestration, and second that no real liberty is to be found outside the institution either. Far from inducing pessimism, in the destruction of certain links in the social nexus attaching institutional spaces to the market and public space, in the *real* circulation of solidarities out of the disrupted circulation of commodities, it becomes possible to join the rebellions of the social pariah to the world of production.

To create ever greater disruptions, the movement entered a new phase in the early 1970s when the therapeutic community was declared, for all intents and purposes, dead weight and a new justification for the institutionalization and rationalization of subtle forms of domination. In 1972, the last remaining group in Gorizia, fed up with the remaining vestiges of unchanging institutional life, penned a collective letter of refusal to continue to hold a "useless" and even "damaging" presence, taking direct inspiration from Frantz Fanon's famous "Letter to a Resident Minister." They no longer found it acceptable to answer the patient's question, "'when can I go home?,' with the lie, 'tomorrow,' knowing full well that for you tomorrow would never come."[46]

It was around this time that the Basaglias moved from Colorno to the San Giovanni Hospital in Trieste, where they acted more decisively and aggressively in the struggle to close asylums. In just six years, in a whirlwind of excitement and activity, they closed the asylum for good. Even more than Gorizia, the asylum in Trieste rapidly became a site of pilgrimage and projects for artists, student activists, leftist militants, and sympathetic professionals. A number of cooperatives were formed, many of them highly unconventional, like the pirate radio station Radio Fragola or the theater troupes that offered new means for patient communication with the surrounding community and beyond. While being destroyed, the halls of the hospital were opened up to new possibilities: a ward became an exhibition hall, a theater, a popular cafeteria, a bar, or a conference center.[47] The site of confrontation would no longer be primarily the privileged internal conflict between the psychiatrist, the nurse, and the patient within the hospital; increasingly, all that was hidden within its walls erupted explosively into the public and was brought to bear on a society hitherto unable to face it.

The walls and fences were torn down, as was the general modus operandi, but more than before, mad parades took to the streets to demand inclusion in the public life of the city. Creative acts of destruction (and destructive acts of creation) were treated as communal rituals knowingly and intentionally presented to the public or the media as scandals and opportunities to create local tensions by exposing the public to the carceral realities of psychiatric hospitals. Artists, filmmakers, photographers, musicians, and theater groups were all invited over the years to bear witness, to spread the word—all in the service of intentionally producing an anti-institutional culture in the public consciousness and to curry favor with sympathetic locals in areas where fascist politics still captured the imagination of some hospital employees and politicians. In 1968, photographers Carla Cerati and Gianni Berengo Gardin were invited by the Gorizian group to produce images documenting the conditions of the asylum in Italy. These were published as a book in 1969, *Morire di classe. La condizione manicomiale fotografata da Carla Cerati e Gianni Berengo Gardin* [*Dying Because of Class: The Condition of Asylums Photographed by Carla Cerati and Gianni Berengo Gardi*], accompanied by essays from the Basaglias, Frantz Fanon, Michel Foucault, Erving Goffman, Primo Levi, and others. That same year, 10 million Italians watched Sergio Zavoli's *The Gardens of Abel*, and were exposed—many of them for the first time—to the voices of patients talking about their experience of institutionalization and the changes taking place.

Democratic Psychiatry repeatedly broke the unspoken yet sacred pact between the madhouse and that nebulous entity "the public" to keep the mad contained: "Come and see," they said. Erika Rossi's film *Trieste Racconta Basaglia* shows how practical this confrontation really was. At times it meant worker-participants of the process venturing out into the city squares and engaging a crowd in discussions or addressing criticisms and fears.[48] Open doors meant that patients were entering town, accompanied or not, and becoming increasingly visible in everyday life. As they did so, people who had never engaged with madness outside of images or books did not magically acquire consciousness and sensitivity. Numerous locals recount in interviews how shocked they were at first engaging with the inmates on city streets, in restaurants and shops. Some of them express anger towards the open-door policy because it made them uncomfortable or because the mad were disruptive in their store. One woman even expresses her sadness that the state didn't just kill all the disabled and

be done with them. Debates about madness in public continued unabated, but Democratic Psychiatry tore madness from its imposed exclusion and succeeded in making it everyone's problem. In that spirit,
in Trieste, the invitation to come to the asylum was literal: hundreds
of people came to work and study there, and 4,000 people came from
around the world to a 1977 meeting held there.[49] In Spring 1974, they
convinced Ornette Coleman to perform in what ended up being the
first of many concerts and film screenings at the San Giovanni hospital.[50] The most famous public incident involved hiring an artist to
help create a large blue horse of papier-mâché named Marco Cavallo.
Legend says that Marco was named for an old laundry horse, which for
many years was the only thing able to come and go from the hospital.
Upon each paper sheet on Cavallo's body was written the dreams of
patients symbolically seizing fugitive freedom outside the walls. Once
the media arrived, it was "discovered" that he couldn't fit through the
gate to get out, so they were forced to smash the fencing down to
make way for the joyous parade. The emancipation of the mad necessarily entails severing the distance between the mad and the normal,
and it concerns the latter just as much as the former. It is by working
through the concrete, often negative, encounter with madness that a
collective creates a social place and role for it. As Franco Basaglia was
fond of repeating about the mad, "We have to keep them among us
and deal with the contradiction *that is us*."[51] Madness' liberation is not
its toleration, but its progressive disintegration as a general signifier
in the abolition of distances and the identification of common needs
that supersede peculiarities.

In 1977, Franco Basaglia held a public press conference in which
he declared that San Giovanni Hospital was closed, even though patients still lived there, in order to create more tension and speed up the
process. Around this time, the words "freedom is therapeutic" were
scrawled on a wall in Trieste. Participants in the anti-asylum movement generally did not lose sight of the fact that to release asylum inmates back into the community was a violation of the unspoken rules
of that community and was experienced as a violent crisis. This, in
turn, was to provoke a crisis in labor, which had already taken its most
advanced form in the factories of Parma where the ex-plumber Ma-
rio Tommasini strove to integrate ex-patients and the developmentally

disabled into union labor. This process was documented in the collectively made film *Matti da slegare* [*Fit to be Untied*] (1975).

In Trieste, the production of various cooperatives diversified the options for incorporation into the labor market, though, unlike in the United States where such integration is the end point for many progressive organizations, this was self-consciously perceived as a steppingstone to transfer patients and the disabled from the enforced poverty and marginalization of mental health services to the enforced poverty and marginalization of capital. On the same day Marco Cavallo was rolled out into the streets, the nurses in Trieste went on strike decrying the starvation wages of the institution and the poverty awaiting patients upon release.[52]

The collapse of institutional barriers and mechanisms of segregation opened new opportunities for collaboration and solidarity while the lived experience of emancipation infused participants with the desire for freedom, but there were no illusions that this was anything but a first step towards the next struggle, the next instigation of crisis. Coordinated strikes by patients, students, and nurses against institutional conditions, asylum construction, work conditions, and sheltered workshop options from the late '60s through the '70s is testament to a general awareness of the connection of labor to the anti-institutional movement.

In May 1978, with the support of the Christian Democrats and Communists, the Basaglias helped draft Law 180, often called the "Basaglia Law," which made psychiatric patients into medical patients like any other, erased nebulous terms like "dangerousness," barred any new entries into Italy's psychiatric hospitals, and set a concrete date for the closure of those that still stood. Despite its enormous consequences, this was considered by many in the movement to be a compromise, since, for instance, it still contained a provision that allowed for up to fifteen days of involuntary commitment in a general hospital. From early on, the law was instrumentalized strictly as a tool for the movement; it had no intrinsic value. Prior to Law 180, using a provision in a 1968 law, the Trieste team designated hundreds of patients as *"ospite"* ["guests"] granting them increased *"contractual* power with which to reenter the social realm, rather than maintaining them under some sort of guardianship."[53]

By the early 1980s, the hospital San Giovanni in Trieste was effectively closed, with just a few patients staying in apartments on the grounds. Everyone else had either returned home or been placed in apartments or small homes where a stay was not contingent upon a medical diagnosis. The hospital had truly been destroyed. Out of its wreckage, over forty health centers emerged in which a new ecology of care networks flourished where former patients or new "guests" could make affective investments in meaningful, and frequently political, projects. The question was always "how to destroy to invent," how to plant new growth in the wreckage of built-up, centuries-old violence, how to get out into the world and find one's place in it. All these dramatic and romantic overturnings, in other words, were not the end of a single protracted battle but the very beginning of a thousand new chapters in mental health care.

Laws do not facilitate the kind of social and political integration that happened in Trieste; that was the result of protracted and dedicated struggle. There are no readymade answers or forms conforming to "practices capable of sustaining the freedom of those in a moment of fragility."[54] Law 180 guaranteed nothing. Franca Ongaro Basaglia makes it clear that, for them, it was conceived of as an opening to opportunity, a chance to change:

> Once the old relationship between psychiatry and the law courts had been broken, Law 180 tended to take the exclusive management of psychic disorders out of the hands of the specialists and to end the hospital bed's dominion as the only place for treatment. Now not only the professional and administrative bodies, but also the whole community was involved in a cultural change concerning the mentally ill and the nature of their illness. The starting point for this change was the realisation that it is primarily the social and psychological processes which the biological elements undergo that determines a patient's fate, rather than the biological elements being considered "natural" and irreversible.[55]

How each place answered that call could not be legislated from elsewhere, so it should come as no surprise that the cities with pre-existing social movements—and therefore years of previous development— were the most successful, and those furthest from the movement— mostly in the South—barely complied at all.[56] "The conflict that Law

180 created is of a much deeper nature than a simple organisational change in a branch of medicine," Ongaro Basaglia continues, "by emphasising the fact that psychiatric problems are not exclusively medical (this does not mean denying the existence of illness), it sought to encourage the professional bodies to assume responsibilities that were not simply custodial. . . . The definitions of normality, illness and deviance were called into question in the context of the multiple nature of needs, citizens' rights and the change in the values of society. It was this something more which produced negative reactions from that part of the medical world, still hidebound by an organicistic culture whose fulcrum was the hospital bed."[57] Much like the confinement threatened by the asylum operates as an "'infection' which is carried down the line to the private clinic, the therapist's office, and the social worker,"[58] formally severing it as a node on the social matrix opens up an opportunity for a total rearrangement by forcing each actor to make a choice to fight for social inclusion or at least recognize their continued reliance on custodial methods.

ALL THOSE WHO STRUGGLE FOR FREEDOM

In some ways, deinstitutionalization in Italy unfolded in an almost diametrically opposite manner to that of the United States, even where so-called "community mental health centers" were established. Where the Italians emphasized co-responsibility in the commons, the US boasted of individual negative rights and consumer choices in treatments or budget-slashing corners cut. Where the Italian groups exposed the class war, misogyny, and racial animus underlying psychiatric diagnosis and subsequent segregation and marginalization, the US discovered ever more subtle forms of micro-deviancy to be intimately managed by technical experts spreading marginalization and isolation into the remotest corners of the country. Where Democratic Psychiatry sought to form new bonds and common languages in struggles that limited and negated the function of institutional power, US-based professionals got lost under the detritus of obscurantist titles, mystifying specializations, and studies that only led to more studies of sole interest to an inarticulate breed of scriveners who trade them for reasons obscure even to themselves. The lesson of Trieste is that extrahospital therapeutics is not a matter of continually inserting psychiatric teams or buildings into a city whose fundamental structure inoculates alienating relations—in this case, the "[o]ld segregational structured are simply miniaturized and . . . internalized."[59] Rather, it is a matter of concrete acts of destruction and reconstruction of space itself, the seizure of new territories where new social forms can take root.

If we want to find a torchbearer of this revolutionary method, we should turn to the Brazilian anti-asylum movement. Given the similar progression of the development of psychiatry in Brazil and Italy, it is unsurprising that movements in these two countries found so much in common with one another. Brazilian psychiatry, like Italian psychiatry, was motivated by an initial utopian enthusiasm that never got its fair shot.

As in the US, the first official medical society in Brazil, the Medical Society of Rio de Janeiro [Sociedade de Medicina do Rio de Janeiro], was largely concerned with madness as a public health problem and made it their priority to construct an asylum.[60] As Brazil transitioned from an imperial to a republican state, free laborers went to market but the mad remained an indigestible kernel whose existence placed the logic of the "free" civil contract into question, as was the case during the French Revolution. In 1841, Emperor Dom Pedro II founded, on the day of his coronation, Brazil's first asylum in Rio de Janeiro by royal decree. After decades of struggling to secure an asylum, the Pinelian utopians in Brazil's moral hygiene movement found themselves stuck in a three-way fight over control with religious (the Santas Casas de Misericórdia) and imperial authorities. It was a tense compromise represented clearly by the statuary chosen to adorn the facade: "two allegorical embodiments of Science and Charity, Emperor Dom Pedro II, José Clemente Pereira, Saint Peter of Alcântara, Philippe Pinel, and his notable student Jean-Étienne Dominique Esquirol."[61]

Within a year of the declaration of the Republic in 1889, the Pinelian group finally wrested power from religious authorities. Decree 206 (The Medical and Legal Assistance to the Alienated) gave psychiatrists privileged authority over the medical care of the insane, and "designated the asylum as the central entry point into the care system for the mentally ill and authorized the construction of two agricultural colonies on the Ilha do Governador, known as the São Bento and Conde de Mesquita colonies."[62] But, unlike the great European reformers, Brazilian psychiatrists received insufficient financial support to attempt widespread reforms for actualizing the rights to "legal representation, due process, and access to expeditious medical treatment" promised by the law.[63] Having inherited a building already brimming with an undifferentiated mass of tortured bodies, long-accumulated misery was like a black hole. Into its inescapable gravity, all hopes and plans were quickly swallowed. Utopianism in Brazil (as in Italy) was only able to persist as an idealized hope on condition it didn't come into contact with the sorry state of care that existed in fact.

What, if anything, was imported into Brazil? Certainly not a model. The anti-asylum movement arose in the 1970s, when Brazil was undergoing massive, rapid transformation as it faced new opposition to the years of autocracy and its repressions from pro-democracy tendencies and the explosion of new subject groups demanding recognition and power—feminism, gay liberation, Black consciousness, Indigenous sovereignty. These movements shared in the spirit of political rejuvenation and experimentation with subjectivity, adopting the strategy of conflict as enculturation and culture as means of conflict typical of the Italian strategy. Despite some humanizing initiatives in the 1940s and '50s like the art therapy practice of Nise da Silveira discussed in the last chapter, Brazilian psychiatry, with some of the most relaxed commitment standards in the world, had earlier embraced a blunt carceral mechanism of control and state-sponsored violence against marginal figures during Vargas' dictatorship, methods that would continue under the *Estado Novo* (1937–1946) in more subtle fashion.[64]

In the years following the military dictatorship of 1964, these trends would rapidly intensify as the mental health system would become reorganized primarily around private care, so that, by 1981, private hospitals hosted 70.9 percent of all psychiatric hospital beds.[65] Speaking as a representative of Brazil at an 1983 conference for the International Network of Alternatives to Psychiatry in Cuernavaca, Mexico, Antonio S. Simone characterizes this coup as the moment when psychiatric hospitals began running themselves explicitly as financial schemes carried out through "increasing hospitalizations, low wages, and the exploitation of professional work."[66] Indeed, between 1965–1968, "the hospital population swelled by 20%" and private hospital beds doubled between 1965 and 1970, tripling again by 1982.[67]

In this unholy alliance, the state could wipe its hands of the mad and all manner of deviants, at once cleaning them off the street and avoiding the consequences of legal responsibility for instances of torture and neglect; on the other hand, the sharks in the business of madness were incentivized to keep more people locked up longer, with as little staff and resources as possible.[68] For the poor, chronification was imposed intentionally, but, as is always the case, *another* psychiatry was offered to the rich, namely a voluntary, slow, and conciliatory form.[69] That this latter form was widely associated with psychoanalysis contributed to its ambivalent position in Brazil's anti-asylum movement, which, much like in Italy, would broadly look at it with indifference or rejection.[70]

The symbol of the country's organized annihilation of outsiders was the Hospital Colônia at Barbacena. Established in 1903, the hospital was a veritable dumping ground for undesirables of all sorts ("alcoholics, syphilitics, prostitutes, homosexuals, epileptics, single mothers, wives who were discarded for mistresses, non-conformists"[71]), though as was common in this country where the founding of the asylum roughly coincided with the abolition of slavery and later so heavily marked by the race science of eugenics, the majority of the inmates were Afro-Brazilian. Daniella Arbex, a journalist whose 2013 book *Holocausto Brasileiro* on Barbacena has rejuvenated public interest in the space, calculates that upwards of 70 percent of inmates never even received a diagnosis.[72] Only in recent years has the extent of the horror of this place become more widely known. Patients were forced to work all day—often naked, having little access to clothing— in what was dubbed "The City of Fools." What little treatment was offered over the decades was simple: antipsychotics to calm the hordes and ECT for the recalcitrant. As the inmates accumulated, the administration removed existing beds to make more space, forcing inmates to sleep on the ground crowded together for warmth or even outside in the courtyard. Food and water were always lacking, so patients took to eating rodents and drinking the raw sewage that ran through the courtyards. Rape was pervasive. Babies born on site were stolen away. It is now thought that at least 60,000 patients died there over its seventy-seven years of operation, as a result of medical experimentation, neglect, malnutrition, torture, sickness, and outright murder. The excess in human bodies led to an active trade in corpses for universities, and the rest were dissolved in acid so that their bones could be harvested for sale.[73] The runaways had the best chance of survival.

As Paulo Amarante, an early participant in the Mental Health Worker's Movement (MTSM), tells it, the group formed in 1978 as an effect of a "chain of solidarity" that eventually led to the *luta antimanicomial*, the anti-asylum struggle. In 1978, a group of three mental health workers (one of whom was Paulo Amarante) working for the National Division of Mental Health, or DINSAM, which was responsible for formulating mental health policy and running four federal asylums in Rio de Janeiro, first raised the alarm about the dismal conditions of Brazil's hospitals and agricultural colonies by exposing "the shortage of physicians on shifts, nutritional deficiencies in patients, and outright violence, mostly deaths from stabbings and beatings, which were not investigated and blamed on other patients . . . even exposing the fact that political prisoners were being confined to these hospitals."[74] DINSAM responded defensively, firing all of them. After a petition was presented in protest, they fired 263 more employees within the course of two months, triggering a strike by the newly formed MTSM, which is believed to be the first public sector strike under the dictatorship. In solidarity, this strike grew to a general strike of the physicians in Rio de Janeiro and, in turn, a national strike.[75]

The MTSM showed up en masse at the fifth Brazilian Congress of Psychiatry in 1978 in Camboriú in the State of Santa Catarina where they pushed through motions for "Broad, General and Unrestricted Amnesty [of the mental health workers]," repudiating the privatization of mental health, and denouncing the "lack of democratic participation in the elaboration of health plans."[76] In October of the same year, the first Brazilian Congress of Psychoanalysis of Groups and Institutions in Rio de Janeiro brought the MTSM and other militants into contact with Franco Basaglia, Félix Guattari, Robert Castel, Thomas Szasz, Erving Goffman, Howard Becker, Armando Bauleo, Emilio Rodrigué, and other major figures critical of psychiatry and members of the International Network of Alternatives to Psychiatry.

In 1979, with the invitation of local partisans, Franco Basaglia returned and did a whirlwind tour around Brazil giving fourteen speeches in ten days around the country, collected later in a volume called "Brazilian Conferences" (currently not translated into English). With Law 180 so recently passed, some participants in the conferences looked to Basaglia for leadership in the international struggle, asking him what was to be done. But he "refused to play the part of a lecturer who comes from abroad to tell stories and give technical advice" reflecting later that "I have become famous because I 'opened up' a psychiatric hospital and the press described me as the 'man who freed the mad' . . . everyone wants to know what to do, what can be done . . . and this is another way of destroying an experience. I think that today, I have become an institution."[77] Sylvia Marcos, who belonged to a group of critical mental health workers in Cuernavaca, Mexico who worked at Ivan Illich's CIDOC (Centro Intercultural de Documentación), said of Basaglia that "the importance of his work resides in the possibility of repeating it, not in crude imitation—servile and repetitive—but rather in the autonomy of a movement that knows 'it cannot be imitated,' that each historical, social, political, institutional context offers different junctures, different possibilities."[78] A patient participant of the annual anti-asylum parades held in Brazil every year on May 18 introduces a whole humorous Basaglian vocabulary: "*Basaglia*: the guy who frees the looneys. *Basaglía*: to become like Basaglia. *Basaglismo*: Basaglian lifestyle. . . . *Basagliaismo*: Study of the Basaglián effect."[79] In order to hold onto the "Basaglian effect," we must actively destroy the myth of Basaglia the liberating saint.

Central to Basaglia's vision was not just the destruction of the mental hospital, but the continuous destruction of psychiatric power, including his own. The psychiatrist paradoxically helps to arrange things through liberalizing measures in such a way that the patients were in a better position to negate them and attain their own liberation, thereby also negating themselves as patients: "as the identity of the institution was destroyed, so all those inside it—staff and patients—lost their own identities too: all were forced to challenge not only their own practice, but their own understandings of this practice, and the result was a constantly shifting flux in which meaningful patterns could only be discerned long after the event."[80] What does the name "Basaglia" represent today? Franco Basaglia was undoubtedly a kind, charismatic, and intelligent figure, but Democratic Psychiatry was not the result of any individual. First, Basaglia is split in two between husband and wife: Franco and Franca Ongaro. The two wrote books and articles together, and she was there every step of the way. Nothing would have happened if there was not a dedicated team of psychiatrists, patients, and nurses involved at every step. If there is a subject, it is not Franco Basaglia and it cannot be Franco Basaglia. Even the books associated with this movement are collective products, most famously the 1968 book *L'istituzione negata* [*The Negated Institution*]. The method of Democratic Psychiatry is unique in its self-conscious aiming towards continuous subjective crises, and yet we still refer to Franco Basaglia as a figurehead and symbol for the Italian situation. This is why, for some, "Basaglia" refers to a person, but for those engaged in political conflict, it first of all refers to a commitment to continual transformation by working through contradictions. It's completely natural that, after seventy years of stagnancy without psychiatric reform, in the wake of the Arab Spring, Egypt's first and only mental health center—the only place offering an alternative to the custodial hospital system—took the name "Franco Basaglia Center."[81] When the name "Basaglia" is sung in joyous anthems in the streets of Belo Horizonte in Brazil, it refers not to a man, but above all to a "detonation of a situation."[82]

Basaglia's tour led to visits at local asylums and more meetings with local militants to raise awareness of their fight. After visiting the hospital at Barbacena with local journalists, students, and anti-asylum partisans, he publicly drew comparisons to a Nazi concentration camp, a common rhetorical analogy in anti-institutional struggles around the world, especially for the generation who survived concentration camps only to discover painful similarities in their own institutions or even met survivors of the camps in cramped hospital quarters. The movement snowballed from this point on. Soon after, the Brazilian filmmaker Helvécio Ratton finished producing *Em Nome da Razão* [*In the Name of Reason*] (1979), a short documentary on Barbacena that lingered on the sense of degradation and brutality there, explicitly framed by quotes from *The Negated Institution*. Despite efforts by the Brazilian government to block its screening, the film was shown to thousands. At the same time, a report by Hiram Firmino called *Nos porões da loucura* [*In the Dungeons of Madness*] about Barbacena was published in the *Diário de Minas* newspaper. Inspired by the film, Paulo Amarante and Jairo Toledo Furtado undertook a major exposé, published in the book *(Colônia): tragédia silenciosa* [*(Asylum): A Silent Tragedy*] (2008).[83]

Capitalizing on the early waves of excitement generated by the exposés, the subsequent public outrage, and the cultural events, the

MTSM and their allies organized a series of congresses and conferences in the late 1970s and 1980s to continue making connections and keep up the pressure.[84] In a June 1986 meeting held in Buenos Aires, the Network of Alternatives to Psychiatry gathered together patients, ex-patients, and mental health workers who proposed a collective motto: *"por uma sociedade sem manicômios"* ["for a society without asylums"], inclusive of anyone opposed to the carceral logic of the institution.[85] The process of opening up was solidified during the MTSM's Second Congress in December 1987 in Bauru when they adopted this motto and decided to open up the movement beyond mental health workers,[86] recognizing that the problems of madness and psychiatry are wholly communal in nature and led to the new group moniker for the movement: "Movement for the Struggle Against Asylums" ["Movimento da Luta Antimanicomial," or MLA].

The Bauru Manifesto produced by the 350 participants of the Congress makes it clear that this was a decisive turning point of the movement from being centered around mental health workers and hospital conditions to being about the social organization of madness.[87] They wrote: "By refusing the role of agents of exclusion from institutionalized violence . . . we inaugurate a new commitment." What ties the Brazilian movement to the Italian one is, among other things, the determination to hold on to tensions and face contradictions in attending to that commitment: "It is clear that it is not enough to rationalize and modernize the services in which we work. The State that manages these services is the same State that sustains the mechanisms of exploitation and the social production of madness and violence. The commitment established by the anti-mental asylum struggle imposes an alliance with the popular movement and the organized working class."[88] Creating a public culture of contestation was acknowledged by the Bauru Congress as a central part of their strategy. Much of these cultural productions centered around the question: what is the place of madness? Where is it excluded and marginalized and where is it welcomed? The Congress participants' designation of May 18th as the "Day of Struggle Against Psychiatric Hospitals" on the tenth anniversary of Law 180 in major cities around the country complete with protests of exclusion and psychiatric violence, but also parades to celebrate the movement and its successes, is one way of bringing this question out into the public arena. In line with this cultural tradition,

Brazil today is host to an exceptionally rich body of musical groups (e.g., Harmonia Enlouquece, Trem Tan Tan, Los Impacientes), films (e.g., director Laís Bodanzky's *Bicho de Sete Cabeças* [*Brainstorm*]), theater groups (e.g., Ueinzz Theatre Company), and carnival groups (e.g., Loucura Suburbana and Tá Pirando, Pirado, Pirou!) that explore the social realities and complexities of madness and the public's response to it. Many of them take the form of boisterous celebrations of difference led by mad people or patients themselves.[89] In 1989, in the midst of a cultural explosion and following the Constitution of 1988, Brazil introduced the broad public health policy Sistema Únio de Saúde (SUS), or the Unified Health System, which included some of the demands and language of the anti-asylum movement. This included the demand to the right to health care.[90]

The new organizational forms corresponding to this continuous public contestation and social place-making crystallized under CAPS (Centros de Atenção Psicossocial), or Psychosocial Care Centers, and the associated NAPS (Nucleus of Psychosocial Care), both founded in 1989 but spreading throughout the early 1990s. Taking inspiration from the model developed in Trieste, CAPS were designed to replace hospitalization and the ambulatory model responses in use in Brazil's largely private psychiatric facilities by integrating patients into a sustaining network that addressed immediate needs like housing and food, but also deeper dimensions of life, like cultural participation and the desire for satisfactory leisure activities. Ideally, CAPS operate first and foremost as social centers where one could, for example, have a meal, talk to a psychiatrist or social worker, apply for a work cooperative, and get signed up for a football league in the same place. CAPS have three different sizes corresponding to their catchment area (with an additional type for substance use management), but only the largest, CAPS III, are open 24 hours a day with the option of overnight stays.[91] While drugs and some overnight care are available, the stated purpose of CAPS is to displace "questions concerning the true nature of psychosis and the best medical way to treat . . . by the problem of how the individual was culturally recognized as psychotic"[92] in order to better integrate people into a broad web of social supports that can sustain someone struggling beyond the clinic.

"Contrary to what many may think," said Paulo Amarante about CAPS, "the anti-asylum struggle is not against psychiatric admission;

it's against institutionalization in models that segregate people permanently."[93] This amounts to saying that the opposite of institutionalization is not the empty freedom of venturing out into the "free" world of the marketplace, it's the robust social cohesion that can withstand disruptions and look to difference as a motive force. These facilities were greatly expanded with the passing of Law 10.216 in April 2001, which also spelled out more extensive and concrete legal rights for mental health service users,[94] while helping the facilities grow from just a few hundred spaces to over 2,000 in the aughts. The number of long-term hospital beds, on the other hand, dropped from 100,000 to just 30,000.[95]

The experience in the city of Santos in the state of São Paulo is both illustrative of the new direction and a turning point for the movement. Spurred to action by reports of extreme violence and death in the Anchieta Clinic, Mayor Telma de Souza and the city's the Sanitary and Health Department put an immediate hold on all segregative and aggressive treatment methods (e.g., electroshock, isolation rooms) and began the process of dismantling the hospital entirely on May 3, 1989. In its place appeared five NAPS focused on different needs, and all open 24 hours: an emergency service in the general hospital; a community radio and TV network; a residential program for former inmates; a work cooperative; and a clinic for substance users.[96] Santos thus marks a point where major reforms were taking place independently of its original social base with mental health workers and nurses and where innovations and strategies of the movement became law independently of direct militant confrontation. In 1990, representatives in the field of mental health from several Latin American countries, including Brazil, met in Caracas, Venezuela for the Regional Conference for the Restructuring of Mental Health Care. Participants declared their intent for a unified stance: to move from hospital care to community care and against the perpetuation of violence. Given that the Latin American resistance movements were, from the outset, internationalist in character, principles of openness and sharing of knowledge and resources were central to the agreement. International correspondence between the Italian and Brazilian movements continued after Franco Basaglia's death in 1980, as did activities at Trieste, which were then directed by Franco Rotelli.

This speaks to the strength of the movement, but it also represents a critical vulnerability: the results may be beneficial, but laws such as those passed in Italy and Brazil are fragile compromises of the state with large, widespread anti-institutional struggles. Given this, they are constantly under threat and rarely adhered to without a strong social support from workers, patients, and neighbors. Throughout the 1980s and 1990s, Franca Ongaro Basaglia became Law 180's fiercest defender against reactionary backlash from the political right and center and the old guard in psychiatry. As she pointed out earlier, the southern regions of Italy without much of a history of movement action had the poorest adherence to the law.

The same is undoubtedly true of Brazil, where scenes in peripheral clinics described by João Biehl in *Vita: Life in a Zone of Social Abandonment* are comparable to the excesses of Barbacena. Brazil's gains are today under extreme strain since the Jair Bolsonaro regime's turn to the right and his alliance with evangelical churches who have been "pushing for the Brazilian state to prioritise private, religious-led therapeutic communities, cutting down harm reduction approaches to drug use."[97] In 2019, he "criticized the current 'ideology' of the system and proposed to replace it with 'scientific methods' based on the 'technical knowledge' of psychiatric hospitals, biological treatments such as electroconvulsive therapy, and the hospitalization of children and adolescents."[98] With Bolsonaro, Brazil had also seen the return of fierce anticommunist state discourse that sees all "others"—all the gays, feminists, leftists, etc.—as pathological deviants in need of conversion. Studies of hospitals under his regime reported drops in environmental conditions and sharp increases in incidents of torture,[99] "including multiple confirmed cases of torture, sexual assault, child abuse, forced labour, forced religious conversion and 'gay cure' practices."[100] Those with hopes that Luiz Inácio Lula da Silva's return to the Presidency in 2023 would decisively reverse these policies were disappointed when he created a "Therapeutic Community Support Department," meaning that "private therapeutic communities—which are typically operated by conservative religious groups—are recognized as credible institutions alongside those that already exist in the national health system."[101]

Our situation looks dire, and yet, in 1961, no one would have thought that the asylums were going anywhere. By 1978, the demolition was unstoppable and international. In Trieste and Barbacena, the stone fortresses of reason fell at the hands of "loonies" and militants who "demonstrated that the impossible can become possible."[102] There is still much to destroy—many asylums both literal and figurative standing haughtily in our path—in the ludicrous war to replace the apocalypticism of the present with the impossibilities we desperately need.

Notes

1. John Foot, *The Man Who Closed the Asylums: Franco Basaglia and the Revolution in Mental Health Care* (London: Verso, 2015), 65.
2. John Foot, "Franco Basaglia: A Man, a Movement, Institutions, and Outcomes," *Basaglia's International Legacy: from Asylum to Community*, ed. Tom Burns and John Foot (Oxford: Oxford University Press, 2020), 7–8.
3. Foot, "Franco Basaglia: A Man, a Movement," 8.
4. Alvise Sforza Tarabochia, *Psychiatry, Subjectivity, Community: Franco Basaglia and Biopolitics* (Oxford: Peter Lang, 2013), 23.
5. Quoted in Tarabochia, *Psychiatry, Subjectivity, Community*, 31.
6. Foot, *The Man Who Closed the Asylums*, 13.
7. Quoted in John Foot, "Photography and Radical Psychiatry in Italy in the 1960s. The Case of the Photobook *Morire di Classe* (1969)," *History of Psychiatry* 26, no. 1 (2015): 21, https://www.ncbi.nlm.nih.gov/pmc/articles/PMC4361699/.
8. Franca Ongaro Basaglia, "Preface," *Psychiatry Inside Out: Selected Writings of Franco Basaglia*, ed. Nancy Scheper-Hughes and Anne M. Lovell (New York: Columbia University Press, 1987), xiii.
9. Franco Basaglia, "Institutions of Violence," *Psychiatry Inside Out: Selected Writings of Franco Basaglia*, ed. Nancy Scheper-Hughes and Anne M. Lovell (New York: Columbia University Press, 1987), 64.
10. Quoted in Chantal Marazia, Heiner Fangerau, Thomas Becker, and Felicitas Söhner, "'Visions of Another World,' Franco Basaglia and German Reform," *Basaglia's International Legacy: from Asylum to Community*, ed. Tom Burns and John Foot (Oxford: Oxford University Press, 2020), 231.
11. Basaglia, "Institutions of Violence," 76.
12. Franca Ongaro Basaglia and Franco Basaglia, "A Problem of Institutional Psychiatry: Exclusion as a Social and Psychiatric Category," *International Review of Psychiatry* 30, no. 2 (2018): 120, https://doi.org/10.1080/09540261.2018.1436324.
13. Quoted in Nancy Scheper-Hughes and Anne M. Lovell, "Introduction: The Utopia of Reality: Franco Basaglia and the Practice of a Democratic Psychiatry," *Psychiatry Inside Out: Selected Writings of Franco Basaglia*, ed. Nancy Scheper-Hughes and Anne M. Lovell (New York: Columbia University Press, 1987), 8.
14. Mauro Serapioni, "Franco Basaglia: biography of a revolutionary," *História, Ciências, Saúde* 26, no. 4 (2019): 9, https://www.scielo.br/pdf/hcsm/v26n4/en_0104-5970-hcsm-26-04-1169.pdf.
15. Quoted in Roberto Mezzina, "Basaglia After Basaglia: Recovery, human rights, and Trieste today," *Basaglia's International Legacy: from Asylum to Community*, ed. Tom Burns and John Foot (Oxford: Oxford University Press, 2020), 44.
16. Brian Barraclough, "In Conversation with Maxwell Jones," *Bulletin of the Royal College of Psychiatrists* 8, no. 9, (September 1984): 166, https://www.cambridge.org/core/services/aop-cambridge-core/content/view/4941C60A0028B6313C5CA1474E070D21/S0140078900000213a.pdf/in_conversation_with_maxwell_jones.pdf.

17. Maxwell Jones, *Social Psychiatry in Practice: The Idea of the Therapeutic Community* (Middlesex: Penguin Books, 1968), 85.

18. Jones, *Social Psychiatry in Practice*, 108–109.

19. Jones, *Social Psychiatry in Practice*, 88.

20. Jones, *Social Psychiatry in Practice*, 87.

21. Maxwell Jones, *Beyond the Therapeutic Community: Social Learning and Social Psychiatry* (New Haven and London: Yale University Press, 1968), 11.

22. Quoted in Foot, *The Man Who Closed the Asylums*, 108. These same basic principles and processes are present in contemporary therapeutic communities and perhaps even more thoroughly in the Soteria model developed by Loren Mosher, designed for treatment of acute psychosis without a reliance on medication. Inspired by phenomenology, Mosher designed a therapeutic community model that emphasized the importance of simply being with one another. To reorient the space around this directive, roles are deemphasized, efforts are made to make the house home-like, tasks are shared, and all activities are seen as having therapeutic potential. For more, see Volkmar Aderhold, Peter Stastny, and Peter Lehmann, "Soteria: An Alternative Mental Health Reform Movement," in *Alternatives Beyond Psychiatry*, ed. Peter Stastny and Peter Lehmann (Berlin: Peter Lehmann Publishing, 2007), 148 and 154.

23. Giovanni Jervis, "Psychiatry in Crisis: Institutional Contradictions," *International Journal of Mental Health* 14, no. 1–2 (1985): 62.

24. Jervis, "Psychiatry in Crisis," 62.

25. Leslie Topp, "Single Rooms, Seclusion and the Non-Restraint Movement in British Asylums, 1838–1844," *Social History of Medicine* 31, no. 4 (November 2018): 772, https://academic.oup.com/shm/article/31/4/754/4934975?login=false.

26. Topp, "Single Rooms, Seclusion and the Non-Restraint Movement in British Asylums, 1838–1844," 773.

27. Topp, "Single Rooms, Seclusion and the Non-Restraint Movement in British Asylums, 1838–1844," 773.

28. Franco Basaglia, Franca Ongaro Basaglia, Domenico Casagrande, Giovanni Jervis, Letizia Jervis Comba, Agostino Pirella, Lucio Schittar, and Antonio Slavich, "Considerations on a Communitarian Experience," in Michael Donnelly, *The Politics of Mental Health in Italy* (London: Tavistock/Routledge, 1992), 109.

29. Topp, "Single Rooms, Seclusion and the Non-Restraint Movement in British Asylums, 1838–1844," 773.

30. Jervis, "Psychiatry in Crisis," 53.

31. Franco Basaglia, "The Destruction of the Mental Hospital as a Place of Institutionalization: Thoughts Caused by Personal Experience with the Open Door System and Part Time Service," *PsychoOdyssey* 1, https://web.archive.org/web/20110722062127/http://www.triestesalutementale.it/english/doc/basaglia_1964_destruction-mhh.pdf.

32. Basaglia, "Institutions of Violence," 62.

33. Scheper-Hughes and Lovell, "Introduction: The Utopia of Reality: Franco Basaglia and the Practice of a Democratic Psychiatry," 18–19.

34. Nancy Scheper-Hughes and Anne M. Lovell, "Breaking the Circuit of Social Control: Lessons in Public Psychiatry from Italy and Franco Basaglia," *Classics of Community Psychiatry: Fifty Years of Public Health Outside the Hospital* (Oxford: Oxford University Press, 2011), 337–338, https://www.academia.edu/7432018/Breaking_the_circuit_of_social_control_Lessons_in_public_psychiatry_from_Italy_and_Franco_Basaglia. Erika Rossi's film *Trieste Racconta Basaglia* uses archival footage of an assembly. One can see dozens of patients sitting in a circle, with Franco Basaglia in the middle, and at least several nurses. Many others stand at the edges. One can assume that some of those sitting or standing were also nurses or psychiatrists, indistinguishable from each other. People are laughing, moving back and forth, and sometimes shouting. Someone finally shouts, "I want to say something," and stands up and people direct their attention to him.

35. Peppe Dell'Acqua and Silvia D'Autilia, "An Architecture to Set Madness Free. San Giovanni is No Memorial," *FAMagazine* (September 2017): 34, http://www.festivalar-chitettura.it/public/Articoli/Allegato/h41Og66fey_224.pdf.

36. Quoted in Scheper-Hughes and Lovell, "Introduction: The Utopia of Reality: Franco Basaglia and the Practice of a Democratic Psychiatry," 17.

37. Quoted in Foot, *The Man Who Closed the Asylums*, 353.

38. Franco Basaglia, "Breaking the Circuit of Control," in *Critical Psychiatry: The Politics of Mental Health*, ed. David Ingleby (New York: Pantheon Books, 1980), 189.

39. Quoted in José Miguel Caldas de Almeida, "The Impact in Latin America of Basaglia and Italian Psychiatric Reform," in *Basaglia's International Legacy: from Asylum to Community*, ed. Tom Burns and John Foot (Oxford: Oxford University Press, 2020), 96.

40. Robert Castel, *The Regulation of Madness: The Origins of Incarceration in France* (Berkeley: University of California Press, 1988), 34.

41. Jervis, "Psychiatry in Crisis," 67.

42. "The programme of Psichiatria Democratica (1973)," in Michael Donnelly, *The Politics of Mental Health in Italy* (London: Tavistock/Routledge, 1992), 121.

43. Anne M. Lovell, "Breaking the Circuit of Control: A Report on the Conference of the European Network: Alternatives to Psychiatry," *State and Mind: People Look at Psychology* 6, no. 2 (Winter 1977): 9. Courtesy of the Oskar Diethelm Library, DeWitt Institute for the History of Psychiatry, Weill Cornell Medical College.

44. Yves-Luc Conreuer, "A Statement from the Psychiatrized," *State and Mind: People Look at Psychology* 6, no. 2 (Winter 1977): 14. Courtesy of the Oskar Diethelm Library, DeWitt Institute for the History of Psychiatry, Weill Cornell Medical College.

45. Basaglia, "The Destruction," 2.

46. Franco Basaglia, "Peacetime Crimes: Technicians of Practical Knowledge," in *Psychiatry Inside Out: Selected Writings of Franco Basaglia*, ed. Nancy Scheper-Hughes and Anne M. Lovell (New York: Columbia University Press, 1987), 166.

47. Dell'Acqua and D'Autilia, "An Architecture to Set Madness Free," 38.

48. Erika Rossi, dir., *Trieste Racconta Basaglia*, Italy: Fantastificio, 2012.

49. Lovell, "Breaking the Circuit of Control," 7.

50. Dell'Acqua and D'Autilia, "An Architecture to Set Madness Free," 35.

51. Rossi, *Trieste Racconta Basaglia*. My emphasis.

52. Scheper-Hughes and Lovell, "Breaking the Circuit of Social Control," 341.

53. Anne Lovell, "From Confinement to Community: The Radical Transformation of an Italian Mental Hospital," *State and Mind: People Look at Psychology* 6, no. 3 (Spring 1978): 9. Courtesy of the Oskar Diethelm Library, DeWitt Institute for the History of Psychiatry, Weill Cornell Medical College.

54. Francesco Salvini, "Caring Ecologies," *transversal texts*, April 2019, https://transversal.at/transversal/0318/salvini/en?hl=basaglia.

55. Franca Ongaro Basaglia, "The Psychiatric Reform in Italy: Summing Up and Looking Ahead," *International Journal of Social Psychiatry* 35, no. 1 (1989): 91.

56. Franco Basaglia and Franca Ongaro Basaglia, "Italy's Aborted Psychiatric Reform," *International Journal of Mental Health* 14, no. 1–2 (Spring–Summer 1985): 12.

57. Basaglia, "The Psychiatric Reform," 92.

58. Basaglia, "Breaking the Circuit of Control," 187.

59. Félix Guattari, quoted in Paulo Amarante and Eduardo Henrique Guimarães Torre, "'Back to the City, Mr. Citizen!' – Psychiatric Reform and Social Participation: from Institutional Isolation to the Anti-Asylum Movement," *Brazilian Journal of Public Administration* 52, no. 6. (2018): 1098, https://www.scielo.br/pdf/rap/v52n6/en_1982-3134-rap-52-06-1090.pdf.

60. Manuella Meyer, *Reasoning against Madness: Psychiatry and the State in Rio de Janeiro, 1830–1944* (Rochester: University of Rochester Press, 2017), 21.

61. Meyer, *Reasoning against Madness*, 35.

62. Meyer, *Reasoning against Madness*, 81.

63. Meyer, *Reasoning against Madness*, 82.

64. Miguel, "Psychiatric Power," 253.
65. Miguel, "Psychiatric Power," 255.
66. Antonio S. Simone, "Locura y Contencion en Brasil," in *Manicomios y prisiones*, ed. Sylvia Marcos (México: Red Ediciones, 1983), 93.
67. Miguel, "Psychiatric Power," 256
68. Gabriel Figueiredo, "Politica de la Salud en Brasil," in *Manicomios y prisiones*, ed. Sylvia Marcos (México: Red Ediciones, 1983), 103.
69. Simone, "Locura," 97.
70. The association of analysts with torture in Brazil also clearly added to this. I'll look at this in Chapter 5.
71. Naiara Galarraga Gortázar, "Barbacena: The Brazilian 'city of madmen' that claimed 60,000 lives," *El Pais*, September 8, 2021, https://english.elpais.com/usa/2021-09-08/barbacena-brazils-city-of-madmen-that-claimed-60000-lives.html.
72. Miguel, "Psychiatric Power," 257.
73. Statistics and accounts can be found in Rodrigo Matos-de-Souza and Ana Carolina Cerqueira Medrado, "On bodies as object: a postcolonial reading of the 'Brazilian Holocaust,'" *Saúde em Debate* 45, no. 128 (May 2021): 165; Ernesto Venturini, Maria Stella Brandão Goulart, and Paulo Amarante, "The Optimism of Practice: The Impact of Basaglia's Thoughts on Brazil," *Basaglia's International Legacy: from Asylum to Community*, ed. Tom Burns and John Foot (Oxford: Oxford University Press, 2020), 113–128.
74. Suelen Gomes, "Anti-asylum Reform in Brazil: From the Horror to Today," *Fiotec*, February 21, 2018, https://www.fiotec.fiocruz.br/en/news/4881-anti-asylum-reform-in-brazil-from-the-horror-to-today.
75. Paulo Amarante, *Madness and Social Change: Autobiography of the Brazilian Psychiatric Reform* (Cham: Springer, 2022), 14.
76. Amarante, *Madness and Social Change*, 15.
77. Quoted in Foot, *The Man*, 388.
78. Sylvia Marcos, "En Recuerdo a Franco Basaglia," in *Manicomios y prisiones*, ed. Sylvia Marcos (México: Red Ediciones, 1983), 16.
79. Venturini, Goulart, and Amarante, "The Optimism of Practice," 123.
80. Basaglia, "Breaking the Circuit of Control," 186.
81. Mustafa Z. Mirza, "Are Psychiatric Hospitals in Egypt Hurting Mental Health Care?," *Egyptian Streets*, December 13, 2016, https://egyptianstreets.com/2016/12/13/are-psychiatric-hospitals-in-egypt-hurting-mental-health-care/.
82. Venturini, Goulart, and Amarante, "The Optimism of Practice," 114.
83. Gomes and Amarante, "Anti-Asylum Reform in Brazil."
84. A list of the most important conferences and their specific focuses can be found in Amarante, *Madness and Social Change*, 17–22.
85. Paulo Amarante and Mônica de Oliveria Nunes, "Psychiatric Reform in the SUS and the Struggle for a Society without Asylums," *Ciência & Saúde Coletiva* 23, no. 6 (2018): 2069; and Rosana T. Onocko Campos, Mark Costa, Mariana Barbosa Pereira, Ellen Cristina Ricci, Giselli da Silva Tavares Enes, Leidy Janeth, Erazo Chavez, Graziela Reis, and Larry Davidson, "Recovery, Citizenship, and Psychosocial Rehabilitation: A Dialog between Brazilian and American Mental Health Care Approaches," *American Journal of Psychiatric Rehabilitation* 20, no. 3 (2017): 313.
86. See Miguel, "Psychiatric Power," 261; Amarante, *Madness and Social Change*, 21–22.
87. Cláudia Braga, "Arguments for Utopias of Reality and the Brazilian Psychiatric Reform Experience," *Saúde Soc. São Paulo* 29, no. 3 (2020): 3, https://www.scielo.br/j/sausoc/a/MZ4V47nnytfHZ9Y9cL3X3dk/?lang=en#.
88. Amarante, *Madness and Social Change*, 23.
89. Paulo Amarante and Mônica de Oliveria Nunes, "Psychiatric reform in the SUS," 2071; Amarante, *Madness and Social Change*, 57–64.
90. Daniel Magalhães Goulart, *Subjectivity and Critical Mental Health: Lessons from Brazil* (London: Routledge, 2019), 14. An account of the mutual influence between the anti-asylum movement and the push for the SUS can be found in Amarante, *Madness*

and Social Change, 19–20. It is worth singling out the Eighth Brazilian National Health Conference where CEBES (the Brazilian Center for Health Studies) proposed an outline for the SUS, which centered around the notion of health care as a right.

91. Goulart, *Subjectivity and Critical Mental Health*, 28.

92. João Biehl, .*VITA: Life in a Zone of Social Abandonment* (Berkeley: University of California Press, 2005), 135.

93. Gomes and Amarante, "Anti-Asylum Reform in Brazil."

94. Venturini, Goulart, and Amarante, "The Optimism of Practice," 124.

95. Amarante and Torre, "'Back to the City, Mr. Citizen!,'" 1104.

96. Amarante, *Madness and Social Change*, 26; Cristina Amélia Luzio and Solange L'Abbate, "The Brazilian Psychiatric Reform: Historical and Technical-Supportive Aspects of Experiences Carried out in the Cities of São Paulo, Santos and Campinas," *Interface – Comunicação, Saúde, Educação* 10, no. 20 (2007): 8–11.

97. Ana Clara Telles and Gabriela Barros de Luca, "Bolsonaro is Destroying Mental Health Care to Favour Evangelicals," *Aljazeera*, September 1, 2021, https://www.aljazeera.com/opinions/2021/9/1/bolsonaro-is-destroying-mental-health-care-to-favour-evangelicals. Note that the term "therapeutic community" has a different meaning in Brazil. It usually describes a small carceral institution and not the democratization of the management of therapy, as in Maxwell Jones.

98. Miguel, "Psychiatric Power," 263.

99. Miguel, "Psychiatric Power," 263.

100. Telles and Barros de Luca, "Bolsonaro is Destroying Mental Health Care."

101. Felipe Neis Araujo,"Lula Quietly Legitimizes Brazil's Forced Drug Treatment Institutions," *Filter*, February 1, 2023, https://filtermag.org/lula-therapeutic-community-support-department/; Abrasme, "Nota de Repúdio à criação do Departamento de Apoio às Comunidades Terapêuticas." *Noticias Abrasme*, January 24, 2023, https://www.abrasme.org.br/blog-detail/post/179604/nota-de-rep%C3%BAdio-%C3%A0-cria%C3%A7%C3%A3o-do-departamento-de-apoio-%C3%A0s-comunidades-terap%C3%AAuticas.

102. Basaglia quoted in Serapioni, "Franco Basaglia: Biography of a Revolutionary," 10.

CHAPTER 4

DREAMS OF ESCAPE

I can envisage a time arriving when we in the field of Psychiatry will entirely forsake our ancestry, forgetting that we had our beginnings in the poorhouse, the workhouse and the jail. —Charles C. Burlingame[1]

WHEN THE OUTSIDE COMES IN, THE INSIDE GOES OUT

The history of madness could be told as a history of acts of delineation, of the gradual or sudden redrawing of lines denoting belonging and exclusion, inside and outside, normal and abnormal that separate the mad from the sane. Michel Foucault's *History of Madness* is the most comprehensive attempt at producing such a history to date, though it is, despite its title, not really a history of madness *per se*—something which remains a dubious prospect—so much as a history of the spaces reason has assigned to it under different systems of production and knowledge, what he calls a "history of limits" and an "archeology of silence."[2] In the Renaissance, madness was characterized as a possible limit experience that was nevertheless internal to the subject: death and madness were the great nothingnesses one confronted within themselves. In this confrontation with the great mysteries of knowledge and life, one discovered deeper meanings and truths, however esoteric they may seem. Like the figurations of hell and the end-times, madness seemed to reveal essential truths and possibilities of the human experience and the order of the world. In this representation, or in similar ones where madness also appeared as the tragic truth of the world, madness was in dialogue with reason, cloaked though it may have been in the habit of Antichrist and Death.

In the sixteenth century, according to Foucault, Europe's relation to madness began to shift: madness and reason increasingly become locked in a reciprocal relation of exclusion as the former begins to appear principally as unreason and the mad become insane.[3] Perhaps more clearly, reason's silencing of madness took the form of material and juridical containment in special hospitals and almshouses, a shift Foucault refers to as "the Great Confinement."[4] Klaus Doerner further argues in *Madmen and the Bourgeoisie* that madmen became stable visible subjects within reason's regime of visibility—or, the "objects of administrative reason"—once the category of "insane pauper"[5] become a public cause for concern, necessitating incarceration and specialized treatment along with the other social rabble. At this point, though madness is conceived of as an outside or as an experience at the limit of intelligibility, it must paradoxically appear so under the persistent surveillance and constant illumination of the floodlights of reason. Human zoos are the historical precondition for psychiatric classifications, which grew in number over the course of the eighteenth and nineteenth centuries.[6]

Assigning to the doctor a near-exclusive dominion over the mad was not the complete break with the past some accounts have held it to be. Physicians have directed their attention to the elusive ailment at least since Hippocrates' *On the Sacred Disease* (written around 400 BCE) and continued to do so through the Middle Ages, particularly in Arabic texts. In the early modern period, doctors were frequently employed in general hospitals to do what they could; even before the dominion of moral treatment, it was widely assumed that madness had some physiological roots or at least significant influence. What shifted with France's 1838 law, over time with the uneven development of mental health law in the United States, with the declaration of the Republic in Brazil in 1890, or with the imposition of psychiatry in colonies around the world, was the production of a medicolegal category of "mad person" and the weaving of a web of technical relations and spaces to correspond with it. Including the mad through excluding them as wards, i.e., as analogous to children, was realized through placement in a "special institution," which in turn required a new "relationship between medicine and hospitalization, the development of a hospital technology, the exercise of a new kind of power within the institution, the acquiring of a new social mandate from practices based at first upon the bastion of the asylum."[7] It's a mistake to view the ascendance of the asylum as a simple coup on the side of medicine over a culturally defined object of madness, In fact, as Robert Castel reminds us, Pinel and his generation prided themselves on the *nonmedical* aspects of their administrative techniques, opposing their social and moral sensitivity to the desperation of heroic medicine (bleeding, purging, etc.). Psychiatry's special historical status lies not in its medicalization of social life, but principally in the socialization of crudely materialist medicine, and further, in having plugged this social medicine into an expansive and productive circuit with the state apparatus. Psychiatry's expertise, its position as the central point around which a social nexus secures relations of exclusion and categorization, pivots around the centralization and progressive rationalization of hospital space by means of medical categories in a continual process of refinement through critique.

If psychiatry managed to integrate the mad only through excluding them, we should be wary of concluding from this—as too often happens in the interpretation of Foucault's *History of Madness*—that the Renaissance or Christian Middle Ages of Europe were therefore inclusive. Perhaps the average pedestrian was more likely to encounter madness on the street without recoiling or be able to imagine it as a general existential possibility rather than as ontological alterity, but the ethics of charity and the poetic Christian allegories of the era, in truth, excluded the mad in their singularity precisely by including them as generic representations in which their madness was positioned as the extreme limit of another imaginal universe. Madness remained *unassimilable*. It was included in the world of reciprocal exchange only by becoming something else: pity for the destitute; lamenting a fall from grace, "a kind of normal deviance in which all must participate because all are born into sin;"[8] visiting it as a foreign territory on the edges of reason where it is equated with everything feminine, primitive, and Black. Psychiatry and its critique remain locked to this strategic game across territories of demarcating the inside and outside of urban space, of legal categories of citizenship, of reason.

More recently, antipsychiatry has been used to describe any force that opposes psychiatry (its categories, status as a medical field, or its treatments) at any level, which is a rather vague concept; or, it is used to describe any project that directs itself at behavioral abnormalities or distress in a radically different way. ("Outside the system," one often says.) There are tendencies among those on the outside (of a legal, spatial, or conceptual boundary) demanding entry into "normal society" or into the rooms where decisions are supposedly made, and others where the inside itself appears as the problem while aspects of that which is excluded are valorized. Often, these two tendencies exist, to varying degrees, side by side in political projects concerning madness and are in tension with one another. Of the former tendency, we could include struggles for the expansion of civil rights, integration into general labor, and the profusion of taxonomies based in supposedly universal categories like suffering or distress. If the desire to be folded into the flow of normal time and space is in the air, various radical therapies simultaneously offer acceptance of marginality and otherness as a source of empowerment against said flows, among them many feminist and antiracist therapeutic models. Few became as famous or as representative of the movements for the countercultural therapeutics of madness in the anglophone New Left as R.D. Laing and David Cooper in England. Despite being assigned the same catchall label of antipsychiatry and lumped together with the legal formalists in the US, these two not only opposed the integration of the mad as bourgeois legal subjects, but even asked at times to what extent the latter can truly be considered superior beings of reason. Laing and Cooper had the clarity of mind to ask: what the hell was so normal about the organization of the social world in its typical form? Weren't the most powerful states in the world—the very arbiters of reason on the world stage—arming themselves for mutual destruction?

A good deal of the positions popularly attributed to R.D. Laing properly belong to his comparatively obscure comrade David Cooper. Cooper was a South African-born communist forced to flee his country of birth due to his membership in the then-outlawed Communist Party and for opposing the Apartheid regime. Cooper deserves special attention, not only because he may be the only person who wholeheartedly championed every stereotype and excess attributed to antipsychiatry, but also since he coined the term in the 1967 book, *Psychiatry and Anti-Psychiatry*. After moving to England to study, he opened Villa 21 in 1962, a therapeutic community at a hospital in Hertfordshire that stretched the model to its limits by scrapping all outward semblances of power inequalities, besides the keys to the prescription drawer. Like the group in Gorizia, he discovered there were hard limits to how much one can change an institutional space and gave up the project in 1966. Cooper lived, and continues to live, in the shadow of R.D. Laing. Laing was a Scottish-born psychiatrist whose captivating book *The Divided Self* used existential and phenomenological theories of experience to render the seemingly alien speech and experience of "psychotics" comprehensible. There, he demonstrated that much of what we stigmatize as psychotic is only made incomprehensible by our tendency to abstract it from context, i.e., from its networks of communication and imminent relations. Psychosis was reframed as a defensive strategy taken up by a person in a crisis of ontological insecurity, itself often enough the result of familial irrationalities.

Prior to this milieu, Wilhelm Reich notably understood the patriarchal family as a material and economic unit whose dynamics and dysfunctions are imminently productive of social activity that set the stage for fascist formations. Reich viewed compulsive heterosexual marriage as the result of prevailing "economic constellations" and not their cause. At the same time, forming a kind of circle, the family is "prerequisite . . . of the authoritarian state and of authoritarian society."[9] By making use of cybernetic theories of communication and Sartre's existential theories of group relations, Laing—at least in the mid to late 1960s when he was most closely associated with the left— was able to scale up the critique of family relations as an analytic tool for unmasking the hidden contradictions and relations of domination in institutions and "society." Implicitly, for the micropolitical analysis of the family to reveal dynamics and problems that were visible on the macro scale of institutional life and geopolitics, he assumed not a circuit of economic relations as in Reich, nor a legally constructed form of filiation guaranteeing property rights in a social system, but a single power relation that adapts to scale and complexity across the whole social world. In this world of mirrors, the state looks like a big extended family and the family is just a small state.

One of Cooper and Laing's shared emphases, at least early on, was on the subjective possibilities of the experience of madness as a risky process of transformation. This is why they were both attracted to the passages in Foucault's work on the Renaissance treatment of madness, sensing therein a possibility for communion with the madness that lurks at the heart of reason. How each pursued this communion gave rise to mounting tensions throughout the 1960s, resulting in the proponents of existential (anti)psychiatry becoming increasingly divergent through the 1970s. Between the two, Cooper remained the most faithful torchbearer of this theme, with an added emphasis on the psychedelic fads and New Left Freudo-Marxism of his time with its total rejection of standard sexual pedagogy and morality, while Laing inched closer and closer to a comparatively tame family therapy model. Cooper's definition of antipsychiatry, as introduced first in *Psychiatry and Anti-Psychiatry* (1967), and further explored in *The Grammar of Living* (1974) and *The Language of Madness* (1978), remains to this day the only cohesive one. According to Cooper, the term refers to "a systematic action against psychiatric repression within the state structure of psychiatry."[10] In this delimited sense, every change in psychiatry is founded on antipsychiatry. The field itself, insofar as it wants to locate its founding in Pinel's unlocking of chains, Tuke's establishment of extra-hospital therapeutics, or any other foundational act, is first and foremost negative in respect to the immediately preceding practice and is, therefore, foundationally negative in character.[11]

Cooper recognized early on that whenever critics of psychiatry seek to establish an extra-psychiatric therapeutics of madness or something akin to it, they reach a fundamental limit. Their new practice is not like psychiatry, they say, because it is founded in the recognition of difference, of social values, and just moral principles. But this is precisely what every founder of a new psychiatry declares. Psychiatry cannot proceed from the vagaries of the moral to the stability of the biological nor from the infernal savagery of dungeons to the humane institution without the gesture and posture of an antipsychiatry, nor does antipsychiatry have any claim to existence outside of the former. The force of the utopian thrust gains its power in relation to the senselessness and brutality of a projected past; liberators arrive on a scene already saturated with chains. One of the great ironies of the term "antipsychiatry" is that the man who coined the term, and who fits the bill better than anyone else, came to forcefully reject it and applied it only to those he distinguished himself from, just as almost everyone does.[12] In Cooper's own time, the great reversal of values was marked at its extreme by the leveling of hierarchies, an openness to experience and difference, full transparency and permissiveness towards the use and effect of treatments (drugs in particular), and the end of sexual repression. Molar periodizations of psychiatry as a single event from Pinel to the 1960s, marked by a coup of state medicine over madness, are partly responsible for this generation's inability to see the continuity of negativity and discontinuities in the field. Despite that, Cooper still saw that antipsychiatry was a pole of psychiatry, and a necessary one. Equivocating madness and revolution, he frantically sought the means to escape this trap of reciprocity.

Cooper's writings are something of a mess—replete with bombast and obscurity, frequent misuse of terms, and circuitous tautologies—but we can't ignore them, for their awkward and circular dancing around a void is the real messiness faced by any attempt to liberate madness or let it speak. "All delusion is political statement,"[13] he wrote in his final book, *The Language of Madness*. How is one supposed to interpret such an assertion? No doubt, it comes across as simple sloganeering of a vacuous and perplexing variety, since one can easily call to mind any number of statements called "delusional" with no apparent political content whatsoever. How does one relate it to the fact that madness frequently occurs in his work as a void made real? He proceeds by way of reversals: madness says the unsayable,[14] it structures language like the unconscious,[15] it does not appear as a positive thing but is that which de-structures experience and empties it out.

The awkwardness and repetitions of Cooper's prose lie in his repeated attempts to cross the void between the nonspace allotted to madness and his political commitments and desire to write. Behind the stage where it performs, at the end of its historical masquerade, does madness have a face? Laing, too, reached a point of no return, but from the opposite direction. After the relatively grounded reversal of the perspective of the clinical encounter in *The Divided Self* (1960), madness was reduced to a mere linguistic effect of intersubjective communication networks in *The Self and Others* (1961), only to be rediscovered as a rare existential possibility of living through the limits of consciousness in *The Politics of Experience* (1967).[16] His search for the Whole and its limits led him on a spiritual quest in the East. Voyages in search of madness-in-itself set sail into wine-dark seas, on nights when the moonless sky swallows the horizon, and end up shipwrecked. Laing mistook Scylla's mountains for the summits of

Wholeness in Sri Lanka and India where all he discovered was an Orientalism made to play the role of mystic that does nothing but say *I am really outside now in the presence of the Other*. Cooper sailed straight into Charybdis' whirlpool of the Great Nothing without hesitation, but came out the other side to find the same old world simply inverted.

Antipsychiatry is not outside psychiatry, but its representation as such has influenced subsequent thought and practice. The search for an outside space was realized in Laing and Cooper's work as the establishing of therapeutic communities or collective homes "outside" of psychiatric logic where one could go mad safely and freely. This led to Laing opening Kingsley Hall in London, where the mad could travel through their experience of madness in a supportive environment. But is there really an "outside" to the system? Is this not a convenient illusion that allows one to ignore the fact that, for instance, the majority of the Kingsley Hall residents were middle-class students, Laingian converts who already had far more social and material support than the average "psychotic" in a mental hospital? In an interview with *Asylum: The Magazine for Democratic Psychiatry* in 1986, Laing contends that psychiatry ought to remain completely apolitical.[17] Laing was unable to see that there is no escaping politics by simply declaring something apolitical, nor can one escape a field of action by nominally positing an outside.

Franco Basaglia critiqued this very notion of the outside in an interview with Laing: "In reality," he said, "outside the system doesn't exist, and there is a continuum between outside and inside."[18] To be apolitical is only to take the side of the present system; to declare oneself "outside" without taking the whole social context into account is to risk reproducing that context in miniature. Robert Castel defines mental health policy as a social system tying together "a theoretical code (for example, in the nineteenth century, the classical categories of illness); a technology of intervention (for example, 'moral treatment'); an institutional set-up (for example, the asylum); a body of professionals (senior consultants); a statute for the 'user' (for example, the insane person, defined in the 1838 law as being a nonadult assisted person)."[19] The specifics can change, but insofar as it still recognizes psychical and behavioral differences or distress as the problematic at the center of a social system of assistance that corresponds to it (even if it valorizes such differences as superior to or as natural consequences of the norm) and designs a social program of intervention around these, the drive for an antipsychiatry conceived of as an "outside" space or "outside" response could also be described as the drive for a new, enlightened psychiatry.

The flight from psychiatry followed through to its end can lead only to "non-psychiatry, a word that erodes itself as one writes it."[20] It being the nature of the "anti" to remain wedded to the thing it opposes, a fealty to strict alterity will continue its fleeing until it finds this otherworldly territory, nonpsychiatry, where madness is "diffused through the whole society."[21] This is nothing short of the absorption of madness in an all-encompassing sanity or the annihilation of sanity in a great madness, which is the same thing. Organic life suffocates without oxygen and comes to a halt without material to metabolize. In the Great Beyond, one encounters only the unnamable and death. It was Cooper's great and terrible discovery that a real repudiation of psychiatry entails relinquishing one's object entirely, along with all the solidarities arising from its powers of abstraction.

Laing and Cooper represent two extremes of the desire for separation and the repudiation of origins so typical of Anglophone movements critical of psychiatry. In this chapter, I will confront various attempts to get outside of the limits of psychiatry or sidestep its demands in the law, in subjective experience, in treatments, or in space. This is a move that, in our present horizon, I am assuming to be impossible, since the social problems we struggle against are products of a social form that we collectively reproduce every day. We are all contaminated by what we try to distinguish ourselves from. If our struggle is against a system, it is a system of which we are the parts. I focus heavily on groups and documents from the United States in this chapter first of all because I live here and am more familiar with the ins and outs of the movements' histories, and also because some of the most famous journals and figures came out of the United States. However, the tendencies I describe are especially present in Canadian journals and statements as well. There was significant exchange between the two to the extent that I believe it is justified to speak of a general North American movement responding to general North American trends in psychiatry, even if Mexican developments simultaneously support and complicate this idea to some extent.

THE AFTERLIVES OF THE ALMSHOUSE

How do we explain the contradictions of the American mental health system? The United States spends billions of dollars on mental health research and treatment each year, and yet, the rate of suicide for the general population[22] continues to rise while having a psychiatric diagnosis makes one three to seven times more likely to be and remain unemployed.[23] Joel Kovel summarizes the complexities of the American system in the essay "The American Mental Health Industry." According to him, we are faced with:

> a massive medical-psychiatric establishment; the lion's share of the world's psychoanalysts; great hosts of ancillary professionals, such as psychologists, family counselors, social workers, etc.; an interminable proliferation of alternate approaches to emotional well-being drawing on virtually every aspect of contemporary culture—in short, an entire industry of sorts, whose business is the production and distribution of emotional order and well-being; an industry, moreover, without substantial physical plant or readily quantifiable commodity, one subject to neither reliable objective analysis nor methodological unity, one whose separate enterprises seem to speak different languages entirely and to deal in matters that had hitherto been the province of myth, legend, superstition and the demonic.[24]

More than anywhere else, psychiatry in the US has repeatedly been set free from both ethical tenets and public regulation to explore every possible arrangement that might increase its technical capacity and social power by further aligning itself with the demands of the market. Nowhere else has the evolution of medicine been so consistently wed to developments in the private sector; nor has it developed in such a disparate and contradictory fashion, remaining deeply dependent on individual states' fiscal budgets. Nowhere else has one's prognosis been so directly dependent on expendable income. For all its superficial dynamism, the mad poor have been subject to a relatively consistent condition: abandonment.

In the decades following the American Revolutionary War, there was a single public asylum in Virginia, the Eastern State Asylum. The almshouses, on the other hand, proliferated rapidly and early, soaking up about two-thirds of funds for public assistance in the same period.[26] Despite initial enthusiasm that the almshouse could serve a similar institutional function for the poor as the prison served for the criminal and the asylum for the mad, it was never imagined to be capable of the same kind of utopian rational reform or transformation of its inmates.[27] It did little more than remove the poor from the streets and force them to labor with no professional pretenses or plan beyond strict discipline. Why, with all the contemporaneous developments in European poor relief, prison reform, and the growing enthusiasm around asylums and boarding schools did we see what Robert and François Castel and Anne Lovell aptly called the "success of the worst"[28] in the US? The answer lies in America's unique and rapid development as a capitalist republic.

As Marx explains in *Capital*, an essential precondition for capitalism is the separation of the worker from everything she needs to survive such that "on the one hand the possessor of value or money, on the other hand the possessor of the value-creating substance—on the one hand, the possessor of the means of production and subsistence, on the other, the possessor of nothing but labour-power—must confront each other as buyer and seller."[29] This process must be repeated *ad infinitum*, by law or by force of arms, in order to ensure that the worker returns to the market to sell their labor-power, to ensure in other words that he remains "bound to his owner by invisible threads."[30] Even more invisibly is domestic and reproductive labor bound to these cycles, as twentieth-century feminist critiques repeatedly pointed out, while being devalued and taken for granted.[31] Periods of expanding industry—the "discovery" of natural material waiting to be processed into commodities, technological leaps and the opening of new markets associated with them—demand an enormous amount of labor. When the demand for labor appears to have no ceiling, capitalists are able to maintain the fiction that the market can absorb all but the most excluded members of the workforce.[32] Post-Revolutionary America appeared to the outsider like an endless expanse of wealth in the form of expropriated land with bountiful resources and abundant work finally free of foreign regulation and oversight over the rapacious appetite for territory, for flesh, for production, for glory. To Europeans, America promised a boundless cornucopia awaiting enclosure; anyone tough enough, clever enough, violent enough and willing to make the treacherous journey and fight all who got in his way would be rewarded with unimaginable returns on their risk and struggle. Naturally, the common and "dominant interest was [. . .] conquest of nature." Gilbert Seldes tells us:

> The dominant methods were self-seeking and guile. This had been so even before the Revolution; but the removal of foreign discipline, the opening of fresh fields of exploitation, the liberation of hundreds of thousands from imposts and disabilities at the close of the war, made the Yankee of the early days of the Republic a man who not only could, but had to, conquer a world. He had to be hard in the forest and smart with his adversaries, and eternally watchful. He had to be ingenious and inventive. Opportunities crowded around him. . . . To exist at all we had to subjugate nature.[33]

As Alexis de Tocqueville makes clear in a pithy reference to the Doctrine of Discovery, in the eyes of the settler-colonist, Indigenous people inhabiting the land were considered part of that nature to be dominated: "Although the vast country we have just described was inhabited by countless native tribes," he explains, "it is justifiable to assert that, at the time of its discovery, it formed only a desert. The Indians took up residence there but did not possess it."[34] By these means, America sold the dream of a life free from wage-labor. The initial demand for labor and the notion of free soil promised an "escape [that], such as it is, takes the (largely idealized) form of becoming a small property owner,"[35] which rested on the representation of genocide and theft as "free land," enslaved labor as "natural" free labor, and the household labor of women as a feminine "natural domesticity." At the end of this chain of naturalizations, we arrive at the central American fiction: the independent individual, the rugged frontiersman, composed of "self-possession, sovereignty, the ability to enter into contractual relations, to see oneself (one's body, one's labor, one's relations with others) as a question of property ownership and propriety."[36]

In the early nineteenth century, the French traveler Michel Chevalier—a contemporary of Alexis de Tocqueville engaged in industrial espionage for the French state—described the anarchic character of American institutions and life deriving from an experience based on conquest, denigration, violence, and capture:

If the movement and rapid succession of sensations and ideas constitute life, here one lives hundredfold; everything is circulation, everything is mobility and frenetic agitation. Experiences chase experiences, enterprises chase enterprises. Riches and poverty follow one another on the track and dislodge one another in turn. . . . An irresistible current seizes all, overturns all, reverts everything to new forms. People change house, climate, profession, condition, party, sect. States change laws, magistrates and constitution. The soil itself, or at least edifices, participates in the universal instability. The existence of a social order alongside this turbulence seems to be a mirage, an inexplicable mirage.[37]

Institutional development and the implementation of public relief were marked early on by the poisonous ideology of free soil in a great wilderness populated by mythical free entrepreneurs in perpetual mutation. A land of endless opportunity and constant change, primed to interpret all but the most extreme cases of impairment as the voluntary idleness of the poor, was fated to place its trust in the almshouse as a universal solution since the latter was designed to sweep up the vagabonds, travelers, and highwaymen and teach them the value of hard labor. Prior to its appearance, local communities had few options for dealing with the unemployed poor: they could support them at home, offer outdoor relief, or arrest and lease them out to a local farmer.[38] Home care became untenable as the scale of the problem increased. Outdoor relief was believed to encourage a stagnant group of loafers who degraded public space, while leasing to a private individual was both a cruel and inexpedient method of control for a burgeoning rational state. Ideally, the almshouse would combine the moralistic injunctions of a society organized around work with the demand to cater services to the needs of a diverse idle population. In its central space, it was supposed to offer care to the old, work for the unemployed, and punishment for the lazy. That the almshouse has been the most successful of all American institutions is clear from the fact that nearly all its other institutions—prison, industrial school, asylum—seem to drop their specific intentions and transform into one at their moments of crisis, becoming repositories for scarcely differentiated outsiders meeting at the nexus of bare subsistence and punishment.

Periods of expansion, growth, high wages, and free soil can't last forever; the expansive mode of capitalist development is drawn, gradually and unevenly, into tension with an intensive mode across its territories. As Marx explains, it is in the capitalist's interest to invest increasing amounts of their surplus into technological improvements, machinery, or other labor-saving mechanisms in order to extract more profit from a smaller group of laborers, which means that the "working population therefore produces both the accumulation of capital and the means by which it is itself made relatively superfluous; and it does this to an extent which is always increasing."[39] Accumulation, then, tends to produce a "a population which is superfluous to capital's average requirements for its own valorization, and is therefore a surplus population,"[40] condemning, in one swoop, one group to enforced idleness and another to overwork. Capital produces and henceforth needs this industrial reserve army to regulate the cost and need for labor: to flood the market with the commodity of labor-power and cheapen it in the process, to maintain a desperate mass who faithfully take up the least protected and deadliest positions at the lowest cost in fear of the empty soup bowl, i.e., a disposable group standing at the ready to be exploited at the most favorable rate. Among this surplus, Marx identifies three subgroups: the floating, the latent, and the stagnant. The floating are the product of the need to replace depleted and superfluous workers for the most adaptable, youthful labor; they form the active industrial reserve army on the lookout for new positions. The latent names those thrown into virtual pauperism by capital's continuous process of "setting free" populations subsistent on means outside of the market: those still living off the land or eking out a living through noncapitalist social relations. But it is the stagnant population that concerns us most, for we must include the majority of the mad in this category, which constitutes "the lowest sediment of the relative surplus population [that] dwells in the sphere of pauperism." Of the subcategories of the surplus population, it's this group which is most likely to be considered chronically unable to work due to their being considered unadaptable to the growing technical and managerial complexity of the workplace on account of some sort of difference or impairment. This includes the "demoralized, the ragged, and those unable to work, chiefly people who succumb to their incapacity for adaptation, an incapacity which results from the division of labour; people who have lived beyond the worker's average life-span; and the victims of industry, whose number increases with the growth of dangerous machinery, of mines, chemical works, etc., the mutilated, the sickly, the widows, etc."[41] In reality, the majority of this group can be called to participate in the labor cycle if the need is great when—*Eureka!*—we are surprised to find, especially in periods of war, that the severely disabled were capable of levels of participation much higher than was assumed. Barring those "opportunities," the disabled and mad are in large part thrown into the least regulated and most informal parts of the economy: temporary work, dangerous jobs, and informal exchanges if not actual pauperism, when they are treated as the "hospital of the active labour-army and the dead weight of the industrial reserve army."[42] That is to say, the obligation to provide care (and the blame for its failure) falls on the shoulders of hyper-exploit-ed and overworked segments of the working population lacking the means and time to provide this labor.[43]

American administrators have long been at great pains to distin-guish between the "able-bodied" and "non-able-bodied" poor. They turned to the almshouse as a natural solution to their problems, as it combined the rational statecraft of populations with the punishing moralism of work. Unqualified assistance was out of the question. As Andrew Scull explains, "Parochial provision of relief to the able-bodied interfered with labor mobility," because it encouraged the retention of a pool of redundant laborers and "by its removal of the threat of indi-vidual starvation, such relief had a pernicious effect on labor discipline and productivity."[44] In other words, the onus has been on the disabled and sick to prove their incapacity to work (so much so it becomes a job in itself) before they receive any provisions. To discourage widespread use of these services by the able-bodied, the process for acquiring and keeping them has been made as unpleasant as possible. Receiving free room and board was either a great indignity or the consolatory of-fering of a machine intended to punish those who'd willingly remove themselves from the labor pool. Though misery is necessary and nat-ural to the process of accumulation, services to support the impover-ished are only "granted" at the last moment. Psychiatry's category of the "mentally ill" progressively justified the production of a system of relief corresponding to needs cast in constitutional terms rather than economic: psychiatry helped the mad who, by reason of their lunacy alone, were incapable of being integrated into the workforce.

America's unique tendencies reached their culmination in what was the defining event of US psychiatry for about a century: Dorothea Dix's failed attempt to pass a federal bill for the provision of land to the care of the indigent insane in 1854. Dix was the most active of a generation of prolific social reformers in the mid-to-late nineteenth century. From 1841 on, she tirelessly traveled around the country visiting institutional sites—prisons, asylums, almshouses—raising the alarm about their terrible conditions and failure to differentiate between the needs of varying populations. Believing that the indigent insane needed large, specialized accommodations ideally regulated by the federal government, she first lobbied Congress in 1848 for 5,000,000 acres of land. After reading a long and detailed list of abuses and cases of the neglect of the mad in jails and almshouses, Dix made the argument that the mad ought to be recognized nationally as a special category of ward, as they already were in some states, arguing that the land should be "appropriated in such manner as shall assure the greatest benefits to all who are in circumstances of extreme necessity, and who, through the providence of God, *are wards of the nation*, claimants on the sympathy and care of the public, through the miseries and disqualifications brought upon them by the sorest afflictions with which humanity can be visited."[45] Though this initial attempt failed, she returned in 1854 with an even larger ask for 10,000,000 acres. Her bill actually successfully passed in both the House and the Senate, but was vetoed by President Pierce for precisely the reason I've outlined above: "If Congress have power to make provision for the indigent insane *without the limits of this district* [District of Columbia]," he claimed, "it has the same power to provide for the indigent who are not insane, and thus to transfer to the federal government the charge *of all the poor in all the States*."[46]

Dix pointed out that her case had precedent: Congress had twice before set aside land for the "deaf and dumb" in Connecticut and Kentucky in 1819 and 1826, respectively, but her argument failed to convince him. The entire debate can be reduced to this question: are the mad sufficiently distinguished from the "normal" (able-bodied) poor to warrant aid (like the "deaf and dumb") or do they in a sense deserve their punishment of the twin horrors of pauperism and custodialism?

Pierce's veto essentially left this question up to individual states for a century, setting in motion a thousand tiny relief measures designed to technically resolve structural faults, creating massive concentrations of specialized services in certain areas (Massachusetts and New York stand out) and neglect in other sites where they resorted to the familiar almshouse with its near-total lack of differentiation (mostly in the South). We have seen similar disputes play out up to today, notably around policy decisions concerning what sort of housing the homeless "deserve." Though we undoubtedly have more than enough empty homes and properties, simply granting them freely is an untenable solution wherever properties exist to be capitalized and "normally" destitute laborers struggle to pay their rents. Therefore, the condition for housing is either enrollment in some form of surveilled, often medicalized, treatment program and placement in low-quality, cramped, and disciplinary shelters or group homes or else an immediate placement with none of the long-term supports that would make it work. Despite structural disjunctions at the national level, the asylum was successful wherever the "indigent insane" were singled out as a special category of the poor for the states, which usually happened earlier than any other category of pauper across the board, giving rise to the first professional medical association in the country, the American Medical Superintendents of Asylums for the Insane (AMSAII), in 1844 and a patchwork of disconnected asylums in just about every urban area of the country.

ARIADNE'S CONSCRIPTION

In 1932, the Connecticut Society for Mental Hygiene described the mission of psychiatry with reference to the ancient myth of the labyrinth and the Minotaur in their newsletter *Mental Hygiene News*. As Plutarch tells it, the Athenians, under advisement of the oracle, were only able to end Crete's plague of perpetual war and ruin if they sent King Minos seven boys and seven girls every nine years as tribute. Upon arrival, these children were sent into an unnavigable labyrinth where they'd either starve to death or be consumed by the great man-bull hybrid, the Minotaur. When the hero Theseus volunteered to enter the labyrinth, Minos' daughter Ariadne conspired to help him escape. With the thread she gave him and the sword he snuck in with, Theseus was able to kill the monster and find his way back out of the winding caverns of the maze.

In *Mental Hygiene News*, the mentally ill, the distressed, and the despairing find themselves in a situation not unlike the Athenian youths: "Having marched into the maze of modern life, they find themselves threatened and bewildered instead of rewarded. They turn to flee."[47] But everywhere they turn, they find more "tortuous pathways" before coming "at last into the presence of devouring terror. With paths all about them, there was no way of escape. The tangle of pathways had become a hopeless barrier between them and freedom." Psychiatry's role is to repeat the labor of Ariadne and unroll the thread "along the path to freedom" for these lost and confused souls. This is an altogether different vision of freedom than the one imagined by the luminaries of the moral treatment movement. Where the latter sought to communally build an intentional and self-conscious social body that absorbed particularities into a whole set apart and against life outside, these mental hygienists defined their mission "in terms of the ability of people to get along together in this world."[48]

In the face of its humiliating failures in the asylums, the utopian spirit in psychiatry fled its walls and was split apart by the force required to separate it from its home, embedding itself into disparate extramural projects (initiatives outside of the asylum walls). Its most successful branches reconciled themselves with the contemporary trends and demands of the economy, embracing the utopia of the subject navigating through a frictionless market ("independence") by making themselves "a useful part of all the forces of society which from birth on, aid in the process of socializing us, of changing us over from savages to civilized human beings—such great forces as the home, the school, the church, and indeed government, organized industry, social work and the like."[49] At the dead end of the asylum, the optimism of psychiatry diluted itself across the whole social field in the form of prophylaxis and hygiene. If you can't defeat the Minotaur, perhaps you can at least outrun it.

The mental hygienists chose this striking image to describe preventive measures proposed in the period between 1860–1945, when the asylum was repeatedly exposed to the world to be miserable and aimless. If the breaking point came after the Civil War near the turn of the century, asylum psychiatry's downfall was already long in the making, such as in the growing generalized ambivalence around the practice of detention and its central position in the psychiatric matrix. Following an insight from Robert Castel, detention could both stand in as a symbol for the system itself as well as its outer limits: it combined a measure for placement, a determinate internal regime, the concept of legal incapacity, the management of property, and the right to treatment in a special form of public assistance.[50] At the same time, its very centrality in the matrix tended to limit the aspirations of the psychiatrist's interface with the general population as a public health expert on psychic sickness. German clinical psychiatry and French outpatient boarding experiments represent two early attempts to escape the gravity of the asylum. In the US, such ideas would be put into regular circulation as a number of crises began to converge around the end of the nineteenth century.[51]

Wherever localities jumped on the asylum craze, their in-patient populations grew dramatically. Already in the 1850s, asylums in or near major urban centers were showing signs of serious overcrowding. Kirkbride and the AMSAII had earlier set the ideal maximum number of patients in a psychiatric hospital at between 200–250; when Edward Jarvis performed a meticulous census of the insane population in 1854, he found that the state institutions in Worcester and Taunton and the municipal hospital in Boston had over 1,000 each.[52] These numbers would only become more appalling through the first half of the twentieth century until some asylums acquired populations rivaling large towns. Central State Hospital in Milledgeville, Georgia was the largest of all, with almost 12,000 patients and a measly one-to-one-hundred staff to patient ratio, but this was merely an extreme example of the general trend. Just as vitally, the internal characteristics of the asylum population began to change as well. From the 1850s on, the proportion of foreign-born and indigent residents accelerated rapidly. By the 1890s, 40 percent of the general asylum population was foreign-born. In industrialized regions, these trends were even more extreme: 77 percent of the Cook County Hospital population were immigrants, for example.[53]

In 1876, Pliny Earle began a sustained attack on the "cult of curability," that crucial ideological justification for early commitment and asylum construction. In numerous publications, Earle proved that the epidemiological statistics being used to demonstrate exorbitant rates of recovery in asylums (up to 90 percent or even 100 percent in the case of the infamous "Dr. Cure Awl") simply by pointing out that repeated discharges, very often of the very same patient over and over, were regularly being counted as individual cases of "recovery," a concept that was more often than not vague and undefined and therefore of little statistical value.[54] His findings effectively ruined the scientificity of the "cult of curability," but more importantly reflected the growing reality that asylum populations tended over time to become older as more and more elderly poor were transferred from the almshouses and became generally more chronic. Asylum caretakers watched as bodies piled up to the point that one deranged lunatic looked just like the next, and they all looked like wild animals, making this—*Opal* author's earlier critique of stigma—an institutional given: "The enstamp of the word crazy, or lunatic, is in the forehead of the one brought. The books are opened: the ear of science is opened too, to hear some of the vilest rigmaroles that ever saluted mortal: no friend to interpose or query: the luna is dumb as a sheep before his shearers."[55] Staff shortages and overpopulation were mutually exacerbated while environmental conditions went into freefall during the Civil War, whisking the call for nonrestraint into the harsh winds of war. Fear of agitated bodies in claustrophobic rooms created a clamor for the most archaic means of controlling the human form, which was put into leather belts, covered with mittens, and contained in camisoles and iron cribs.

When the dust from the Civil War finally settled over the blood in a thin layer barely covering the raw brutality of this so-called nation, psychiatrists were called to long overdue public summons for their shortcomings. The most forceful call came from the newly formed ranks of neurologists who'd just recently proved their mettle during the war, treating nervous tissue wounds and stress problems in their mostly private practices.[56] S. Weir Mitchell, the most reputable among them, upon being invited to critique his psychiatric colleagues at the fiftieth annual conference of the American Medico-Psychological Association (formerly AMSAII) in 1894, accused them of being out of touch in their little fiefdoms.[57] Out there on their own, the neurologists claimed, psychiatrists had ceased to march in line with the progressions of science, becoming mere administrators, and bad ones at that, with mystical notions about the power of the institution: "You have for too long maintained the fiction," Mitchell said, in a reversal of psychiatric wisdom, "that there is some mysterious therapeutic influence to be found behind your walls and locked doors. We hold the reverse opinion and think your hospitals are never to be used save as a last resort. Upon my word, I think asylum life is deadly to the insane."[58]

Similar proposals and critiques had been made from inside psychiatry for decades. Notably, in 1855, John M. Galt, the superintendent of the Eastern Lunatic Asylum in Virginia published "The Farm at St. Anne" in *The American Journal of Insanity*, in which this enlightened manager of slave labor argued that a tiered plantation-style labor farm, where a farmer overseeing "working men—those of quiet demeaner[sic]—laboring under chronic insanity"[59] could potentially replace the drudgery of congregate asylums with a happier and more "useful" mode of existence. What good it would do to breathe the clean country air! How much disease would be avoided if they lived in smaller, homier cottages instead of cold wards! How much expenditure could be balanced if they worked to reproduce their own welfare!

Like most reformers of psychiatry, Galt ultimately enjoyed a bitter victory. All of these proposals were adopted but soon absorbed into the asylum, becoming mere appendages of its central towers, making it all the more massive and town-like. Agricultural plots grew up around the asylums themselves. Cottages were built and rapidly filled to the brim with patients who lived in the paradoxical state of hyper-concentration and isolation. Though it never became a profitable source of capital accumulation like prison labor, patient labor became so pervasive that some institutions almost broke even, such that the patients basically worked off the costs of their own institutionalization without ever getting paid for this service.[60]

Herein lies the miracle of psychiatry: right at the point of its widest condemnation and discredit in the eyes of medicine, it swallowed up every attempted reform. Therapeutic communalism became impossible as the chasm between all yawned ever wider and the masters of madness stealthily adorned the mad in their primal attire once again. The most basic social relations made transparent just years before were cast once again into a mysterious fog. Lost and unwilling or unable to protest conditions that might be producing this sad state of affairs, the overseers became more concerned with justifying its existence and their treatment modalities. For this, they turned to eugenics and Social Darwinism. The masses congregated in asylums were a kind of social waste, the necessary byproduct of capitalist production cycles and the structural incapacity to incorporate them into barebones subsistence measures that go into reproducing its social relations every day. But to recognize this would entail confronting the contradiction at the heart of psychiatry. In the US, many professionals preferred to embrace notions of constitutional defect, tautologically justifying the physical and mental ruin of the asylum by reference to hereditary theorems of corrupted germ plasms or the biological generation of species of monsters.

The best they could offer the monsters of heredity was management through drugs, sterilization to prevent any further "generations of imbeciles,"[61] or, at a seemingly impossible remove from their origins, mass murder in Germany. Throughout the twentieth century (well past revelations of Germany's attempts at exterminating "race degeneracy"), over 70,000 sterilizations were performed by US doctors on the mad, the disabled, Puerto Ricans, Indigenous people, and Black recipients of welfare—a practice which continues in prisons and ICE detention facilities.[62] Alienation was no longer at issue; instead, psychiatrists turned their attention to conquering the clever "aliens" among us—those racial, sexual, congenital Others who really existed and threatened the social body constitutionally with their degenerate genes or tendency to act violently.

Desperate to do something about the hordes of inhuman stock accumulating in the state hospitals, psychiatrists began advocating a "total push" in the early-to-mid–twentieth century to get them out. Coined by Abraham Myerson, total push referred to the utilization of any means necessary to rouse chronically slothful humans from their waking slumber. Whatever Abraham may have had in mind, the term captures the bellicose mood of the extended period when asylum psychiatrists around the world threw every physical treatment thinkable at the wall to see what stuck. It was always at the expense of patients: soak them in water, shock them, lobotomize them, sterilize them, pull their teeth out in the chance an infection caused psychosis. Patient accounts from 1890 to 1960, from Clifford Beers to Jane Ward, are startlingly similar in their indictments, and not just in the US.

Journalist Nellie Bly describes the mixture of cruelty and drudgery of asylum life in "Ten Days in a Mad House," an investigative article about her stay at the Women's Lunatic Asylum on Blackwell's Island in New York in 1887. Though she was only there for a brief time and knew she'd be able to leave, in a chapter about the choking and beating of patients, she tellingly chooses to describe points when she despaired at the boredom of asylum life: "People in the world can never imagine the length of days to those in asylums," she wrote; "They seemed never ending, and we welcomed any event that might give us something to think about as well as talk of. There is nothing to read, and the only bit of talk that never wears out is conjuring up delicate food that they will get as soon as they get out."[63] Janet Frame knew the asylum quite well from her years of being locked up in New Zealand in the 1940s and 1950s: "Every morning I woke in dread, waiting for the day nurse to go on her rounds and announce from the list of names in her hand whether or not I was for shock treatment, the new and fashionable means of quieting people and of making them realise that orders are to be obeyed and floors are to be polished without anyone protesting and faces are made to be fixed into smiles and weeping is a crime."[64] Anna Kavan, who underwent treatment during the same period in London, Switzerland, and elsewhere, situates the asylum as a special prison in a massive juridical conspiracy. It was a place that punished people for their very existence as aliens: confronted by men with a "pale blue form [with] some unintelligible legal phrases, and my own name embellished with elaborate scrolls and flourishes in the old-fashioned style," she assumes that "some secret court must have tried and condemned me, unheard, to this heavy sentence."[65]

For their part, in a cycle that continues today, many psychiatrists indulged in the tragicomical melodrama of playing the martyr instead of analyzing the material factors that determine their situation. In 1855, Charles Nichols, superintendent of St. Elizabeths, wrote to Dorothea Dix: "I feel as if I was living over a volcano all the time, and cannot command the security necessary either to happiness or the highest usefulness."[66] Unwilling or unable to drop the facade and throw their lot in with patients, psychiatrists became lords who administered treatments from their isolated chambers based on knowledge hidden even from nurses, tilling soil for myriad conspiracisms at all levels, and instilling a great reign of silence over territories weighed down with boredom although paradoxically infused with dread.

Just as the negative dream of eugenics began to capture the minds and spirits of those fretting about chronicity, the positive-idealist utopian vision of mental hygiene directed itself to "acute" forms of madness and its prevention in the healthy, normal population. The story of Clifford Whittingham Beers is central to this narrative. Beers was a psychiatric patient from Connecticut who spent time at three different hospitals. In his eyes, there was no substantial difference between them since "hell is hell the world over, and I might also add that hell is only a great big bunch of disagreeable details anyway. That's all an Insane Asylum is."[67] His 1908 autobiography, *A Mind That Found Itself*, describes beatings following beatings, which followed periods of neglect and deprivation, outlining a general program of institutional terrorism. After being subjected to beatings time and again and even witnessing a probable murder, this remarkable character actually acted out with the explicit intention of being placed in the violent ward to "conduct a thorough investigation of the institution" and to combat it at a later date. With the support of psychologist William James, settlement house activist Jane Addams, and the influential psychiatrist Adolf Meyer, Beers launched the National Committee for Mental Hygiene in 1909. While his initial focus was to advocate for institutional reforms like nonrestraint and improved conditions, mental hygiene's utopianism expressed itself elsewhere. Indeed, at the heart of the global mental hygiene movement was the idea that pathology was a spectrum including everyone; the goal ought to be to institute points of contact in every corner of society to prevent people from ever going into an asylum at all. In line with the Progressive Era's pivot towards the malleable and away from the intractable, they dedicated themselves to educational programs, training teachers and social workers, pushing for juvenile delinquency programs in the criminal justice system, and helping to form preschool and other child guidance programs. If chronic psychosis was incurable, maybe "mental disease is preventable."[68] No doubt this early mental health movement is an early instantiation of the much-criticized tendencies to psychiatrize social problems and pathologize small differences, and to institutionalize the world to marginalize the institution.

Mental hygiene never strayed too far from the conceptual universe of eugenics. Both based themselves on the power of detection and preventive action to rout population problems formerly excluded from the purview of public health. At the 1930 International Congress of Mental Hygiene, none other than Ernst Rüdin gave a speech on eugenics as a model for preventing mental disease to great applause. Rüdin was the renowned German eugenicist who cofounded the German Society for Racial Hygiene in 1905, and later served as the President of the Society of German Neurologists and Psychiatrists from 1935 to 1945. He even earned an audience's laughter when he said, in the manner of a joke, if we theoretically wanted only light-skinned people in the world, we could institutionalize all the darker people "so as to purify the population of brunette skins."[69]

The audience's laughter was no fluke; it represented the broad support that eugenics had earned by the 1930s in the Western world, so that "[p]roposals to institute a eugenic killing program in the United States were openly debated in a 1942 edition of the official journal of the American Psychiatric Association, *The American Journal of Psychiatry*."[70] Colonial authorities in Korea,[71] North Africa,[72] and the US found in the tenets of eugenics and prophylaxis a twin pathway out of their narrow German-style clinics that would open up interfaces with the "dangerous population" at large, hitherto under the exclusive domain of the police. The mental hygiene movement denounced the dream of control over a social institution just as it was losing ground. Through that negative move, the new generation, in their aspiration to control the very development and unfolding of species and life itself, helped clear a path for theories of degeneration and racial science to transgress the narrow bounds of the asylum and the clinic.

Even as it did so, mental hygiene was the first movement to offer a substantial alternative vision to state psychiatry, being the first to challenge the centrality of the asylum in the psychiatric social matrix. It was therefore also the movement that set in motion the typical reform cycle, where the idea that the problem of public mental health could be resolved through some technical intervention or integration legislated from above—in professional jargon, intellectual production at the site of research, or legal statutes and codes—is put into circulation again and again.[73] In the context of the myopia in asylum psychiatry, their utopian vision of psychiatry as a public hygiene program with promises to reduce state expenditure on public assistance through early action; improve the general working force's "mental health" and resilience in the face of economic depression and especially war; and detect and weed out weak links in the armed forces, schools, or industrial force before they became a liability brought mental hygiene to the conceptual center of an alternative technological circuit of state psychiatry.

Each of these goals pointed to the necessity of individualizing psychiatric vision away from the problem of the chronically ill, congregated masses and towards the complexity of the individual in society. To this end, the case study and life chart were ideal technologies. Adolf Meyer insisted on accumulating as many facts about the patient as possible onto a life chart that began with age and name and continued indefinitely collecting anything one could glean about the patient from conversation and interviews with friends and relatives in the belief that an extensive chart would "help them to evaluate the individual's psychological assets, to analyze the conditions under which they would fail, and to devise ways to strengthen them."[74]

This attention to individual detail and developmental narrative dovetailed nicely with the growth of social work at its infancy in the early twentieth century, at that point still in the grips of Mary Richmond's social diagnostics that used casework to develop a picture of the individual's social network in order to determine the most rational adjustments. Both were part of the growing effort to professionalize the dispensation of relief and, ultimately, psychologizing problems proved the most rational way to organize populations according to need in their social environments, as it offered a more internally rigorous and consistent theoretical model seemingly free of the contradictions of social diagnostics.[75] Social work and mental hygiene, from their first early contact, formed a spiraling mutual feedback loop so tight and expansive, they began to resemble one another until psychiatric social work effectively edged out the earlier settlement house model in the tradition of Jane Addams.[76] Social workers became the key actors of projects to organize aftercare for patients leaving the hospital. Those trained in mental health work would be introduced to working with risky populations in schools or workplaces, and they could act as sentinels identifying potential signs of mental unwellness early on in community placements.

At the heart of their reforms stood the psychopathic hospital. This hospital was to be distinguished from the asylum by a number of features: 1) it would provide short, intensive treatment for acute cases of mental illness; 2) it would offer diagnostic services and link the patient up with numerous community resources; 3) it would be located in easy-to-access locations closer to the city (sometimes standing independently, but other times attached to a university or existing hospital). For the mental hygienists, such a space would encourage voluntary visitations because of its convenience and the reduced stigma attached to a short trip to a clinic. It would be curative, since they'd be treating acute and borderline cases of madness rather than chronic ones. It could be an educational and research hub for students. Finally, it would serve as an essential community resource, offering referral services and a smooth, transactional approach to receiving care. The psychopathic hospital was imagined as the central hub for a whole range of progressivist interests—child guidance, juvenile delinquency, and social work—and would serve as a diagnostic center individualizing and rationalizing care and education for a broad range of deviants.

But if mental hygiene is to be identified with Ariadne and her thread, it must be said that, at some point, she was conscripted into the services of the labyrinth itself, deceptively marking trails that led one in circles before depositing them back at the entrance. By its own metrics, mental hygiene was roundly a failure. Few psychopathic hospitals were built. Those that were built tended to operate as clearinghouses, not for a rational dispensation of services, but for the asylum. In Massachusetts, in order to facilitate easier movement in and out of the Boston psychopathic hospital, professionals lobbied to pass a temporary commitment period that would allow them to observe a patient for seven days (contemporary iterations of which exist around the country today). This quickly became the preferred means to obtain commitments, for both acute and chronic patients, who, at the end of the observation period were either sent home or to the state hospital.[77] Aftercare was never systematically implemented, but its technique of "psychiatric parole" under the auspices of social workers became yet another way to draw patients back into detention with little fuss. In the end, the reforms of mental hygiene either served to strengthen the network of detention and custodial care, were absorbed into the private sector to the exclusive benefit of patients with disposable income, or they failed to get off the ground past the research phase. Despite their efforts, the asylum population kept growing right through all attempts to make the move to extramural care, reaching its peak in 1955 with over 550,000 inpatients.

Mental hygiene, with its expansive alliances and federal support, was unable to soften the psychiatric matrix and reduce its reliance on detention, but tended in fact to facilitate precisely its worst aspects. One of the most enthusiastic and promising reform movements became an auxiliary to what it proposed alternatives to. This cycle of reform might be why later activists concluded that if education, influence, and research wouldn't work, perhaps hard and fast laws and legislation would.

DISSOLVING LUNACY INTO CRIME

One of the distinguishing marks of the psychiatric turn in the nineteenth century is the inscription of a boundary between the mad and the sane in the law, like the French law of 1838 marking the mad as the legal equivalent of children deserving of medical treatment and the English Lunacy Law of 1845 that did the same. Such distinctions have been drawn and justified in accordance with two related doctrines: *parens patriae*, or legal guardianship over the incapable and undeveloped, and the police power with the discretion to handle threats, risks, and dangers to the state. Prior to the infamous M'Naughten case that established the first modern insanity defense in 1843, the courts of Europe and the colonial US made use of the "wild beast test," which excluded the *furiosi*, the raving lunatics, from legal culpability, considering them to be of the same mental level as beasts. The legal test corresponding to this figure was of a zoological order: English general physician Richard Mead warned that such a madman was likely to "attack his fellow creatures with fury like a wild beast."[78] The court's rationale for exculpating the mad could be summed up in the phrase "'*furiosus solo furore punitur*,' a lunatic is punished by his madness alone."[79] Subsequent tests and criteria remained wed to the basic principle that madness and legal culpability were irreconcilable, even as knowledge of and the characterization of madness shifted.

In the nineteenth century, madness was no longer principally negatively defined in relation to reason in the shape of unreason, but appeared positively in the form of disease as "mental illness." Increasingly, insanity, the foil to reason, ceded to taxonomies of observable and classifiable medical entities. Mirroring this domestication by science, the courts, beginning with the M'Naughten test in England, integrated more sensitive tests that registered momentary lapses of judgment and losses of reason connected to specific medical symptoms. Subsequent tests became even more subtle: the Model Penal Code of 1962 exempts lawbreakers who lack some *substantial* means to *appreciate* the criminality of an act, softening the lines by including emotional state and interpretative capacity into simple understanding. Despite these substantial changes in the representation and status of madness, the act of exempting a person from the punishments determined by law on account of unreason—though rarer—remains a litmus test for the boundary separating the legal citizen from the insane. The fact that, among all the various contingencies and accidents of life, insanity has consistently appeared as a special category warranting tests and operational procedures probably explains why insanity defense trials have long aroused great interest in the public, which is equally horrified and fascinated by the deeds of mad criminals and their eventual fate.

Perhaps this legal continuity and popular wonderment helps to explain why the fight for recognition in the law has historically been of such central concern in the United States and England. Two figures tower above the rest in what has come to be known as "antipsychiatry," each with their own legal concerns: Thomas Szasz and Judi Chamberlin. Chamberlin is probably the most significant and central figure of the psychiatric survivor movement in the English-speaking world from the 1970s on. Her 1978 book *On Our Own* describes how she went from a voiceless, depressed madwoman shuffled between six different hospitals over the course of five months to a fiery, politically engaged madwoman and a leader of a social movement. After giving birth, she fell into a deep, unforgiving sadness, eventually self-electing to enter the hospital to receive help. Instead of receiving help in becoming the person she used to be, she was stripped of all control over her own life and talked down to for years until she began to believe that she truly was a helpless, hopeless mental patient. Chamberlin was a dedicated activist who spent her life forming connections, attending conferences, supporting the creation of new groups and projects. Hers is a remarkable story of appropriating enormous suffering and the imposition of a deficient status. Her story resonates with scores of people whose interface with psychiatry has been mystifying, disempowering, and abusive.

Thomas Szasz was born in Hungary, but left in 1938 to escape the Nazis' eastward encroachment and to find new opportunities in the United States. He studied psychiatry in Chicago and, even early on during his residency, adopted a principled and unwavering stance against coercion in his field. This stance, over time, solidified into a single-minded crusade. Between the two of them, Szasz was more singularly fixated on a formal legal critique. In his work, we find the distillation of positions that are generally representative of the critique of law in Anglophone antipsychiatry from 1960 on. Szasz's critique of the concept of mental illness and his strong focus on legal categories have made such indelible stamps on the antipsychiatry movement, on psychiatric survivor groups, and rights-based organizations that it's entirely fair to say that the Szaszian understanding of psychiatry has become one of the central pillars for opposition in the United States and Canada and the main point of entry for those seeking out a critique.

It's not hard to understand why: Szasz offers a very simple, appealingly schematic understanding of modern psychiatry and its categories. Mental illness, he says, does not exist, at least not in the same way cancer and diabetes do. What does it mean for an illness to exist? According to Szasz, an illness is something quite clear: a disease is a histopathological lesion, or, in layman's terms, tissue damage. Because mental illnesses cannot be traced to clearly observable cellular or molecular pathology, the "illness" in "mental illness" is better described as a metaphor for "problems of life" than as an observable somatic entity or process. Psychiatry's original sin is in having construed behavioral patterns as symptoms of an underlying disease entity the psychiatrist presumes exists where none presented itself. Being essentially "problems of life," there's nothing inherently wrong with seeking help to deal with issues normally classified as psychiatric; the problem is that contemporary psychiatry forces patients to undergo treatment. Hence the entire problem of psychiatry can be reduced to the question of coercion, and Szasz correspondingly divides psychiatry into two types: Institutional Psychiatry, which is characterized by the use of forced treatment it justifies with the assumption of a mythical disease entity, and Contractual Psychiatry, which is voluntary and ideally discusses its clients' problems in a mutually agreed-upon manner.

The word "contractual" is the key to understanding Szasz's political worldview, based as it is on the abstractions of classical liberalism. Szasz has never claimed to be against coercion *tout court*; like Hobbes, Szasz believes humans to be essentially evil beasts that must be tamed by the law. Unlike the ambiguous, discretionary power exercised by the medical police making up what Szasz calls a "Therapeutic State," the real police hold citizens accountable to clearly defined laws in exchange for protection from the brutality of natural law. To save us from the horror of being singled out as beasts, Szasz makes us all monsters, and yet some, strangely enough, are still more deserving of punishment than others.

Szasz's underlying libertarianism and professional connections to the Church of Scientology make him an odd bedfellow with the many feminist, antiracist, and anticapitalist groups and authors that have made use of his work. His psychiatry is the capitalist form *par excellence* with all its attendant cruelties and irrationalities on full display, bizarrely packaged as a heroic sword of justice against arbitrary power. The faith in a theoretically pure legal system of rules and punishments explains his continuous preoccupation with forensic psychiatry, which introduces vague categories where there should be simple rules and discretion where there should be mechanical sentencing procedures. Szasz is at his most naive here. So far as the criminal is concerned, according to Szasz, the only question "is whether or not the person committed the act and whether he committed it within the definition of what constitutes a criminal act."[80] But that is not how policing or courts work. The police and courts have an enormous amount of discretion such that the ascription of criminality onto their victims is in no way clearer or better defined than that of mental illness.

In Minnesota, where I live, Philando Castile is one of a long line of young Black men killed because police have the discretion to murder people when they feel scared. Police officers Mark Ringgenberg and Dustin Schwarze were able to execute a handcuffed twenty-five-year-old Jamar Clark in North Minneapolis in 2015 and face no charges.

Meanwhile, youth who threw stones or were presumed to have destroyed property during rebellions against these state-sanctioned murders potentially face decades of incarceration. The determination of "criminal" is plastic—the effect of a long social chain of determinations—and does not in reality have a mechanical relation to any specific law. The powerful and the rich can break many laws without being punished, while deviants and the marginalized can be punished without breaking any or be punished severely for property destruction or drug possession.

Szasz's psychiatry is simply the inverse of Isaac Ray's (or Cesare Lombroso's in Italy). Ray, a member of the AMSAII, was the foremost US expert on forensic psychiatry in his time. He was the first to import from France the concept of "moral insanity"—the precursor to psychopathy and sociopathy—that posited a form of insanity where one's intellectual faculties remain untouched while the emotional state or impulse control is substantially altered. Moral insanity, like Cesare Lombroso's doctrine of criminal degeneracy, substantially increases psychiatry's domain over criminal law, since they hold that there are states of derangement essentially invisible to the untrained eye, requiring the presence of an expert in the courtroom. Szasz and Ray are simply two poles of a spectrum of criminal responsibility and the limits of citizenship. In this battle of domains, the legal relationship remains the same, but one side's relative discretionary power increases or decreases. Szasz attempts to eliminate madness' exteriority by claiming that no one is outside the law and the contract forms of capitalist society. Everyone is granted access to adequate social services to aid them with interpersonal or social problems, so long as they can pay for them. Forget how social positions are established; or how wealth is obtained, produced, and distributed; or how territory is stolen and divided up into properties; rich and poor alike *theoretically* have access to the same services. In our abstract equality, we all have the same relation to rights, property, and family. But we know this isn't even remotely true: in the grand libertarian tradition of the US, the poor, daily impoverished by expropriation and exploitation, are free, without a single law being violated, to starve to death, be exposed to deadly diseases at their workplaces, rot in a prison cell for stealing goods, or be shot dead in the street by the police.

This striving for change through hard rules is doubtless connected to the essentially decentralized development of US psychiatry following President Pierce's 1854 veto of Dorothea Dix's bill. In spite of, or perhaps on account of, this failed strategy and the therapeutic anarchy it unleashed, North Americans have attempted to unite the moral shock of scandal to the promotion of broad policy or legal changes in hopes of finally toppling the domino that could knock down the whole structure of coercion. A consistent thread can be traced from Elizabeth Packard in Illinois decrying her incarceration at the hands of her husband and successfully lobbying for stricter commitment criteria in the 1860s–1880s, to the mid-twentieth century writings of Albert Deutsch, Albert Q. Maisel, Mary Jane Ward, Nellie Bly, and Kate Millett exposing the conditions of American hospitals in intentional media campaigns to effect broad reforms. At the same time, popular films that cast mental institutions and psychiatrists in a negative light, like *One Flew Over the Cuckoo's Nest* and *The Snake Pit*, contributed to a cultural suspicion of the field, lending personal accounts even more emotive power through common images of horror.

With few exceptions, the earliest groups that organized themselves as psychiatric patients or anti-asylums activists were trying to *escape* their status as mad. The nineteenth-century English group of activist ex-patients, the Alleged Lunatics' Friend Society, was mainly composed of upper-class gentlemen who exploited shock at men of their stature being mistreated, holding that they "should be provided with care commensurate with their station in life, private lodgings with personal attendants."[81] More sympathetically, Elizabeth Packard in the US created the Anti-Insane Asylum Society and lobbied for stricter commitment laws to prevent the common practice, of which she herself was a victim, of husbands locking up their wives in insane asylums for their own gain. In both cases, as was common in the nineteenth and early twentieth centuries, they did not take up the cause of the mad *as mad*, but only of those who were *not actually* mad. These groups aimed high in their policy aspirations to try and change commitment policies, or the panoply of legal recourse afforded to patients, but they substantially differ from the movements in the 1970s in that they steadfastly refused such rights *as mad*, seeking rather a strengthening of the criteria dividing (deserving) wards from citizens.

Judicial activism was even more pronounced from the 1960s on, as high-profile Supreme Court cases followed one another around the country, issuing major challenges to asylum administration, at times hastening the closure of institutions that couldn't meet the new standards or sustain themselves without patient-labor. An early and exemplary case was *Rouse v. Cameron* in 1966. In 1960, Charles Rouse was found not guilty by reason of insanity in a weapons possession case and was placed in a security hospital where he spent the next six years with only nominal treatment. Judge David Bazelon held that patients who are committed have a "right to treatment" and cannot be indefinitely held in psychiatric facilities for the purposes of simple removal. Some years later, in the early 1970s, *Wyatt v. Stickney* reaffirmed that patients are entitled to more than custodial care, and further, it established baseline standards for quality of food, environmental conditions, and more at asylums. Though far from the last significant case, 1974's *Souder v. Brennan* held that patients could no longer be expected to perform institutional peonage and amended the Fair Labor Standards Act (FLSA)[82] to protect institutional laborers and secure them at least a partial wage. Later cases established a right to refuse treatment,[83] increased judicial oversight of civil commitments,[84] the requirement to seek out less restrictive alternatives to institutionalization,[85] and more. Taken together, these cases dealt a major blow to the economic viability of the supermassive congregate institutions by forcing them to implement environmental improvements that were virtually impossible to meet without bankrupting the institution, to either pay incarcerated laborers (who worked up to twelve hours a day) or hire outside staff,[86] and placed bulwarks in the way of the smooth commitment process.

Taking direct inspiration from the civil rights movements of the 1960s and '70s and emboldened by early and continuous legal wins in the courts recounted above, psychiatric users, patients, and ex-patients in North America made the law a central concern of their activism from this point on. This is especially evident in their publications and public statements. A 1972 issue of the radical therapy/psychiatry journal *Rough Times* focused on "Mental Patients' Rights & Organizing." It featured a four-page spread with statements from twelve groups around the country. Of the twelve groups, eight of them had legal strategies at the center of their practice. The group statements are followed up by a two-page spread outlining the basic legal rights of mental patients while in the hospital, written by an organization in Philadelphia. This follows from the fact that many such groups adopted the Szaszian position that coercion is *the* central question in psychiatry. Psychiatry is to be distinguished from other branches of medicine around the central axis of force, for having a mental illness and being detained is fundamentally different from having a broken leg, as is often said. It is also the special relation to force that separates it from the mechanical law, as Kate Millett argued in a 1992 lecture at Queen's University in Ontario. In a normal "prolonged criminal trial," she argues, there is an "elaborate and concrete . . . presentation of evidence, the jury system . . . the adversary process . . . constitutional guarantees and civil rights,"[87] all of which precedes and justifies the use of force. Armed with the pathological object "mental illness," forensic psychiatry brushes all that away and allows the law to act outside of itself, extra-legally, to confine or discipline individuals who have committed no crime. The law "is prostituted before the claims of psychiatric medicine."[88] In response, anti-psychiatric and c/s/x (consumer/survivor/ex-patient) groups have long been organized as legal-aid societies and advisory committees, like the Committee Opposing Abuse of Psychiatry (COAP), Women Against Psychiatric Assault (WAPA), and the Center for the Study of Legal Authority and Mental Patient Status (LAMP) in 1970s Berkeley; the Network Against Psychiatric Assault (NAPA) in San Francisco; or MindFreedom internationally.

In the United States, the largest conferences for activists were the Annual Conferences on Human Rights and Psychiatric Oppression. These were organized by ex-patients along with legal groups and focused largely on the law. In 1976, participants at the fourth conference in Boston adopted a set of positions that sums up the points of contention for the movement before and after, remaining basically the same to this day: they opposed involuntary psychiatric interventions, forced psychiatric treatment, the psychiatric system generally, its concept of mental illness (specifically "because it justifies involuntary psychiatric treatment") and psychiatric terminology.[89] The legal protest movements were centered in California and major cities in New England. Their primary shared activity consisted in doing research on psychiatric law and disseminating this through journals in small handbooks.[90] The high point of the strategy focused on the force of law came in

1973, when ex-patients (some of them under COAP) banded together with Black Panthers, feminist organizations, and labor groups to
oppose the construction of an experimental Center for the Study of
Violence at the Neuropsychiatric Institute at UCLA.[91] The purpose of
such a facility was to study "the incidence of violent disorders in a state
penitentiary for men; estimate their prevalence in a non-incarcerated
population; and improve, develop and test the usefulness of electro-
physiological and neurophysiological techniques for the detections of
such disorders in routine examinations."[92] The Panthers and psychiatric patients were united in their fear that such an institute would
biologize social violence and develop psychosurgery procedures to be
used as a disciplinary tool against prisoners or patients.

The Institute was not built, and some of the grant money that
would've been allotted to it ended up in the hands of the Panthers.[93]
What set this moment aside was that it embraced a much broader and
flexible concept of the force of law that integrated opposing positions
in a strategic whole focused on movement goals rather than forcing
them into a logical binary. Other major actions in the '70s followed
a similar tack, embracing the tactic of occupation above all, but were
usually smaller and generally a return to a logical-binary composition
of law. For example, ex-patients occupied: hospitals, mainly in California, to protest involuntary treatments;[94] the offices of psychiatrists
known to use especially aggressive treatments; and California Gover-
nor Brown's office in Sacramento, to demand the right to refuse treatment and unpaid labor in psychiatric hospitals.[95]

A number of paradoxes attend this kind of judicial activism. The
first is simple: when we appeal to the law to help us improve conditions or acquire protection from harm, psychiatric law scholar Bruce
Arrigo points out, it is largely the law itself from which we are asking
for protection.[96] It has been *the legislature* that provided the funds for
the hospital system, *the courts* that established the precedent and justifications of forced treatment, *the police power* of the state and its collaboration with psychiatrists of various stripes (forensic, hospital-based,
outpatient) that formed the necessary conditions for the possibility of
custodial care and forced treatments. In a legal appeal, who else is
supposed to prevent an agent of the law from intrusions besides some
other agent of the law? Positioning the law as a shield *against* force
conceals the ways in which the law acts *as* force and is grounded in

it. The foundations of law historically lie outside of itself, lest it be self-positing. The law, in order to function, always has the means to act outside of itself (extralegally) against threats (terrorism, inchoate crimes, conspiracy, etc.) to its fundamental applicability. North American movements' liberal categories of citizenship are universalized as natural facts, when in fact, they emerged from the need to regulate the market activity of "free" laborers in the most developed parts of the world. These were quite far from universal, premised as they were on the explicit exclusion of slaves, Indigenous peoples, and women among others. One cannot accurately characterize the antipsychiatry movements of the 1970s as a form of legal activism against psychiatry in the United States, for in truth, they pitted one medico-legal construction ("rights-bearing patient," or the dissolution of patient into a more universal category of "citizen,"[97] along with a necessarily broader concept of "criminal" purged of the insanity defense or *parens patriae* power[98]) against another medico-legal construction (the ward).

This leads us to the second paradox. Judicial activists sometimes talk of rights gained as if they were positive entities in the world. Once created, it seems to be implied, they envelop the vulnerable like an invisible wall. But when we examine the real state of things, we can see that rights must, in each and every situation, be claimed and seized before a receptive audience. One may always say "this violates my right" (past) or "I have a right to [blank]" (future), but such statements must meet certain conditions to have a real effect in the world. If one says "I have rights" to the prison guards while detained in solitary confinement, the right does not effectively exist; put another way, it has no possibility of actualization. One can nominally have the right to happiness, to protection, or to privacy, but what good are any of these latent rights if the police can enter your home for a welfare check and shoot you on your own couch? The declaration of a right must, in other words, be heard by another who can and will respond to this call. Furthermore, the declaration of rights usually happens after the supposed right has already been violated. In that sense, rights are, for the most part, remedial and not protective. The antipsychiatric legal groups, by contrasting forensic psychiatry with criminal law, place too high a faith in the law to respect rights on the streets, in the courts, or elsewhere. As it stands, the vast majority (between 90–95 percent) of criminal cases in the United States are decided by plea bargains without a lengthy trial or the consideration of evidence.[99] If this enormous punishment machine stopped functioning and defendants each demanded trials, the courts would fall apart at the seams. Fear and the threat of a lengthy sentence are the real motive forces regulating these trials where the idea of the "mechanically applied law" is a blurry mirage in the distance.

At the heart of the ambivalence around rights and the limits of discretion is the relation between madness and danger. Dangerousness is one of the standards regulating who can receive psychiatric treatment against their will, but what is danger and who makes that determination? Depending on who you ask, madness and violence are either the best of friends or Cain and Abel. Syrian author Ghada Samman, in her novel *Beirut Nightmares*, places a strikingly clear metaphor at the center of a story about the Lebanese Civil War: the doors of the psychiatric hospital are flung open, heralding the reign of irrationality in the form of daily bombings unleashed on civilians. War is hell, goes an ancient adage, and hell is madness. This couldn't be further from the insanity portrayed in a film like *King of Hearts*, where the inmates of the psychiatric hospital in a French town escape during the German invasion in WWI only to form a peaceful, loving commune despite the circumstances, precisely on account of their madness inuring them from investments in global warfare. At the end, when the psychiatric patients are locked behind closed doors again, the Scottish soldier on scouting duty opts to intern himself in with them rather than stay outside in a violent society. When the doors of the psychiatric hospital open, we may either have the paradise of perfect fools, victims of the world without, or we may see the greatest evils ever known feast on unsuspecting prey.

Perhaps this is why the British writer Colin King thinks about his schizophrenia diagnosis through the lens of the Gemini sign: it is always a diagnosis with an "other side." Even schizophrenia, supposedly the most alienated form of contemporary madness, involves a measure of performance, following a script.[100] Borrowing from Fanon, King suggests that even in conditions of extreme distress and alienation, Black patients adopt a whole series of masks to navigate daily violent encounters where the mask of madness can lead to both internment, abuse, and fear on the one hand or increased understanding and empathy on the other. Black men specifically have historically been associated with the most violent forms of madness,[101] and, when under investigation for a criminal or antisocial deed, have found themselves differentiated from madness only to be placed in the camp of irremediably violent criminals. Awareness of these representations deepens what W. E. B. Du Bois called the "double consciousness" of Black people, or "this sense of always looking at one's self through the eyes of others, of measuring one's soul by the tape of a world that looks on in amused contempt and pity."[102] Even as the mad role is associated at times with violence and terror, in the case of police shootings, it can be the key to a script of innocence: *the police shot and killed a mentally ill person, who was therefore innocent of any possible crime.* Blackness, like madness, has a deep-seated association with violence and criminality, and it is with, through, or against these terms that individuals in a profoundly violent situation have to negotiate a strategic relation with identity in a deadly serious masquerade.

The drive to distance madness from violence and crime using sociological categories can obfuscate this strategic field when this action does nothing to question *what violence is* or under what context it appears as such, and, most importantly, *who gets to define what violence is* in a world saturated with acts of brutality, daily murder, deprivation, exposure to viruses or dangerous chemicals, or pollution of native homelands and waterways. With the 1967 Lanterman-Petris-Short (LPS) Act in California, and later the Supreme Court cases *Jackson v. Indiana* (1972) and *O'Connor v. Donaldson* (1978), the criteria for mental health commitments—both the initiation of an observation period and the requirements for continual involuntary treatment—around the country began to contract to "danger to self or others" or being "gravely disabled." Though this made commitments generally more difficult, it also effected a significant demographic shift in the process, as Anne Parsons has shown: a study of five states around the country showed an increase of commitments in men with a prior arrest from 38.2 percent in 1968 to 55.6 percent in 1978, a decrease in the average age from 39.1 to 33.3, and national statistics showed a 7 percent increase in Black representation between 1960–1980.[103]

None of the above suggests that judicial activism is counterproductive or that negative rights have not substantially improved many peoples' lives and provided a means of remedial corrective action where none existed. What it does seem to suggest is that, if the goal is communal empowerment or liberation, legal goals are to be understood in terms of their instrumental usefulness and contingent applicability for a social body that can ensure their application or fight against their transgression. Otherwise, the legal apparatus can and will change its relation to those rights depending on external economic or political demands. Ruthie-Marie Beckwith's *Disability Servitude*, a study on institutional labor, has provided much evidence to support Marta Russell's thesis on disability and capitalism[104]: states and institutions will do everything in their power to skirt the laws when facing a crisis like a labor shortage, where masses of disabled peoples' subminimally or uncompensated labor suddenly becomes more essential. In the wake of antipeonage laws, Supplemental Security Income (SSI) maintains disabled people in the US on a meager allowance requiring burdensome documentation of one's productive capacity, forcing receivers into a precise state of poverty within a small window between not working enough to survive and working for wages that exceed a maximum cap to receive any benefits.[105] Sheltered workshops, adult day centers, and major corporations alike continue to pay subminimum wages to disabled people, and, along with high schools and universities who exploit this labor for their most menial reproductive requirements, frequently (and successfully) petition to suppress wages.[106] Rights, in the final account, apply only to full citizens and in the eyes of the state in crisis, this category can become as fluid as need be. Threats can and will be stripped of their rights, as will the "severely disabled," the "vulnerable," or those with "extreme mental illness" who can be warehoused or killed with impunity given a sufficient rationale.

Confronted with danger, the psychiatric establishment and the state that requires its services have reacted with progressive euphemization, sometimes with the support of activists themselves. Minnesota is a case in point: in 1985, asylums that still stood and operated, though on a smaller scale, had their names changed to "Regional Treatment Centers" and, in 2020, wards of the state were renamed "person subject to guardianship"[107] without changing any of the functions of their referents. The reorganization of the US movements around legal campaigns means that they more or less collapse, sharply retracting into a devoted hardcore after the major cycles play out in the courts. Even our successes wound us, and, when the economy falls into crisis, even our most inalienable rights are like stones thrown into a river; they may displace the flow of water in that spot, but only for a moment.

10,000 PARADIGM SHIFTS AND COUNTING

In part due to the excessive and tangled mess that constitutes the legal production around psychiatry and the status of the mentally ill, professionals looking for a coherent picture of the state of American psychiatry or a more streamlined means to affect change often turn to large professional groups like the American Psychiatric Association (APA). Over time, a few current or ex-patients who are public about their status (we can safely assume that there are many more who are not) have brought this approach to the elite palaces of the academy with various epistemological critiques of social and psychological disciplines, probing the productive circuits that join these with psychiatric research or the training of social service providers. Such groups, in alliances with disaffected ex-patients, have just as often turned their attention to the production of alternatives "outside" the system. These two trends (professional reform and the production of alternatives) converge in their desire for the social reorganization of care or healing, and diverge on the question of organization, with one facing the professionals and hoping to effect a paradigm shift and the other facing away from the mainstream to the fringes where they hope to create viable alternatives that will form a sort of federated network to provide care. These two methods of effecting change have taken on increasing centrality, from being primarily North American tendencies to representing dominant models for struggle in the twenty-first century.

ANOTHER NAME FOR LOSING OUR SHIT

Their common background lies in the rise in social movements formed around marginalized subjectivities like Black Power, feminism, and Gay Power in the 1960s and '70s. In 1965, a Black Caucus of the American Psychiatric Association formed to demand greater inclusion in positions of influence and that the association advocate for the desegregation of all mental health facilities and develop special training corresponding to the needs of the Black population.[108] In 1968 and 1969, some Black psychiatrists in these groups and a new "radical caucus" of the American Psychiatric Association directly inspired by them disrupted the APA conferences in Boston and Miami, accusing their colleagues of pacifying righteous anger and failing to take a principled stance on domestic anti-Black racism and the war in Vietnam. A group marched in with signs accusing their fellow psychiatrists of excusing and normalizing racism, pacifying dissent in the cities, and stabilizing soldiers to continue to fight unjust wars, and made their way to the front of the room where they tried to lead a discussion.[109] In 1970, a group of feminists disrupted the American Psychological Association's annual conference, demanding one-million dollars in reparations to support deinstitutionalizing women locked in mental hospitals.

Borrowing from this tactical repertoire, gay activists began disrupting APA conferences beginning in 1970. Until 1973, homosexuality was widely classified as a mental disorder, specifically as a personality disorder in the *DSM*, or *Diagnostic and Statistical Manual of Mental Disorders*. At its core, this is a descriptive handbook of psychiatric nomenclature for professionals, taken by the public and activists alike to represent the most contemporary and accurate reflection of the field's epistemological understanding of problems in the field. Its origins lie in the 1943 US War Department's creation of a technical bulletin used to aid in the classification and management of masses of complex psychiatric cases during World War II, called *Medical 203*. In 1952, an APA committee was tasked with producing a manual to standardize psychiatric nomenclature for American professionals directly modeled on *Medical 203*. From being a relatively marginal statistical tool like the census and an optional diagnostic aid for professionals, the *DSM* has grown into a multimillion-dollar publication that serves as a standard for statistical research and drug trials and the gatekeeper for social aid, school resources, housing options, and the possibility of medical or therapeutic interventions for patients.

Resistance against the classification of homosexuality reached its peak at the significant turning point when psychiatry was pivoting from its peculiar American brand of ego psychology claiming roots in Freudian psychoanalysis into its nascent medical guise. For the individual gay person in "treatment," they were asked to believe that their desire itself was pathological at the less-invasive end. Others were either convinced or forced to participate in extreme aversion therapies like those that administered electroshocks to the genitals when excited by the wrong imagery or therapies of a more subtle variety that sought to exploit the gay person's guilt to break down their defenses and create a personality crisis from which a new, straight, person could emerge.[110] Gay prisoners fared even worse: at the Vacaville Prison in California, inmates received intensive psychotherapy, experimental drug treatments (including chemical castration), and even psychosurgery.[111] At the first handful of conferences, activists would enter and heckle speakers who were known to espouse homophobic positions, shouting them down or storming the stage and stealing the microphone to speak. The struggle reached its climax at an APA conference in Dallas in 1972, where activists had secured a panel slot for "Psychiatry: Friend or Foe to Homosexuals (a Dialogue)," during which, a heavily disguised gay psychiatrist named John Fryer recounted a life of fear and loathing amidst intolerant colleagues. Declassification of homosexuality became a central goal for the whole movement to coalesce around, embodying as it did the key points of contention in radical psychiatry and ex-patient activism: the pathologization of deviance, forced treatment, normalization, and social control.

The move to depathologize homosexuality is also exemplary for some of the unintended consequences that can attend such movements. Justly championed by many antipsychiatric critics as a progressive move to depsychiatrize a form of deviance, it is worth noting that psychiatrists too celebrate the declassification as a major turning point for the purification of the biomedical framing of mental disorder and the public revaluation of the field as a medical discipline, something looked on with great suspicion by these same activists. While the first two *DSMs* were steeped in the psychodynamic theories that still betrayed a strong psychoanalytic influence in the 1950s, the APA's approach to mental disorders took on increasingly medical pretensions as these new protest movements grew. The APA—and US psychiatry in general—found itself in a crisis of legitimacy, facing attacks from many sides at once, and pursued medicalization as a way to position themselves as the arbiters and gatekeepers of what constitutes a disease or syndrome worthy of intervention and what is a normal behavioral divergence from the norm. Psychiatry's prospective scientists seized upon the controversy surrounding homosexuality as an opportunity to dissociate their field from the vagaries and endless depths of the psyche, hoping to replace Freudian couches with laboratories as the avant-garde of mind-doctoring.[112] Scholar Abram Lewis suggests that "[r]ather than 'depathologizing' sexuality, as the revision is often memorialized today, the campaign might instead be read as facilitating a more nuanced psychiatrization of sexual and gender difference."[113] As it turns out, the removal of homosexuality in the *DSM-III* was accompanied by a general rise in the total number of sexual deviations as well as a section on gender identity disorders for the first time.

Campaigns to alter or remove specific diagnoses or to change the approach towards taxonomy have continued unabated from more targeted campaigns to remove schizophrenia or personality disorders[114] from the nosologies to proposals to replace the generic concept of "mental illness" with comparatively nonmedical terms like "distress." The opposition to medical conceptions of mental suffering has proved to be a sufficient unifying point for a number of groups (e.g., A Disorder for Everyone in the UK). In the 2010s in Britain, a group of psychologists (Lucy Johnstone, Mary Boyle, John Cromby, David Harper, Peter Kinderman, David Pilgrim, and John Read) together with patient advisors (Jacqui Dillon and Eleanor Longden) developed the exemplary Power Threat Meaning Framework (PTMF), which, instead of collecting symptoms as evidence of an underlying illness in the person,[115] seeks first to collaboratively identify the kinds of power and threats that an individual faces in their daily environment, figure out how the person makes sense of it, and responds. From there, the client is empowered to identify their strengths and weave their own narrative out of their experience, rather than being asked to accept a label with considerable stigma attached.

Users and ex-patients have long demanded that "experts by experience" be included in major decisions affecting treatment or the construction of knowledge about madness and illness, embodied in the popular slogan from the disability rights movement "Nothing About Us Without Us." On the surface, this movement has seen remarkable success since the 1970s. Peer support workers are increasingly perva-sive in major cities in the US and globally. Peers can provide a level of empathy and understanding difficult to replicate for those who haven't gone through extreme experiences that are, by definition, considered hard to relate to and highly stigmatized in everyday life. The benefits to a mental health program are conspicuous and well-documented. Studies on the efficacy of peer support tend to emphasize the reduc-tion in hospitalizations, an improved subjective experience of care (and therefore a higher likelihood of follow through), and increased use of outpatient services. This translates to significant savings in the cost of services,[116] which has meant that major research and policy organizations along with governmental agencies like the Substance Abuse and Mental Health Services Administration (SAMHSA) in the US and the National Health Service (NHS) in the UK have pro-gressively embraced and even come to require user-involvement in research and program implementation.[117]

There are now departments of Mad Studies at Toronto Metropol-itan and York Universities in Canada—something that would have been inconceivable in Chamberlin's time. Numerous academic con-ferences on Mad Studies have taken place in the twenty-first centu-ry, hosted by universities in Canada and the UK,[118] providing a use-ful metric for the significant inroads user-generated knowledge have made into academic and professional knowledge production. Despite these apparent successes, Diane Rose and Jayasree Kalathil have ar-gued that "'co-production' implies equality not just in the sense of persons or statuses but at the level of how knowledge itself is valued," something which they believe "is not possible in current configura-tions which demarcate elite sites of privilege in knowledge generation and accord value to what results."[119] Their concern finds resonance in other user accounts: Peter Beresford, who has been involved in user advocacy since the late 1970s, and Suzy Croft point to the "consulta-tion fatigue"[120] felt by user-participants who feel overworked with little reform to show for their efforts.

While there is consistently a disposition towards bringing patients or users into the production of knowledge around and development of responses to mental illness/distress/difference, there seems to be an equally strong propulsion outwards, a desire to be separate and distinct from psychiatry, the university, or normality itself.

B. THE GERMOPHOBIA OF GROUPUSCULES

Alternatives to normal psychiatric therapeutics have been attempted around the world, but North American projects—especially in the United States—have placed an unusually high premium on ensuring that their alternatives are "true" or "real." The central texts of both the radicals in psychiatry/therapy and the ex-patient movement emphatically and repeatedly insist on their distinction from their historical forebears, their colleagues, and contemporaries. Radical therapists and ex-patients alike held strong to the belief that certain kinds of knowledge were only possible in strict isolation from any contamination from the "establishment." Claude Steiner, a central figure of the radical psychiatry movement in Berkeley, claimed that "in the absence of oppression, human beings will, due to their basic nature or soul, which is preservative of themselves and their species, live in harmony with nature and each other."[121] This particular image of an Eden lost to civilization is but one of the more theological (though not necessarily uncommon) variations on the theme of alienation of the sort explicitly put forth by the radical psychiatry movement and implicitly by the antipsychiatry movement. Judi Chamberlin repeatedly restated divisions between "real" alternatives versus "false" ones while Steiner made lists of "radical psychiatrists" versus the false "alpha," "beta," and "gamma" psychiatrists that are only faking radicalism or falling short.

This extrusive propulsion manifested itself similarly between the two groups. Like so many others, Steiner was politicized by World War II and its aftermath and, after finishing school, threw his support behind psychiatric projects at the crossroads of therapy and countercultural subcultures in the Bay Area, like the RaP Center (Radical Approach to Psychiatry) at the Berkeley Free Clinic, where they "offered drug, welfare, and draft counseling services, group psychotherapy, and some individual one-to-one therapy to the young people who were crowding the streets of Berkeley."[122] Along with the founder of Transactional Analysis, Eric Berne, and feminist therapists like Hogie Wyckoff, Steiner helped found the radical psychiatry approach and released their manifesto in 1970. Their medical ideology and methods scarcely differed from the tradition of social psychiatry,[123] except perhaps in their explicitly leftist political stances on war, racism, and sexism. They were drawn early on to the group around *The Radical Therapist* journal, which was founded in 1970 by Air Force psychiatrists in Minot, North Dakota. Almost immediately, Steiner and others began to split apart from this newly formed collective, which was itself a split from the broader progressive activist element that met at APA conferences. In 1972, *The Radical Therapist* dissolved, and the main group changed their name to *Rough Times*, explaining that they needed to move away from those who "are too comfortable in their professionally detached attitudes, pseudo-hip lifestyles, and removed position from world revolution as well as personal change. We began to see our position in terms of being part of a revolutionary movement. Our goals were more linked to a broad-based socialist movement than to a radical caucus at a professional convention."[124] *Rough Times* later changed to *State and Mind* around 1975, reflecting a shift into pop psychology and self-help, while Steiner went on to form *Issues in Radical Therapy*.

In a 1983 interview with ex-patient activist Allen Markman, on his program *Madness Network* on community radio station WBAI in New York, Judi Chamberlin described the North American movement as having two branches: one focused on legal rights and another on developing alternatives. These two branches of the c/s/x or the antipsychiatry movement, in its modern, post-1960s iteration, arose from the concrete experiences of being subjected to unwanted treatments—oftentimes repetitive and brutal like the dozens of shock treatments Leonard Roy Frank underwent[125]—or in the loss or weakening of civic rights. Using phone networks and self-printed journals, ex-patients were able to forge sufficient connections to organize conferences or mobilize actions between groups, usually in response to specific laws or APA meetings. These networks were quite small and, if the journals and conference speakers are any indication, largely limited to cities on the coasts with a long history of progressive psychiatric currents or large countercultures (Massachusetts, New York, and the Bay Area in California). At times, there were some attempts to build links between psychiatric hospital attendants and patients. For example, in the first issue of *Our Journal* (Fall 1977) produced by Mental Patients' Liberation Front, the editors maintain a cautious openness to building class alliances: "We can easily become so immersed in the specifics of individual oppression that we lose sight of the realization that hospital workers and mental patients are really on the same side of a larger struggle." They recast the ward environment as one defined by crisscrossing lines of class hierarchies and struggle so that "[l]ow-paid workers and miserably oppressed mental patients are left to fight it out on the wards, while the psychiatrists and the big-wig Department officials just lay down the rules and then drive off in their Cadillacs with their fat paychecks." In this context, it makes sense "that so many hospital workers become hardened to human suffering, and become perpetrators of mental patients' oppression." But still, the authors admit, the forces that structure the lines of power are obscured by daily struggles, and it is quickly forgotten "that radical changes in the mental health system and generally in the whole society are in the interests of the workers as well as the patients."[126] Core participants and journals, in their attempts to build positive alternatives to psychiatric treatments, adopted instead an anti-solidaristic separatist position from the outset. The central conferences for American activists, the annual Conference on Human Rights and Psychiatric Oppression, were the sites of deepening distinctions. At the 1974 meeting in Topeka, Kansas, the organizers made a point to declare the meeting would be "action oriented" and excluded professionals from participation. In 1976, these tendencies were made formally explicit when ex-patients locked themselves in a separate room to hold parallel meetings and stuck a "keep out" sign on the door.[127]

Just one year after the Mental Patients' Liberation Front article, Chamberlin would propose a radically different strategy towards building an alternative mental health system that much more closely aligns with this separatist impulse. "What I define as a true alternative is one in which all basic decision-making power is in the hands of those the facility exists to serve,"[128] she wrote early on in *On Our Own: Patient-Controlled Alternatives to the Mental Health System* (1977), a point she reiterates multiple times in similar variants. At the macro level, democratic peer alternatives would form "a network of community facilities for people in acute crisis and for people with long-term difficulties [which] would eliminate mental hospitals entirely."[129] As we've seen, horizontal decision-making has been proposed in psychiatry in various formulations since the moral treatment movement. What sets Chamberlin's proposal apart from the therapeutic community, for instance, is the emphasis that all significant decisions can *only be made* by those on the receiving end of services and the insistence that they operate according to expressed need rather than through medical categories. Though this seems simple enough, she runs into problems whenever she tries to describe what exactly this entails. She suggests at various points that a distinct class of patients should be giving support, comparing her ideal to situations where "healthy and vigorous" elderly people help the "less able" and stable gay people "could provide role models for other, troubled gay people."[130] Healthy elderly people aiding the less able elderly and non-troubled gay individuals caring for the troubled ones implies criteria for distinguishing between user and professional, even if Chamberlin resists framing it in that way. Given that all decision-making power would be in the hands of clients, our first question must be: who are the clients and how are they identified as such?

Radical psychiatric and c/s/x separatists define themselves and their course of action in the tension between two countervailing poles: a drive towards the erasure or leveling of distinctions and hierarchies and a drive towards a furious taxonomical redrawing of the lines between micropolitical factions. The collective around *The Radical Therapist* held that "[j]ust as all people are potentially patients, so all are potentially therapists. All can attack the roots of emotional distress. We invite support from all concerned people, not just from a professional elite. We repudiate divisions among ourselves on the basis of sex, class, training, and status: we are more alike than different."[131] It's hard to reconcile this with the fact that their group was, from the get-go, broken up into splinter groups that split into smaller groups within just a few years of being formed. For its part, the separatist peer model "doesn't divide people into fixed categories of sick and well, since everyone experiences stress and reacts in different ways. Rather than setting up one group of people as 'experts,' people are seen as equals who can help one another."[132] At the same time, the strict criteria for inclusion was having been or currently being a patient in the psychiatric system: "All nonpatients and professionals are excluded because they interfere with consciousness raising and because they usually have mentalist attitudes."[133]

The two poles in question are joined in a shared concept of alienation (explicit for Radical Psychiatry, implicit for the c/s/x movement) as the fall from true knowledge or the incapacity to realize it. According to Claude Steiner, the radical psychiatric formula for overcoming alienation is "awareness + contact = liberation." For Chamberlin, this appears in the need for "consciousness raising," which differentiates it from "conformist" therapy because it "helps people to see that their so-called symptoms are indications of real problems."[134] Crucially for both, any and all possible change hinges on *ways of knowing*, realized not in a social practice that joins self-consciousness to its own reflexive activity, but rather, in a determination made in advance based on the assumption of shared experience of categories defined in relation to psychiatric administration. In essence, Steiner's equation scarcely differs from the equation "faith + good will = salvation."

It must be restated that the two movements arose from real social needs of patients (pain, lack of control, etc.) and practitioners. But their eventual distance from these basic needs does not make it true that they were coopted by a consumerist wing that gravitated towards conservative organizations like the National Alliance on Mental Illness (NAMI) or a conciliatory reformist element in their midst. Consumerism was present from the beginning and is implicit throughout, and it's unclear how separatist proposals escape the domain of psychiatric practice.[135] On the contrary, the Radical Psychiatrists and c/s/x separatists view the entire social world as a field open to questions of therapeutics, health, and care at the very moment establishment psychiatry strove for the same. Intense contractions in the proposed scope of mental therapeutics here coincide with the point of their widest potential applicability.

Like the mental hygiene movement and the community psychiatry movement, these two tendencies fought to detach psychiatric power from its sites of control, but this tended to free it up to flow into new, untouched territories and markets, carrying it further and further from the exclusive domain of "mad paupers" and into the daily life of all. Lucas Richert summarizes the effects: "The movement condemned the arrogance of mental health practices not because of objections to therapeutic conceptions of reality but because it wanted to diffuse them more widely than ever, rooting them in popular understanding and daily practice. Expansion, not reduction. Growth, not limitation. Instead of confining therapy to medical practice, radical therapists proposed to import it into every activity: model education, law enforcement, and the like. They also sought to break down barriers between elites with specialized knowledge and the mainstream."[136] Nor does it mean that they failed because of "false ideas" that could be corrected on an individual basis (e.g., through education). False knowledge as a central problem brings with it an implicit bias for individual moral and intellectual reform, tending to invoke reactions and attitudes that are "virtuous, self-sacrificing, moralizing, individualistically voluntarist, hyperactivist, and frankly neurotic."[137] A moral imperative in the discourse analysis of psychiatry left to levitate long enough will simply drift to the outer edges of the universe where no reality, no sensuousness, no conceivable imagery takes hold. It would be a mistake for pedagogical efforts in nonprofits and the academy to offer this floating "you should" without first building a social assemblage that can receive it.

AMERICAN HYDRA

Ironically, *prior* to the organization of protest movements seeking an outside to the system, the US psychiatric establishment itself began to accelerate a transition outside its traditional hospitals after World War II. When the US entered the war, the incorporation of mental hygiene was delayed but eventually resulted in the creation of a department of neurology and psychiatry within the Surgeon General's office, entrusted to the National Committee for Mental Hygiene. Under the guidance of Karl Menninger, they instituted a systematic vetting process, resulting in the denial of over a million recruits categorized as risky; created facilities to care for soldiers awaiting discharge on account of neuropsychiatric disorder; and prepared services to care for soldiers following their return home. These innovations, and the fiscal realism of a wartime economy, forced interested parties to consider the possibility of extramural care. The passage of the National Mental Health Act in 1946 seemed to solidify the gains of mental hygiene by setting aside federal funds to nonprofits, public and private, for scientific studies on nature, cause, and treatment of mental illness; to community psychiatry services and the training of professionals; and for the creation of the National Institute of Mental Health, the federal mental health research agency.[138] Instead, the Act signaled the end of mental hygiene as states continued to invest in hospitals—often with the intent to improve them—for another ten years. In the second half of the twentieth century, it was the community mental health movement that rose to the task of producing an extramural network.

Community mental health's theory and policy proposals appear at first sight to be the next repackaging of extramural social psychiatry, with the major difference that, in the era of "deinstitutionalization," it was formulated in the context of a real exodus out of the asylums. Deinstitutionalization is not an event, it's a name applied retroactively to a series of complex interlocking processes. Because it is simultaneously a conspicuous turning point in our national history and yet resists easy narration, one's characterization of the patient migrations in the era offers itself up as an inexhaustible fuel for the most divergent ideological positions, as Liat Ben-Moshe's *Decarcerating Disability* shows so well.[139] Some central facts are incontrovertible, regardless of the rhetorical excesses of pundits. Asylum populations began to significantly and regularly shrink for the first time in the late 1950s (about 15 percent between 1955–1965, 59.4 percent between 1965–1975, and another 28.9 percent until 1980).[140] Notably, this emptying began before the major court cases and the appearance of anti-institutional leaders post-1960, largely in response to continuous state surveys revealing both the wretched conditions and, more importantly, the enormous cost of inpatient care, which increasingly came under question in the reassessments of a wartime economy.[141] Amendments to social security—Medicaid and Medicare—were passed in 1965 and resulted in a shifting of costs for long-term care (especially of the elderly) from the states to the federal government. Through the 1960s, when the resident population of psychiatric hospitals most rapidly declined, the nursing home population skyrocketed from around 470,000 to 928,000, and by 1985, they held over 600,000 patients diagnosed as mentally ill, i.e., those who most likely would have fallen in the camp of the "chronic" population.[142] In the 1970s, neoliberal administrations divested large sums from mental hospitals and community care and invested heavily in prisons, incentivized private industry, ultimately offloading services onto the latter and nonprofits. What happened to the objects of administrative reason during these momentous transformations?

In short, they multiplied. Psychiatry is like the hydra: every time you cut off a head, two grow to take its place. Anne Lovell describes it well: "The wider the range of available programs—and it is constantly expanding—the greater the likelihood that any problem identified as being of concern to society will match up with some program ready to take charge of a new segment of the population. It is this constantly shifting clientele that constitutes the jurisdiction of the mental health system. The unity of the system really lies in the diversity of the services it undertakes to provide." This need not suggest that psychiatric power as a form of social control is constantly on the ascent, but only that psychiatric space, discourse, and law shifts to serve different needs in the nexus of public assistance and punishment, which requires more or less intensive direct authority over clients depending on circumstance. Psychiatry, in other words, is neither a simple tool to be picked up and used by a political or economic class, nor is it a unified system with clear directives and shared understanding. It is not purely vertical (i.e., from the psychiatrist down to the patient), nor is it entirely horizontal; "its connotations are both general and specific;"[143] and its language is everywhere.

Rachel Jane Liebert has analyzed how adolescent psychiatric diagnostics are progressively moving into the realm of future securitization, comprising a tendency she ingeniously calls "psycurity." Chief among these new interests is the figure of the "prodromal psychotic," i.e., those who show signs of being potentially psychotic in the future as a site for intervention,[144] something that feels like it must have been the product of a mental hygienist's fever dream. Everywhere we look, psychiatric language is put in service of detection and security: in schools, in their search for deviants and "problem children," especially in the wake of mass shootings; in social work, insofar as it has progressively interpreted of the problems of welfare assistance and homelessness in psychological terms; and in the sacrificial public health directives of the state, particularly during the COVID-19 pandemic, which offers up the mentally ill as natural victims of a preventable disease.

Alternative therapeutic models proliferated widely in the countercultural milieus of the 1960s, most notably in California in the so-called Human Potential Movement. Such alternatives thrived in the new markets opened in psychiatry's fracture. Spaces like the Esalen

Institute, founded in 1962, offered eclectic combinations of body work, Gestalt therapy and massage, promising a retreat from the vulgarities of modern life. Vaguely mystical intonations about body and spirit appealed to their largely affluent base, for whom the alternative health movement continues to isolate various therapeutic practices from around the world—meditation, yoga, life coaching, encounter groups, tantra, mantra chanting, primal scream, transactional analysis, Zen, artistic work, psychedelia—from the centuries of tradition that birthed them in order to sell them as combinable elements of an individual health program. Such medical programs are quickly integrated into a private economy of health virtually inaccessible for the "indigent insane" that state psychiatry was invented to track and deal with. This parallel world is, as Peter Sedgwick put it, not so much an alternative to mainstream healthcare as an alternative to communal forms of care.[145]

For the contemporary conservative wing of reform (E. Fuller Torrey of the Treatment Advocacy Center is the most visible in this camp), deinstitutionalization signaled a collective abandonment of the mad, who now "die with their rights on." The latter phrase refers to the Supreme Court cases described above that increasingly made standard state hospital institutionalization financially unviable as a reflexive recourse. Though disingenuous in claiming that this abandonment began between the 1960s–1980s, they aren't wrong to point to an abandonment of the mad. If there is any condition constantly faced by the mad in capitalism, it is abandonment: on the street and in the basement, yes, but also in asylums, hospital wards, and group homes on the peripheries of cities. Along these lines, we should probe the meaning of the "community" in "community psychiatry." Where is this so-called "community?" As Anne Lovell and Nancy Scheper-Hughes, and, more recently Liat Ben-Moshe[146] have stressed, it is not immediately clear what "community" refers to. Is it simply the place one finds oneself? Well, then the institution is surely a community. Is it belonging to a religious, ethnic, or racial group? This is completely possible in a prison or psychiatric hospital. Often, "community" is simply a negative term meaning "not in the mental institution or prison." A group home located in an isolated area outside city limits with locks on the bedroom doors is, according to this logic, "in the community," but in reality, it translates the carceral, exclusionary logic of the asylum into a micro-institutional domestic environment. Community treatment sounds nice, but it doesn't compare to adequate housing, access to resources, the absence of coercion, or even permission to access the public spaces we often think of as community spaces.

Given that increased privatization of our public space coincided with the supposed movement "into the community," it must be stated that for many people in the atomized US, the word "community" evokes little more than the people we work with or our immediate family. Early on, the character mask of the "independent citizen" was available strictly to property-owning white men, but its symbolic range slowly increased over time such that, even today, when the average American is so entirely dependent on the labor of a veritable army of farmers, truckers, shippers, packers, stockers, etc. that they would surely starve were the supply chain to break down, the nonsensical ideal of "independence" is set down as the goal for discharged inmates, mental patients, and the disabled in the social services. Those who own this property, "independence in the community," i.e., the sane, normal citizens, supposedly offer the gift of access to this impoverished community to the disabled and mad, but they themselves do not know what it is or where to find it. If the lunatic takes a seat on the steps of these welcoming peoples' homes, the citizen calls the police; when they step into the lobby of a building, they are met with security; fine, they'll go to the parks, and then find that locals act indignant "as if the homeless were violating their own living rooms when they pass time in public."[147]

Just as the absolute populations of mental hospitals fell and the length of stays fell below a month, the admission rates, especially to the subsidized psychiatric wards of general hospitals, nearly doubled. Now, the vast majority of crises are filtered through this system, oftentimes over and over, with no real purpose except to process this social waste and provide emergency services.[148] The poor lucky enough to be granted services are forced to trade symptoms for aid and access to public space as the "vulnerable or homeless mentally ill" or on condition of an Involuntary Outpatient Treatment order, but wherever they go in this freedom, they hear a resounding call "we don't want the crazy criminals on our doorstep." Craig Willse has noted that the image of the "mad homeless" is a product of material circumstances—the "bag lady" carries bags because she does not own property, the "disheveled crazy guy" likely does not have access to regular baths or other essentials[149]—that are denied and objectified as ontological features. Consenting to a psychiatric program is the passport into the community, which then excludes them on account of their dangerous insanity or unsightly disability.[150] Existing networks of services have proved inadequate to break past this circular trap. Nor are they incentivized to do so. The madness industry is alive and well; it feeds on its own tautologies, providing its own means of reproduction.

Theoretically, community psychiatry shares with mental hygiene a faith in the power of strengthening the resources of those at risk of developing psychiatric illness, but its object of observation and intervention changed: instead of the complex individual, community psychiatry directs its attention towards typified populations.[151] In the absence left by the states' relinquishing of responsibility for these redundant populations, nonprofits, charitable organizations, and private industries have emerged to fill in the gap, soaking up federal subsidies and waivers without having to meet the same standards of care. At the core of this "neoliberal shift from the social welfare state is a thorough reimagination of social programs as economic problems,"[152] bringing with it a whole social services industry full of welfare entrepreneurs who compete with one another to find the most efficient means of exacting the widest margin between waivers, grant funds, federal subsidies, and charitable donations and the exploitation of laborers (making even less than they would from the state, with fewer securities and opportunities for organizing in their separation) and cutting corners whenever possible to meet the minimal standards of care.

Capitalism goes on producing redundant surplus populations as social waste, but here we see them opened up, "[by] clever capitalist alchemy,"[153] not for discipline in hopes of a reintegration into labor (except for the younger, most promising users), but for turning permanently managed social waste into a source of competition and profit.[154] This field is labor-intensive as opposed to capital-intensive; that is, the social services resist automation and in the main require semiskilled workers. After extracting federal or state waivers for services and SSI for rents in residential buildings, these companies have few avenues for growth. They can cut corners, try to fit as many bodies in a building as possible without breaking the law (or getting caught), and save when they can force fewer workers to compete for lower wages, but otherwise their sustainability is tied to competing for foundation grants and philanthropic donations, giving rise to the bizarre spectacle of every cash-strapped NGO, barely offering the minimal essentials, hosting fine-dining events and rolling out new flashy slogans and pretty new "person-centered" models every year in the hopes of acquiring that big donation that will keep them going. Private psychiatric hospitals, where holding patients as long as possible (intentionally producing chronicity) is financially incentivized, are only the most extreme product of a network of services structurally antagonistic to the provision of aid. For the capitalist, mental health services are hardly a commonsense first choice to grow an empire, though there are definite exceptions. For the worker's part, year after year, we see progressive professionals in the US mortify their bodies and psyches going round in circles in a kind of purgatory hoping only to come across a new model or training to save time and allow them to offer something meaningful beyond mere subsistence and still see all their clients on time. The best they can hope for in our current predicament is a gilded cage for two where the patient's basic needs are met, but they remain without autonomy, love, sex, and happiness while the professional suffers in overwork and terrible conditions but content at least to have guaranteed the other's continued existence in incrementally improved circumstances. All the while, the user is still positioned by forces outside of their control, tugged this way and that through the byzantine labyrinth. Ultimately, everyone here is dominated by the impersonal market and its demands.

In Brazil, CAPS have been criticized for their overreliance on drugs to return the mad person to a state of equilibrium in alignment with the staff's desires, where their search for fast and easy solutions leads to an emphasis on efficiency over best care. Daniel Magalhães Goulart has called this the "new institutionalization" of community care.[155] Similar critiques have emerged from Italy, along with the assertion that patient voices are seldom included in exported documents from Trieste or other centers of the movement. These critiques certainly resonate with those made in this chapter, but a straightforward comparison would serve to obfuscate the underlying conditions and the distinction between nominal and substantial community. For one, many of Brazil's and Italy's local mental health systems have invested a much larger proportion into substantial integrative arrangements like worker's cooperatives composed of patient laborers. In Trieste, they work at "cafes at the opera house, the public radio station, a historical bathhouse, all museums, public gardens," while a comparatively miniscule fund goes into inpatient services and pharmaceuticals.[156] Cities with a concentration of services in both Italy and Brazil have public radio stations run by patients and ex-patients. Most importantly of all, they grounded their activities in self-reflexive social movements oriented principally around strategic questions of power and ethical affinities. On this account, they are more prepared to face their shortcomings. In a very basic sense, although North America has produced much more developed literary and scholarly oeuvres by mad authors, we are lacking similar physical spaces to *simply exist* or to encounter an excluded other except in indifferent passings-by. Authorship and scholarship are not representative criteria to measure the level of inclusion in a social group; there may even emerge a negative relation between substantial inclusion in social life and the proliferation of literature. As it stands, the US has only periodically seen the introduction of organizational forms that place at the center ethical affinity and the necessity to produce a new kind of sociality capable of providing sustained care: the Hearing Voices Network is one such initiative, as are the spaces associated with the flexible Wildflower Alliance in Massachusetts,[157] or the various clubhouses modeled on the Fountain House in New York. How to multiply these socializing initiatives and spaces and resist the pull of the market is the most immediate task facing mental health workers and patients in North America.

Notes

1.   Quoted in Gerald Grob, *The Mad among Us: A History of the Care of America's Mentally Ill* (New York: The Free Press, 1994), 189.
2.   Michel Foucault, *History of Madness*, ed. and trans. Jean Khalfa (London: Routledge, 2009), xxviii–xxix.
3.   Foucault, *History of Madness*, 28.
4.   Foucault, *History of Madness*, 55. This concept has come under fire in recent years due to the inaccuracy of Foucault's periodization regarding when this took place in England or how large the confinement was. These critiques may be correct in the details. The "Great Confinement" is not a quantitative concept that earns its title after a specific amount of people are locked up but describes a qualitative shift in how the mad were administratively and juridically categorized. Whether or not the policing machinery was sufficient to affect this split is another matter. The fact is that nearly every country would have a period of accelerated commitments at some point thereafter.
5.   Doerner, *Madmen and Bourgeoisie*, 46–47.

6. Comparing the psychiatric hospital to a zoo may sound harsh, but early hospitals in England, the US, and elsewhere put lunatics on display as a moralizing lesson for the public and charged fees to reduce the cost of confinement. See Doerner, *Madmen and Bourgeoisie*, 21.

7. Robert Castel, *The Regulation of Madness: The Origins of Incarceration in France* (Berkeley: University of California Press, 1988), 46.

8. Allen Thiher, *Revels in Madness: Insanity in Medicine and Literature* (Ann Arbor: University of Michigan Press, 1999), 48.

9. Reich, *The Sexual Revolution*, 71.

10. David Cooper, *The Language of Madness* (London: Penguin Books, 1978), 130. Cooper coined many new terms using the prefix "anti-:" "antifamily," "antipsychoanalysis," etc. With each of these, he named a form of the thing itself turned against its own stale ideological givens. For example, an "antifamily" was a family that questioned the unspoken givens within the family.

11. One could argue that psychiatry only came into existence in these acts (as I did earlier), so that it can't yet be called "antipsychiatry," but my point is that there is a foundational connection to negativity that repeats itself. All subsequent negative acts of separation (from moral treatment to clinical forms, or from ward to community psychiatry) proceed through a negative turn that could more accurately be called "antipsychiatric."

12. Thomas Szasz wrote numerous articles and a book condemning antipsychiatry, which he associated with leftist "commies." R.D. Laing denied ever being in this camp while still drawing on many influences that are commonly associated with it. The same is generally true for most of the Italian reformers. American psychiatric survivor and ex-patient groups sometimes embrace it as a catchall, but some reject it because of its association with professionals or academics, opting instead for "mad pride" or "c/s/x (consumer/survivor/ex-patient)." Cooper rejected it for the same reason.

13. Cooper, *The Language of Madness*, 116.

14. Cooper, *The Language of Madness*, 28. This is a reversal of Ludwig Wittgenstein's proposition in *Tractatus Logico-Philosophicus*: "What can be said at all can be said clearly, and whereof one cannot speak, thereof one must be silent."

15. Cooper, *The Language of Madness*, 22. This reverses Lacan's formulation that the unconscious is structured like language.

16. Zbigniew Kotowicz, *R.D. Laing and the Paths of Anti-Psychiatry* (London: Routledge, 1997), 30.

17. Lyn Bigwood, "Lyn Bigwood Talk to R.D. Laing—Sanity, Madness and the Psychiatric Profession," *Asylum: The Magazine for Democratic Psychiatry* 1, no. 1 (Spring 1986): 16.

18. Franco Basaglia, "Peacetime Crimes: Technicians of Practical Knowledge," in *Psychiatry Inside Out: Selected Writings of Franco Basaglia*, ed. Nancy Scheper-Hughes and Anne M. Lovell (New York: Columbia University Press, 1987), 196.

19. Castel, *The Regulation of Madness*, 4.

20. Cooper, *The Language of Madness*, 116.

21. Cooper, *The Language of Madness*, 117.

22. "Suicide Rising across the US," Centers for Disease Control and Prevention (CDC), 2018, https://www.cdc.gov/vitalsigns/suicide/index.html; "Suicide," National Institute for Mental Health (NIMH), 2019, https://www.nimh.nih.gov/health/statistics/suicide. Every few years, we see a small decrease (in 2019, it fell less than 1 percent), but in general, the trend is rising.

23. E. P. M. Brouwers, "Social Stigma is an Underestimated Contributing Factor to Unemployment in People with Mental Illness or Mental Health Issues: Position Paper and Future Directions," *BMC Psychology* 8, no. 1 (2020): 36, https://doi.org/10.1186/s40359-020-00399-0.

24. Joel Kovel, "The American Mental Health Industry," in *Critical Psychiatry: The Politics of Mental Health*, ed. David Ingleby (New York: Pantheon Books, 1980), 72.

25. Robert Castel, Françoise Castel, and Anne M. Lovell, *The Psychiatric Society* (New York: Columbia University Press, 1982), 7.

26. Rothman, *The Discovery of the Asylum*, 193.

27. Castel, Castel, and Lovell, *The Psychiatric Society*, 3.

28. Marx, *Capital, Vol. 1*, 715.

29. Marx, *Capital, Vol. 1*, 719.

30. Two prominent groups that stressed this theme in divergent contexts are the Wages for Housework movement in Italy and Black Feminism in the 1960s and '70s. See Silvia Federici, *Wages against Housework* (London and Bristol: Power of Women Collective and Falling Wall Press, April 1975); Frances M. Beal, *Black Women's Manifesto; Double Jeopardy: To Be Black and Female* (New York: Third World Women's Alliance, 1969), http://www.hartford-hwp.com/archives/45a/196.html.

31. My analysis of this dynamic between the demand for labor and the capacity for absorbing deviant or disabled people is strongly indebted to Richard Warner, *Recovery from Schizophrenia: Psychiatry and Political Economy* (Hove: Brunner-Routledge, 1997), especially Chapter 5, "Madness and the Industrial Revolution," and Chapter 6, "Labor, Poverty and Schizophrenia." Warner offers a convincing thesis as to why both the boom and the bust of capitalist cycles can have negative effects on incident and recovery rates of schizophrenia. This is because the most consistent factor between them is not the level of national prosperity but rather the general demand for labor and the broader effects of capitalist development on social cohesion and stability: "Significant treatment efforts will only be expended on those skilled workers who are acutely mentally ill and whose disappearance from the work force involves the loss of a substantial investment in training. Efforts to rehabilitate and reintegrate the chronically mentally ill will only be seen at times of extreme shortage of labor (such as in the boom years of the late 1990s in the US)—after the other battalions of the industrial reserve army have been mobilized." See Warner, *Recovery from Schizophrenia*, 136.

32. Gilbert Seldes, *The Stammering Century* (New York: New York Review of Books, 2012), 38.

33. Alexis de Tocqueville, *Democracy in America and Two Essays on America* (London: Penguin Books, 2003), 36.

34. Angela Mitropoulos, *Contract and Contagion* (Wivenhoe: Minor Compositions, 2012), 171.

35. Mitropoulos, *Contract and Contagion*, 172.

36. Michel Chevalier, *Letters on North America* [1836], trans. Steven Rowan (St. Louis: University of Missouri, 2014), 302–303.

37. Rothman, *The Discovery of the Asylum*, 187. For a longer discussion of therapeutic eclecticism, see Chapter 1, "Caring for the Insane in Colonial America," in Gerald Grob, *The Mad among Us: A History of the Care of America's Mentally Ill* (New York: The Free Press, 1994), 5–17.

38. Marx, *Capital, Vol. 1*, 783.

39. Marx, *Capital, Vol. 1*, 782.

40. Marx, *Capital, Vol. 1*, 797.

41. Marx, *Capital, Vol. 1*, 787.

42. In his comparable analysis of the rise of psychiatry in England, Andrew Scull points out that early psychiatric commitment was much more dependent on *lay* conceptions of madness than professional ones, since asylum commitments were entirely dependent on family and parish usage. He argues that the presence of the asylum worked to loosen traditional understandings of madness by the simple fact that it could work as a release valve of domestic pressure. See Andrew Scull, *Museums of Madness: The Social Organization of Insanity in Nineteenth-Century England* (New York: St. Martin's Press, 1979), 238–239.

43. Andrew Scull, *Decarceration: Community Treatment and the Deviant—A Radical View* (Englewood Cliffs: Prentice-Hall, 1977), 2.

44. Albert Deutsch, *The Mentally Ill in America: A History of Their Care and Treatment from Colonial Times* (New York: Columbia University Press, 1949), 177.

45. Deutsch, *The Mentally Ill in America*, 178.

46. *Mental Hygiene News* 11, no. 6 (September 1932): 1.

47. Adelaide Nichols Baker, "The Challenge of The Labyrinth," *Mental Hygiene News* 11, no. 6 (September 1932): 2.

48. Baker, "The Challenge of The Labyrinth," 2.

49. See Castel, *The Regulation of Madness*, 188.

50. These efforts were concentrated in Massachusetts and New York in the 1890s and, like their European counterparts, made frequent reference to the family boarding tradition in Geel, Belgium. See H. R. Stedman, "The Family or Boarding-Out System—Its Uses and Limits as a Provision for the Insane," *American Journal of Psychiatry* 46, no. 3 (1890): 327–338; Nana Tuntiya, "Free-Air Treatment for Mental Patients: The Deinstitutionalization Debate of the Nineteenth-Century," *Sociological Perspectives* 50, no. 3 (2007): 469–487.

51. Grob, *The Mad among Us*, 104–105.

52. David Rothman, *Conscience and Convenience: The Asylum and Its Alternatives in Progressive America* (New York: Aldine de Gruyter, 2002), 23–24.

53. Lawrence Goodheart, "'The Glamour of Arabic Numbers': Pliny Earle's Challenge to Nineteenth-Century Psychiatry," *Journal of the History of Medicine and Allied Sciences* 71, no. 2 (2015): 187, https://www.ncbi.nlm.nih.gov/pmc/articles/PMC4887602/.

54. Anonymous, "On the Claims of the Insane to the Respect and Interest of Society," *The Opal* 2, no. 4 (April 1952): 242. Courtesy of the Oskar Diethelm Library, DeWitt Institute for the History of Psychiatry, Weill Cornell Medical College.

55. Grob, *The Mad Among Us*, 132; Deutsch, *The Mentally Ill in America*, 277.

56. Deutsch, *The Mentally Ill in America*, 279.

57. Rothman, *Conscience and Convenience*, 296. A similar critique was leveled by German, university-based clinical psychiatrists in the 1860s against the superintendents of asylums located outside the cities. See Engstrom, *Clinical Psychiatry in Imperial Germany*, 6.

58. John M. Galt, "The Farm at St. Anne," *The American Journal of Insanity* 11 (1854–1855): 352.

59. See especially, Ruthie-Marie Beckwith, *Disability Servitude: From Peonage to Poverty* (New York: Palgrave Macmillan, 2016); Scull, *Decarceration*, 112–113; and Segrest, *Administrations of Lunacy*, 154–156. As the authors highlight, patient labor was clearly divided along racial and gendered lines. For instance, in Georgia, white men worked in the gardens while Black men were overwhelmingly farmhands; white women mostly worked as seamstresses and Black women worked the laundry.

60. *Buck v. Bell*, 274 U.S. 200.

61. Sanjana Manjeshwar, "America's Forgotten History of Forced Sterilization," *Berkeley Political Review*, November 2020, https://bpr.berkeley.edu/2020/11/04/americas-forgotten-history-of-forced-sterilization/.

62. Nellie Bly, *Ten Days in a Madhouse* (New York: Ian L. Monroe, nd), University of Pennsylvania, http://digital.library.upenn.edu/women/bly/madhouse/madhouse.html.

63. Janet Frame, *Faces in the Water* (North Sydney: Vintage, 2008), epub.

64. Anna Kavan, *Asylum Piece and Other Stories* (London: Peter Owen, 2001), 90.

65. Quoted in Nancy Tomes, *A Generous Confidence: Thomas Story Kirkbride and the Art of Asylum-Keeping, 1840–1883* (Cambridge: Cambridge University Press, 1984), 277.

66. Clifford Whittingham Beers, *A Mind That Found Itself: An Autobiography* (1908), available at Project Gutenberg, https://www.gutenberg.org/cache/epub/11962/pg11962-images.html.

67. This slogan appeared at the bottom or in the headline of many volumes of *Mental Hygiene News*, the newsletter of the Connecticut Society for Mental Hygiene started by Beers in 1908.

68. Ernst Rüdin, "The Significance of Eugenics and Genetics for Mental Hygiene," *Proceedings of the First International Congress of Mental Hygiene* (New York: International Committee for Mental Hygiene, 1932), 489.

69. Jay Joseph and Norbert A Wetzel, "Ernst Rüdin: Hitler's Racial Hygiene Mastermind," *Journal of the History of Biology* 46, no. 1 (Spring 2013): 4.

70. Theodore Jun Yoo, *It's Madness: The Politics of Mental Health in Colonial Korea* (Oakland: University of California Press, 2016), 74.

71. Richard C. Keller, "Taking Science to the Colonies: Psychiatric Innovation in France and North Africa," *Psychiatry and Empire*, ed. Sloan Mahone and Megan Vaughan (New York: Palgrave Macmillan, 2007), 20–21.

72. The most thorough historical account of this policy activism is Gerald Grob, *From Asylum to Community: Mental Health Policy in Modern America* (Princeton: Princeton University Press, 1991).

73. Rothman, *Conscience and Convenience*, 304. For a more biographical account of Meyer and his work, see Andrew Scull, *Psychiatry and Its Discontents* (Oakland: University of California, 2019), 95–133.

74. For example, in the aftercare movement, according to David Rothman, the emphasis shifted from financial assistance to mental health resources around 1910. See Rothman, *Conscience and Convenience*, 313.

75. Deutsch, *The Mentally Ill in America*, 320–322.

76. Rothman, *Conscience and Convenience*, 328–331.

77. Andrew Scull, *Social Order/Mental Disorder: Anglo-American Psychiatry in Historical Perspective* (University of California Press, 1989), 58.

78. Samuel Polsky, "Present Insanity – From the Common Law to the Mental Health Act and Back," *Villanova Law Review* 2, no. 4 (1957): 509, http://digitalcommons.law.villanova.edu/vlr/vol2/iss4/4.

79. Studs Turkel, "Dr. Thomas Szasz discusses his book *The Manufacture of Madness: A Comparative Study of the Inquisition and the Mental Health Movement*," 1970, Studs Turkel Radio Archive, https://studsterkel.wfmt.com/programs/dr-thomas-szasz-discusses-his-book-manufacture-madness-comparative-study-inquisition-and?t=NaN%2CNaN&a=%2C.

80. Quoted in Hervey Nicholas, "Advocacy or Folly: The Alleged Lunatics' Friend Society, 1845–63," *Medical History* 30 (1986): 255, https://www.ncbi.nlm.nih.gov/pmc/articles/PMC1139650/pdf/medhist00070-0005.pdf.

81. Formerly, the original draft of the FLSA in 1938 stipulated that disabled workers could be paid less than the minimum wage. The amendments restricted when and by how much this subminimum wage could be lowered, but did not efface the rule, which is based on the idea that the disabled are objectively less productive over time than the nondisabled. See Beckwith, *Disability Servitude*, 89.

82. *Mills v. Rogers*, 457 U.S. 291 (1982) and *Rennie v. Klein*, 462 F. Supp. 1131 (D.N.J. 1978), among others.

83. *O'Connor v. Donaldson*, 422 U.S. 563 (1975) and *Addington v. Texas*, 441 U.S. 418 (1979).

84. *Olmstead v. L.C.*, 527 U.S. 581 (1999).

85. Beckwith, *Disability Servitude*, 2.

86. Kate Millett, "The Illusion of Mental Illness," *Alternatives Beyond Psychiatry*, ed. Peter Stastny and Peter Lehmann (Berlin: Peter Lehmann Publishing), 29.

87. Millett, "The Illusion of Mental Illness," 29.

88. "The Statement," *State and Mind: People Look at Psychology* 5, no. 4 (December 1976): 7. Courtesy of the Oskar Diethelm Library, DeWitt Institute for the History of Psychiatry, Weill Cornell Medical College.

89. *Madness Network News* 4, no. 4 (Fall 1977), for example, includes one such report.

90. Lucas Richert, *Break on Through: Radical Psychiatry and the American Counterculture* (Cambridge, MA and London: MIT Press, 2019), 64; Michael Staub, *Madness Is Civilization: When the Diagnosis Was Social, 1948–1980* (Chicago: University of Chicago Press, 2011), 126.

91. Staub, *Madness Is Civilization*, 126.

92. Alondra Nelson, *Body and Soul: The Black Panther Party and the Fight against Medical Discrimination* (Minneapolis: University of Minnesota Press, 2011), 179.

93. Richert, *Break on Through*, 64–67.

94. For accounts of these actions see *Madness Network News* 4, no. 1 (October 1976), https://madnessnetworknews.com/archives/archives-vol-4/.

95. Bruce Arrigo, *Punishing the Mentally Ill: A Critical Analysis of Law and Psychiatry* (Albany: SUNY Press, 2002), 39.

96. But even here, it is admitted that patients will continue to exist and ought to have certain rights, so it still pits the "average" medico-legal entity, "normal patient" versus the illegitimate one, "psychiatric patient."

97. In a retrospective on the mental patients' movements, Chamberlin lists the abolition of all legal categories specific to the mentally ill as one of the goals that set the liberation movements apart from the consumer rights groups. See "The Ex-Patients' Movement: Where We've Been and Where We're Going," *Journal of Mind and Behavior* 11, no. 3 (Summer 1990 – Special Issue, Challenging the Therapeutic State): 323–336.

98. Lindsey Devers, *Plea and Charge Bargaining* (US Department of Justice, 2011), 1, https://bja.ojp.gov/sites/g/files/xyckuh186/files/media/document/PleaBargainingResearchSummary.pdf.

99. Colin King, "They Called Me a Schizophrenic When I Was Just a Gemini. 'The Other Side of Madness,'" in *Reconceiving Schizophrenia*, ed. Man Cheung Chung, K. W. M. Fulford, Bill Fulford, and George Graham (Oxford: Oxford University Press, 2007), 15.

100. This is the story at the center of Jonathan Metzl, *The Protest Psychosis: How Schizophrenia Became a Black Disease* (Boston: Beacon Press, 2011).

101. W. E. B. Du Bois, "Strivings of the Negro People," *The Atlantic*, 1897, https://www.theatlantic.com/magazine/archive/1897/08/strivings-of-the-negro-people/305446/.

102. Anne E. Parsons, *From Asylum to Prison: Deinstitutionalization and the Rise of Mass Incarceration After 1945* (Chapel Hill: University of North Carolina Press, 2018), 105.

103. Marta Russell (1951–2013) was one of the preeminent theorists of disability and capitalism in the US. Her books *Beyond Ramps: Disability at the End of the Social Contract* (1989) and *Capitalism & Disability: Essays by Marta Russell* (2019) are major influences on my thinking around disability, unemployment, and the financing of services. In the 2020s, there has been a rejuvenation of interest in her works, likely on account of their relevance to governance and economy in the COVID era and because of the popularizing efforts of Liat Ben-Moshe, Beatrice Adler-Bolton and Artie Vvierkant of the podcast *Death Panel*, Nate Holdren, and others. For an intro to her work and its continued relevance see: Beatrice Adler-Bolton, and Artie Vvierkant, "Capitalism & Disability: A Symposium on the Work of Marta Russell," LPE Project, October 3, 2022, https://lpeproject.org/blog/capitalism-disability-a-symposium-on-the-work-of-marta-russell/. I write about her political economic work extensively in a forthcoming text entitled "Belacqua Syndrome: A Report on the Mental Health Industry" to be released sometime in 2024/2025.

104. Beckwith, *Disability Servitude*, 141.

105. Beckwith, *Disability Servitude*, 144.

106. "Guardianship," Minnesota Judicial Branch, 2020, https://www.mncourts.gov/Help-Topics/Guardianship.aspx.

107. Paul Lowinger, "Radicals in Psychiatry," *Canadian Journal of Psychiatry* 17 (1972): 194.

108. Richert, *Break on Through*, 17.

109. Castel, Castel, and Lovell, *The Psychiatric Society*, 241–242.

110. Castel, Castel, and Lovell, *The Psychiatric Society*, 185.

111. Castel, Castel, and Lovell, *The Psychiatric Society*, 86.

112. Abram J. Lewis, "'We Are Certain of Our Own Insanity': Antipsychiatry and the Gay Liberation Movement, 1968–1980," *Journal of the History of Sexuality* 25, no. 1 (January 2016): 98, https://blogs.brown.edu/hman-1973p-s01-2019-spring/files/2019/02/Lewis-Antipsychiatry-GayLiberation.pdf.

113. Emily Reynolds, "The People Who Want to Get Rid of the Term 'Personality Disorder,'" *Dazed*, May 15 2018, https://www.dazeddigital.com/life-culture/article/40036/1/bpd-borderline-personality-disorder-diagnosis-label.

114. Lucy Johnstone and Mary Boyle with John Cromby, David Harper, Peter Kinderman, David Pilgrim, John Read, Jacqui Dillon and Eleanor Longden, *The Power Threat Meaning Framework: Towards the Identification of Patterns in Emotional Distress, Unusual Experiences and Troubled or Troubling Behavior, as an Alternative to Functional Psychiatric Diagnosis* (Leicester: British Psychological Society, 2018), 17–18, https://www.bps.org.uk/guideline/power-threat-meaning-framework-full-version.

115. *Evidence for Peer Support* (Mental Health America, 2019), https://www.mhanational.org/sites/default/files/Evidence%20for%20Peer%20Support%20May%202019.pdf; *Global Evidence for Peer Support: Humanizing Health Care* (Peers for Progress, 2014), https://www.mhanational.org/sites/default/files/140911-global-evidence-for-peer-support-humanizing-health-care.pdf.

116. Nev Jones, *Peer Involvement and Leadership in Early Intervention in Psychosis Services: From Planning to Peer Support and Evaluation* (SAMHSA/CMHS, 2015) 2–4, https://nasmhpd.org/sites/default/files/Peer-Involvement-Guidance_Manual_Final.pdf.

117. Lucy Costa, "Mad Studies – What It Is and Why You Should Care," Mad Studies Network, 2014, https://madstudies2014.wordpress.com/archive/.

118. Diana Rose and Jayasree Kalathil, "Power, Privilege and Knowledge: The Untenable Promise of Co-Production in Mental 'Health,'" *Frontiers in Sociology* 4 (July 2019), https://doi.org/10.3389/fsoc.2019.00057.

119. Peter Beresford and Suzy Croft, "Service Users' Knowledges and the Social Construction of Social Work," *Journal of Social Work* 1, no. 3 (2001): 296, https://citeseerx.ist.psu.edu/viewdoc/download?doi=10.1.1.864.7176&rep=rep1&type=pdf.

120. Claude Steiner, "Radical Psychiatry: Principles," in *The Radical Therapist*, ed. Jerome Agel (New York: Ballantine Books, 1971), 4.

121. Richert, *Break on Through*, 51. For instance, the principles of Transactional Therapy are a much-simplified version of the therapeutic social optimism of moral treatment: "1. People are born ok, 2. People in emotional difficulties are nevertheless full, intelligent human beings, and 3. All emotional difficulties are curable, given adequate knowledge and proper approach." See also Richert, *Break on Through*, 80.

122. Richert, *Break on Through*, 45.

123. Richert, *Break on Through*, 55–60.

124. Leonard Roy Frank, "The Journey of Transformation," *Mad in America*, May 2013, https://www.madinamerica.com/2013/05/the-journey-of-transformation/.

125. Mental Patients' Liberation Front, "Mental Health Workers," *Our Journal* (Fall 1977): 28. Courtesy of the Oskar Diethelm Library, DeWitt Institute for the History of Psychiatry, Weill Cornell Medical College.

126. This scene is described in Richert, *Break on Through*, 66; and in Linda Morrison, *Talking Back to Psychiatry: The Psychiatric Consumer/Survivor/Ex-Patient Movement* (New York: Routledge, 2005), 77, with other examples of separatist gestures.

127. Judi Chamberlin, *On Our Own: Patient-Controlled Alternatives to the Mental Health System* (National Empowerment Center, 1977), 15.

128. Chamberlin, *On Our Own*, 20.

129. Chamberlin, *On Our Own*, 20.

130. The Radical Therapist Collective, "Manifesto," *The Radical Therapist*, xvii.

131. Chamberlin, *On Our Own*, 105.

132. Chamberlin, *On Our Own*, 93.

133. Chamberlin, *On Our Own*, 71.

134. For discussion of the question of "cooptation," see Morrison, *Talking Back*, 80–85.

135. Richert, *Break on Through*, 69. This is also one of the conclusions of Michael Staub's *Madness is Civilization: When the Diagnosis Was Social, 1948–1980* (Chicago: University of Chicago Press, 2011) and Kovel's "The American Mental Health Industry."

136. Franco Basaglia, Franca Ongaro Basaglia, Domenico Casagrande, Giovanni Jervis, Letizia Jervis Comba, Agostino Pirella, Lucio Schittar, and Antonio Slavich, "'Considerations on a Communitarian Experience' (1967–8): 'Reality and Contradictions in the

Process of Institutional Renewal,'" in Michael Donnelly, *The Politics of Mental Health in Italy* (London: Tavistock/Routledge, 1992), 118.

137. See Chapters 1–3 of Grob's *From Asylum to Community* for a detailed account of these events.

138. Liat Ben-Moshe, *Decarcerating Disability: Deinstitutionalization and Prison Abolition* (Minneapolis: University of Minnesota Press, 2020). Various narratives are recounted, complicated, and critiqued throughout, but see 38–42 for an early example.

139. Bernard E. Harcourt, "Reducing Mass Incarceration: Lessons from the Deinstitution- alization of Mental Hospitals in the 1960s," *Ohio State Journal of Criminal Law* 9, no. 1 (2011): 54, https://chicagounbound.uchicago.edu/cgi/viewcontent.cgi?article=1509&- context=journal_articles.

140. Parsons, *From Asylum to Prison*, 25–26; 52. Hospitalization cost taxpayers about $3 million a day in 1954, near the peak.

141. Grob, *The Mad among Us*, 290.

142. Castel, Castel, and Lovell, *The Psychiatric Society*, xxi. See also Grob, *The Mad among Us*, 167. Grob points out that there were (and are) massive disparities in the portion of states' budgets dedicated to mental health services, between 2 percent and 33 percent.

143. Scheper-Hughes and Lovell, "Breaking the Circuit of Social Control," 380.

144. Rachel Jane Liebert, *Psycurity: Colonialism, Paranoia, and the War on Imagination* (Lon- don: Routledge, 2018).

145. Peter Sedgwick, *Psycho Politics* (London: Unkant, 2015), 213.

146. Ben-Moshe, *Decarcerating Disability*, 214–215. It is here where she also discusses the idea of "community" as a purely negative term, which I have also adopted in my anal- ysis.

147. Scheper-Hughes and Lovell, "Breaking the Circuit of Social Control," 353.

148. Grob, *The Mad among Us*, 291.

149. Craig Willse, *The Value of Homelessness: Managing Surplus Life in the United States* (Min- neapolis: University of Minnesota Press, 2015), 100.

150. Historically, this exclusion can be understood in the context of the "ugly laws" analyzed in Susan Schweik, *The Ugly Laws: Disability in Public* (New York: New York University Press, 2009), 25–26, which were designed to clear the streets of the beggar, the "poor, miserable, crazy vagabond," and the "diseased, maimed, mutilated, or in any way de- formed" as if they were clearing away obstructions.

151. See Grob, *The Mad among Us*, 250.

152. Willse, *The Value of Homelessness*, 46.

153. Marta Russell and Jean Stewart, "Disablement, Prison, and Historical Segregation," *Monthly Review*, July 1, 2001, https://monthlyreview.org/2001/07/01/disablement-pris- on-and-historical-segregation.

154. More precisely, this alchemy turns the fixed sums allotted to such people by law through public health insurance and waivers rather than the people themselves into exchangeable commodities.

155. Daniel Magalhães Goulart, *Subjectivity and Critical Mental Health: Lessons from Brazil* (London: Routledge, 2019), 24.

156. Elena Portacolone, Steven P. Segal, Roberto Mezzina, Nancy Scheper-Hughes, and Robert L. Okin, "A Tale of Two Cities: the Exploration of the Trieste Public Psychiatry Model in San Francisco," *Culture, Medicine, and Psychiatry* 39, no. 4 (December 2015): 684–685, https://escholarship.org/uc/item/1144b1h9. Just 6 percent of the budget went into each, compared to 40 percent into employment.

157. Of course, there are others, but these seem to be two of the more visible forms that have produced real, physical spaces for socializing with a simple model for replicability.

CHAPTER 5

VIOLENCE AND THE WARD

But mine, my destiny is full of doubt, full of doom. I am being dragged down, without my willing, into a whirlpool of horrors. I prefer nobility and goodness but a preference isn't enough; there are forces who make a mockery of my preferences. —Bessie Head[1]

DISSENSUS IN CUERNAVACA

Just south of Mexico City, in the centrally located city of Cuernavaca, a strange pedagogical institute, CIDOC, became a center for critical psychiatric activity in North America in 1966. CIDOC, or Centro Intercultural de Documentación, was a small pedagogical institution founded by Ivan Illich, the Austrian-born priest known for his series of anti-institutional polemics (*Deschooling Society, Medical Nemesis, Tools for Conviviality*), that began as a uniquely anti-missionary missionary school. CIDOC has its origins in Illich's rejection of Pope John XXIII and John Kennedy's combined efforts to combat Marxism, Protestantism, and the success of the Cuban Revolution throughout Latin America in 1961 by renewing missionary efforts and supplying $10 billion in conditional aid. Illich, who'd moved to Cuernavaca just a year earlier, received and promptly castigated would-be missionaries at CIDOC as unwitting agents of imperialism, a critique he later made more publicly in articles and talks.[2] After the Vatican prohibited priests from participating in the programming at CIDOC, it further entrenched itself in a radical ethos, and came to establish itself as a language program, an open school, and a hub for Latin American critical psychiatry, among other functions.[3]

Unlike the US and Canada, Mexico in the 1960s and '70s did not have a sprawling mental health system. Cash-strapped and ruthless, the state seemed to always have more *abandonados* ("the abandoned" who disappeared into the dark confines of the asylum) on its hands than it knew what to do with, leading to repeated denunciations of the familiar mixture of overcrowding and neglect in its psychiatric system with few moments of optimism.[4] But 1968 was a watershed: Mexico's student movement had gathered numbers and momentum up until the massacre of protestors at the Olympics, while Mexico's largest centralized mental hospital—the symbol of carceral mental health care, La Castañeda in Mexico City[5]—closed down, events which a generation of medical students and practitioners could not help but be involved in.

Sylvia Marcos was one such person. A psychologist by training, Marcos became involved in CIDOC in the early 1970s, and was especially stimulated by the 1974 visit of Franco Basaglia and her meetings with Félix Guattari, with whom she became good friends. Shortly after Basaglia's visit, she traveled to Trieste, in the first of multiple trips to Italy. The very next year, Basaglia, David Cooper, Robert Castel, Félix Guattari, and Mony Elkaïm, a Belgian-Moroccan psychiatrist who became especially involved in family therapy in the Bronx among others formed le Réseau-Alternative à la psychiatrie, or the Network of Alternatives to Psychiatry. The Network was formed in response to the technical reorganization happening in psychiatry—particularly in the US,[6] described in part in the last chapter, and in France with *secteurization*[7]—as a loose and mobile form for sharing information between projects, communicating across borders from within rapidly shifting therapeutic territories. In line with this model, membership was expansive and theoretically included any patients/the psychiatrized, workers who refuse repression functions of their role, and anyone trying to make alternatives or destroy current psychiatric service who participated in meetings. Coordination and information sharing was the main purpose of the Network, specifically around the questions of the creation of alternatives and circulation of their practices, analysis of local political situations and dismantling of repressive apparatuses, how to support struggles at psychiatric sites, research into the means of dissolving psychiatric power at various sites, and concretizing rela-tions between research and real practices.[8] Central to this vision was the desire to enlarge the Network's base to the struggles of the psychia-trized and mental health workers, make contact with groups who were already trying experiments, multiply exchanges, create regional coor-dinations to counter the concentration of power, open the network beyond the narrow confines of "mental health," and establish rapid channels of intervention to counter repression.[9]

Sylvia Marcos was one of the most active in the extended Network, having organized a community psychology program in Cuernavaca, helped put together multiple conferences in Mexico, edited antholo-gies based off these, and generally remained very active through the 1970s and the beginning of the '80s throughout the Americas.[10] The 1981 conference in Cuernavaca on the theme of "Prisons and Asy-lums" was declared the "I Encuentro Latinoamericano y V Internacio-nal de Alternativas a la Psiquiatría" ["First Latin American and Fifth International Meeting of Alternatives to Psychiatry"]. From the outset, Marcos and the Latin American Network made a point, in a preface labeled *"insistimos"* ["we insist"], to distinguish themselves from oth-er branches of "antipsychiatry." Without "denying that we emerged from it," they distance themselves from other approaches that go by that name by affirming "mental illness" as a concept that has political connotations and a sociohistorical reality going beyond the individu-al. Since madness, or mental illness, is not solely or even primarily a question of individual pathology and cure, they refuse the hypostatiza-tion of madness as a journey of self-discovery along with all proposals to erect alternative structures isolated "from the macrostructure" on the grounds that they would be "elitist, economically and culturally."[11] In her introduction, Marcos states this more emphatically by posit-ing that the struggle against the asylum is but one piece of the fight against marginalization in general; it is a struggle that cannot survive when severed from its links to general political struggle.[12] Marcos sug-gests that such a position is unavoidable in the specific conditions and needs of the Latin American Network. For one, with the exceptions of Argentina and Brazil, mental health systems tended to be small and have limited reach outside of the cities. In this context, a program of molding a population via psychiatry by a conscious elite was highly improbable, given the meager resources allotted to state psychiatry, its inability to compete with other forms of healing, and its limited technical capacity to affect the masses. On the asylum question, some participants suggested they should aim to prevent their spread through Latin America and strengthen already existing therapeutic systems before they become psychiatrized, but most had other problems on their minds.

Among their most pressing issues was the fact that psychiatric discourse, technology, justifications, and spaces were being put to use by military leaders and dictators to aid in the torture of political militants. There was no pretense here of "treatment": psy-knowledge was valued to the extent that it could theoretically provoke a prisoner to betray their comrades. Political questions were absolutely unavoidable, the question of madness overdetermined. There was both an incapacity to evade chaos and violence and a willingness in politics to use any technique or category to achieve discrete goals—a combination which effectively polarizes every therapeutic activity. Even choosing to treat a certain client (say, a militant or a military officer) is inscribed into a political field that could result in exile or death. And so, they came together as "militants of different origins"—psychiatrists and psychiatrized, militants and nurses—with the goal of discovering the link between torture and segregation, asylum and prison, not just in Latin America, but globally.[13] What ties violence to psychiatry and psychiatry to politics?

A SHORT HISTORY OF PSYCHIATRIC VIOLENCE

The title of this chapter is a play on the title of the jurist Robert Cover's 1986 article "Violence and the Word," in which he contends that the law's power is constitutionally reliant upon its capacity to enact violence and inflict pain. Of course, we are not like Kafka's prisoners in the penal colony: our crimes are not inscribed in our dying flesh with torturous writing machines. In the US, most of the accused take a plea bargain and simply wait, severed from what constituted life up to that point and bored out of their mind. Cover's point is that this metaphor of carving the sentence into the dying flesh of the accused materially circumscribes the limits of a viable system of law; without having the available means to inflict pain and kill, there would be no security for the catastrophic "no" of the prisoner who refuses to walk peaceful-ly into prison for "it is unquestionably the case in the United States that most prisoners walk into prison because they know they will be dragged or beaten into prison if they do not walk."[14] This reliance on pain and death might be called the operational security of violence, or what Walter Benjamin termed "law-preserving violence."[15] I can think of no better example of law-preserving violence for our purposes than the trial of Bobby Seale. Seale, on trial for conspiracy in Chicago in 1969, repeatedly disrupted the court proceedings, jumping up and shouting "I object! My lawyer's not here. He's mentioning my name." When Seale refused to follow the judge's demand to sit, calling him "a racist, a fascist and a bigot," Judge Julius Hoffman was faced with a blunt, radical challenge to his legal authority. There's absolutely no need for him to acknowledge this challenge as part of a reciprocal exchange by justifying himself and his law; not when he could have Seale "bound up":

> I was bound up with ACE bandages. . . . And they brought me in the courtroom. My arms are strapped down to the chair. My legs are strapped to the legs of the big heavy wooden chair, the last day of gagging. . . . I was losing blood pressure, circulation. And it caused a big commotion in the room. And then the judge says, 'Well, take him out.' And they tried to pick me up in this heavy chair, three guards. And the big guard started beating me in the head. Jerry Rubin jumped up out of his chair. Abbie jumped up out of their chair, trying to help me. Guards slammed them back in their chairs. I'm trying to turn my hand over, my right hand over, to get my—to get my fingers up to the top of the gag. And then the other guard would turn my hand down and then hit me and knock me back, you know, and stuff like that. They really brutalized me.[16]

At its limit, the law makes and preserves itself in blows and blood. Similarly, I want to underscore that, at the end of the day and barring all other enticements, psychiatric legal decisions rely, at their limits, on force, threat, and the infliction of pain. The introduction of psychi-atry into the courts was, in part, supposed to ameliorate the exposure to pain and death, but it also brings the courts closer to another em-barrassing reality: that their decisions are normative, contingent—as much a matter of morals, discretion, and custom as consensus and fact. It opens a broad multitude of spaces where the law acts not on account of a mechanical infraction, but due to the expression of an unbearable eccentricity or a mutual incoherency. It is always possible to say that it is friendlier when a judge orders the afflicted and the raving to see a therapist, rules that they must take prescribed medications, or sends them off to a hospital, but what if they refuse? Naturally, they will be forced, and this threat hovers over the whole exchange from the jump. In such cases, the title "therapeutic" does not erase the violence which underlies the possibility of administering court decisions, no matter the ends they may have in mind.

Beyond the "law-preserving" violence in psychiatry that secures its efficacy as a legal relationship, pain and shock have played a deeper, more ambivalent, and often contradictory role in psychiatric treatment dating to its origins. Leonora Carrington's harrowing description of a personal apocalypse is entirely legible in the annals of psychiatric theory. Lost and confused in France, with her lover Max Ernst being held in a concentration camp, the surrealist painter and novelist wept and soon fell sway to horrifying visions of an apocalypse to come. She spent weeks alone in solitude, dreading the onslaught of the German forces. In Madrid, she met a Dutch man, Van Ghent, who she believed to have Nazi ties and thereafter accused him of using "hypnotic powers" to aid Hitler and his party. She repeated these accusations at the British Embassy, where the medical authorities were promptly called. Carrington was locked in a hotel room until, after a brief stay in a "sanitarium of nuns," she was "handed over like a cadaver to Dr. Morales, in Santander" in a place she called Down Below. Here, she seems to have lived through a death of sorts in the throes of a Cardiazol-induced epileptic seizure:

A new era began with the most terrible and blackest day in my life. How can I write this when I'm afraid to write about it? I am in terrible anguish, yet I cannot continue living alone with such a memory [. . .]

The next morning a stranger entered my room. He carried in his hand a physician's bag of black leather. He told me that he had come to take blood for a test and that he had to be helped by Don Luis. I replied that I was willing to receive one of them, but one at a time only, for I had noticed that the presence of more than one person in my room brought misfortune to me; moreover that I was going to leave for Down Under and that I would not allow an injection to be given me under any pretext. . . . Each one of them got hold of a portion of my body and I saw the *centre* of all eyes fixed upon me in a ghastly stare. Don Luis's eyes were tearing my brain apart and I was sinking down into a well . . . very far. . . The bottom of that well was the stopping of my mind for all eternity in the essence of utter anguish.

With a convulsion of my vital centre, I came up to the surface so quickly I had vertigo . . . I howled: 'I don't want . . . I don't want this unclean force'. . . .

I confessed to myself that a being sufficiently powerful to inflict such a torture was stronger than I was: I admitted defeat, the defeat of myself and of the world around me, with no hope of liberation. I was dominated, ready to become the slave of the first comer, ready to die, it all mattered little to me. When Don Luis came to see me, later, I told him that I was the feeblest creature in the whole world, that I could meet his desires, whatever they were and that I licked his shoes.[17]

The bleakness of the passage becomes more apparent after one has become acquainted with Leonora the fighter, who just days before negotiated her unstrapping from the hospital bed and immediately defended herself from an attacker, who "jumped with joy among the apple trees, sensing again the strength, the suppleness and beauty of [her] body."[18] So quickly this aspect fades and we find her prostrate, broken, and ready to lick the shoes of anyone who could save her. The loss of a world is brought about in the institutional encounter through, among other things, *shock*.

I have absolutely no pretensions to accurately describe the physiological effects of one or another treatment of shock; I am merely suggesting that there is a symbolic attachment to the idea of destructive leveling, a long predilection for shock as the symbol of that which clears away brush, leaving behind a mental *tabula rasa*, either for effective management or treatment.[19] Sometimes this is the literal shock of electroconvulsive therapy, or the diverse array of shock treatments described by Daniel Paul Schreber: "The attendant M. repeatedly threw me back into the bath when I wanted to leave it after a time, or in the morning when it was time to get up and I want to, threw me back into bed for reasons unknown to me; or in day-time when I was about to doze sitting at the table, he wakened me out of my sleep by pulling my beard."[20] In his article "The Psychiatric Sublime," Nicholas Tromans cataloged a number of strange and seemingly disconnected treatments, united solely in the idea of shock.[21] Among the first means of shocking patients was Francis Willis' terrible piercing eye, which "seemed to read [maniacs'] hearts and divine their thoughts as they formed."[22] Willis was the physician called in to treat King George III's madness in 1788. In a single moment, ideally upon first glance, the physician must establish the terms of the relationship *through the eye*, a technique whose importance is underscored by William Pargeter in his *Observations on Maniacal Disorders* on a section about "the government of maniacs:" "As maniacs are extremely subdolous, the physician's first visit should be by surprize. He must employ every moment of his time by mildness or menaces, as circumstances direct, to gain an ascendancy over them, and to obtain their favour and pre-possession. If this opportunity be lost, it will be difficult, if not impossible, to effect it afterwards; and more especially, if he should betray any signs of timidity. He should be well acquainted with the pathology of the disease—should possess great acumen—a discerning and penetrating eye—much humanity and courtesy—an even disposition, and command of temper."[23] In the case which follows, he describes his approach in confronting a maniac raving alone in his room: "I then suddenly unlocked the door—rushed into the room and caught his eye in an instant. *The business was then done*—he became peaceable in a moment—trembled with fear, and was as governable as it was possible for a furious madman to be."[24] Add to this the "surprise bath" (dunking the lunatic into cold water without warning); Rush's "rotary chair" (swinging them around to overwhelm their sensation and sense of place); or, most bizarrely, Johann Christian Reil's *Katzenklavier*, a fantastical instrument composed of living cats "arranged in a row with their tails stretched behind them. And a keyboard fitted out with sharpened nails would be set over them. The struck cats would provide the sound. A fugue played on this instrument—when the ill person is so placed that he cannot miss the expressions on their faces and the play of these animals—must bring Lot's wife herself from her fixed state into conscious awareness."[25] Reil, for his part, in his recommendations to apply irritants to the feet of hysterics, hot wax onto the chests of maniacs, deprivation of food, whipping with nettles, or even dropping one into a tub of eels, did not hesitate to describe these methods as "torturous."[26] In the twentieth century, theories of "antagonist agents" share in this symbolism of the destructive breakdown or overwhelming force as condition or course of treatment: Julius Wagner-Jauregg's intentional inoculation of general paresis patients with malaria that killed about 15 percent of patients and, of course, the use of electroconvulsive treatments to induce seizures in the belief that schizophrenia and epilepsy were irreconcilable.

A shock is a vibration, a shaking at a high frequency. At all times, living beings gently vibrate by virtue of their own internal processes and their sensual contact with the objects in their world. Sound is perceived and understood via an organ in our ears, which vibrates in reception. Our bodies' most invisible and most immediate extremities alike hum in a sweet unity while we go about our daily business. Shock is not like this: it seizes matter. Some shocks animate, like an electric current running through a motionless body returning it to life. A quick jolt of this sort can wake one up, like a jump scare in a horror movie does to the sleepy spectator. But enough shock will decimate that same matter. One of the most common negative side effects of electroconvulsive treatment is memory loss: the loss of history, of what constitutes a world. Looking beyond this literal method of shock, removing the insane to a rural institution was intended to shock and break the familiar patterns of the ill. Patients sat down on their beds on the first day of their new life, knowing that the world they've come to know and move within will remain at an unattainable distance, perhaps for years. Intentionally scaring and shaming them were even more favored means to achieve submission by Kirkbride and Pinel, as the correct course arose from an internalized domination over the instincts.[27] Restraint alone precipitates a violent psychic breakage, and even though some, like John Connoly, did away with mechanical means of restraint, his preferred method of solitary confinement has its own means of breaking the resistor. As the walls close in ever more, the body itself transforms into a weapon. Inmates learn to experience the body as an antagonist against whom they must struggle to survive. One's own body is objectified into another horrid fixture of a hostile world—brutal and unforgiving, weak and torturous—bent on pathetically inflicting pain to a mind that has ceased to remember its having once belonged to such an unrelenting sadist. Shock may dissolve matter, but it simultaneously brings into being a "whole inward electric body . . . an immense turning outward in flames, monads of nothingness bristling to the limits of an existence held prisoner in my lead body."[28] Violence and pain do not fully eradicate worlds but become a world unto themselves.

At first glance, shock treatments seem to come in two varieties, divided according to their ends: some seem geared towards the management of the mad, or breaking them to establish the conditions (at best) for therapy or (at worst) for quietude; others appear to be *the treatment itself* or a significant part of it. Electroconvulsive therapy and fever treatments often appear in this way. Such a distinction, however, is an illusion. Moral treatment has long established that the effective management of mental disorder is, in itself, the treatment. With madness, it is not possible to extrapolate a manner of living from the expression of an illness as these elements are more often than not one and the same, or, to speak less ontologically, indistinguishable in practice.

In his *Psychiatric Power* series of lectures, Foucault notes how, with Francis Willis, and especially in the nineteenth century, psychiatric theory began to reorganize itself around the question of "force," transforming asylum space into a "battlefield."[29] Pinel went so far in this direction as to assert that the therapeutics of madness is "the art of, as it were, subjugating and taming the lunatic by making him strictly dependent on a man who, by his physical and moral qualities, is able to exercise an irresistible influence on him and alter the vicious chain of his ideas."[30] If the eighteenth century was generally taken up with Lockean theories of "false belief"—the madman is someone who errs in the order of ideas—the nineteenth was caught up in the imaginary of "force." Now madness arrives through the flow of sensations, distorted instincts, the *force* of incorrect ideas (as opposed to false reasoning), and the persistent permeation of bad influences.[31] Naturally, stimulants of a soothing variety were introduced in equal measure: sweet music, warm baths, and pleasant walks were mainstays of moral treatment. Reil again took this to romantic extremes, which were naturally not realized, but give one a sense of the direction this manner of thinking took, recommending intercourse with sex workers to expend one's excessive energies, or exposure to the "heartbreaking" singing voice of a donkey to enrapture their mind.[32]

Among the causes, as we've seen many times already, we find the intensity of the environment and the speed of civilization, joined by Reil into an imaginative metaphoric universe:

> It is a remarkable experience to step from the whirl of a large city into its madhouse. One finds here repeated the same scenes, though as in a vaudeville performance; yet, in this fool's system there exists a kind of easy genius in the whole. The madhouse has its usurpers, tyrants, slaves, criminals, and defenseless martyrs, fools who laugh without cause and fools who torture themselves without cause. Pride of ancestry, egoism, vanity, greed, and all the other idols of human weakness guide the rudder in this maelstrom, just as in the ocean of the large world. Yet every fool in Bicetre and Bedlam stands more open and innocent than those from the great madhouse of the world. In the world, the vengeful ravage, so that fire falls from the heavens; and the cultivated leader of armies believes, in light of a madly bold plan, that he can destroy half the world with the sword. But there [in the madhouse] no villages smolder, and no men whimper in their own blood.[33]

Following Laure Murat in *The Man Who Thought He Was Napoleon*, I don't think it's a coincidence that analogies of political force and revolution appear so widely in psychiatry following revolutions, often by spectators themselves—Pinel witnessed the beheadings of the terror, Rush lived through the American Revolution. Murat makes this very clear:

> The revolutionary 'shock' had been beneficial, and Pinel the clinician was the first to recognize the 'salutary effects of the progress of liberty.' New energy was stimulating human character and giving the 'animal economy' the spur it needed. 'I feel better since the revolution,' has been said by several persons honored by that sentiment; and indeed, how could the enjoyment of rights derived from well-ordered nature and which seem to enlarge and brighten the soul, do anything other than revive the organic function of the viscera and penetrate, as though by some electric virtue, the system of nerves and muscles of a new life?[34]

She calls attention to the very peculiar, specific terminology Pinel chose to describe his methods of psychological intimidation and shock: "a formidable show of terror should convince them that they are not free to pursue their impetuous willfulness and that their only choice is to submit."[35]

Around this notion of "violence," psychiatry has generated a number of contradictory, ambivalent traditions tying it, on the one hand, to practices of surprise, overwhelming sensual intensity, force, shame, intimidation, and torture as the means of shaking loose, through shock, a self from the petrified reef of the interior; and, on the other, to regulatory mechanisms of coercion for the proper management of an administrative machine. More often than not, these are virtually inextricable from one another.

It's hard to imagine what salutary effects arise from electrocuting students through a wearable device when they act out, but, in 2021, the US Court of Appeals for the DC Circuit refused to ban this practice at the Judge Rotenberg Educational Center for developmentally disabled children on the grounds that "the ban was a regulation of the practice of medicine, which is beyond the FDA's authority."[36] Equally troubling is the insurrectionary break of revolution and its relation to the mental functions. None other than Frantz Fanon, the psychiatrist and anticolonial revolutionary whose work is examined in more detail below, was optimistic about using shock treatments, at least during his time in Saint-Alban under the guidance of Tosquelles. In a series of papers written together, they referred to shock treatments as "annihilation therapy," referring to its capacity to destroy the barriers to effective treatment. All too aware that shock treatments were "performed out of convenience or, in the best cases, as a symptomatic medication for agitation, as if agitation was a behaviour with a univocal cause," they nevertheless found it useful in "a complementary, not an essential, fashion." Shock was seen as a means of breaking down a fixed personality—annihilating all barriers—and returning the patient to a plastic state from which they can reconstitute themselves in a new way.[37] It's not hard to imagine that he had this therapy in the back of his mind when he wrote about the cleansing force of violence in a colonial society. As it's objectively impossible to be apolitical, in psychiatry or otherwise, one's role in the political order or revolution directly shapes the practice of therapy (or the psychological justification of torture) in politically disturbed times. In such times, the rift dividing opposing accumulations of force becomes so wide that to simply stay put is to already choose one's side.

NO LONGER LYING TO OURSELVES

Marie Langer was born in 1910 in Vienna into a wealthy Jewish family. After being radicalized at her college prep school in Red Vienna, she pursued medical training during the rise of the Nazis around the same time she joined the Communist Party. Langer served as a nurse in the Spanish Civil War, was forced to flee multiple countries throughout her life, formed multiple psychoanalytic organizations throughout her time in Argentina, participated in clandestine activity, was put on a kill list, and helped set up mental health services in revolutionary Nicaragua. A child of the twentieth century, a practicing analyst in states of political turmoil and extreme violence on multiple continents, a clandestine revolutionary—for Langer, a "neutral" therapeutic stance was simply a denial of reality. Therapy, she reiterated time and again, will not cure you, it is not subversive in itself, nor does it equate to revolution. So, what's analysis for? Simply "in order not to lie to oneself any more."[38]

In retrospect, as she tells it, Langer's life appears like a series of choices laid before her where she was called to take a position. The first came in 1932 when she saw Hitler speak at a mass rally in Kiel. She was horrified by his power over the crowd. Soon after, she joined the Communist Party, and, when the state barred Jewish citizens from clinical training, she turned to psychoanalysis.[39] "When I was asked why I chose the Communist Party and not the Socialist Party," she wrote later, "I could answer that I joined because the Communist Party promised revolution."[40] When the party was banned, she received a crash course in clandestine organization, though she never did more than agitprop work at this stage. A revolution was what was needed to counter the Nazi turn in Europe, which made the official reaction of the *Wiener Psychoanalytische Vereinigung* [Viennese Psychoanalytic Society] all the more devastating. They not only refused to take a principled stance, they decided, in 1934, that no analyst could be active in any clandestine or banned political organizations, nor treat patients who were.[41] This fostered an absurd and surreal atmosphere which "presented analysts with the alternatives of either interrupting their patient's treatment, which goes against medical ethics—what's more, the vast majority weren't in training analysis, there were patients with serious problems—or avoiding the subject with patients during their sessions and going against the most elementary rules of psychoanalysis; or violating the regulations of the institution of analyst-analysand."[42]

In 1936, at the outbreak of the Spanish Civil War, she was presented with an opportunity to serve as an anesthetist alongside her partner Max, who worked as a surgeon, and she eagerly accepted. In 1937, then well into her pregnancy, she was asked to travel to Paris to acquire the machinery required for a prosthesis workshop, a task she'd never finish. In Paris, it was clear that the situation in Spain was not improving, and the couple traveled to Nice to wait for the money, but only tragedy found her there: "the money didn't arrive, the baby had died, so many comrades as well, and not only Spain but all of Europe was falling apart."[43] Europe was closing in. Austria disappeared with the Anschluss. Assured that things would get worse before they got better, the two of them fled to Mexico on the way to Uruguay.

This turned out to be a brief stopover on the way to Argentina where she arrived in 1942 and remained for most of her life. Buenos Aires was a felicitous place for a politically militant therapist to join her two passions, therapy and politics, hitherto kept at a remove. Though the state aspired to develop a sprawling asylum system comparable to Europe's, it was plagued by political turmoil through the eighteenth and nineteenth centuries. Dreams of one regime to raise palatial madhouses built fast enough to keep pace with a commitment rate to rival those of England's or France's were periodically dashed by the next rulers. In the 1820s, Bernardino Rivadavia, Minister of Government and Foreign Affairs, began the process of liberalizing the country's few hospitals, establishing commissions to examine their conditions and reduce the influence of the church over welfare provisions. He fell in 1827 to Juan Manuel de Rosas as ruler of Buenos Aires, who immediately reversed the little progress made, condemning the system to remain a small, clerical, segregative patchwork. Rather than simply abandoning the mad, Rosas transformed them into "an instrument of political terror," as Jonathan Ablard reports: "Most galling was the dictator's reputed use of poor non-whites, including many supposed 'lunatics,' as henchmen and propagandists to humiliate his elite opponents. Roving gangs on his payroll were sent out into the streets to announce victories, harass the opposition, and sow fear in the populace."[44] It is this peculiar pattern, alternating between pretenses of benevolent governance emulating European liberalism and periods of unmitigated, guileless political terror, that makes the Argentine psy-complex unique.

From the early 1940s on, this cycle would accelerate, widening its reach in the process. This decade was the official turning point marking psychoanalysis' entrenchment into Argentine public life, beginning with the founding of the Argentine Psychoanalytic Association (APA) in 1942, but its diffusion began much earlier in the 1920s and '30s, making Argentina the psychoanalytic capital of the Americas.[45] In 1943, a nationalist group of military officers took control of the state. With the ascendance of Perón from this corps in 1946, the contradictions that animated the Argentine psy-complex were both heightened and suspended in tension in the same state apparatus. Militarist authoritarians promised secular welfare reform and repressive heads of state bolstered therapeutic services.[46] Though they tended to favor construction of grand hospitals, some smaller and more imaginative projects were established as well. Most important among them, the experimental psychopathology unit in the Lanús general hospital, established in 1956, was outfitted with social workers, psychologists, therapists, and an outpatient section.[47] During this ambiguous period, Langer strayed from political work, focusing instead on developing Kleinian analysis. That changed in the late 1960s. Escalating inflation, rising unemployment, and the concentration of wealth fomented a formidable protest movement both among general Argentine workers who led a general strike in 1969 and specifically in mental health workers, leading to breaks with professional organizations like the APA.

Frustrations came to a head at the World Congress of the Psychoanalytic Association in Rome in 1969, which eventually led to the creation of two splinter groups: Plataforma and Documento. After hanging a banner mocking the greed and complacency of mainstream psychoanalysis, future members of these groups formed a para-conference at a beer hall nearby and formulated their opposition.[48] Chief among their concerns was the sense that psychoanalysis had become more and more elitist and isolated from the political realities of the world. The Plataforma Declaration reads:

> What essentially divides us is that these models of societal function-
> ing, . . . isolate the different groups from each other with respect
> to internal policy, and the institution from reality with respect to
> the external. They gradually encase psychoanalysts from reality,
> with their acquiescence in their long wait for a promotion, in the
> bastion of a strictly apolitical and asocial profession. This painful
> condition is rationalized with the criteria of the 'valuable neutrality'
> of the scientist, supposedly possible and necessary, which is part of
> a utopian concept that includes deluded hopes for social change to
> which we cannot contribute as people because we are engrossed in
> professionalism, nor as psychoanalysts because any attempt in that
> regard is accused of being an 'ethical violation' and 'mixing science
> and politics.'[49]

"True psychoanalysis" and science, they held, "cannot and must not be used to build an isolating barrier which alienates it from social reality or from its theoretical instrument, thus converting it into a mystifying and mystified tool at the service of the status quo. . . . Psychoanalysis is wherever psychoanalysts may be, understanding 'being' as a clear definition that has no connection to an isolated and isolating science, but rather with a science committed to the multiple realities it attempts to study and transform."[50] Langer made a similar intervention at the Vienna Congress of 1971, a historic event marking the return of Anna Freud after her exile during the Nazi period. When the Congress asked for papers on the history of psychoanalysis, Langer saw an opportunity to address the historic failure of the Viennese Psychoanalytic Society's apoliticism in the face of National Socialism and polarization with a paper titled "*Psicoanálisis y/o revolución*" ["Psychoanalysis and/or Revolution"].

On the surface, this shift in mindset brought with it few practical innovations: there were training centers established with the goal to reduce the false divisions and hierarchies between mental health professions; teams of mental health workers were sent into working class neighborhoods to provide preventive care and diagnostics; and, mental health workers were encouraged to participate in unions and political activity out in the open.[51] At the same time, the interventions recounted above all respond to the demand made on therapists (and scientists) to "remain neutral," which affects all therapeutic encounters. In *From Vienna to Managua*, Langer responds directly to a biting criticism directed at psychoanalysts by Robert Castel: "The 'analysand' is at the same time encouraged and enticed by the process of subjectivization, induced by the analytical situation, to put the political and social dimension into parentheses. The psychoanalyst directs from his position of 'neutrality.'"[52] Politics was unavoidable, for "reality was imposed upon you, and our supposed 'neutrality' would have become absurd"[53]; politics constituted the *conditions* under which any therapeutic relationship was formed. What trust could a Jewish analysand have if the analyst was sympathetic to Nazis? How could "reality principles" be addressed if it was not understood that the state was torturing or murdering its citizens? How, in short, could you pretend to understand someone without understanding the conditions in which they live, conditions which the therapist cannot help contributing to or opposing?

This does not mean that politics are collapsed into therapy or that therapy is subsumed by politics. The recognition that therapy is political does not mean political action is exhausted or even effectively pursued in therapy. The latter plays a few very specific roles, none of which constitute a change of conditions in themselves. Analysis aids in the process of demystification, that is, it gives one the means not to lie to oneself by recognizing one's own contradictions and the real conflicts one struggles with. At times, it can feel like an unburdening, a freeing up of tension to do work, something which is not neutral since there exists no abstract situation in which humans "just work:" the therapist can help to unburden a worker of the tensions associated with their exploitation,[54] or unburden a militant of the guilt stemming from their capture and torture, which requires a certain level of trust. In either case, the therapist colludes with the patient as a partisan with a concrete position, for the first could just as easily direct such an unburdening towards political activity rather than productivity schemes and the latter could affirm or deny that the state has the political right to capture dissidents (even if they try to remain neutral, by helping, they are already, in the eyes of the state, colluding with a militant). Therapy is always social because, alongside the bipersonal relation of therapist-client, a multiplicity is always present as a third, or all the others who inform the session and condition it. In respect to this third, it's always in collusion simply in the act of recognition—with the status quo or with something that opposes it.

With the military coups of the 1960s and '70s, political militants, including many psychoanalysts, were targeted by the military police and tortured or killed by death squads,[55] which made the above considerations around collusion all the more urgent, as psychoanalyst Marcelo Viñar argued at a 1970 conference in Caracas: "[As] more of our patients began to be affected by military and police actions, we postulated that when a patient or those close to her are directly affected by political repression and she doesn't speak about it, the analyst's refusal to raise the subject does not reflect therapeutic neutrality but collusion with the patient's denial of reality."[56] The purpose of torture is very rarely to extract useful information; or, if this is its function, it is generally ineffective. Torture acts in part upon the individual, trapping them in a game of dominance and resistance, but it also acts upon communal bodies like neighborhoods, political parties, or social classes. Its final goal is separation, or alienation, as Elizabeth Lira makes plain in Nancy Caro Hollander's book *Love in a Time of Hate*: "this policy of disappearing people evoked extreme states of anxiety in the community related to the sense that mysterious and uncontrollable forces were at work whose power everyone was impotent to contain."[57] An analyst, therapist, or psychiatrist can serve a few functions in this respect, as Langer and others did in Argentina and later in Nicaragua. On the individual level, they can help prepare militants for the possibility of torture[58] or provide a much-needed opportunity for catharsis. On the social level, groups of mental health workers, in Nicaragua for example, can help to socialize "grief for the dead, the permanent burden under which people there have to live and also—why not?—. . . the hatred towards the enemy who is invading the country."[59]

Psychoanalysis, then, is political in the sense that it cannot distance itself from its political conditions, but we must be careful not to extend the connotations of this too far by collapsing political action and therapy into a single category. Sometimes we just need to talk. Other times, we need to fight and the therapeutic lens is insufficient. Talking can strengthen the resilience and capacity to struggle, it can help one to accept one's own madness and learn to live with it, it can diminish the guilt and shame that get in the way of participation, or it can affirm one's unease in a horrifying situation. In these limited senses, therapy can "make change," but the therapist can just as often be a "changemaker" in the opposite sense, that is, they can reinforce guilt and confusion, weaken the desire to make connections, or even collude directly in torture. In the final account, therapy plays a vital but ultimately ancillary role: it won't put food on the table, kill slave owners, or expropriate any expropriators.

RESOUNDING FAILURES

The question of conditions and the limit became a point of contention at the two-week-long July 1967 Dialectics of Liberation Congress in London, organized by Laing and Cooper with Joe Berke and Leon Redler (psychiatrists from the US). The Congress featured an impressive roster of speakers beloved by the New Left, among them Herbert Marcuse, Kwame Ture (known at the time as Stokely Carmichael), Allen Ginsberg, and Gregory Bateson. Some of the contradictions and shortcomings were readily apparent on the surface: there were almost no women invited to speak at the conference. Others emerged once the delicate thread uniting various "countercultural" forces was torn up by conflicting presuppositions about the problem at hand.

According to the poster for the event, the purpose of the Congress was "to demystify human violence in all its forms, the social systems from which it emanates, and to explore new forms of action."[60] How can we understand the enormous cruelty and depravity of the Vietnam War, the genocide of Indigenous populations, and anti-Black violence? In Cooper's introduction to a collected volume of speeches from the Congress, he ties the theme to processes of dehumanization. He and his colleagues are familiar with the theme, because this, he asserts, is central to the function of psychiatry: once we label someone schizophrenic, we medicalize and objectify their behavior, and thereby sanction the use of violence against this subhuman other.[61] At the same time, there was a good deal of conceptual spillage from the participants, who, when they weren't comparing political systems or modes of violence to psychiatry, were analogizing them to madness.[62] Laing proposed that we approach "the obvious," which in this case means approaching the question of violence in small interpersonal encounters (micro-situations) between a wielder and a victim and scaling up to "the *total social world system*"[63] (macro-situations). Laing wanted to understand individual violence within a context. He thought it would otherwise remain unintelligible, but his phenomenological and cybernetic theory of the "context" rarely goes beyond decrying the division of groups into "US versus THEM" or "Have and Have-Nots" binaries.

The scene shifted as soon as Kwame Ture took to the stage. Abstract binaries were moot and bizarre to this man who had just lost his notes for the speech because he was arrested a few days prior and the cops stole them.[64] All the talk of individuals and getting over personal complexes and prejudices sounded to him like a "cop out." Instead, he brought Fanon into the debate and said that if Black people are alienated, it's not due to some vague notion of society or familial dysfunction, nor interpersonal dynamics that separate people into one of two categories based on their immediate action and position in a situation, but on account of centuries of colonial violence and the everyday functioning of a white-supremacist capitalist society. But the biggest scandal of the whole event was that he, in his talk and repeatedly elsewhere, asserted the necessity of counterviolence. Peter Davis' film on the proceedings, *The Anatomy of Violence*, accords us a unique vantage point to witness how this disturbing intervention was received. At a panel talk with Allen Ginsberg, Ture becomes irate with the mainly white, liberal audience who talk of violence in the abstract, who view it as a philosophical possibility one can take up or refuse as opposed to the air one breathes or the environment one lives in. One audience member even accosts him and the wider Black Power movement for failing to assuage white liberals' fears and goes so far as to accuse him of being a totalitarian using fascist methods.[65]

Comparisons like this are no fluke in either critical psychiatric literature or the New Left. Thomas Szasz once sustained an absurd comparative analysis between psychiatry and the institution of chattel slavery;[66] Goffman does not bother to mention that St. Elizabeths (the federal asylum where he did his ethnography) was a segregated institution in his analyses of Total Institutions; and, at the Congress, Ginsberg called for a "calm, peaceful, tranquil equilibrium"[67] as a response to Ture's acceptance of counterviolence in the face of thievery and brutality.

"Whether or not violence is used is not decided by us." Ture (plus a few others who acknowledged this, like Herbert Marcuse) and the flower children confronted each other from one side or another of the insurmountable gulf opened up in this clause. Only when the question of violence is reduced to phenomenological situations or disruptions in communication does it become possible to compare slavery, apartheid, patriarchy, or colonialism to psychiatry. The central problem with such comparisons at the systemic level is that psychiatry (and psychiatric violence) has existed in concrete and contradictory relations with each of them throughout its history, certainly as a supporting structure but at times as a counterforce. Equating the dispensation of medicine in relation to a political system (ignoring also the diverse historic forms this relationship has taken) to the system itself is more confounding than illuminating.

Few have examined the contradictory nexus between psychiatry, violence, and race more forcefully than the Martinican psychiatrist and anticolonial militant Frantz Fanon. As with Ture, the immediacy of their connections forced itself upon him in his daily life. In 1943, at the age of eighteen, Fanon signed up for the French Free Forces and left his native Martinique to fight the forces of fascism in North Africa. This turned out to be a humiliating and disillusioning experience for the young soldier, who found that he and the other Black soldiers, far from being recognized as comrades in a common struggle with their white peers, "without their berets . . . were treated as wild savages, and, with them, as domesticated servants."[68] The anti-Blackness of his "allies" only increased when he was stationed the next year on the European front lines. On the occasion of major victories, Fanon and his Caribbean compatriots were excluded from the festivities. Spilling blood for France or the US was not enough to win love or even reciprocal acknowledgement of common humanity from white citizens.[69] After he returned, he studied at the Lycée Schoelcher where he met the anticolonial poet and politician Aimé Césaire and was hired in 1945 to support the latter's unsuccessful communist ticket in the parliamentary elections. In 1947, Fanon decided to travel to Lyon, France to study medicine, which was then a center for radical political activities. Out of his training as a student of medicine and frequent experiences of anti-Black racism in France, he produced two major works in the early 1950s upon completion of his studies: his dissertation

"Mental Alterations, Character Modifications, Psychic Disorders and Intellectual Deficit in Spinocerebellar Heredodegeneration: A Case of Friedreich's Ataxia with Delusions of Possession" in 1951 and his more well-known phenomenological and psychoanalytic analysis of anti-Blackness, *Black Skin, White Masks* in 1952.

In 1952, after finishing his studies in Lyon, Fanon worked as an intern under François Tosquelles at Saint-Alban. He was very active during his brief time there, teaching classes, co-authoring clinical texts with Tosquelles and others, and contributing to the collective journals. Institutional Psychotherapy's emphasis on "spontaneous, everyday lived experience" where "the psychotherapist is at once materially absent and present in the hospital institution"[70] must have been appealing for Fanon, who recommended we place "sociogeny" on the same plane of importance with phylogeny and ontogeny.[71] In November 1953, Fanon was hired to head the psychiatric team at the Blida-Joinville hospital in French-colonized Algeria. Blida-Joinville was at that time segregated by gender and ethnicity with distinct "European" and "native" wards. In the worst of conditions, Fanon still attempted ambitious experiments in line with what he learned in France, but over time, Fanon paved his own path, parallel but divergent, responsive to the peculiar position of psychiatry in the colonies.

As director at Blida-Joinville, Fanon set out straightaway to implement some of the key principles of sociotherapy or Institutional Psychotherapy. He faced an uphill battle: firsthand accounts of the hospital describe decrepit conditions, overcrowding, and the liberal use of restraints. In some versions of the story, Fanon himself went around like an anticolonial Pinel and removed the chains from patients before introducing himself to every patient personally.[72] This story seems to only be partially true: he did begin removing some restraints immediately, but not all at once, with some remaining in straitjackets for an indeterminate time.[73]

Between 1953–1954, Fanon and his staff introduced film nights with discussions, a journal for the patients to publish in, a music club, biweekly ward meetings, reading groups, sewing workshops, and more in an attempt to give patients increasing opportunities for participation and self-directed activity.[74] As Fanon and his intern (and dear friend) Jacques Azoulay report in their 1954 paper "Social Therapy in a Ward of Muslim Men: Methodological Difficulties," and Alice Cherki recalls in her biography on Fanon, the resounding successes recorded in the European women's ward—the diminishing incidents of agitation, the widespread participation—were contrasted with the Algerian ward which was "a resounding failure, with the patients indifferent to a man. Further attempts to repeat the strategies that had worked so well for the European women did not fare any better. The male patients did not engage with the collective games that were intended to resocialize them—the ball games and the games of hide-and-go-seek—nor were they interested in the parties or the attempts at choir singing. Even the basket-weaving workshop was deserted."[75] Since, as Fanon says elsewhere, "the essential weapon of psychiatry is psychotherapy, which is to say a dialogue between the mental patient and the doctor [and] in Algeria, most psychiatric doctors do not know the local language,"[76] the prospect of sociotherapy was ruled out from the start. The idea that the psychiatrists, from a position of authority and speaking French, could introduce a therapeutic model imported from France in a ward of colonized Arabic-speaking Muslim men placed too many barriers between the healer and the patients. For one, the synchronicity of the speaking with its reception was off, making it hard "to begin a dialogue, a dialectical exchange of questions and replies." Second, knowing no Arabic, they were unaware of the affective weight or rhythm of speech so central to a productive and trusting dialogue.[77] Worse, by employing an interpreter, Fanon and his colleagues resembled the dreaded judicial language interpreter, government officials with whom nothing good is associated, a situation which "spontaneously triggers a distrust that makes all 'communication' difficult."[78] For all intents and purposes, the hospital staff (regardless of their racial or religious make-up) represented the colonial order and reproduced the colonizer-native relation, since the "colonized perceives the doctor, the engineer, the schoolteacher, the policeman, the rural constable, through the haze of an almost organic confusion."[79]

In accounting for their failure, Fanon and Azoulay employ a central Fanonian concept: reciprocity. In the colonial situation, there is no reciprocity, only absorption, for when the Algerian is asked to adopt European culture, "[i]t is up to one entire culture to disappear in favour of another."[80] Briefly outlining the ways French settlement dissolved nomadic Algerian social formations through binding them to towns where they rent their labor, leading to the rise of large shanty towns notorious for pervasive poverty and hunger, they make it clear that assimilation means nothing to the French settler women, but signifies acquiescence to destruction (of place, lifeways, culture) for the Algerian patient. "It is not possible," Fanon wrote elsewhere, "for the colonized society and the colonizing society to agree to pay tribute, at the same time and in the same place, to a single value" since, when the colonized recognizes any benefits of Western medicine, this person is perceived to be "successfully integrated" and grateful for their domination.[81] Alice Cherki suggests that Fanon was actually partly pleased with the failure since it was "as a positive sign of resistance by a culture that refused to bend when faced with its own denial." For Fanon and Azoulay, the failure outlined the necessity of a novel approach:

> The patients could not abide the interpreter because he embodied the link between them and colonial authority, administrative or legal as the case may be, and because of his inclination to be complicit with that authority. The planned festivities had failed so miserably because the only meaningful holidays, at least in 1953, were the ones that held religious significance. The lack of interest in forming a choir followed from the cultural perception of performers as professionals who do not pertain to the group, individuals who, especially in rural areas, are viewed as itinerant. The basket-weaving workshop had found no takers because the making of baskets had traditionally been women's work.[82]

Observations derived from their failures opened a wealth of possibilities, leading to the more successful implementation of appropriate interventions. But they were fully aware of how such a failure was typically interpreted and what it would lead to: the colonial doctor would find confirmation that the North African was naturally lazy, indifferent, and childish, concluding that they were naturally fit to be ruled by a benevolent colonial patriarch.

THE USES OF ETHNOPSYCHIATRY

The ethnopsychiatric establishment in Algeria was marked by vulgar racial stereotypes sufficiently advanced to be congealed into medical orthodoxy. Fanon takes direct aim at this school of thought in a short article from 1955, "Ethnopsychiatric Considerations." From the 1910s on in Algeria, Antoine Porot and the "Algiers School" of psychiatry placed the North African *as a racial group* into measurable standards of mental acuity and wellness, and furthermore posit a psychophysiological unity between all Africans.[83] Porot identified the African's main characteristics: he has no emotional life, he's naturally untrustworthy, prone to forgetting, mistakes, and accidents. In short, the North African as a general type occupied the place of the "idiot" on the traditional European scheme for degeneracy.[84]

For Porot, this is not a political statement, but a scientific and medical fact: the North African is not just culturally primitive, but constitutionally. According to him, the regions of the brain associated with higher cognitive functioning are undeveloped, so that their behavior relies on the most basic—"vegetative and instinctive"—functions of the nervous system. Such a construction proffers a biological explanation for the historical appearance of the colonial relationship, which is construed as basically inevitable given any contact between the races—"[primitivism] has far deeper foundations and we even think it must have its substratum in a particular disposition of the architectonics, or at least of the dynamic hierarchizing of the nervous centers."[85]

In 1954, these ideas gained international recognition with the publication of John Colin D. Carothers' *The African Mind in Health and Disease: A Study in Ethnopsychiatry* by the World Health Organization (WHO). Carothers—without formal psychiatric training—was hired by WHO in 1954 to study the psychological condition of Black Africans in English-speaking Africa and concluded that the African *naturally* had little frontal lobe activity, and was therefore equivalent to a lobotomized European.[86] Given that there were few asylums and psychiatrists, what was the purpose of this kind of medical knowledge when guns seemed to do just fine keeping things the way they were? In Fanon's eyes, the psychiatrist in the colony was tasked with pathologizing and medicalizing both the noxious effects of colonialism and naturalizing vulgar stereotypes of the settler-colonists,[87] thus easing their conscience and justifying brutal occupation. Psychiatric universalism was first premised on the universalization of patriarchal racial developmentalism, where the primitive is equated with the child on equal footing with the "idiot" and the settler is a father whose violence is actually a form of benevolence (etymologically, "idiot," in its Greek origins, refers in part to an incapacity to participate in public affairs as a citizen). Colonial psychiatry is first and foremost *for* the colonist, not the colonized, even when it speaks *about* the latter.

In the colonial situation analyzed by Fanon, the naturalization of racial hierarchy and racial difference was barely veiled in theory or in the few existing asylums, in which Native patients (often political prisoners) were simply locked to walls and Europeans received modern treatment. Psychiatry was likewise a key discipline in the nineteenth-century project of grounding the naturality of slavery, though it's often hard to tell what various disciplines individually contributed, in a situation where all of mainstream science agreed on the superiority of the white race. Samuel George Morton's massive *Crania Americana* is a case in point. His book was an attempt to ground racial difference in craniometry, or observable physical differences in skull/brain size. Morton partially appealed to psychiatry for his explanatory apparatus, but craniometry relied just as much on biology, anatomy, and anthropology as well. Even theology was mobilized into his pro-slavery ideology: he, like Thomas Jefferson and others, propounded the theory of "polygenism," or the idea that humans have divergent racial origins. A deeper look at psychiatry's involvement in constructions of race in the US or in the colonies can help demonstrate how complex this involvement can be.

One of the most analyzed mechanisms at racial capitalism's disposal is to pathologize the resistance of slaves and colonized peoples. Whenever mental illness becomes more closely aligned with the concept of danger, there is a noted increase in the labeling of nonwhite people as insane, as we saw in the last chapter with the juridical turn towards "danger" as a commitment criteria. Jonathan Metzl's *The Protest Psychosis: How Schizophrenia Became a Black Disease* (2011) is one of the most compelling narratives of this type. In it, he traces the way the diagnosis of schizophrenia changed from describing a condition of docility and alienation to one of aggression and violence during the Black Power movement in the 1960s. Subsequently, the stereotypical image of the schizophrenic shifted from listless white wives to militant young Black men who were then hospitalized and committed at significantly higher rates.

The most famous example of the pathologization of racial difference and rebellion is the work of Samuel A. Cartwright. Cartwright claimed that slaves who ran away suffered from a disease he called "*drapetomania*" (or "runaway slave disease") and "*dysaesthesia aethiopica*" or "Black laziness." Much has been made over Cartwright's classifications, but it's important to note: (1) he was not taken very seriously by many psychiatrists;[88] and (2) he did not actually recommend any psychiatric treatments specific to a clinic or hospital, but only those which could be administered on the plantation. These so-called treatments—whipping and social isolation—are indistinguishable from normal discipline on the plantation. Rhetorically, this constitutes a pathologizing of rebellion, but without even the veneer of a medical response. Nor would an enslaved person be aware of this pathologizing, so again we must ask: who exactly was such a construction for?

On the whole, Cartwright's influence is almost definitely overstated, as psychiatric incarceration was not a widespread form of social control in the antebellum South. And why would it be? Psychiatry was practically of little use to slave owners in the South. Instead, as slavery was enshrined in law and sanctified in religion, psychiatrists joined the chorus of physicians embedding slavery into natural order at a time when psychiatry was beginning to gain significant social status and political power in the region. The fact that "there are no records suggesting that slaves were admitted to the Eastern Lunatic Asylum for running away nor were enslaved patients ever whipped" but "the same cannot be said for enslaved attendants"[89] significantly complicates the idea that psychiatric power will be concentrated upon specific groups in a predictable way or solely along the vector of pathologization. Its function is far more strategic; racial psychiatry can speak out of both sides of its mouth using frankly irrational, imaginary logic to achieve its goals. Though the Civil War stunted the spread of asylums in the South and concentrated it in a few congested hospitals like the Milledgeville Asylum in Georgia, it was only at this point that psychiatrists outside of the South devoted widespread attention to the question of race, but even the antebellum Southern asylums were inconsistent and eclectic in their responses, united only in consigning the comparatively small Black inpatient population to the worst care across the board.[90]

Crucially, antebellum pro-slavery psychiatry theoretically condemned Black people to slavery through *denying* them the capacity to go mad as people with primitive minds. This denial, which in some variations supports and in others contradicts the first, is one that characterizes civilization as pathogenic. According to this theory, Black and Native peoples in their "natural states" do not go mad because their primitive minds are too simple and undeveloped. This is a pro-slavery psychiatry that theoretically operates by depsychiatrizing nonwhite peoples.

In 1840, this line of thinking was brought to a limit when national census workers were required to ascertain whether citizens were "idiots" or "insane" in order to measure the need for asylum construction. What these census takers found, was that free Black people were insane and idiotic at numbers far above that of white people; astoundingly, insanity was about ten times more common for free Black people than for slaves. For pro-slavery ideologues in the North, this huge leap in numbers suggested that it was exposure to civilization and freedom driving these Black people—who are "naturally primitive"—insane. Of course, the numbers were totally falsified and statistically impossible, but the census became a useful tool of propaganda: even critics of the statistics like Francis Galt couldn't help but cite them for their implicit suggestion that "more free blacks meant more insanity, and the further north an asylum, the greater number of insane of all races and social classes."[91]

Pro-slavery psychiatries could sustain the contradictions of simultaneous under- and over-diagnosis of Black madness, because the interests of one or another anti-Black psychiatric ideology were not de facto equivalent. In one case, psychiatry pathologized difference and rebellion but without proscribing treatment. In another, involuntary treatments of Black patients rose once psychiatrists shifted a diagnosis towards the description of violence and the space for commitment determinations to the courts, all of which is associated in the US with the fear of "Black aggression." And in yet another, psychiatrists depathologized the so-called "natural state" in the service of decerebralizing the "native," preserving slavery and the racial hierarchy in the laws of nature.

Where is insanity really located in the long history of racial violence accompanying the history of capitalism? Our history books are full of the names of white men on wanton murder sprees, but we don't psychologize distant national forefathers, nor ascribe depth where the truth is right on the surface. Settler-colonists and white supremacists are not insane by virtue of their racism unless we mean to extend that word into the infinite, even though many might find it convenient to think of them as such. The capture of territories, the impudent desecration of ancient cultures, the sale and purchase of human beings, even the eradications of whole peoples for mere land and profit are *rational* acts within colonial and plantation economies. Bonaventure Ndikung writes: "Despite its obvious imprudence, violence, irrationality, absurdity, ludicrousness, and the mayhem and disorder it caused on colonized societies, colonialism is not madness, but rather a generator, facilitator, and catalyst of and towards madness."[92] To read Bessie Head's masterful *A Question of Power* is, in this light, to experience the vertigo of an excursion through the internal ruins made by colonial violence, in her case in Apartheid South Africa. Elizabeth, the main character, is wracked in turmoil in her search for God, describing her descent into madness that led up to her move to Botswana. Head's story suggests that the search for God in the colony can be experienced as the travel through hell, guided, or perhaps tormented, by figures she calls Dan, Sello, and Medusa, each of whom appears in different forms to either torture or soothe. Her torment is often described as the experience of falling: "She had a clear sensation of living right inside a stinking toilet; she was so broken, so shattered, she hadn't even the energy to raise one hand. How had she fallen in there? How had she fallen so low? It was a state below animal, below living and so dark and forlorn no loneliness and misery could be its equivalent."[93] Ndikung reminds us that sanity and sanitation are related through the Latin root *sanus*: sanity is what results when the social world has been sanitized, cleansed of corrupting influence.[94] Dan's visions of distortions and filth suggest debasement experienced by the individual, but presented in a universal that "began to make all things African vile and obscene. The social defects of Africa are first the African man's loose, carefree sexuality."[95] That Elizabeth is here and throughout subjected to the common base stereotypes of what it is to be African and Black in the deepest throes of her insanity suggests that this is a case of colonial insanity, perhaps not unlike those described in the chapter on the mental disorders of colonial wars in Fanon's *Wretched of the Earth*. The truth of inner turmoil is on the historical plane: "the things of the soul are really a question of power" since "[t]here is no God like ordinary people."[96]

Only the words and actions of people can account for the peculiar shape of our toils and strain.

With the zoological articulation of madness, we appear to arrive at another point of convergence with colonized people, since, as Fanon describes:

> the terms the settler uses when he mentions the native are zoological terms. He speaks of the yellow man's reptilian motions, of the stink of the native quarter, of breeding swarms, of foulness, of spawn, of gesticulations. When the settler seeks to describe the native fully in exact terms he constantly refers to the bestiary. . . . Those hordes of vital statistics, those hysterical masses, those faces bereft of all humanity, those distended bodies which are like nothing on earth, that mob without beginning or end, those children who seem to belong to nobody, that laziness stretched out in the sun, that vegetative rhythm of life—all this forms part of the colonial vocabulary.[97]

Madness pictured as a descent into subhumanity has been buffered by the figures of "savagery" and primitive Blackness, which are the true "other side," the absolute nonhumanity or added to the latter to intensify the effect of alterity. Despite experiencing an obvious and sometimes dramatic fall in status, white people interned in segregated psychiatric hospitals in early colonial Africa were given games to play and meat to eat while the Natives did hard labor and ate grains and vegetables.[98] Debasement through madness is not a linear descent when other determinations affect one's status in the orders of human, animal, or alien. As Mab Segrest demonstrates throughout *Administrations of Lunacy*, the segregated Milledgeville asylum in Georgia could not have been built or expanded without its supply of slave labor, which made it the cheapest asylum to run in the world. While it is true that asylum inmates are debased in their status as mad, what does this say about the slave cleaning up after them or the Native or Black patient in the lowliest segregated wards? Madness, as a distorted reflection of a broken segment of humanity, can, to the bewilderment of those who have been stripped of their badge of humanity in its name, paradoxically and in a roundabout way, offer a remnant of humanity to those already denied it just as it can, at another time, describe the fall into savage animality and the ranks of the nonhuman.

Outside of participating in the legal and medical production of racial difference, psychiatry in the settler colony has a few limited but important roles. Just as capitalism does not begin anew wherever it is introduced but brings with it industries of variable organic compositions (machinery, managerial innovations, etc. in varying ratios to labor) accumulated over centuries, so too colonial authorities tend to introduce only those developed forms appropriate to their aims. In practice, this means that asylum psychiatry was rarely a primary mechanism of early colonial domination. Across Africa's colonial territories, only a handful of small asylums were ever constructed, generally for the purpose of treating mad Europeans, though the majority of their inmates were African. By 1960, Ghana, to take a typical example, had a single mental hospital in Accra.[99] The capacity and function of these asylums was materially limited and the conditions were abysmal, especially for the African patients. Incidents of death by infectious disease were very common, particularly for the Africans, who received meager rations and were forced to work on farms. As in Europe and the Americas, the asylum was accepted as a pressure release by newly proletarianized families in the towns and cities to relieve themselves of troublesome family members they could no longer care for. Very little thought was given to questions of treatment. Perhaps their most useful function was to allow colonial authorities to differentiate between captive populations, rationalize the state's repressive apparatus, and make the prison more manageable in the process.[100] It was a place to get rid of those who caused problems, but for whatever reason, couldn't readily be sent to prison.

Similar patterns can be seen in the US. In the antebellum period, asylum psychiatry was designed for whites, while Black and Native patients, especially in the North, were mainly positioned as an unfortunate complication or as an interesting point of comparison. Even though peonage was rampant in mental institutions in the postwar period, vagrancy laws, sharecropping and debt, and convict leasing made the carceral network the more effective mechanism of controlling the movements of and extracting value from "free" Black people. Similarly, the rise of the Industrial School/Residential system (along with missions, prisons, and the patriarchal structure of the reservation system itself) helps to account for why the Canton Asylum for Insane Indians (the only asylum designed specifically for Native American patients) was not widely replicated and treated as an auxiliary prison with few therapeutic pretenses. Brazil was something of an exception in this regard. Like Europe and the US, psychiatrists in Rio de Janeiro viewed the agricultural colony as a possible saving grace from overcrowding since it combined beneficent labor, open air, and was theoretically self-sustaining. Renowned as a major center for mental health care in the Americas, ships from around Latin America would carry cargo loads of madmen and dump them in Rio de Janeiro where they'd be picked up by the police and deposited in the asylum.[101] Similarly, slave owners would readily free insane (unproductive) slaves in the city, forfeiting financial and legal responsibility over them. Correspondingly, Black patients made up the majority of the asylum population. When the agricultural colonies were implemented post-abolition, overseers were reluctant to let go of their best laborers in order to sustain the operation, which means they were holding onto these "insane" captives performing forced labor indefinitely, making the therapeutic claims of a space "reminiscent of the colonial plantation" misguided at best.[102]

Psychiatrists in the early colonies did not have the tools nor the support to regularly employ commitment as a strategic mechanism beyond a small sphere of control, but that does not mean that they weren't implicated in the colonial structure. In the "Medicine and Colonialism" chapter of 1959's *A Dying Colonialism*, Fanon explains the "ambivalent attitude" towards doctors like himself in the colonies. Having arrived with the soldiers, the torturers, the policemen, the judges, the landowners and the rest, the colonial doctor may genuinely apply himself to the art of healing, but it won't matter. More specifically, the European doctors in the colonies, being settlers, have a vested interest in the maintenance of colonial society, principally in maintaining their property rights. Their direct complicity manifests itself in the form of false autopsy reports clearing colonial officials of foul play, in their work as expert consultants in the methods of torturing suspects, or when they give reports to colonial authorities of private medical information. They could never be perceived as neutral agents of healing; they represent nodes in a vast surveillance network, the handmaidens of torture, and sometimes even its direct perpetrators, like when psychiatrists in Algeria used ECT to weaken suspects' resistance to confession.[103]

Psy-professionals in repressive states made similar compromises in their situations. In Brazil, psychoanalysts were directly complicit with the military government of 1964, working with teams to torture political prisoners. One of these analysts, Amilcar Lobo, was publicly denounced by Marie Langer, but the story was buried when the International Psychoanalytical Association (IPA) and other psychoanalytic societies dismissed the accusations.[104] In Uruguay, psy-professionals handed over private medical documents to the authorities, hid evidence of torture, and even prescribed medication to exacerbate its effects.[105] There is only a difference in degree between such debased actions and those of American psychiatrists who train police or lawyers in how to recognize the signs of and use the diagnosis of "excited delirium"—a remarkable diagnosis that appears to have no clinical or historical reality outside of its forensic use in excusing extralegal police executions—or those who collaborate with the police in the implementation of untested drugs like ketamine in crisis situations because it is easier or beneficial to them (for research purposes or to sedate agitated patients), regardless of the enormous risk involved.[106] Mutual distrust and dishonesty form the core of a toxic therapeutic relation; to engage in such is to renounce the calling to render care and accept a role as the loyal handmaiden of whoever foots the bill. In their eternal bowing posture, they never have to look in the eyes of those whose lives they destroy.

A VIOLENT AWAKENING

When it comes to colonial, racist, or pro-slavery psychiatry, madness and violence share the common condition of being overdetermined and ambiguous. To deny their existence is to indulge in fantasy, but to assign them a single operative mode or a moral value enlarges a discrete element to the point of distortion. Violence is undoubtedly an indispensable tool for colonial authorities and racial terror, but this tends to produce a Manichean situation where violence serves as the common language between diametrically opposed parties. Madness is a predictable result of a reign of terror, but, whatever reality it may have in the lives of the afflicted, it's also a useful currency of regulation and the inevitable character mask of all possible resistance.

This is how Fanon comes to describe the process of decolonization as the encounter of two forces, mirroring closely the nineteenth century's presentation of a psychiatric relationship:

> Decolonization is the meeting of two forces, opposed to each other by their very nature, which in fact owe their originality to that sort of substantification which results from and is nourished by the situation in the colonies. Their first encounter was marked by violence and their existence together—that is to say the exploitation of the native by the settler—was carried on by dint of a great array of bayonets and cannons. The settler and the native are old acquaintances. In fact, the settler is right when he speaks of knowing 'them' well. For it is the settler who has brought the native into existence and who perpetuates his existence. The settler owes the fact of his very existence, that is to say, his property, to the colonial system. [107]

Violence is inscribed in a starkly descriptive account of a situation. There is no recommendation or celebration here, only brutal recognition:

> When the native is tortured, when his wife is killed or raped, he complains to no one. The oppressor's government can set up commissions of inquiry and of information daily if it wants to; in the eyes of the native, these commissions do not exist. . . . The native's work is to imagine all possible methods for destroying the settler. On the logical plane, the Manicheism of the settler produces a Manicheism of the native. To the theory of the 'absolute evil of the native' the theory of the 'absolute evil of the settler' replies. The appearance of the settler has meant in the terms of syncretism the death of the aboriginal society, cultural lethargy, and the petrification of individuals. For the native, life can only spring up again out of the rotting corpse of the settler. This then is the correspondence, term by term, between the two trains of reasoning. [108]

How could a practice of healing be implemented where such a vicious logic reigned supreme? The more involved Fanon became with the FLN and anticolonial resistance, the more pessimistic he became about the possibility of social therapy alone. Between 1954–1956, Fanon regularly went out in the field alone or with interns to observe local methods of conceiving of and treating madness, believing it vital to "to go from a position in which the supremacy of Western culture was evident, to one of cultural relativism,"[109] but, from the end of 1956 to the end of the decade, his optimism for cultural relativism within a colonial society ceded ground to commitment to an active resistance to colonial domination as the necessary condition for a therapeutic relation. Fanon came to a similar realization as Sylvia Marcos did decades later on the question of Indigenous "alternatives" to psychiatry. She held that Indigenous healing practices were neither an alternative to psychiatry (as if another item on the grocery store shelf) nor a "'return' to the past" but really a form of healing with its own values and history to which *psychiatry* is an alternative.[110] This is not a question of two equal "alternatives" on offer in the market, but of a hegemon consuming everything in its path. For his part, Fanon began harboring rebels at home and in the hospital, procuring needed medicines for networks of isolated militants, providing basic medical care for the wounded, and advising criminal suspects on the best ways to prepare the mind and body both for being tortured and for committing acts of violence against colonial administrators.[111]

As the war intensified, being both a revolutionary and a colonial psychiatrist became too intolerable to sustain. Fanon finally broke in December 1956 and submitted his resignation from his position at Blida-Joinville with his "Letter to the Resident Minister." He begins by asking, "what are a man's enthusiasm and care if daily reality is woven with lies, acts of cowardice and scorn for humankind? What are intentions if their embodiment is made impossible by an indigence of heart, sterility of spirit and hatred for this country's natives?"[112] Psychiatry as the "medical technique that sets out to enable individuals no longer to be foreign to their environment" was finally grasped as an impossible task in "a state of absolute depersonalization" where "lawlessness, inequality, and multiple daily murder of humanness were erected as legislative principles."[113] Years of the double experience as a psychiatrist and as a Black man in a colonial state troubled his ideal of psychiatry as the means of healing from alienation. In the colony, where psychiatry was part of the structure of alienation, where "normal" meant acquiescence to brutal domination and torture, "going mad" appeared more and more ambivalent a state.

In Fanon's lectures on "Social Psychopathology" in Tunis, which he gave in 1959 after fleeing Algeria, he characterized the mad person as "one who is 'foreign' to society. And society decides to rid itself of this anarchic element. Internment is the rejection, the sidelining of the patient. Society asks the psychiatrist to render the patient able again to reintegrate into society. The psychiatrist is the auxiliary of the police, the protector of society. . . . The social group decides to protect itself and shuts the patient away."[114] Madness is no longer just a state of alienation, but appears as an anarchic element the psychiatrist, *as an auxiliary cop*, seeks to defend society against.

Fanon's final works on madness and medicine, the chapter on medicine and colonialism in *A Dying Colonialism* (1959) and the final chapter of *The Wretched of the Earth* on "Colonial Wars and Mental Disorders" (1961) argue just that: the only hope for a psychiatry as disalienation in the colony—a "factory where madness is manufactured"[115]—is through the decolonizing revolution. All social relations are transformed through revolutionary struggle, so the only way to undermine "notions about 'native psychology' or of the 'basic personality'" is through a program of total disorder. The final chapter of *The Wretched of the Earth* on madness has been relegated to near invisibility in the shadow of the opening chapter on violence. This is a grave mistake: the two belong together, as bookends of a single thread tying political activity together directly to psychological states. The basic premise of Fanon's thought on violence is laid out quite clearly in the first pages of *The Wretched of the Earth*: the colonial encounter is founded and maintained in visceral acts of brutality and violence; murder, torture, and all manner of mutilations and humiliations are everyday parts of life. Surrounded—indeed, constituted—by violence, the colonized is fated to turn their own psychic frustrations and muscular tensions against themselves, animated by a hatred that offers only suicidal actions for an outlet[116] wherever resistance is foreclosed. With the threat of imminent death and imprisonment closing in with every step, the Native carries an implacable guilt divorced from the chain of cause-and-effect and dreams only of revenge.

Disalienation cannot, in such a situation, be disaggregated from overwhelming violence; this is what Fanon means when he says that "violence is a cleansing force" for it "frees the native from his inferiority complex and from his despair and inaction; it makes him fearless and restores his self-respect."[117] In a context defined by force, only a matching force can reveal the true state of things and open the path to another future. Colonialism's terrible diagnosis shocks and repulses many readers, as does Fanon's equally clear prognosis: the colonized will either appropriate the violence of the native-settler relation and turn it against the colonizer or be daily degraded by the twin violence of the police baton and their own minds in what amounts to a gradual annihilation. Fanon's theory of decolonial violence is equally about the practical political necessity of committing acts that will themselves be characterized as violent and destructive as it is about the psychological/existential necessity of appropriating overwhelming violence, directing it outwards towards its fount so as not to be extinguished by it:

> It has always happened in the struggle for freedom that such a people, formerly lost in an imaginary maze, a prey to unspeakable terrors yet happy to lose themselves in a dreamlike torment, such a people becomes unhinged, reorganizes itself, and in blood and tears gives birth to very real and immediate action. . . . After centuries of unreality, after having wallowed in the most outlandish phantoms, at long last the native, gun in hand, stands face to face with the only forces which contend for his life—the forces of colonialism. . . . The native discovers reality and transforms it into the pattern of his customs, into the practice of violence and into his plan for freedom.[118]

Fanon affirms, in no uncertain terms, that "liberation must, and can only, be achieved by force."[119] Wherever human interaction is determined by lines of force normalized and sedimented into daily interaction, the creation of a new "species," or the complete replacement of one form of human interaction with an entirely different one can only be the result of widespread breakdown and disorder.

Fanon's final words on madness and sanity in the last chapter of *The Wretched of the Earth* betray a level of therapeutic pessimism about the psychological outcome of the struggle against colonialism.[120] "We will have to bind up," he concedes, "the many, sometimes ineffaceable, wounds that the colonialist onslaught has inflicted on our people."[121]

Decolonization is neither the immediate unburdening of the conflicts that animate the struggle nor the magical smoothing of scars, but an "indispensable condition for the existence of men and women who are truly liberated,"[122] the struggle for which creates such "ineffaceable wounds." Throughout the war, before he went in exile in Tunisia, Fanon received many patients carrying these wounds at Blida-Joinville and whose case studies constitute the bulk of the final chapter. These patients are the victims of what Fanon calls "reactionary psychoses," by which he means, in less clinical terms, that "the events giving rise to the disorder are chiefly the bloodthirsty and pitiless atmosphere, the generalization of inhuman practices, and the firm impression that people have of being caught up in a veritable Apocalypse."[123] In a footnote, he recalls a young man who bombed a cafe, which was "a meeting place for notorious racists," who was later haunted by his action after meeting some friendly nationals of the colonial state. His thoughts swirled down into a vortex as he realized he may have inadvertently murdered some potential friends. Unable to shake the terror of vertigo, he became his own harshest judge, even though his country was now independent.[124] "In other words," writes Fanon, "we are forever pursued by our actions. Their ordering, their circumstances, and their motivation may perfectly well come to be profoundly modified a posteriori. This is merely one of the snares that history and its various influences sets for us. But can we escape becoming dizzy? And who can affirm that vertigo does not haunt the whole of existence?"[125]

The idea that *The Wretched of the Earth* argues that torture victims, children who murdered their French classmates, men who fell into a frenzy and killed French nationals, or militants and bombers would be miraculously healed through mass acts of violence deliberately ignores these more difficult complimentary passages. As Nigel Gibson and Roberto Beneduce put it their 2017 book *Frantz Fanon, Psychiatry and Politics*, in the midst of this intense and risky text testing the limits of the contemporary political imaginary, Fanon the psychiatrist "could not forget the wounded society on which the new nation would be built."[126] Violence is a dangerous eruption, a force with "a dimension of incalculability" that forms part of its strength and capacity for regenerative forms. It is simultaneously "that which was liable to save and that by which the peril penetrated the abode."[127] The energy and creative force unleashed in revolt—something readily called "madness"—is countered by the psychic and physical wounds the dominated carry in their blood and bones. Our mental and emotional states, our very sense of self, are tethered to history's tumults.

Notes

1. Bessie Head, *A Question of Power* (Long Grove: Waveland Press, 2017), 86.
2. Ivan Illich, "To Hell with Good Intentions," Conference on InterAmerican Student Projects (CIASP) in Cuernavaca, Mexico, April 20, 1968, https://www.uvm.edu/~jashman/CDAE195_ESCI375/To%20Hell%20with%20Good%20Intentions.pdf ; Ivan Illich, "The Seamy Side of Charity: From January 21, 1967," *America Magazine*, https://www.americamagazine.org/issue/100/seamy-side-charity.
3. Gordian Troeller and Claude Deffarge (dir.), *Im Namen des Fortschritts – Kein Respekt vor heiligen Kühen* [*No Respect for Sacred Cows*], Germany: ARD, 1976, https://www.youtube.com/watch?v=epD932IBF_Y&t=1397s.
4. On the "abandonados," see *Human Rights & Mental Health* (Washington, DC: Mental Disability Rights International, 2000), 36, https://www.driadvocacy.org/wp-content/uploads/Human-Rights-Mental-Health-English.pdf.
5. I learned of this historical coincidence through Adriane Hunsberger Gelpi, "Priority Setting for HIV and Mental Health in Mexico: Historical, Quantitative and Ethical Perspectives," PhD diss., Harvard University, 2014, https://dash.harvard.edu/bitstream/handle/1/11744449/Gelpi_gsas.harvard_0084L_11290.pdf.
6. See François Dosse, *Gilles Deleuze & Félix Guattari: Intersecting Lives*, trans. Deborah Glassman (New York: Columbia University Press, 2010), 336. Though the Network officially formed in 1975, its seeds were planted in a meeting organized by Elkaïm in the Bronx in 1974, in which Guattari, Giovanni Jervis, and Robert Castel participated.
7. Susana Caló, "Network of Alternatives to Psychiatry # 0 – Project presentation," Chaosmosemedia, May 2021, https://chaosmosemedia.net/en/2021/05/15/network-of-alternatives-to-psychiatry-o-project-presentation/.
8. "Statement of Purpose Concerning the International Network," in David Cooper, *The Language of Madness* (London: Penguin Books, 1978), 166–167.
9. Robert Castel and Mony Elkaïm, "Excerpts from the Introductory Statement to the Network, Trieste, September 1977," *State and Mind: People Look at Psychology* 6, no. 2 (Winter 1977): 15–16. Courtesy of the Oskar Diethelm Library, DeWitt Institute for the History of Psychiatry, Weill Cornell Medical College.
10. See Francisco Javier Dosil Mancilla, "La Locura Como Acción Política. El Movimiento Antipsiquiátrico en México," *Revista Electrónica de Psicología Iztacala* 22, no. 1 (2019): 634–635, https://www.medigraphic.com/pdfs/epsicologia/epi-2019/epi191zf.pdf.
11. "Insistimos," *Manicomios y prisiones* (México: Red Ediciones, 1983), 8.
12. Sylvia Marcos, "Introducción al Primer Encuentro Latinoamericano Alternativas a la Psiquiatría," *Manicomios y prisiones* (México: Red Ediciones, 1983), 19.
13. Marcos, "Introducción al Primer Encuentro Latinoamericano Alternativas a la Psiquiatría," 13–14.
14. Robert Cover, "Violence and the Word," *The Yale Law Journal* 95 (1986): 1607, http://digitalcommons.law.yale.edu/fss_papers/2708.
15. Walter Benjamin, "The Critique of Violence," in *Selected Writings, Volume 1, 1913–1926*, ed. Marcus Bullock and Michael W. Jennings (Cambridge: Harvard University Press, 1996), 241.
16. Amy Goodman and Juan González, "Black Panther Bobby Seale Was Bound and Gagged at His 1968 DNC Protest Trial," *Democracy Now!*, August 28 2018, https://truthout.org/video/black-panther-party-chair-bobby-seale-describes-his-trial-after-1968-dnc-protest/.
17. Leonora Carrington, *Down Below* (New York: New York Review of Books, 1988), 39–41.
18. Carrington, *Down Below*, 26.
19. This may play a role in determining which directions treatment research pursues or the criteria for effectiveness, but, beyond that, I am pointing out a symbolic unity that is expressed in material treatments rather than a material unity connecting each to actual effects on the body.
20. Daniel Paul Schreber, *Memoirs of My Nervous Illness* (New York: New York Review of Books, 2000), 139.

21. Nicholas Tromans, "The Psychiatric Sublime," in *The Art of the Sublime*, ed. Nigel Llewellyn and Christine Riding, Tate Research Publication, January 2013, https://www.tate.org.uk/art/research-publications/the-sublime/nicholas-tromans-the-psychiatric-sublime-r1129548.

22. Doerner, *Madmen and Bourgeoisie*, 74.

23. William Pargeter, *Observations on Maniacal Disorders* (Reading: Smart and Cowslade, 1792), 49.

24. Pargeter, *Observations on Maniacal Disorders*, 50–51.

25. Robert J. Richard, "Rhapsodies on a Cat-Piano, or Johann Christian Reil and the Foundations of Romantic Psychiatry," *Critical Inquiry* 24, no. 3 (Spring 1998): 702.

26. Richard, "Rhapsodies on a Cat-Piano," 721–722. See Doerner, *Madmen and the Bourgeoisie*, 205 for an even longer list of recommended methods of torture.

27. See, for example, Nancy Tomes, *A Generous Confidence: Thomas Story Kirkbride and the Art of Asylum-keeping, 1840–1883* (Cambridge: Cambridge University Press, 1984), 30.

28. Antonin Artaud, "ELECTROSHOCK," in *Artaud Anthology*, ed. Jack Hirschman (San Francisco: City Lights, 1965), 185.

29. Michel Foucault, *Psychiatric Power: Lectures at the Collège de France, 1973–74*, ed. Jacques Lagrange and trans. Graham Burchell (New York: Palgrave Macmillan, 2006), 7.

30. Quoted in Foucault, *Psychiatric Power*, 8.

31. Foucault, *Psychiatric Power*, 7–8.

32. Richard, "Rhapsodies on a Cat-Piano," 720–722.

33. Quoted in Richard, "Rhapsodies on a Cat-Piano," 714.

34. Laure Murat, *The Man Who Thought He Was Napoleon: Toward a Political History of Madness* (Chicago: University of Chicago Press, 2014), 37.

35. Quoted in Murat, *The Man Who Thought He Was Napoleon*, 42.

36. Brendan Pierson, "D.C. Circuit Overturns FDA Ban on Shock Device for Disabled Students," *Reuters*, July 2021, https://www.reuters.com/legal/litigation/dc-circuit-overturns-fda-ban-shock-device-disabled-students-2021-07-06/.

37. Frantz Fanon and François Tosquelles, "Indications of Electroconvulsive Therapy within Institutional Therapies," in Frantz Fanon, *Alienation and Freedom*, ed. and comp. Jean Khalfa and Robert J.C. Young, trans. Steven Corcoran (London: Bloomsbury Academic, 2018), 292–294.

38. Marie Langer, *From Vienna to Managua: Journey of a Psychoanalyst*, trans. Margaret Hooks (London: Free Association Books, 1989), 230.

39. Langer, *From Vienna to Managua*, 76; see also Nancy Caro Hollander, "Introduction to the English Translation," in Marie Langer, *Motherhood and Sexuality*, trans. Nancy Caro Hollander (New York: The Guilford Press, 1992), 6–7.

40. Langer, *From Vienna to Managua*, 66.

41. Langer, *From Vienna to Managua*, 78.

42. Langer, *From Vienna to Managua*, 78.

43. Langer, *From Vienna to Managua*, 89–90.

44. Jonathan D. Ablard, *Madness in Buenos Aires: Patients, Psychiatrists, and the Argentine State 1880–1983* (Calgary: University of Calgary Press, 2008), 23.

45. For general knowledge of Argentine psychoanalysis and its relationship to psychiatry, I rely heavily upon Mariano Ben Plotkin, *Freud in the Pampas: The Emergence and Development of a Psychoanalytic Culture in Argentina* (Stanford: Stanford University Press, 2001) and to a lesser extent on Andrew Lakoff, *Pharmaceutical Reason: Knowledge and Value in Global Psychiatry* (Cambridge: Cambridge University Press: 2005). Langer was among the six who founded the APA, and the only woman.

46. Jonathan D. Ablard, "Authoritarianism, Democracy and Psychiatric Reform in Argentina, 1943–83," *History of Psychiatry* 14, no. 3 (2003): 364.

47. Ablard, "Authoritarianism, Democracy and Psychiatric Reform in Argentina, 1943–83," 365.

48. Langer, *From Vienna to Managua*, 112.

49. "Declaration of the Plataforma Group to Mental Health Workers," in Langer, *From Vienna to Managua*, 246.

50. "Declaration of the Plataforma Group to Mental Health Workers," 246.

51. See Nancy Caro Hollander, "Afterword," in Marie Langer, *Motherhood and Sexuality*, trans. Nancy Caro Hollander (New York: Guilford Press, 1992), 274–277; and Langer, *From Vienna to Managua*, 121–123.

52. Langer, *From Vienna to Managua*, 167.

53. Langer, *From Vienna to Managua*, 181.

54. Langer, *From Vienna to Managua*, 161.

55. For a clandestine psychiatric organization operating under an authoritarian state in Europe, see Victor Aparicio Basauri, "The Critical Movements and the Influence of Franco Basaglia and 'Democratic Psychiatry,'" in *Basaglia's International Legacy: from Asylum to Community*, ed. Tom Burns and John Foot (Oxford: Oxford University Press, 2020), on the Psychiatric Coordinator, which was active between 1971–1975 in the final years of Franco's rule in Spain.

56. Nancy Caro Hollander, *Love in a Time of Hate: Liberation Psychology in Latin America* (New Brunswick: Rutgers University Press 1997), 87.

57. Hollander, *Love in a Time of Hate*, 102–103.

58. Langer, *From Vienna to Managua*, 151.

59. Langer, *From Vienna to Managua*, 217.

60. Peter Davis, dir. *Anatomy of Violence*, Villon Films, 1967. Kanopy.

61. David Cooper, "Introduction," in *The Dialectics of Liberation* (London: Verso, 2015), epub.

62. Sarah Marks, "Dialectics of Liberation," *Hidden Persuaders*, October 25, 2017, http://www7.bbk.ac.uk/hiddenpersuaders/blog/dialectics-of-liberation/#_edn6.

63. R.D. Laing, "The Obvious," in *The Dialectics of Liberation* (London: Verso, 2015), epub.

64. Stokely Carmichael, "Black Power," in *The Dialectics of Liberation* (London: Verso, 2015), epub.

65. Peter Davis, dir. *Anatomy of Violence*, Villon Films, 1967. Kanopy.

66. See especially Thomas Szasz, "Chattel Slavery and Psychiatric Slavery," in *Psychiatric Slavery* (Syracuse: Syracuse University Press, 1977), 133–139.

67. Davis, "Anatomy of Violence."

68. Hussein Abdilahi Bulhan, *Frantz Fanon and the Psychology of Oppression* (New York: Plenum Press, 1985), 27.

69. Bulhan, *Frantz Fanon and the Psychology of Oppression*, 28.

70. Frantz Fanon and François Tosquelles, "Indications of Electroconvulsive Therapy within Institutional Therapies," in Frantz Fanon, *Alienation and Freedom*, ed. and comp. Jean Khalfa and Robert J.C. Young, trans. Steve Corcoran (London: Bloomsbury Academic, 2018), 296.

71. Frantz Fanon, *Black Skin, White Masks* (London: Pluto Press, 2008), 4.

72. Bulhan, *Frantz Fanon and the Psychology of Oppression*, 214.

73. Jean Khalfa, "Fanon, Revolutionary Psychiatrist," in Frantz Fanon, *Alienation and Freedom*, ed. and comp. Jean Khalfa and Robert J.C. Young, trans. Steve Corcoran (London: Bloomsbury Academic, 2018), 189.

74. Alice Cherki, *Frantz Fanon: A Portrait* (Ithaca: Cornell University Press, 2006), 69.

75. Cherki, *Frantz Fanon: A Portrait*, 69.

76. Fanon, *Alienation and Freedom*, 405.

77. Fanon, *Alienation and Freedom*, 368.

78. Fanon, *Alienation and Freedom*, 367–368.

79. Fanon, *A Dying Colonialism*, 121.

80. Fanon, *Alienation and Freedom*, 362.

81. Fanon, *A Dying Colonialism*, 126.

82. Cherki, *Frantz Fanon: A Portrait*, 69–70.

83. Fanon, *Alienation and Freedom*, 407.

84. Fanon, *Alienation and Freedom*, 406.

85. Fanon, *Alienation and Freedom*, 407.
86. Fanon, *Alienation and Freedom*, 408.
87. Bulhan, *Frantz Fanon and the Psychology of Oppression*, 90–92.
88. Wendy Gonaver, *The Peculiar Institution and the Making of Modern Psychiatry* (Chapel Hill: University of North Carolina Press, 2019), 7.
89. Gonaver, *The Peculiar Institution*, 7.
90. Segrest, *Administrations of Lunacy*, 36–37.
91. Gonaver, *The Peculiar Institution*, 31.
92. Bonaventure Soh Bejeng Ndikung, "Ultrasanity: On Madness, Sanitation, Anti-Psychiatry, and Resistance," in *Ultrasanity: On Madness, Sanitation, Anti-Psychiatry, and Resistance* (Berlin: Archive Books, 2020), 25.
93. Head, *A Question of Power*, 6–7.
94. Ndikung, "Ultrasanity," 28.
95. Head, *A Question of Power*, 145.
96. Head, *A Question of Power*, 212.
97. Frantz Fanon, *The Wretched of the Earth* (New York: Grove Press, 1963), 42–43.
98. Jock McCulloch, *Colonial Psychiatry and 'the African Mind'* (Cambridge: Cambridge University Press, 1995), 15.
99. McCulloch, *Colonial Psychiatry*, 35.
100. McCulloch, *Colonial Psychiatry*, 41–42.
101. Manuella Meyer, *Reasoning against Madness: Psychiatry and the State in Rio de Janeiro, 1830–1944* (Rochester: University of Rochester Press, 2017), 83.
102. Meyer, *Reasoning against Madness*, 86.
103. Fanon, *A Dying Colonialism*, 138.
104. Aline Rubin, "Collusion with Torture – A Case from Brazil," *Hidden Persuaders*, February 6, 2017, http://www7.bbk.ac.uk/hiddenpersuaders/blog/torture-brazil/.
105. Hollander, *Love in a Time of Hate*, 107.
106. Minnesota, where I live, has been the site of multiple high-profile scandals involving each in the past few years, especially in connection to the Hennepin County Medical Center in downtown Minneapolis. See Andy Mannix, "Minneapolis Police Department Still Teaching Controversial 'Excited Delirium' Syndrome—despite Claiming It Had Stopped," *Star Tribune*, February 12, 2022, https://www.startribune.com/minneapolis-police-still-teaching-excited-delirium-syndrome-despite-claiming-it-stopped/600146112/; Andy Mannix, "Patients sedated by ketamine were enrolled in Hennepin Healthcare study," *Star Tribune*, June 23, 2018, https://www.startribune.com/patients-sedated-by-ketamine-were-enrolled-in-hennepin-healthcare-study/486363071/. The same hospital reports some of the highest uses of medical force in the country and faced protests from employees in 2021: Andy Mannix, "Hennepin Healthcare Workers Demand Hospital Reduce Use of 'Medical Force' on Patients," *Star Tribune*, May 23, 2021, https://www.startribune.com/hennepin-healthcare-workers-demand-hospital-reduce-use-of-medical-force-on-patients/600060524/?refresh=true.
107. Fanon, *Wretched of the Earth*, 36.
108. Fanon, *Alienation and Freedom*, 92–93.
109. Fanon, *Alienation and Freedom*, 363.
110. Sylvia Marcos, "Introducción al Primer Encuentro Latinamericano de Alternativas a la Psiquiatría," in *Manicomios y prisiones* (México: Red Ediciones, 1983), 18.
111. Bulhan, *Frantz Fanon and the Psychology of Oppression*, 237–238.
112. Fanon, *Alienation and Freedom*, 434.
113. Fanon, *Alienation and Freedom*, 434.
114. Fanon, *Alienation and Freedom*, 517.
115. Achille Mbembe, "Frantz Fanon and the Politics of Viscerality," John Hope Franklin Humanities Institute at Duke University, April 27, 2016, https://www.youtube.com/watch?v=lg_BEodNaEA.
116. Fanon, *Wretched of the Earth*, 52.
117. Fanon, *Wretched of the Earth*, 94.

118. Fanon, *Wretched of the Earth*, 56–58.
119. Fanon, *Wretched of the Earth*, 73.
120. Nigel C. Gibson and Roberto Beneduce, *Frantz Fanon, Psychiatry and Politics* (Lanham: Rowman and Littlefield, 2017), 233.
121. Fanon, *Wretched of the Earth*, 243.
122. Fanon, *Wretched of the Earth*, 310.
123. Fanon, *Wretched of the Earth*, 251.
124. On this, see Gibson and Beneduce, *Frantz Fanon, Psychiatry and Politics*, 233–235.
125. Fanon, *Wretched of the Earth*, 253.
126. Fanon, *Wretched of the Earth*, 232.
127. Achille Mbembe, "Fanon's Pharmacy," *Necropolitics* (Durham: Duke University Press, 2018), 129.

CONCLUSION:

ILLNESS AND ECONOMY

Confronted with the form of unreality our broken world assumes, psychiatry can function as a soporific tranquilizer in a conspiracy of medicine (caught in Kurelek's choice between a malevolent persecution and a benevolent conspiracy), or as a means of rousing oneself and the other from our dream of ourselves. That is to say, it can function as a process of demystification. Whatever uses it may be put to, psychiatry orients itself around the question of alienation. Even in the darkest ward cells, for the lonely nurse driving all day delivering pills to isolated subsidized apartments, or on the outdated computer screen of the doctor who talked to you for two minutes before shuffling you out of the room. The field, and everyone in it, is determined by the contradiction between disalienation and separation, between the openness of mutual care and guardianship's leash, between the familiarity of close relationships and the protective walls of custodialism. I have called projects "radical" that realized disalienation is an ongoing process in an ethico-political struggle rather than the automatic result of technical development. There is, however, no substantial essence dividing psychiatry from its radical iterations, as the very same contradictions are at play regardless of the approach. To conclude this book, we will briefly examine psychiatric currents that pushed the field to its conceptual limits by redefining the limits of biology and economy. First, those that tried to short circuit all contradictions by essentializing illness and elevating it as a racialized universal (the absolute conspiracy); and finally, a group that exploded the category of illness to apply it to the economy as a whole (demystification as the ultimate aspiration to the point of self-destruction).

NIHILIST PSYCHIATRY AND THE RACIAL UNIVERSAL

> Is it my fault that I am born this way, and that they do this to me?
> —Anonymous German woman quoted boarding a Gekrat bus on the
> way to a euthanasia site[1]

Racial hygiene is the dream of the final cure. It is the attempt at an absolute resolution of the social problem of madness. We've already encountered the basic building blocks of racial hygiene throughout this book: the objectification of the recipients of psychiatric administration into a problem of chronicity; the objectification of the problem of alienation into the question of aliens; the growth of eugenics and its productive encounter with mental hygiene; and the development of a technical network capable of widespread detection, detention, sterilization, and killing. Under racial hygiene, these elements were formalized into a biological explanatory schema and pattern of response implemented most infamously and thoroughly in Nazi Germany, but, as we shall see, racial hygiene, or aspects of it, made significant inroads around the world.

German psychiatry's peculiarities are best understood considering its belatedness in comparison with its neighbors to the West. Like other European states, Germany's multiple states sequestered the nonworking poor in eclectic facilities of greater or lesser differentiation (depending on the state), but, unlike the others, it never produced a national humanist hero like Pinel at its point of origin. Where psychiatrists working in the anglophone or francophone tradition could not evade the question of emancipation in their late-eighteenth-century origin stories, Germany's activity in the same period is marked by the economism and spatialization of territorial mercantilism born from desperation and political fracture, ultimately failing to produce a "chainbreaker." Absolutist princes competed to extract the greatest value from small tracts of land, necessitating the coercive mobilization of all available hands and the strict policing of possible obstructions. Madness' danger was therefore emphasized far above the public duty to care for the poor, marginalized outsider to a degree unmatched elsewhere; this explains why one of the few technical innovations in Germany was the *Doll-* or *Narrenkisten*, boxes that completely immobilized the madman's body for transport, and why "institutional regulations prohibited the release of the insane from their chains even in the event of a fire because of the public danger they presented."[2] Perhaps due to Germany's lagging, protracted industrialization, asylum physicians preserved a greater degree of the patriarchal protectionism of the absolutist states into a changing political-economic era than was present in the rapid developments of England or the Revolution in France.[3] In practice, this meant that the moral and ethical ideals of moral treatment, however flimsy or short-lived they may have been in reality elsewhere, were dismissed as unrealistic along with its attendant optimistic spirit by a domineering economic rationality seeking to determine the fitness or unfitness of populations normally excluded from labor. Correspondingly, conditions broadly remained the same or worsened through bourgeois revolution and industrialization alike as reforms were limited by the conservative devotion to safety and economy.

In terms of theory, Germany is again an exception. The first original, progressive works to emerge from the region were written in relative isolation from asylums by men from other medical fields, like Reil (a surgeon and ophthalmologist) or even theology like J. C. A. Heinroth (a military physician who studied theology), giving them a distinctly literary and philosophical—often fantastical—character. There is a poetic truth contained in the fact that the national tradition responsible for coining the word "*Psychiatrie*" held itself from the start at an enormous remove from the social conditions it made pronouncements about in its numerous journals. Moral theories stemming from the philosophy of Immanuel Kant treated the problem of delusion as the result of logically rational deductions from false sets of premises. Not far off, Christian psychiatrists like Heinroth portrayed lunacy as the consequence of sin. He equated the insane with Hegel's "rabble," seeing little more in madmen than a distillation of the incoherency and idiocy of the mob, construed as the congenitally weak mass threatening society.[4] Similarly, for Carl Wilhelm Ideler, the psychogenesis of unreason could be in man's unfettered drives and passions. In the normal man, the passions balance one another and are tamed by the knowing hand of reason, but let one of these drives develop too far and you may find yourself enveloped in the impenetrable husk of a florid madness, which is why Ideler joined the chorus of "mad doctors" warning society that madmen and revolutionaries were united in an "unconcealed striving to destroy all order and coherence of the situation."[5] Incredibly, these diverse abstract pronouncements about the nature of madness all tended to agree on the inherent dangerousness and alterity of insanity (especially when figured as "idiocy") as well as the value of torture to contain, to train, or to heal the insane pauper.

Idealist, romantic, and psychological doctrines retained hegemony until the 1860s, when a younger group based in new university clinics rallied around the battle cry of their leader, Wilhelm Griesinger: "mental illnesses are brain diseases." Under this glorious banner, they declared: out with groundless moral and religious grandstanding, in with pathological anatomy and clinical observation in wards attached to universities or in the heart of the city. No more bad conscience and long nights after applying restraints or torture; the "Somaticists" looked forward to the tranquil sleep that would come with applying treatments derived solely from the mechanical laws of the human body in its natural state. Griesinger's followers somaticized the soul by framing it as the "the sum of all cerebral states," which were, in turn, the products of the "immense reflex apparatus," the brain.[6] Griesinger himself was genuinely motivated by the extension of empathy to the crestfallen. His theory did not rest on a strict determinism between physical and psychic mechanisms, but rather opened each up to a dialectical and indefinite process; if he mechanized the soul, he also seems to have ensouled the mechanism. Whatever his intent, the engineers of the somatic turn who followed him took up his battle cry as a call to subordinate the mental functions to biological reflexes, promising a new era marked by the technical resolution of psychic distress and alienation. At first, this was wrapped in the guise of a progressive impulse, even as it mechanized the soul: being scarcely more complex than a giant clock, the mad know not what they do; to torture or restrain the insane for impulsive acts is tantamount to striking an animal for bad table manners. Over time, neuropsychiatrists like Emil Flechsig (Daniel Paul Schreber's psychiatrist) progressively stripped whatever human qualities were still attached to the surface layer of patients in experimental clinics, leaving only an epidermal sheath wrapped around a misfiring machine and the brief moratorium on gratuitous violence was lifted. Meal times became force-feedings for resistant patients who were watched 24-7 under a strict principle of constant surveillance for the subtlest variations and aberrations. If the treatment failed to have the desired effect, they were simply sent away to the asylum as a chronic patient, more hopeless than ever. Once they were dead, their corpses were traded to universities eager for a constant supply of fresh cadavers to verify their anatomical hypotheses.[7] Even the small successes of clinical psychiatry seemed to prove to its leaders that there was a subclass of patients, the chronics, who were beyond help, whose idle vegetation was supported by precious state funds.

Throughout this book, I have tried to show how the contradictions of psychiatry in a capitalist society tends to create a surplus of chronicity. We have seen manifold responses to this problem: psychiatrists like da Silveira or Basaglia self-reflexively construed chronicity and the attendant environmental or treatment degradations as a problem related to psychiatry's institutional organization and its structural position within the economic order (facing the contradiction head on as the main issue at hand); mental hygiene and positive eugenics turned towards prophylaxis in the hopes of preventing chronicity from forming (reducing the surplus to as small a category as possible by dramatically expanding the field's points of contact with pathology); the faithful placed their hope in an always-forthcoming technical or theoretical revolution that would finally show them the way (maintaining chronicity in rotten conditions today so that tomorrow they may be saved). Racial hygiene is a more proficient abstract machine that works by ontologically binding typologies of mental illness and disability to the status of chronic and hereditary degeneration and subsequently locating these problems as inherent biological features of subpopulations defined by race.

In 1905, Alfred Ploetz, along with the psychiatrist Ernst Rüdin, the lawyer Anastasius Nordenholz, and the anthropologist Richard Thurnwald, founded the Society for Racial Hygiene [Gesellschaft für Rassenhygiene] in Berlin. At its early stage, the beliefs and concerns of the racial hygienists—as historian Robert Proctor recounts them— were no different from those of pessimistic asylum superintendents or eugenics proponents around the world: "the declining birthrate and the growing number of mentally ill in state institutions . . . the importance of population growth for maintaining national strength and the links between 'racial fitness' and national efficiency." Alfred Grotjahn linked racial hygiene with the "rationalization of sexual life." Erwin

Baur spoke of the "rational economy in human life." Racial hygienists worried that feminism and World War I had destroyed the family;
racial hygiene was proposed as one way to reverse this destruction.[8]
The "race" of most racial hygiene discourse was still a human race
construed as a linear range, i.e., the developmental universal we encountered in the last chapter that made the civilized white man the
benevolent and cultured "father" and the native or disabled person the
helpless child. Even within madness itself, they subscribed to a linear
developmental schema in Albert Zeller's popular somatic theory of the
"unitary psychosis" [*Einheitspsychose*] that understood the variegated
types of madness to be expressions of the temporal progression of a
single disease. The melancholic was only partly mad, but on their way
to total dementia and idiocy. Lacking a substantial reform movement to
look to, German psychiatrists never had much of a local counterweight
to patriarchal management and economic pessimism. Come World
War I and the environmental and economic devastation it wrought
in psychiatric hospitals—it's possible that 30 percent of the prewar
German asylum population died from neglect and hunger during the
war[9]—their pessimism took on the unvarying visage of fate. Only the
prospect of saving money convinced Weimar Republic bureaucrats to
finally implement some social reforms including, above all, a network
of outpatient clinics and Hermann Simon's work therapy. Simon was
the most influential German social psychiatrist of his era (1867–1947).
His emphasis on the importance of occupational therapy as a way to
activate dormant potentialities even reached Tosquelles and others at
Saint-Alban. And yet, his professional development was sadly typical.
Since "not all patients were capable of rolling cigars, weaving baskets,
running errands or answering the telephone," the work therapy programs tended to leave behind "a quantity of 'incurables' languishing
in unproductive hebetude," further concretizing a subclass of chronics
who, economically speaking, were "useless."[10] By the 1930s, Simon too
had lost hope in this subclass and, like so many of his colleagues, wondered why the healthy should have to pay for them to simply exist.[11]

Through combining these pessimistic economic insights with
Bénédict Morel and others' theory of hereditary degeneration and
Mendelian genetics, German psychiatrists chipped away at environmental causation on the road to therapeutic nihilism. With this last
remaining impurity in the perfect tautological circle defining the

incurable smoothed over, asylum populations could finally appear as purely inhuman stock: they lived inhuman, filthy lives not on account of any specific decision, but due to an inherent congenital defect. Nazism wholeheartedly embraced this position, making it central to their political ideology. Hitler was "the great doctor of the German people" and his party's activity was "nothing but 'applied biology.'" The National Socialist Physicians' League described this shift as clearly as possible when they declared as one of their principles "the primacy of national biology over national economy."[12] They may have medicalized chronicity to a higher degree than elsewhere, but it's important to stress first that Nazi ideology worked here as an intensifier of a discourse long present in psychiatry, and second that German doctors and economists were not at all alone in worrying about this "useless" subclass. As we've seen, it is produced wherever capitalism and psychiatry exist together. Once this problem had been determined to pertain to a population's biological being, states in the twentieth century attempted to resolve it by means of three methods: sequestration and segregation to prevent miscegenation (the propagation of degenerates and racial hybrids), permanent prevention of the same through sterilization, and, in the case of Germany, elimination.

Segregation is the least controversial of these, since institutional psychiatry has always been premised on some level of segregation. In its synthesis with eugenics and racial hygiene, when defect is less a learned engagement with the world and more an attribute of the blood, protecting the quality of the biological pool meant preventing intercourse between the healthy and weak. In South Africa, eugenicists expressed special concern around the threat of "poor whiteism," for such a class (and their commingling with Africans in the slums) existentially threatened the white supremacist state's elevation of race solidarity over all others. In the eyes of the eugenicist, the "emergence of a healthy white labouring class" therefore required effective segregation carried out by the state.[13] In US immigration policy, race and chronicity have walked in unison since 1882, when the Chinese Exclusion Act and the Immigration Act barring "convicts," "lunatics," and "those likely to become a public charge" were passed within a few months of one another. Alfred Binet's intelligence scale—an early IQ test—offered administrators a regular measure for systematically classifying mental deficiency and was quickly taken up by schools for separating low-scoring children into special education classes or institutions for the "feeble-minded" and by the military for weeding out the unfit. In the twentieth century, racial restrictions on immigration have included literacy tests or, as was the case for the 1924 Johnson-Reed Act that placed caps on both Southern and Eastern European and Jewish immigration while effectively halting Asian immigration, were justified on the grounds that some populations scored lower on intelligence tests.

Fear of miscegenation and defective genes was inextricably intertwined with fear of sexual depravity and disease in the ambiguous discourse of "hygiene." Argentina's 1876 Ley de Inmigración, for instance "prohibited the admission of anyone suffering from contagious disease, those unable to work, the demented, beggars, criminals, and those over sixty years of age unaccompanied by their families."[14] It's scarcely possible to completely extricate the biological, racial, and mental elements of restrictions on movement based on the principle of "hygiene" where blanket immigration and internal population restrictions blend the *cordon sanitaire* and the racial ghetto so that they appear like identical twins. Few states have demonstrated this as directly as Australia with its so-called "White Australia Policy" beginning with the Immigration Restriction Act 1901 simultaneously barring:

(a) Any person who when asked to do so by an officer fails to write out at dictation and sign in the presence of the officer a passage of fifty words in length in an European language directed by the officer;
(b) any person likely in the opinion of the Minister or of an officer to become a charge upon the public or upon any public or charitable institution;
(c) any idiot or insane person;
(d) any person suffering from an infectious or contagious disease of a loathsome or dangerous character;
(e) any person who has within three years been convicted of an offence, not being a mere political offence, and has been sentenced to imprisonment for one year or longer therefor, and has not received a pardon;
(f) any prostitute or person living on the prostitution of others.[15]

Because, as Alison Bashford points out, these restrictions were put in place "at the moment of nation-formation in the Australian instance,

. . . the connections between racial hygiene, national hygiene and the constitution of a white civic body by exclusion (as well as selective inclusion) [were] both formative and tight."[16]

Exclusionary policies like these (or others like marriage restrictions) could only ever have limited efficacy. Degeneracy concealed itself in the swelling masses like the diseases it was compared to, spreading easily, but hard to detect. More extreme measures would need to be taken to prevent the unchecked propagation of any more "generations of imbeciles."[17] Foremost among methods of negative eugenics was sterilization. In Europe, Switzerland and Denmark passed sterilization laws in 1928 and '29, respectively, preceding the Nazis by years.[18] Many regimes that otherwise embraced eugenic ideals resisted these more extreme measures. This was the case for eugenics proponents in Latin America who largely failed to wrest control over the process of reproduction from the Catholic Church and the broader scientific community.[19] Veracruz in Mexico stood alone in implementing sterilization laws, and only for a brief time. US policy was a guiding light for global sterilization policy (and its effective, though only implicit, racialization[20]) in the early twentieth century after Indiana passed the first such law globally in 1907, which targeted criminals, the mentally ill, idiots, and rapists.[21] More than thirty states would come to pass similar laws to control the reproduction of "defectives" and other degenerate classes, sterilizing close to 70,000 individuals, though the practice continued past this initial phase in welfare programs for Native and Black women, who were sterilized in even larger numbers.[22] To this day, courts can still mandate it as a condition of release for prisoners or in ICE facilities.[23]

Hitler and his cabinet passed the Law for the Prevention of Offspring with Hereditary Diseases [*Gesetz zur Verhütung erbkranken Nachwuchses*] within a few months of taking office, in July 1933, which took effect in January of 1934. The law was based in part on the voluntary sterilization policy of the Weimar Republic and the American model sterilization law, but it reached much further than any previous laws in its dual aim, as a contemporary commentary put it, to "purify the body of the people and completely obliterate pathological genetic tendencies" and to "irrevocably secure the primacy and authority of the state over life, marriage, and the family as a field of activity."[24] In order to effectively "dry up the springs that feed the torrent of defective and degenerate protoplasm,"[25] as American eugenicist Charles Davenport put it, the Nazis established a "genetic health court" [*Erbgesundheitsgericht*], which heard requests for and could ultimately mandate sterilizations if the defendant had one or more "genetic" illnesses outlined by the law: "feeblemindedness, schizophrenia, manic-depressive insanity, genetic epilepsy, Huntington's chorea, genetic blindness or deafness, or severe alcoholism."[26] Requests arrived in droves from "physicians of the public health service or, for patients and prisoners, by directors of hospitals, homes, and prisons," resulting in nearly 400,000 procedures largely carried out against the will of the law's victims (individuals could still apply for their own sterilization under the law), the great majority of whom were labeled "feeble-minded" and "schizophrenic."[27] Extending the procedure to Jews or other racially defined groups was considered and experimented with—notably in the case of the secret extralegal experiment with sterilizing 500 so-called "Rhineland bastards," offspring of Black French occupation troops and native Germans[28]—but ultimately not generalized or legalized. This helps to underscore that coercive birth control measures were, in terms of public law, aimed at mental or physical "defectives," rather than explicitly at racial groups, so that when politicians in white supremacist states like South Africa or Australia proposed sterilization policies, they usually imagined institutionalized people and poor whites as their primary target groups.[29] Most of these proposals failed or were granted a relatively limited reach.[30]

Japan's path to national genetic purity is closely tied to Germany's. During the Meiji Restoration, imperial leaders looked to Germany for inspiration politically and medically. Naturally, psychiatrists imported Griesinger and Flechsig's clinical model that was dominant at the time, though it failed to escape the gravity of the universities in the largest cities where it was concentrated. As it rose to dominance as a colonial power following the colonization of Okinawa in 1874, Japan attempted to export this model, using their colony in Korea to test strategies to more fully involve a resistant population into psychiatric services,[31] but with only limited success. As in Germany, psychiatrists emphasized acute treatment grounded in biological ideology over institutional or social reform, likewise relegating the "incurables" to ignominious doom. Myths of the superiority of the Yamato ethnic clan provided fertile soil for the spread of eugenics. Japan soon became the center of the movement in the region, with Racial Hygiene societies popping up beginning in the 1910s.[32] Like most eugenicists, Japanese proponents focused on positive breeding habits among the fit by hosting "healthy babies" contests and materializing the myths of pure blood by encoding them in citizenship laws.[33] It was in their negative policies and attitudes that the German influence revealed itself most strongly, particularly in the 1940 National Eugenic Law and 1948 Eugenic Protection Law, designed to "to prevent birth of inferior descendants from the eugenic point of view, and to protect [the] life and health of [the] mother."[34] Articles 4 and 12 of the latter authorized a "Eugenic Protection Commission" to permit involuntary sterilization "for the public interests in order to prevent hereditary transmission of the disease" resulting in over 16,000 coerced operations, most of which were on patients in psychiatric hospitals and facilities for the intellectually disabled.[35]

Nazi psychiatry's true innovation was to transform the category of "incurable" juridically and institutionally, inscribing it into an extremely efficient abstract machine that reproduced and dispensed with its own product. We've already recounted the economism and distance from patients marking early German psychiatry. As the clinical model entered its waning phase, Adolf Jost published *The Right to Die* in 1895, arguing first for the right of the private individual to choose medical euthanasia in case of severe disability, before pivoting to the case of the incurable who supposedly cannot advocate for their own death:

> When we see someone incurably ill squirming with unendurable pain on his bedstead with the dire prospect of a further maybe month-long deterioration without hope of recovery; when we walk through the rooms of a bedlam house and the sight of the raving mad or the paralytic fills us with all the pity humans are capable of, then—in spite of all the prejudices we have absorbed—the thought must stir in us: 'do not these people have a right to die, does not human society have the duty to offer this death to them as painlessly as possible?'[36]

For the hopeless, the decision to carry out a mercy killing cedes to the state as guardian, where "the diagnosis of incurability is sufficient in itself to justify killing."[37] A possible blueprint of this theory's combination with effective statecraft came in 1920 with the publication *Permission for the Extermination of Worthless Life* [*Die Freigabe der Vernichtung lebensunwerten Lebens*], written by the popular lawyer Karl Bindung and the forensic psychiatrist Alfred Hoche, which, citing Jost, asks: "Are there human lives that have lost the quality of legally protected entities to such an extent that their continuation has permanently lost all value for the bearer of that life and for society?" They answer:

> If one imagines a battlefield strewn with thousands of dead young men, or a mine in which firedamp explosions have trapped hundreds of industrious workers, and if, at the same time, one juxtaposes that image with our mental asylums, with their care for their living inmates – one is deeply shaken by the shocking discordance between the sacrifice of the finest examples of humanity on the largest scale, on the one hand, and by the greatest care that is devoted to lives that are not only absolutely worthless, but even of negative value, on the other hand.[38]

The notion of "lives unworthy of being lived" can be seen as a rational product of the legal category of guardianship with the biopsychiatric theory of hereditary degeneration and idiocy, the intentional degradation of institutional environments, accountings of human life as a questionable expense on the state's budget, and the exploitation of the transhistorical/transcultural aesthetic of grotesque body horror in connection to the disabled and mad in propaganda films that exposed the life of the mentally ill to be an "existence without life" [*Dasein ohne Leben*].[39]

Disgust and mercy, burden and potential savings, vegetation and suffering were the productive couplets that fueled the machinery of mass murder. As grotesque and shocking as it was, Satoshi Uematsu's serial murder of nineteen disabled people at a care facility in Japan in 2016 is entirely legible in this tradition. In his eyes, the "disabled can only create misery." If one considers the "tired faces of guardians, the dull eyes of caregivers working at the facility" or the person who cannot "carry out household and social activities," murder was not only merciful, but done "for the sake of Japan and the world" because ridding the world of them might "revitalize the world economy and . . . prevent World War III."[40] The stigma associated with (even a proximate relationship to) disability or mental illness is still so pervasive that only one parent allowed the name of her daughter to be released publicly.[41]

Chronicity is both the product and the target of the psychiatrists' feverish theorization and activity. Spending money on the mentally ill was a waste, so they promptly divested institutions of their funds, closing specialized institutions, and cramming custodial ones to the brim with bodies forced to live in tortured proximity. Food, hygiene, and activities were all cut. Nazi officials organized "freak show" tours of these snake pits "to illustrate the inherent uselessness of the patients . . . including 6,000 members of the SS, some of whom came out recommending setting up machine guns at the entrance to mow down the inmates."[42]

This bloodlust would be satiated come the outbreak of war. In September 1939, Hitler authorized the mercy killing of incurables in psychiatric institutions. To protect the future of the race, the murder of children began in October. From the beginning, the medical euthanasia program was thoroughly bureaucratic and cooperative. It required the broad participation of physicians, local officials, parents, and others to report and classify defective children before moving them to one of the designated killing facilities where they would be starved to death, or, more likely, given a fatal overdose of barbiturates. Not every parent was aware of what was happening, especially because the physicians went to great lengths to disguise deaths as natural, but at least some explicitly requested mercy killings.[43] In January 1940, the elimination of adults began under a hail of bullets in occupied Poland, where accumulated hatred unbound from supervisory restraints was let loose from the rifles of the *Einsatzgruppen* [literally, operational groups; SS "mobile killing units"] on 4,400 mental patients.[44]

A massive legal bureaucracy was established at Tiergartenstrasse 4 in Berlin, hence the name "Aktion T4," made up of "economists, agronomists, lawyers and businessmen, with an expanded pool of academics and psychiatrists" tasked with classifying, transferring, and murdering psychiatric patients with the preferred industrial method of toxic gas.[45] When Hitler, facing protest from the church and relatives, ordered the gas to stop in August 1941, over 70,000 people had perished.[46]

The decision to kill patients was decided on the basis of a short questionnaire called "*Meldebogen* 1" ["Reporting form 1"] sent out to asylums by the Ministry of the Interior in 1939. Asylum staff were instructed to catalogue patients according to whether they had 1) a psychiatric or neurological condition and were unemployed, 2) been institutionalized for longer than five years, 3) were "criminally insane," or 4) "do not possess German nationality or do not have German or related blood."[47] The goal was to discover those cases where "low or merely mechanical productivity, irremediable illness, or the duration of institutionalization sufficed effectively to sign a person's death warrant."[48] There is not a single criterion present external to the pessimistic strains of institutional psychiatry. As journalist Ernst Klee put it, "German psychiatry was not abused by the Nazis. It used the Nazis. The National Socialist state made possible what psychiatrists had already long proposed: the classification and elimination of lives not worth living."[49] Though he ordered the gassing to stop, Hitler never actually ordered the gassing of mental patients to begin; he unofficially *authorized* it and left its implementation up to the discretion of patriotic physicians.[50] Being a product of internal desire rather than external compulsion, "wild," i.e., unofficial, euthanasia and sterilization continued *after* Hitler reversed the legal authorization to kill the disabled and mentally ill in a spurious fashion by means of poisoning and starvation.[51]

Some institutions killed so many that they built crematoriums to dispense with the corpses more efficiently; others built special vacation homes for the murderers to relax in. Most of the physicians who murdered children and gassed patients survived the war and the war crime trials. After 1945, Ernst Klee (among others) recounts, some became heads of regional psychiatric services (Willi Baumert and Gerhard Kloos), obtained high positions in pharmaceutical companies (Georg Renno), university departments (Kurt Pohlisch, who selected patients for the gas chamber, became head of psychiatry at the University in Bonn), or heads of medical associations (Klaus Endruweit). Doctors responsible for the murder of children were not just left responsible for children, but even promoted after the war: Elisabeth Hecker, in charge of youth euthanasia in Lubliniec, became head of youth psychiatry in Hamm; Margarete Hielscher was promoted after consigning children to death to director of children's psychiatry in Stadroda; Werner Catel was appointed Professor of Pediatrics in Kiel, after being exposed as overseeing the killing of children in Leipzig; Catel's assistant, Hans Christoph Hempel, became the head of a children's clinic in Chemnitz (Karl-Marx-Stadt until 1990).[52]

ILLNESS IN OR AS ECONOMY

Young people growing up in Germany in the 1960s and '70s were confronted with the reality that many of the parents, grandparents, schoolteachers, nurses, and psychiatrists who willingly participated in euthanasia programs or concentration camps (or blissfully ignored them) managed to secure cushy university or hospital positions. In the late '60s, facing an economic crisis, the coalition parliament formed an emergency government that nullified the parliament. To the growing German left and student movements, the fear that the West German government could slip back into its fascist mode in a crisis was seemingly confirmed when, in response to large protests against a visit by the shah of Iran to Berlin in June 1967, the state's security forces implemented far-reaching emergency orders banning demonstrations, shutting down highways, and sending in thousands of police. The murder of student protestor Benno Ohnesorg exacerbated the crisis into a fever pitch.[53] 1968 represents both the climax of the collective rage of the student movement and the beginning of its disaggregation: soon after, it splintered into numerous Maoist and Marxist-Leninist cadres, autonomists and *Spontis*, feminists and antinuclear activists, squatters and queers, and, of course, the big bads, urban armed-struggle groups.[54] All this coincided with the rediscovery of Wilhelm Reich's work and the translation of critical and antipsychiatry texts by David Cooper, R.D. Laing, Franco Basaglia, and Félix Guattari around the same time, bringing with them a new lexicon of desire and an emphasis on psychopolitics.[55]

Amid generational clashes, new youth movements, and the growth of antipsychiatry, there emerged in Heidelberg, a city in southwest Germany, what Jean-Paul Sartre called "the only possible radicalization of the antipsychiatry movement": the Socialist Patients' Collective [*das Sozialistische Patientenkollektiv*], or SPK. The continuous hostility of local media and a healthy dose of self-mythologization have led to factual disputes that shroud their development through the 1970s in murkiness and fog. What is certain is that the group began organizing actions around 1970 out of the Department of Psychiatry at the University of Heidelberg.

Heidelberg's psychiatry department offers a microcosm of Germany's psychiatric legacy: it was the workplace of one of the most important psychiatrists of all time, Emil Kraepelin, whose classificatory system serves as a prototype for modern taxonomies; it was and is home to the Prinzhorn Collection, one of the earliest and largest collections of patient artwork, which has preserved works for over a century; and, during the Nazi years, under Carl Schneider's directorship, the staff helped organize euthanasia killings. In 1955, the university made a gesture towards a new direction by hiring Walter von Baeyer, a Jewish professor with a progressive agenda. Influenced by the social psychiatry currents in Britain and the US, he decried the still wretched conditions of Germany's mental hospitals, advocated for community care and psychotherapy over custodialism and aggressive physical treatments, and talked positively of radical psychiatrists like R. D. Laing and Franco Basaglia. At the same time, the university kept multiple nurses and psychiatrists who served in the SS and were involved in the Nazi euthanasia program,[56] a situation which led to a split between a more traditional psychiatric milieu and the social psychiatric one. The SPK represents the extreme limit of this split. They first began to take shape around Wolfgang Huber, an intense and prickly assistant in the Psychiatric and Neurological University Clinic hired in 1964. Between 1964 and 1969, Huber started to skip conferences and meetings while simultaneously extending his meeting hours late into the night to avoid supervision before frequent clashes with colleagues resulted in having him moved to the undesirable polyclinic in 1969 where acute patients were observed, sorted, and likely moved elsewhere after a brief time.[57] Despite the barriers, he began to amass a number of supporters who organized large therapy sessions that more closely resembled political rallies than conventional group therapy meetings. These became unmanageable and thus a target for the administration around 1970, who feared that this man was so lost in his work he "might prescribe dynamite!"[58]

Things came to a head on February 5, 1970, when the university finally tried to evict Huber and about sixty patients. But the patients refused to leave. Instead, they called a general assembly in the clinic and hunkered down for an occupation. This continued until February 29th, when they struck a compromise with the university, never fulfilled, which promised the patients the renovation and use of a work room and a lump sum payment for development. Out of frustration, in July the SPK occupied the Rector's office and increased the scope of their demands: they wanted patient control over all care, over right to residency, over the clinics' funds, and over a house to use as a crisis or refuge house. Though they attained official recognition on July 9th, 1970, they were repeatedly attacked in the media and by the university in public statements until they were formally evicted on November 14, 1970, which was not effectively acted upon until a second order was given in May 1971. After being evicted, many SPK members were arrested in late June on suspicion of being involved in a shootout with police. Throughout this period, their primary collective activity consisted of what they called "agitations," as opposed to therapy, the main point of which was to identify individual needs and both denaturalize them—situating them in a historical context—and collectivize them. On top of that, they collected a few Deutsche Mark at every meeting to allow poorer members to participate in basic care functions: they offered free childcare for those who needed to work; performed home visits to diffuse tension between partners and roommates or to help solve crises; tutored students who were falling behind; secured medications without the mediation of the clinic when possible; and helped to work out labor or housing disputes by pressuring bosses and landlords.

In terms of their activity and material demands, the SPK were militant and impressive but not so different from similar groups around the world that demanded patient control and offered alternative support structures. Their uniqueness lies rather in their conceptualization of psychiatric/medical power and illness in relation to the economy and the reconceptualization of political and personal identity this brings about. There is much confusion around what the SPK actually wrote, due in part to their own proclivity for falsifiable hyperbole and crude sloganeering.[59] The notion that mental illness is socially determined is often attributed to them, but this is actually disputed on the very first page of their primary text *Turn Illness into a Weapon* on the concept of illness: "it was clear to us from the outset that it's completely unsatisfactory to look for a single bodily cause according to the model of scientific medicine. It also quickly became clear to us that it's not enough simply to speak of the social cause of illness, that it's too simple to pin 'responsibility' for illness and suffering on 'evil capitalism.' And it became clear to us that it's a completely abstract and ineffective affirmation simply to say that society is ill."[60] They hold that illness is not reducible to the purely biological, but it does not follow, as it's often said, that it is socially determined; outside of these two dominant narratives, what are we left with? Notice that the SPK does not speak here of mental illness, madness, nor disability. Instead, they use the generic term "illness." Why? One must contextualize their reclamation of illness within the more common refrain that mental illness is not a disease like any other because it lacks a localized cellular or molecular lesion or because of its legal ramifications. Illness, for the SPK, is not a thing nor a state, but it is, nonetheless, very real and a constituent part of contemporary capitalist society. Illness is the crux of their argument and works on multiple levels at once, both abstract and empirical, general and highly specific, and it bears an essential relationship with capitalism: "Illness is the essential condition, the presupposition and the result of [the] capitalist process of production."[61] This is not the same as saying *capitalism alone causes illness* or *illness didn't exist until capitalism*, but it is to deny a "natural, objective" illness existing free of material context.

Early on in *Turn Illness into a Weapon*, they make it clear that illness can be understood as alienation, in the terms set out by Marx: it "*is* the alienation [*Entfremdung*]" as it's experienced "subjectively, as the experienced condition of physical and psychological needs of the individual."[62] In the capitalist mode of production, the worker is estranged [*entfremdet*] and alienated [*entäussert*] from their activity. In *The Economic and Philosophic Manuscripts*, Marx explains what this means: first, he says, because labor is not freely chosen, but is taken up as a forced necessity for survival, it exists outside of the worker. Though they make the world, the worker is denied the capacity to freely choose their mental or physical activity. Therefore, the more they work and produce, the more alienated they are from themselves and from the things they create, the less time they have to undertake their own endeavors and develop themselves—the more their "own time" is reduced to mere reproduction (eating, sleeping, drinking). The type and intensity of work does not arise from one's own desire or capacity, but from the necessity of survival, which means that working beyond one's own physical or mental limits or in terrible conditions is, for most, an inevitability. Work is experienced as organized mortification and denial, an exhausting expenditure for products that oppose the worker as an inaccessible and alien world of things fulfilling none of their immediate needs.[63] The world is so arranged that, in pursuance of the *means* of survival, one must alienate themself from their own power of production and sell it off to another, eventually resulting in physical or mental degradation, as Marx argues in *Capital, Vol. 3*: "a certain crippling of the body and mind is inseparable from the division of labor in society as a whole. But since the age of manufacturing pushes this separation of kinds of work much further, and in its way of dividing the individual attacks him at the roots of life, it is the first age to supply the material and the start to industrial pathology."[64]

Illness can be understood in this multifaceted sense of alienation/estrangement from the product of labor, from one's own capacity to produce, which in turn presents this alienated world as a natural one. For the SPK, that mortification of the self from the world whereby one "becomes merely a fragment of [one's] own body"[65] *is* illness, something which becomes particularly apparent in those cases when this persistent, endemic mortification is subjectively experienced as pain and destruction, e.g., in the form of workplace injury, psychic crisis, or immiseration. Capital sets one part of us out against another. Illness describes the "damaged life, life that contradicts itself"[66] that lives through such an experience.

We may seem quite far from the question of madness or psychiatry at this point. Indeed, part of the SPK's strategy is to despychiatrize madness and present it as a specific type of the alienation process inherent to capitalism. But there is also a historical precedent for their organization in that psychiatry initially confronts madness as "alienation" and ties it to the question of civilization and industry. This brings us back prior to the totalizing medicalization of madness, when what we would call "psychotic" types were conceived of in terms of delirium, or forms of alienation from reason. The mad person has a privileged position in this schema, in that they confront society either as *the alienated* who have lost contact with civil society and need a shepherd to guide them back or as *aliens* who are so far gone as to appear as animals. The SPK reverse the terms: to be ill/alienated is actually to wield the potential of increased consciousness of the estrangement of the world. To be healthy is not at all possible; those who believe they are healthy are unaware of their real estrangement from the world. The healthy ideal only describes readiness for exploitation and further mortification,[67] which is itself a state of illness.

To better explain this, the SPK divides illness into two possible elements: the progressive element [*das Moment*] and the reactionary element. Take the example of paranoid delusion discussed in the book. In the common representation, the paranoid person feels themself beset by unknown forces (voices, visions, or mysterious figures) that assault them as an omnipresent force, as if from the environment itself. This differs only in the specifics from the explication of alienation recounted above, and, indeed, "delusion," the SPK say, "is the product of the individual's objectification in capitalist society, it's the expression of the polarized relationship of life and capital, of organic and living matter with inorganic, dead matter."[68] Paranoia as a totalizing sense of estrangement from the world that antagonizes the individual as an alien force *expresses the truth of the world*. Let's say the paranoid feels followed or surrounded by murderers and holes up in their apartment to escape the horrors outside. Another truth is barely under the surface: murder is the norm of the capitalist mode of production, both immediately in the form of domestic police executions and clearing the way for imperial accumulation, and over time with avoidable accidents or exposure to viruses and diseases at the workplace. Even so, illness having a basis in social reality does not determine its outcome and expression; it is merely a starting point. Normally, the patient's illness is objectified as schizophrenia or bipolar disorder, freezing it as a manipulable and stigmatized property of a person, or, at times, even supplanting the person as their primary form of identification. One's adaptive *condition of living* is seized, frozen, turned inward, made into the central property, the primary *condition*, of the individual while bizarrely remaining outside of them at a remote distance as the discrete cause of increasing magnitudes of guilt and fear and confusion. In its reactionary moment, that which connects us to the social world is repressed and the illness is experienced as a limitation, an "inner prison"[69] belonging to us, in a way, but experienced as if we belong to it.

The only *real* right one can count on in a capitalist society is the right to sell labor power; when one is perceived to be incapable of doing so due to being depleted by or excluded from the market, they are no longer the bearer of rights and face the law nakedly, as a "human wreck"[70] or a waste product. Healthcare is organized so as to either maintain the exploitability of the ill or at least to contain and manage illness in its repressed form by molding them into patients dependent on the most profitable, and not necessarily the most effective, medical techniques and medications.[71] "Hospitals are places of production in the same way that factories are," one member said in 1970, "the patient must turn in everything he has produced there: stool, blood, urine, bile . . . headaches, hallucinations. . . . These products translate to medical bills, lab bills, administrative costs . . . thus the illness flows back into the state treasury."[72] The SPK write:

> Illness is collectively produced: that is, insofar as the worker creates capital in the work process, which encounters him as an alien force, he collectively produces his own isolation. It's therefore only logical that healthcare produced by capitalism perpetuates this isolation in that it doesn't treat these symptoms as collective but rather treats them as individual bad luck, fault, and failure. However, capitalism produces, in the form of illness, the most dangerous threat to itself. Therefore it has to fight against the progressive moment in illness with its heaviest weapons: the healthcare system, the legal system, the police.[73]

Illness is Janus-faced, that is, it looks forwards and backwards; it is potentially both a beginning and an end, process and product. These passages speak to the surreality of the last few years when: more than 6,000,000 people are dead from COVID-19, so many of whom were forced to work in positions that put them at high risk of contracting the virus or were living in nursing homes or other facilities designed to manage the ill, old, and debilitated, along with the prisons and hospitals; schools are expected to stay open so parents can go to work, no matter the risk; in the midst of slow catastrophe, pharmaceutical companies were allowed to privatize vaccines and withhold them from poorer countries, even though this is tantamount to murder. Our bodily and mental integrity is being held hostage by the very system that makes the world work. We live in the fever dream of humanity, in a giant unreality of our own making trampling on us every day. States rationalize eugenic measures about who is worth sacrificing in the name of the market; all we get in return for integrating our bodies into this machine is the bare minimum of care necessary to preserve the flow of commodities. In more extreme crises, when the sick surplus cannot be maintained at low costs or adjusted forcibly to a norm, they are simply dispensed with in slums or institutions, one way or another, by slow exposure to deadly conditions or rapid liquidation. Our unreality is *produced*, our disunity is remade daily in the linkages that make things we need and keep things moving, all united and organized under the sign of general accumulation in a dream world traveling along a fateful path where there are no real accidents: we can reasonably expect a thousand water crises, cascading extinctions, cancer epidemics, and widespread famines in the coming years.

We live in a big open pit mine; its poison seeps into our blood at different speeds, but it's in everyone. There is no discrete suicide epidemic here or there; we are all in a massive suicide cult inching towards an ignominious mass death of humanity. Located in the polyclinic, the function of which was to observe, sort, and ship mental patients to their next destination at the very same university where they once sent them off to be murdered, the SPK were uniquely well-situated to make such observations.[74]

Turn Illness into a Weapon can be read as the search for a counter-universal capable of organizing medicine under the sign of process relations and material conditions in a form that confronts the National Socialist concept of illness as a racial universal with the utmost force. They certainly weren't alone. As the war came to an end, Ana Antić writes, "a different and genuinely global psychiatry" was called for "to alleviate the cataclysmic effects of pathologies and prevent the suicide of humanity."[75] Global health agencies like WHO, UNESCO, and WFMH were called upon to produce research and theories that united humanity rather than divided it, setting in motion a hunt for universals. Theories of universal development, which we encountered in the last chapter, inscribed alterity more creatively by equating "primitive" humanity and the mad with the figure of the child, which is excluded from civic participation. Other "transcultural" approaches assumed that their categories of schizophrenia or depression were the "real" ones and only sought to find how other cultures defined them.[76] More subtle (though not necessarily actually "universal") theories were also in circulation in the colonial world: Wulf Sachs' *Black Hamlet* sought out the patterns and constructions that underlie and constitute mental life for everyone without implying the universality of any diagnostic constructs, but even this humanist effort struggled to retain a balance between political and cultural determinism that didn't reek of a colonial attitude. The decolonizing world was not short on proposals for humanist, cross-cultural psychiatry that took up the mantle of the universal mind as a clarion call against Eurocentric ones that only subtly reimagined the superiority of the white Western mind.[77]

A middle position between the humanist universalist one and the SPK's are the contemporary critiques of neoliberalism and the Global Mental Health movement that view psychiatry as a tool for molding psychiatric subjectivity by subtly coaxing wounded individuals—stressed out and anxious from the instability of the economy or the climate—into medical consumerism under the guise of treatment.[78] From this angle, one of the main drivers of psychiatric theory and practice is the consumer market, specifically the market in psychiatric drugs since the rise of psychopharmacology in the 1950s with the introduction of the antipsychotic Thorazine. In this view, psychiatric diagnoses are forms of subjectivity essentially wedded to the flux and growth of the drug market, which ties the rapid proliferation of new diagnoses (each with a variable assortment of potential drug regimens) to the neoliberal notion that certain market decisions can shape one's identity and solve (or mitigate) personal crises and traumas. Here, the consumption of psychiatric drugs necessitates a prior, more significant, transformation into a dependent self that requires the drug for reproduction, a self that ties its notion of wholeness or presence to a compound that can actualize it.

Drugs have come to play such a central role in psychiatry that they sometimes appear to be *the* central question of both the practice and its critique. This singular focus can be perplexing from the outside, for drugs are just drugs. Like alcohol or heroin, Lamictal and Olanzapine are, in the end, mere chemical compounds, inert in themselves with neither benevolent nor evil properties. Putting aside all attendant controversies over efficacy and danger, it's easy to see that the reason drugs elicit such an extreme response is that they, too, facilitate ways of being human in relation to other humans. Indeed, the dispensation of drugs may be the largest or at least fastest growing way in which mental illness as an identity has been mediated in the United States since the mid-twentieth century, and now globally. Drugs ask things of the individual who ingests them, or they act as facilitators for questions asked by another. Their effects, good or bad, beg the question: who or what is being acted upon, corrected or corrupted when I take this thing and feel different? With psychiatric medication, one is asked to swallow and digest, not just a drug with this or that material effect, but an identity altered, managed, stabilized, or even only actualized on account of a chemical solution. Unsurprisingly, drugs are a productive and always contentious turning point in the recalibration of mad subjectivity, actualized through tapering, experimentation with psychedelics or other nonpsychiatric drugs, or a purely instrumental usage that strips them of deeper pretensions. This demonstrates above all that the way we take drugs changes the experience of them entirely. I drink alcohol regularly, and, like any drinker, I know that having a drink alone after work is an entirely different experience than taking it in the company of friends on the weekend. In the Spinozist sense, we can say that drugs are a body that either agrees or disagrees with mine under certain conditions. But that's too easy. A large part of why it agrees or disagrees has to do with the way it's dispensed. An antipsychotic taken voluntarily in full awareness of its limitations, its side effects, and its instrumental (rather than ontological) uses for the explicit goal of making social life more fruitful is a different drug than the very same antipsychotic ingested due to a court order shrouded in mystifications like "it helps your brain work better" in service of calming one down. Drugs are about who we are and how we become who we are in the company of others, but the pro- and antidrug literature does not reflect that in the back and forth about whether they are good or bad in themselves.

The critique of neoliberalism and psychiatry appears especially persuasive when one takes note of the way psychiatric language has so thoroughly permeated the broader public's way of discussing everyday problems, thanks in part to the ubiquity of anti-stigma campaigns on bus stops and football commercials, the unbridled bloating of diagnostic manuals heavy enough with ailments to be used as weapons, the drug industry's bold advances into the unconquered territories of youth and banal deviations, and the shift in mental patient status from being overwhelmingly involuntary to largely voluntary. In other words, there has been a rise in a participatory, common psychiatrization of increasingly microscopic deviations that would, in times past, not have come onto the radar of psychiatrists except for the wealthiest patients. Psychiatric imperialism reigns supreme and not just in the most developed economies: Ethan Watters[79] and China Mills[80] have written about the voracious advance of psychiatric diagnostic categories exported and introduced into markets in the Global South, often with funding and advertising by pharmaceutical companies without concern for local exigencies or traditions of diagnosis and healing. These are new processes, but they are dramatic: the market in psychiatric medications is expected to become a $40 billion industry by 2025 (nearly double its current size) in response to the expected rise in patients due to the COVID-19 pandemic.

But it's hard to see how these could be determining factors for the field prior to the end of the twentieth century: throughout most of its history, most psychiatric hospitalizations were involuntary, and, even when this started to shift in the 1960s, voluntary hospitalization remained at around 20 percent until just the last few decades. In the past, most people who became regular users of psychopharmaceuticals did so following the experience of being hospitalized. It wasn't until the late 1990s that the FDA moved to allow drug companies to market directly to consumers with ads that encourage people to go to their doctors and ask to receive specific diagnoses and medications.

Complicating this further is the fact recounted by Liat Ben-Moshe that—contrary to the idea that psychopharmaceuticals were the turning point from institutional psychiatry to a diffuse, capillary mode catering to private consumers—Thorazine was originally marketed to skeptical psychiatrists as a managerial tool to keep the ever-growing morass of human beings in overcrowded asylums a half-sleeping collectivity.[81] While plenty of people are making a good deal of money off of psychiatric research and treatment, particularly in the largely unregulated private facilities in the United States and the introduction of a new drug market in countries without substantial psychiatric infrastructure outside of the major cities, the profit motive cannot be the sole nor even dominant driver of change and adaptation in psychiatry, nor would it explain its origins or major shifts prior to the growth of the pharmaceutical market. As far as training goes on an individual level, while entering the field may provide the psychiatrist with a comfortable salary and plenty of opportunities to exploit prospective patients, there are manifold simpler and more economical ways to ensnare and fraud a consumer base in twenty-first-century capitalism. Becoming a stock trader, an alternative health guru, or a snake-oil salesman doesn't require years of postdoc residency training. In this light, the idea of psychiatrists getting into the field because they have conscious aspirations to be social engineers and control their patients through medications is equally untenable when one could become a police officer with far less training and schooling, even less oversight, and no requirement to pretend to do anything besides guarantee the status quo by means of force. That's not to say that psychiatrists aren't today motivated by the prospect of making money or that they don't enjoy leveraging power over patients, but that these are not likely the central enticements of the work for most, and thus exist in tension with whatever intentions individuals bring to it. Nor is drug market expansion sufficient for explaining the rapid growth of global psychiatry's client base. Psychiatry is a historically contingent phenomenon tied up with the spread of market relations, the complexities of urban life, and the destruction of traditional means of mitigating stress and absorbing difference. Drug companies certainly have a vested interest in inserting themselves as the simplest solution in vast untouched reservoirs of human misery. Lacking other cheap and easily applicable means of attenuating the speed and violence of this destruction, it is not hard to imagine why psychiatry and its tools would be in demand by states rushing headlong into exponential growth seeking to manage the excessive suffering of humanity left in its wake.

Health and illness as we encounter them on the pages of *Turn Illness into a Weapon* are fundamentally unlike other universals, for what unites humanity here is no longer a constitutional design nor a series of innate patterns, but our common condition under capital. For the SPK, these theorists may believe they are inching ever closer to the innate reality of brain and mind, but they don't theorize the fact that all reality we encounter is transformed by the conditions under which it is produced. As damaged life, illness confronts not just consumption but capitalist production and circulation as an absolute limit: if too many bodies are ruined beyond repair, the work stops; if illness completely permeates the social world, nothing moves without enormous risk. The bodies and minds of a sufficient quantity of workers must be sustained to the degree that enough of them can get up and work again the next day; the working day is limited in part by the hours of the day, in part by the reproducibility of laborers. This is the fulcrum of the revolutionary potential of illness and where the possibility of the "progressive" element presents itself, when "fear will turn into a weapon."[82] Illness, insofar as it is an expression of the real contradictions that permeate our social world, contains within it the seeds of a form of protest, a potential rejection of one's conditions and the expression of the need for transformation. At that point, one can manage it, repress its call, or "turn illness into a weapon." At its base, the SPK offer a variation of the Marxist theme of *immiseration*: capitalism, said Marx, "far more than any other mode of production is a waster of people, of living-work, a waster not only of flesh and blood but also of nerves and brain."[83] Sartre was spot on when he quoted Friedrich Engels' 1845 *Condition of the Working Class in England* in his preface to *Turn Illness into a Weapon*, for the theory of illness under capitalism stays close to his theory of "social murder":

When one individual inflicts bodily injury upon another, such injury that death results, we call the deed manslaughter; when the assailant knew in advance that the injury would be fatal, we call his deed murder. But when society places hundreds of proletarians in such a position that they inevitably meet a too early and an unnatural death, one which is quite as much a death by violence as that by the sword or bullet; when it deprives thousands of the necessaries of life, places them under conditions in which they cannot live—forces them, through the strong arm of the law, to remain in such conditions until that death ensues which is the inevitable consequence — knows that these thousands of victims must perish, and yet permits these conditions to remain, its deed is murder just as surely as the deed of the single individual; disguised, malicious murder, murder against which none can defend himself, which does not seem what it is, because no man sees the murderer, because the death of the victim seems a natural one, since the offence is more one of omission than of commission. But murder it remains. I have now to prove that society in England daily and hourly commits what the working-men's organs, with perfect correctness, characterise as social murder, that it has placed the workers under conditions in which they can neither retain health nor live long; that it undermines the vital force of these workers gradually, little by little, and so hurries them to the grave before their time. I have further to prove that society knows how injurious such conditions are to the health ano the life of the workers, and yet does nothing to improve these conditions.[84]

By necessity, our economy functioning makes masses of people more miserable (and, in this case, sick). By doing so, the revolutionary hopes, it digs its own grave, for these degraded and humiliated masses won't put up with it forever.

We are on fire, and so is the Earth we stand on. Everyone is burning, forced to watch as their bodies diminish, their mental state degrades, the ground gives way beneath their feet. Our lives slip away from under our noses as if they belonged to someone else, because they do. Can we wield that fire, our pain, and use it to destroy our conditions or will it just obliterate us all the quicker? Like most incendiaries, the original SPK couldn't burn for too long: the first group broke up in 1971, with some eventually fleeing to Italy to work with Basaglia or France to work with Guattari, and others ended up in prison or deceased. It has been claimed and contested that a few others were involved with the Red Army Faction (RAF) armed struggle in the 1970s.[85] Though they represented an extreme reaction to psychiatric power, the SPK were something of a harbinger for a reckoning with Germany's psychiatric past, though one without their broader social critique. In the coming years, between 1971–75, the Federal Republic under Willy Brandt produced a major report of the state of Germany's institutions called the *Psychiatrie-Enquete*, which revealed continued devastation: "denial of privacy in mass sleeping rooms with no individual cupboards; deprivation of dignity by shaving the hairs of patients and letting them wear grey asylum clothes; brain operations; electro shock therapy and sterilisation practices; hazardous medicalisation . . . meals were withheld and disciplinary measures were inflicted."[86] It would take the remainder of the decade for the profession and the public to seriously reckon with their activities under Nazi rule in the way the SPK already had in 1970.

In practice, the formal SPK was a failed experiment, but their theory rings true wherever illness, debilitation, disability, or brokenness are appropriated as a condition of solidarity. It rang true for the Young Lords in 1970 when they occupied the Lincoln Mental Health Center in the Bronx along with paraprofessionals, locals, some doctors and patients, decrying the disconnection between the mostly affluent white staff and their clientele, and the fatal consequences of medical care based on efficiency and profit. They demanded destigmatized drug treatments, noncarceral and consensual care relations, and propagandized about the political nature of health. Despite major conflicts with the police, they actually won funding for their People's Program, which they used to fund acupuncture treatments and lead testing, and offered some diagnostic services with a mobile chest X-ray vehicle they seized from the city until they were permanently booted from the hospital by the police in 1978.[87]

One hears echoes of the solidaristic potential of illness in the productions of the International Network of Alternatives to Psychiatry when, in their founding statement from 1975, they characterized the mad and disabled as workers out of work, the unemployed, and therefore fundamentally part of any movement against capitalist form of life.[88] A similar spirit is infused in the marvelous "Statement from the Psychiatrized" delivered by Yves-Luc Conreur at the 1977 meeting for the Network in Trieste:

> We, a group of psychiatrized, do not claim to exercise a monopoly over 'what is to be done.' We owe our importance and our force to the fact that we have victoriously opened a path that was unimaginable until now, thereby freeing us from a desperate situation. We do not intend to act in the place of anyone, but to demonstrate concretely to certain people that the real field of possibilities is greater than it might have seemed. We reject magical forms of conduct, we reject artificial and voluntary misery, mysticism, suicide and madness as forms of liberation. But in order to struggle, in order to give birth to the force necessary to struggle, we must participate personally in the political struggle that leads to the transformation of reality; for that is the only way of discovering the mechanisms of oppression. And once we have understood that that repression is growing in all domains, prisons, class forms of justice, the rhythms of factory life, buying on credit, suburban life, the ghettos of immigrant workers,

etc., we can no longer fortify our position behind the fetish of legal-
ity. Our truth is not to be found in the projects of our benefactors
but in our own always renewed struggles. There will always be an
alternative to the alternative.[89]

Normality may be built of stone or steel, but one day, it will crumble
and rust. We are all disabled or on our way there; we all have a little
bit of madness or will soon. We are united in the dynamism of our
separations, our failures, and our shortcomings, limited only by our
inability to appropriate them against a common nightmare.

CODA ON THE MADNESS OF MADNESS

An enigma which Oedipus could not have solved. It is to establish a
definition of insanity. That is, to discover one form of words expressive of the nature of a hundred different things. —W. A. F. Browne[90]

Illness both is and is not madness. It can serve as neither a container
nor a character mask for madness. Mental illness has its own reality
and parameters, but both images incorrectly posit a madness tangible
enough to hold or maneuver. If madness at times appears *as* illness,
it is necessary to ask how this "as" works in a category that lacks any
semblance of stable presence.

Antonin Artaud's career as a madman began in Ireland, from
which he was deported in a straitjacket in 1937, before being handed
over to authorities on French soil. It's fitting that the quintessential
mad poet's story would start on the amorphous territory of the sea,
calling to mind one of most enduring myths in the history of madness: the ship of fools. After spending nine long years in asylums
throughout France, the playwright and poet was invited to visit and
review an exhibit of works by Vincent Van Gogh at the Orangerie in
Paris in 1947. He was spellbound by what he saw. Van Gogh's work
confirmed Artaud's conviction that the mad are those whose fevers
are torments of bitter truth driving those sick with sanity out of their
wits, under whose skins' boil the waters of "an over-heated factory,"[91]
whose spirits rise and fall like cosmic fireballs, living and dying in
the scorching heat of "a thousand summers,"[92] exploding and fizzling

out in the course of a single day. Artaud, the madman's madman, declared the quasi-spiritual right of madness and sickness to exist. "My existence is beautiful but hideous," he wrote, "Hideous, dreadful, constructed of hideousness. Curing a sickness is a crime."[93] Civil society, having abandoned any mechanisms for incorporating the alterity that lies in its heart "invented psychiatry to defend itself against the investigations of certain visionaries whose faculties of divination disturbed it."[94] To hold an apocalypse seething within one's guts, to have all attempts to convey one's volcanic relation to reality met with disapproval and hostility, ends, as you might expect, in lethal nonreciprocity: Van Gogh, Artaud said, was "suicided by society." Van Gogh's death wasn't solitary. We are not born alone and we don't die alone. Separation is but a modification of our being with others. Relative isolation always bears some relationship to the form in which social life is organized, or where opportunities to be in common present themselves. Therefore, even the most extreme act of self-destruction is, in part, a wound inflicted by a collective to itself.

Within this strange system of relays, the seeming incoherency of madness reveals a deeper, silenced truth of an insane society, which in term claims the right to make sane, to "cure" the former of his dangerous relation to an unspeakable reality. It was up to the mad, like Artaud and Van Gogh, "to cure all doctors . . . and not up to doctors ignorant of my dreadful states of sickness to impose their insulin therapy on me, their health for a worn out world."[95] The madman is contained "[f]or if his way of thinking, which was sane, were unanimously widespread, Society could no longer survive."[96] Outside the walls of the asylum, a war raged through Europe. Neighbors wantonly murdered each other, and for what? Artaud was interned in the period when the Vichy government unofficially implemented their program of passive-negative eugenics, allowing patients to die of disease and malnutrition. In 1939, when he was moved to 'hôpital psychiatrique de Ville-Evrard , where patients had their heads and pubic hair shaved (to prevent infestations), were left to sleep on the floor "withering from starvation [and] dropped like flies."[97]

Who's the mad one in this "atmosphere of prurience, of anarchy, of disorder, of delirium, of dementia, of chronic lunacy, of psychic anomaly (for it isn't man but the world that has become abnormal), of deliberate dishonestly and downright hypocrisy"?[98] In the 1986

Argentinian cult classic film, *The Man Facing Southeast*, a man claiming to be an alien appears one day in the asylum on a mission to understand humankind. He endears himself to everyone, including the psychiatrist, whose interest is split between genuine love for the man and a clinical fascination with figuring out what's wrong with him. Rantes, the alien, snaps at him one day:

> I'm more rational than you. I respond rationally to stimulus. If someone suffers, I console him. If someone needs my help, I give it. Why, then, do you think I'm crazy? If someone looks at me, I respond. If someone speaks, I listen. You have slowly gone mad by ignoring those stimuli, simply by looking the other way. Someone is dying and you let him die. Someone asks for your help and you look away. Someone is hungry and you squander what you have. Someone is dying of sorrow and you lock him up so as not to see him. Anybody who systematically behaves this way, who walks among them as if the victims weren't there . . . may dress well, may pay taxes, may go to Mass, but you can't deny he is sick. Your reality is terrifying, Doctor. Why don't you end your hypocrisy and look at the madness out here for once? And stop persecuting the sad ones, the poor in spirit, those who don't want to buy or can't buy all that shit you would gladly sell me. If you could, that is.[99]

In this sinister light, the mad are saner than the sane, what Bonaventure Ndikung calls the "ultra-sane,"[100] a "space explored and inhabited by those that have broken out, that have delivered themselves from the ordinariness, as well as the staleness and sogginess of the norms of society."[101] They see and tell the truth where mere appearances reign supreme.

A common representation of the mad is that they lack feeling; they are unaffected. For Artaud and for Rantes, the opposite is the case: the mad are those who feel the intricate movements of the cataclysms that put this world into motion so deeply that they radiate out from their pores, burning passersby like the heat from the torrid desert sun. They feel *too much* to the point of abolishing all sense, like when King Lear, overwhelmed by the irrationalities of his position, could only scream impotently into a storm as his power dissolved in full appraisal of reality's horror. It's an experience even the sovereign cannot override, so that the real King George III was beaten and hounded like a common pauper when he lost all good sense. Madness as folly appears in the mania of a *danse macabre*, a chorus of dancing skeletons, i.e., when the truth of the human's future confronts him in laughter. Unlike other romantic visions of madness as an explosive creative power, this representation of madness' power, like Artaud's, does not back away from describing it as illness, and illness as destruction, even if health, its supposed opposite, is positioned as a "plethora of deep-seated ills, of a tremendous zest for living, through a thousand corroded wounds, which must be forced to live."[102] What remains of madness in this hall of distorted mirrors?

It is seductive to simplify all this and simply represent madness as a chaotic tide of creative energy waiting to burst from the belly of the beast or as a quasi-natural tendency towards breakdown in structures of power, but this is deceptive. For if madness is definitely outside or beyond the order of the norm, it is not clearly as an opposing force, as is evidenced by the more sedative role of the town, court, and holy fools. Here is a deeply ambiguous figure appearing time and again through the history of madness: behind their iconoclastic turns of phrase and unsightly behavior is a conservative principle of preservation. Isolated from social life on account of their reputation for urinating out of windows and communing with beasts, courts from Europe to India nevertheless kept fools near the throne and granted them special permissions to speak clearly when others would be harshly punished. It is *because* of their disgraced status, unsightly appearances, and unstable relation with reality that they were granted these inverted privileges: only the court fool may reflect an image of power back as it truly is, pointing out, as no one else can, the prince's royal warts and sores. Their singular lack of concern for appearances and flattery made them especially trustworthy aides: as 'Abdallah ibn Mubarak said of the most famous Arabic fool Buhlul: "Oh Shaykh! The madman knows his own soul. True discourse must be heard from a madman."[103] This truth-telling does not necessarily threaten or undermine the sovereign but enables him to ingest what escapes him as jest. What could get an advisor killed could be said loud and clear by the bumbling fool. The same is ultimately true of the holy fool: in the *hadith* of Islam, it is stipulated that the holy fool is the only figure permitted to criticize God directly. They may say anything they please. His recording angels do not inscribe the deeds of fools, as they do for everyone else, since fools are excluded from the punishments laid out in the Quran.[104] Generally speaking, the prophet bears an ambiguous relationship to madness in the Jewish, Muslim, and Christian medieval traditions, but their madnesses were integrated as the mouthpieces of gods. Along these lines, in the *Phaedra*, Socrates judges madness in the arts and in the prophets to be of much greater value than sanity. Fools revel in disclosing the falsity of appearances, painting the world topsy-turvy so that kings look like fools and wild passions run amok in place of reason. But this piercing image of the contradictions and irrationality saturating the world is laughed at viciously and thus held in suspended animation by mirth and the simulation of transgression.

A tension between soothsaying and silence animates the movement of madness or unreason throughout history. Thucydides, one of the great historians of ancient Greece, told, like all the others, the deeds of great men. His narrative was sealed and confined to the stories of heroes and generals—until the arrival of the maddest of wars, the civil war, and the subsequent destabilization of the Athenian colonial holdings. Here, and only here, in tumult and chaos, do we bear witness to women and slaves acting as subjects.[105] *Logos*, reason, was a property of the head of the household, the patriarch, in a material way: only he was permitted to speak in the public forum, fight in wars, and vote. The association of women and slaves with madness and childhood is ancient and rooted in this patriarchal form of organization. In conditions of breakdown and disorder, where reason fails and *logos* cracks, the subordinate objects of management within the household—the slaves, the women, the children—find agency in the historical narrative. In Greece, the most revered of these prophets, the oracle to Apollo Pythia at Delphi, was also a woman. The cult of madness around Bacchus—the god of theater, wine, and madness—in Greece and Rome is yet another sanctified form. Mysterious bacchanalias, sometimes exclusive to women and held outside of the city, were believed by the nonparticipating public to be occasions of excess, disturbing enough to earn bannings from local politicians. Euripides, in his play *The Bacchae*, tells the tale of King Pentheus in Thebes who snubs Bacchus and his sacred rites, symbolically shunning irrationality along with him, as all foolishly rational leaders do. The dancing women in the mountains, driven mad by the wine god himself, seize upon Pentheus and rip his body limb from limb. These tales trace the outlines of an uneasy bond between madness and women. Madness first appears as a condition of possibility for the common woman's speech, but is it her own voice, or a formulaic projection of an animal irrationality? If the madwoman speaks, what does she actually say? If the history of psychiatry is, as Foucault suggested, actually a "monologue of reason about madness,"[106] on what conditions are mad subjects included and permitted to speak?

As often as madness has appeared as a condition for women's speech, it has also appeared as a mark of their absolute servitude in the terror of imposed silence. This duality of feminine madness has led to a debate in its feminist histories: Hélène Cixous, in *The Laugh of the Medusa*, interprets hysteria, the quintessential feminine madness, as a kind of (contained) revolt; others, like Marta Caminero-Santangelo and Shoshana Felman, see little in it but powerlessness, silence, and despair. There is a third element here as well: the popular photos of hysterics from Charcot, we know now, were staged. Those arms and legs in tortured knots and eyes looking deep into another world were the conscious postures of patients performing distress.[107] If once fools mobilized madness' fakery and wit to show us the world as it really was, here male doctors manipulate human clay to show us "real" madness by simulating it in the eyes of suffering women who stand before photographers in medical theaters. The other popular form of psychiatric photography showed women in recovery, portrayed in images as a smiling woman in the loving arms of a husband or dressed in the typical garb of a housewife.[108]

Anna Kavan's work is full of this central contradiction. Not long after she finished her first stint in a sanitarium, the English writer Helen Woods changed her name to Anna Kavan and committed herself to a new sparse, enigmatic writing style. Her novels dwell in the muddy waters of feminine madness where protagonists appear at one time as privy to the workings of the underworld—privileged visionaries of what lies behind the curtains of our dream world—and at another time as the lowest miserable creatures on Earth. Her revelatory visions of the sun, animals, and plants in *Asylum Piece* tending to cede to a relentless industrial swell of machinery and violence visit her so frequently she wants "to batter my head on the walls, to shatter my head with bullets, to beat the machines into pulp, into powder, along with my skull."[109] In *Who-Are-You?* the protagonist's husband, a

British colonial officer she was forced to marry, is seen solely as "Mr Dog-Head," a ferocious creature capable of little more than violation and brutality, whose acts of rage are announced by the flash of lightning. Moments of illumination, as often as they are a source of power and knowledge, simultaneously appear in Kavan's work at the precise moment of the most extreme disempowerment, when her characters feel "the queer empty sensation of having run down like a clock that needs winding."[110] Compare this to what occurs to Barbara O'Brien in her autobiographical *Operators and Things: The Inner Life of a Schizophrenic* when the world of work appears as one big game of manipulations following only the "rich, oily smell of money."[111] This, at the same moment as the "Hook Operators," little gremlin-like creatures, drive hooks into her back and turn her into a drivable "Thing." In a flash, the world appears as it really is, but its prophet is reduced to the status of an animal or a clock, objects denoting the need for an operator or owner to take charge in the form of the doctor or husband.

But must it be silence *or* power? Marleen Gorris' 1982 film *A Question of Silence* complicates this binary. Her film depicts three women, Christine, Annie, and Andrea—all strangers to one another—who one day all happen to enter the same dress shop. With quick knowing glances, they brutally murder the male shopkeeper after one is caught shoplifting while a few other women in the store simply observe, idly and approvingly. Throughout the course of the film, the forensic psychiatrist, Janine van den Bos, tries, to no avail, to find the crucial detail that would explain their spontaneous outburst. She comes to realize— both in her conversations with the women and in her own life—there was no inciting incident, no revelatory flash, no deep conspiracies, no *folie à trois*, just a life of indignities, humiliations, and many, many moments of silence in a man's world. Silence appears in many guises in the film: the silence of Christine, a housewife who refuses to speak through most of the film; the silence of Annie's lonely home; the silent reception of Andrea's contributions at work; until finally, the silent decision to take a life. Over time, even though "the women are all isolated in their varying conditions of silence . . . the silence gradually becomes more collective, and more like an active practice,"[112] especially in its confrontation with law, which is the man's world. The film depicts this literally by contrasting the psychiatrist with her husband, the lawyer, who one night at dinner casually calls the Dutch legal system "undemocratic" and doubts the utility of recounting one's backstory to the jury (his male friend sitting opposite calls it "a blanket in which the system can wrap up its sense of guilt"[113]), along with the court itself with its robed masculine judges. The climax comes in the courtroom, where the accused sit in disciplined silence. Van den Bos delivers the first blow: they're of sound mind, not crazy, which is to say, their actions are legible. Brutal, yes. Horrible, yes. Indefensible, perhaps. But incomprehensible . . . ? The second blow comes soon after, in tension with the first: after the prosecutor suggests that gender played no role in the attack seeing as it could have been perpetrated by three men against a woman without making a difference, the women in the courtroom (including, finally, the psychiatrist) erupt into the disorderly laughter of the fool. Sanity gives way to madness; the meaningful saturation of silence to blurting out everything all at once. At their extreme limits, they meet again at the axis of unsayable truth.

One of the big paradoxes of mad peoples' history—if such a phrase even makes sense—is that so many of its "maddest" representatives repudiate madness, desiring some other form of recognition. When James Tilly Matthews entered the House of Commons and accused the English ministry of "traitorous venality," believing them to be under the influence of a mysterious machine called an "air loom," he by no means imagined himself as mad. What does it mean to claim such figures for the history of madness or "mad pride" who had no pride in madness, or, at best, a deeply ambivalent relationship with it? Janet Frame's autobiography *An Angel at My Table* (1984) captures the ethical murkiness of this question. When she first received her schizophrenia diagnosis, she immediately scoured her psychology textbooks trying to decipher this strange word. What she found horrified her: "It seemed to spell my doom," she wrote, "as if I had emerged from a chrysalis, the natural human state, into another kind of creature, and even if there were parts of me that were familiar to human beings, my gradual deterioration would lead me further and further away, and in the end not even my family would know me."[114] But still, its logic began to take hold: "That the idea of my suffering from schizophrenia seemed to me so unreal, only increased my confusion when I learned that one of the symptoms was 'things seeming unreal.' There was no escape."[115] Even after a near-lobotomy and numerous dreaded shock treatments, when her diagnosis was finally reversed, all she could think to ask was:

"Oh why had they robbed me of my schizophrenia which had been the answer to all my misgivings about myself? Like King Lear I had gone in search of 'the truth' and I now had nothing. 'Nothing will come out of nothing.'"[116] Without it, she writes at another point, she was deprived of "the unexpected warmth, comfort, protection. . . . And even when I did not wear it openly," she continued, "I always had it by for emergency, to put on quickly, for shelter from the cruel world." Mental illness denied becomes a longing for just that. How could one communally internalize endless suffering without discrete and recognized cause? Whom do we turn to when we have no specific problem that needs solving, but need help and security nonetheless?

There is a strange categorization game at play: when madness is identified only to be explained or denied, is it still mad? A series of photographs, published in a Canadian collection called *Shrink Resistant*, about the author Persimmon Blackridge's experience of being labeled mad as a lesbian is called "Still Sane." *Madness Network News* has likely devoted more time than other journals to the question of madness. In the first article of vol. 1, no. 4, the author starts out with the kind of obscure contradictory definition so common in the history of madness: "Madness is not madness."[117] The poem that follows takes the more ambiguous position that "everyone is mad at times,"[118] explaining that what we call madness is coherent as a common, though strange or extreme, experience. These are representative of positions that remain among the most popular in antipsychiatry: denial, contextualization, normalization. What remains of madness? Is it only the name others use to identify problem people? With enough time and attention—on the scale of geologic time, with divine access to all known facts in the universe leading up to the present—could not every madness be explained away as a meaningful, even reasonable, condition? By being made comprehensible and normalized, is it not therefore also sanitized and rendered sane? Such are the contradictions at play when one sets out to politicize or organize around "madness" or psychiatric status (and surely I have only scratched the surface), comprising what Hel Spandler recently called the "uncomfortable truths of survivor narratives."[119] It seems madness cannot make contact without inverting and scattering what it strikes, like a reverse Midas touch that converts gold back into shit. "Mad" is a cognate of the Gothic words for "exchange" and "adulterate," evoking a process of transforming while making impure through mixture. Around it, a linguistic constellation of contradictions took shape: Icelandic connects it to "crippled"; Old High German to "vain" and "boastful"; English to "happy" and "brave." A craze denotes a new fad, a new derangement; crazing in pottery refers to a network of tiny cracks that form on the surface of the product.[120] I am tempted here to say that madness is not a break from reason, like sickness is a fall from health, but that reason is but a modification of irrationality, a particular form in which it appears. Crazy makes so many cracks on the surface of things—is there anything underneath?

An Arabic proverb tells us *al-junun funun* [madness is of many kinds]. "What is madness?" asks Najib Mahfuz, "It appears to be a mysterious condition, much like life and death. You can learn a lot about it if you look at it from the outside, as for its interior, its core, it's a suppressed secret."[121] If there is an inside of madness, it could only be like the inside of a circus tent on a moonlit night. Circus, from circulus, evokes circularity and the weightless rush around racetracks. It is described by Jean Clair as "that magic space in which bodies escape gravity. Under the sky of the big top, bodies describe precise arcs, stretch out figures that, being akin to those of the zodiac, hint at fate."[122] If it does have a sign, it would be that of the moon, the celestial body whose phases—shrouding us in illuminative light or leaving us in the deepest darkness—govern the states of lunatics; literally, those whose madness is tied to the position of the moon. Down below, beneath the acrobat who defies the physics of ground and sky, clowns defy the physics that govern the space of the interior, making light of all depth psychologies, investing enormous weight to the trivial loss of a flower before gleefully rushing headlong into the clearest sign of danger. The rolling of drums preceding a great feat calls to mind the spectacular execution of the criminal; but now, joy erupts when the performer escapes their pronounced fate. Destiny is overturned; the law is bounced around like a ball for a cheap thrill.

According to Henry Miller, the clown is identical to "the story which he enacts." He invites us to partake of life's constant flux, offering us the "gift of surrender."[123] The clown inhabits a world where the lowest scoundrels can find love just before the haughtiest king falls plopping into muck. And yet, if it is a space imbued with magic, we also know that not all magic is benevolent. The English word for clown originally referred to an uneducated peasant. The veil of irreality enshrouding the spectacle of clownery may subvert the expected, but, at its worst, it merely ritualizes it, allowing an audience to guiltlessly laugh at the physical deformity of "freaks" or to revel in the cruelty of watching the *Auguste* character, the "one who gets slapped," cry out in pain. That captive human beings have been put on display under the big tent in colonial expositions and the Jim Crow South shows it to be a place where the deepest malevolence dwells.

Responding to the question "can the mad organize themselves?" there are, at this juncture, three equally true answers. Yes, the mad already informally organize themselves wherever they talk openly about their pain and strengths, meet in group homes or on street corners, exchange cigarettes or secrets. The mad organize themselves in every psych ward, every clubhouse, and every asylum in the world. No, not towards new horizons, because madness is so thoroughly awash in the phantasmagoria of a million mental health markets that present few openings for anything beyond the modification of the language used by service providers. And, finally, not for long, because "the mad" cannot organize themselves without madness itself negating the effort and transmuting it to new forms. Without question, it is folly to gather under the circus tent of madness to plot the end of the world, ludicrous to imagine finding resonance surrounded by distorting funhouse mirrors. Efforts to think madness *as such* or to organize around it in the past quickly evaporated. The fact is: there has been no mass movement of the mad *as mad*, there have been few psych ward riots, few sustained revolts of genius and fantasy against tyrannical reason that didn't come to settle into their own form of reason. The *madness of madness* absolutely forbids this as it deviously transforms all efforts to make it appear into its exact opposite, sanity. Madness beckons from an elsewhere that's here and now and expects a response. Madness may in the end be nothing, but it has been, and it will become the fate of millions. If it's nothing, then it's a nothing that grabs hold of boundaries and corrodes them with its acidic drool while polarizing opposing terms to the farthest imaginable reaches. Perhaps one day we crushed ones, we losers, we self-destroyers, we rats will pile up into a rat king and move like a wave of ten million would-be suicides across the Earth, obliterating our labyrinth in the process. On that day, we'll chew up all the money and spit it out of our rabid, frothing mouths into the drain, gleefully sending it back to the nothingness from which it came—in place of our friends, for once. Understood through the weeping gaze of the clown, to set out with and through madness as a process belonging to all of us—somewhere between common exchange and adulteration—is to adopt a fundamentally ethical posture. From the position of a captive humanity forever whirling around in its circulus—the vortex-like racetrack from which the circus derives its name—madness reveals the essential truths of the world only to parade them in a blurry masquerade making its way around a winding orbit. But, unlike the cosmic powerhouses churning at the axes of Andromeda and the Milky Way, activating systems of thermodynamic relays, there is only stale air in the center. It is here—denied the assurance of soil, flung round with glee or nausea, glimpsing only ephemeral markers to guide our passage—where we are called together by some mad howl to act and to find each other.

Notes

1. Henry Friedlander, *The Origins of Nazi Genocide: From Euthanasia to the Final Solution* (Chapel Hill: University of North Carolina Press, 1995), 170.
2. Doerner, *Madmen and Bourgeoisie*, 166.
3. See Doerner, *Madmen and Bourgeoisie*, 133–134 for more on German psychiatry's tight-knit relationship with and higher degree of reliance on the state compared to other European traditions.
4. Doerner, *Madmen and Bourgeoisie*, 242.
5. Quoted in Doerner, *Madmen and Bourgeoisie*, 254.
6. Griesinger, *Mental Pathology and Therapeutics*, 6.
7. Engstrom, *Clinical Psychiatry in Imperial Germany*, 132.
8. Robert N. Proctor, *Racial Hygiene: Medicine under the Nazis* (Cambridge, MA: Harvard University Press, 1988), 20.
9. Michael Burleigh, "Psychiatry, German Society, and the Nazi 'Euthanasia' Programme," *Social History of Medicine* 7, no. 2 (August 1994): 214.
10. Burleigh, "Psychiatry, German Society, and the Nazi 'Euthanasia' Programme," 216.
11. B. Walter, "Hermann Simon – Psychiatriereformer, Sozialdarwinist, Nationalsozialist?," *Nervenarzt* 73 (2002): 1053.
12. Proctor, *Racial Hygiene*, 64.
13. Saul Dubow, *Scientific Racism in Modern South Africa* (Cambridge: Cambridge University Press, 1995), 169.
14. Jonathan D. Ablard, *Madness in Buenos Aires: Patients, Psychiatrists, and the Argentine State 1880–1983* (Calgary: University of Calgary Press, 2008), 28. He notes, however, that very few were effectively restricted on account of this law. For more on Argentinian eugenics and immigration laws, see Nancy Leys Stepan, *"The Hour of Eugenics:" Race, Gender, and the Nation in Latin America* (Ithaca: Cornell University Press, 1991), 142.
15. "Immigration Restriction Act 1901," Australian Federal Register of Legislation, https://www.legislation.gov.au/Details/C1901A00017.
16. Alison Bashford, *Imperial Hygiene: A Critical History of Colonialism, Nationalism and Public Health* (Houndsmills: Palgrave Macmillan, 2004), 138. See also Stephen Garton,

"Eugenics in Australia and New Zealand: Laboratories of Racial Science," in *The Oxford Handbook of the History of Eugenics*, ed. Alison Bashford and Philippa Levine (Oxford: Oxford University Press, 2010), 243–257.

17. *Buck v. Bell*, 274 U.S. 200 (1927).

18. Stepan, *"The Hour of Eugenics,"* 30.

19. On the reluctance to implement extreme negative eugenics measures, see Stepan, *"The Hour of Eugenics,"* 111–112.

20. In California, the state that performed the majority of operations (over 20,000), Black and Mexican women accounted for 4 percent and 7 percent of the total—despite only representing 1 percent and 4 percent of the per capita population, respectively. See Alexandra Minna Stern, "Sterilized in the Name of Public Health: Race, Immigration, and Reproductive Control in Modern California," *American Journal of Public Health* 95, no. 7 (July 2005): 1128–1138, https://www.ncbi.nlm.nih.gov/pmc/articles/PMC1449330/.

21. See Lutz Kaelber, "Eugenics/Eugenic Sterilizations in Indiana," in online research project *Eugenics: Compulsory Sterilization in 50 American States*, Department of Sociology, University of Vermont, https://www.uvm.edu/~lkaelber/eugenics/IN/IN.html.

22. Numbers differ, but usually land in the range between 100,000 to 200,000. See Segrest, *Administrations of Lunacy*, 274. The numbers are also tricky to pin down because the line between voluntary and forced sterilization can be elusive. Decisions made under extreme duress or when the state makes it a precondition for services or liberty may be chosen, but they are not totally free.

23. Sanjana Manjeshwar, "America's Forgotten History of Forced Sterilization," *Berkeley Political Review*, November 2020, https://bpr.berkeley.edu/2020/11/04/americas-forgotten-history-of-forced-sterilization/.

24. Klaus Doerner, "Nationalsozialismus und Lebensvernichtung," *Jahrgang* 15, no. 2 (1967): 130.

25. Friedlander, *The Origins*, 7.

26. Proctor, *Racial Hygiene*, 96.

27. Proctor, *Racial Hygiene*, 107.

28. Proctor, *Racial Hygiene*, 107. Friedlander recounts other cases where the Nazis illegally sterilized racial minorities solely on account of their race, but this was never written into law. See Friedlander, *The Origins*, 247.

29. Dubow, *Scientific Racism*, 153.

30. Stephen Garton, "Eugenics in Australia and New Zealand," 247–248. Garton argues that segregationist and sterilization policies failed partly because of opposition from the scientific community and the Catholic Church, but more so because policy tended to focus on the threat of external contagions from Asia, for example.

31. Theodore Jun Yoo, *It's Madness: The Politics of Mental Health in Colonial Korea* (Oakland: University of California Press 2016), 65–71.

32. Sumiko Otsubo and James R. Bartholomew, "Eugenics in Japan: Some Ironies of Modernity, 1883–1945," *Science in Context* 11, no. 3–4 (1998): 547–552.

33. Jennifer Robertson, "Blood Talks: Eugenic Modernity and the Creation of New Japanese," *History and Anthropology* 13, no. 3 (2002): 194–199.

34. Takashi Tsuchiya, "Eugenic Sterilizations in Japan and Recent Demands for Apology: A Report," *Newsletter of the Network on Ethics and Intellectual Disability* 3, no.1 (Fall 1997): 1.

35. Tsuchiya, "Eugenic Sterilizations in Japan and Recent Demands for Apology," 2–4.

36. Gerrit Hohendorf, "The Extermination of Mentally Ill and Handicapped People under National Socialist Rule," case study, Mass Violence and Resistance – Research Network, Sciences Po, November 17, 2016, https://www.sciencespo.fr/mass-violence-war-massacre-resistance/en/document/extermination-mentally-ill-and-handicapped-people-under-national-socialist-rule.html#title1.

37. B. M. Z. Cohen, *Psychiatric Hegemony: A Marxist Theory of Mental Illness* (London: Palgrave Macmillan, 2016), 179.

38. Karl Binding and Alfred Hoche, *Permitting the Destruction of Life Unworthy of Living* (1920), in *German History in Documents and Images*, Volume 6: The Weimar Republic, 1918/19–1933, https://ghdi.ghi-dc.org/sub_document.cfm?document_id=4496.

39. Propaganda films regularly used footage of real asylum inmates. *Dasein ohne Leben* lit the patients from beneath in dark rooms to emphasize their strangest facial features. See Stewart Lansley, Joanna Mack, Michael Burleigh (dirs..), "Selling Murder: The Killing Films of the Third Reich," London: Domino Films, 1991, https://www.youtube.com/watch?v=c2kV83nPWnM&t=1007s.

40. "Letter by Man Accused of Mass Stabbings Carried Eerie Warning," *The Asahi Shimbun*, July 26, 2016, https://web.archive.org/web/20160726124743/http://www.asahi.com/ajw/articles/AJ201607260083.html.

41. Kwiyeon Ha and Linda Sieg, "Japan Confronts Disability Stigma after Silence over Murder Victims' Names," *Reuters*, September 16, 2016, https://web.archive.org/web/20160917162306/http://www.reuters.com/article/japan-disabled-idUSL-3N1BS0AV.

42. Burleigh, "Psychiatry, German Society," 217–219.

43. Hohendorf, "The Extermination."

44. Proctor, *Racial Hygiene*, 190.

45. Burleigh, "Psychiatry, German Society," 223.

46. Proctor, *Racial Hygiene*, 191.

47. The English translation is from Charlie English, *The Gallery of Miracles and Madness: Insanity, Modernism, and Hitler's War on Art* (New York: Penguin Random House, 2021), 181–182. The original can be seen in Ernst Klee, *Dokumente zur Euthanasie* (Frankfurt am Main: Fischer Taschenbuch Verlag, 1995), 95–96.

48. Burleigh, "Psychiatry, German Society," 224.

49. Ernst Klee, *Sichten und vernichten – Psychiatrie im Dritten Reich*, Germany: Hessischer Rundfunk, 1995, https://www.youtube.com/watch?v=f9cEbCe5Mos.

50. Friedlander, *The Origins*, 67.

51. Proctor, *Racial Hygiene*, 192.

52. These are all recounted in Klee's film *Sichten und vernichten – Psychiatrie im Dritten Reich*.

53. Geronimo, *Fire and Flames: A History of the German Autonomist Movement* (Oakland: PM Press, 2012), 27–28.

54. George Katsiaficas, *The Subversion of Politics: European Autonomous Social Movements and the Decolonization of Everyday Life* (Chico: AK Press, 1997), 60–63.

55. Christian Pross, "Revolution and Madness – The 'Socialist Patients' Collective of Heidelberg (SPK)': An Episode in the History of Antipsychiatry and the 1960s Student Rebellion in West Germany," self-published, 2016, 7–8, http://christian-pross.de/pross-revolution-and-madness1.pdf; Hugo Bütrer, "From the Pleasure Principle to the Wolves' Philosophy," *The German Issue*, ed. Sylvère Lotringer (Los Angeles: Semiotext(e), 2009), 197. For more, see Cornelia Brink, *Grenzen der Anstalt. Psychiatrie und Gesellschaft in Deutschland 1860–1980* (Göttingen: Wallstein Verlag, 2010), 434.

56. Pross, "Revolution and Madness," 6.

57. Brink, *Grenzen der Anstalt*, 435.

58. Socialist Patients' Collective, "Turn Illness into a Weapon," *Indybay*, 2013, 7–8, https://www.indybay.org/newsitems/2013/11/14/18746394.php. I have opted to use the unofficial translation posted on *Indybay* as opposed to the one Huber himself put out in 1973. The latter is, by his own admission, very unsatisfactory and borders on unreadable in parts. The more recent unofficial translation is much more accurate and smooth. Sometimes, I will include the original German in brackets, if it makes my argument clearer or if there is an ambiguous meaning.

59. This unfortunately still continues with a group calling themselves PF-SPK (Patient Front-Socialist Patients' Collective). Texts from recent decades released under that name are broadly and stereotypically medical-conspiratorial, which in my view is a major departure from the contributions of the SPK in *Turn Illness into a Weapon*. This

newer group has gone so far as to deny the existence of AIDS, COVID-19, and other conditions as mere "machinations" of doctors. They seem to be very keen on revising the past by claiming the SPK had no involvement with the movement of '68, antipsychiatry, or other social movements, something which is easily falsifiable by looking at their own texts and participant observations. To that end, they have published statements denouncing individuals who write about their past in a way they disapprove of. I don't reference or discuss these newer texts in the main body of the book because I see no reason to believe this new formation is representative of the group that formed around 1970 and published *Turn Illness into a Weapon*.

60. Socialist Patients' Collective, *Turn Illness into a Weapon*, 1.
61. Socialist Patients' Collective, *Turn Illness into a Weapon*, 59.
62. Socialist Patients' Collective, *Turn Illness into a Weapon*, 2.
63. Karl Marx, *Economic and Philosophic Manuscripts of 1844* and the *Communist Manifesto* [also by Friedrich Engels], trans. Martin Milligan (Amherst: Prometheus Books, 1988), 74.
64. Quoted in Socialist Patients' Collective, *Turn Illness into a Weapon*, 59.
65. Socialist Patients' Collective, *Turn Illness into a Weapon*, 59.
66. Socialist Patients' Collective, *Turn Illness into a Weapon*, 2.
67. Socialist Patients' Collective, *Turn Illness into a Weapon*, 6.
68. Socialist Patients' Collective, *Turn Illness into a Weapon*, 79.
69. Socialist Patients' Collective, *Turn Illness into a Weapon*, 8.
70. Socialist Patients' Collective, *Turn Illness into a Weapon*, 26.
71. Socialist Patients' Collective, *Turn Illness into a Weapon*, 60.
72. Unidentified member speaking in Gerd Kroske (dir.), *SPK Komplex*. Germany: Realistfilm and Rundfunk Berlin-Brandenburg (RBB) 2018, Vimeo, https://vimeo.com/ondemand/spkkomplex.
73. Socialist Patients' Collective, *Turn Illness into a Weapon*, 59.
74. Dora García and Carmen Roll, "An Interview with Carmen Roll," *Mad Marginal, Cahier #1: From Basaglia to Brazil* (Milan: Mousse, 2010), 150, http://theinadequate.doragarcia.org/wp-content/uploads/2011/04/MM01.pdf.
75. Ana Antić, "Decolonizing Madness? Transcultural Psychiatry, International Order and Birth of a 'Global Psyche' in the Aftermath of the Second World War," *Journal of Global History* 17, no. 1 (2022): 24.
76. Antić, "Decolonizing Madness?," 27.
77. Antić, "Decolonizing Madness?," 31.
78. For a summary and critique of the arguments presented here, see Chapter 3 of Nikolas Rose, *Our Psychiatric Future* (Cambridge: Polity, 2019).
79. Ethan Watters, *Crazy Like Us: The Globalization of the American Psyche* (London: Robinson Publishing, 2011).
80. China Mills, *Decolonizing Global Mental Health: The Psychiatrization of the Majority World* (London: Routledge, 2014).
81. Liat Ben-Moshe, *Decarcerating Disability: Deinstitutionalization and Prison Abolition* (Minneapolis: University of Minnesota Press, 2020), 60–62. Richard Warner offers further quantitative evidence for this claim in *Recovery from Schizophrenia: Psychiatry and Political Economy* (Hove: Brunner-Routledge, 1997), 87.
82. Socialist Patients' Collective, *Turn Illness into a Weapon*, 83.
83. Quoted in Socialist Patients' Collective, *Turn Illness into a Weapon*, 102.
84. Friedrich Engels. *The Condition of the Working-Class in England* (Moscow: Progress Publishers, 1980), 120–121.
85. The most up-to-date history and literature overview on the controversy in English is in Beatrice Adler-Bolton and Artie Vierkant, *Health Communism* (London: Verso, 2022), 154–178.
86. Anne Klein, "Governing Madness—Transforming Psychiatry: Disability History and the Formation of Cultural Knowledge in West Germany in the 1970s and 1980s,"

Moving the Social 53 (2015): 24, https://moving-the-social.ub.rub.de/index.php/MTS/article/view/7471/6643.

87. Sessi Kuwabara Blanchard, "How the Young Lords Took Lincoln Hospital, Left a Health Activism Legacy," *Filter*, October 30, 2018, https://filtermag.org/how-the-young-lords-took-lincoln-hospital-and-left-a-health-activism-legacy/.

88. David Cooper, *The Language of Madness* (London: Penguin Books, 1978), 171.

89. Yves-Luc Conreur, "A Statement from the Psychiatrized," *State and Mind: People Look at Psychology* 6, no. 2 (Winter 1977): 1. Courtesy of the Oskar Diethelm Library, DeWitt Institute for the History of Psychiatry, Weill Cornell Medical College.

90. W. A. F. Browne, *The Asylum as Utopia: W. A. F. Browne and the Mid-Nineteenth Century Consolidation of Psychiatry*, ed. Andrew Scull (London: Routledge, 2014), 8.

91. Antonin Artaud, *Artaud Anthology*, ed. Jack Hirschman (San Francisco: City Lights, 1965), 158.

92. Artaud, *Artaud Anthology*, 158.

93. Artaud, *Artaud Anthology*, 192.

94. Artaud, *Artaud Anthology*, 135.

95. Artaud, *Artaud Anthology*, 193.

96. Artaud, *Artaud Anthology*, 147.

97. Sylvére Lotringer, *Mad Like Artaud* (Minneapolis: Univocal, 2003), 15.

98. Artaud, *Artaud Anthology*, 135.

99. Eliseo Subiela, (dir.), *Man Facing Southeast*, Argentina: Cinequanon 1986, DVD.

100. Ndikung, *Ultrasanity*, 21.

101. Ndikung, *Ultrasanity*, 21.

102. Artaud, *Artaud Anthology*, 157–158.

103. Michael Dols, *Majnun: The Madman in Medieval Islamic Society* (Oxford: Clarendon Press, 1992), 149.

104. Dols, *Majnun*, 397.

105. Nicole Loraux, *The Experience of Tiresias: The Feminine and the Greek Man* (Princeton: Princeton University Press, 1995), 235–236.

106. Michel Foucault, *History of Madness*, ed. and trans. Jean Khalfa (London and New York: Routledge, 2009), xxviii.

107. Showalter, *The Female Malady*, 150.

108. Showalter, *The Female Malady*, 86.

109. Anna Kavan, *Machines in the Head* (New York: New York Review of Books, 2019), 140.

110. Anna Kavan, *Guilty* (London: Peter Owen, 2007), epub.

111. Barbara O'Brien, *Operators and Things: The Inner Life of a Schizophrenic* (Los Angeles: Silver Birch Press, 2011), 40.

112. Amelia Groom, "'Eruptions of Silence': The Unheard, the Unsaid, and the Politics of Laughter in Marleen Gorris' A Question of Silence," Another Screen, https://www.another-screen.com/silence-laughter.

113. Marleen Gorris (dir.), *A Question of Silence [De stilte rond Christine M.]*, The Netherlands: EYE Film Institute Netherlands, 1982, digital.

114. Janet Frame, "1945," in *An Angel at My Table* (London: Virago, 1989), epub.

115. Frame, "The Boardinghouse and the New World," in *An Angel at My Table* (London: Virago, 1989), epub.

116. Frame, "The Investigation and the Verdict," in *An Angel at My Table* (London: Virago, 1989), epub.

117. John Lilly, "Madness or 'The History of Religion is the History of Madness,'" *Madness Network News* 1, no. 4 (1973): 1.

118. Wade Hudson, "On Madness," *Madness Network News* 1, no. 4 (1973): 1.

119. Ayurdhi Dhar, "Uncomfortable Truths in Survivor Narratives: An Interview with Helen Spandler," *Mad in America*, February 24, 2021, https://www.madinamerica.com/2021/02/uncomfortable-truths-survivor-narratives-interview-helen-spandler/.

120. Anatoly Liberman, "There Are More Ways than One to Be Mad," *OUPblog*, July 4, 2007, https://blog.oup.com/2007/07/mad/.

121. Quoted in Dols, *Majnun*, 1.
122. Jean Clair, "Parade and Palingenesis: Of the Circus in the Work of Picasso and Others," in *The Great Parade: Portrait of the Artist as Clown* (New Haven: Yale University Press, 2004), 21.
123. "Workshops," hopkins/workshop for clown research, https://www.clownforschung.de/seite/406522/workshops-events.html.

BIBLIOGRAPHY

Ablard, Jonathan D. "Authoritarianism, Democracy and Psychiatric Reform in Argentina, 1943–83." *History of Psychiatry* 14, no. 3 (2003): 361–376.

———. *Madness in Buenos Aires: Patients, Psychiatrists, and the Argentine State, 1880–1983*. Calgary: University of Calgary Press, 2008.

Addington v. Texas, 441 U.S. 418 (1979).

Aderhold, Volkmar, Peter Stastny, and Peter Lehmann. "Soteria: An Alternative Mental Health Reform Movement." *Alternatives Beyond Psychiatry*, edited by Peter Stastny and Peter Lehmann, 146–160. Berlin: Peter Lehmann Publishing, 2007.

Adler-Bolton, Beatrice and Artie Vierkant. Beatrice Adler-Bolton and Artie Vvierkant. "Capitalism & Disability: A Symposium on the Work of Marta Russell," *LPE Project*, October 3, 2022. https://lpeproject.org/blog/capitalism-disability-a-symposium-on-the-work-of-marta-russell/.

———. *Health Communism*. London: Verso, 2022.

Alighieri, Dante. *The Divine Comedy*. Translated by Allen Mandelbaum. New York: Alfred A. Knopf & Everyman's Library, 1995.

Amarante, Paulo. *Madness and Social Change: Autobiography of the Brazilian Psychiatric Reform*. Cham: Springer, 2022.

Amarante, Paulo and Eduardo Henrique Guimarães Torre. "'Back to the City, Mr. Citizen!' –Psychiatric Reform and Social Participation: From Institutional Isolation to the Anti-asylum Movement." *Brazilian Journal of Public Administration* 52, no. 6 (2018): 1090–1107. https://www.scielo.br/pdf/rap/v52n6/en_1982-3134-rap-52-06-1090.pdf.

Amarante, Paulo and Mariana Rangel. "Freedom is Therapeutic: Reinventing Lives in Psychiatric Reform." *Revista Eletrônica de Comunicação Informação & Inovação em Saúde* 3, no. 4 (December 2009): 10–16. https://www.reciis.icict.fiocruz.br/index.php/reciis/article/view/747/1760.

Amarante, Paulo and Mônica de Oliveria Nunes. "Psychiatric Reform in the SUS and the Struggle for a Society without Asylums." *Ciência & Saúde Coletiva* 23, no. 6 (2018): 2067–2074.

Antić, Ana. "Decolonizing Madness? Transcultural Psychiatry, International Order and Birth of a 'Global Psyche' in the Aftermath of the Second World War." *Journal of Global History* 17, no. 1 (2022): 20–41.

Araujo, Felipe Neis. "Lula Quietly Legitimizes Brazil's Forced Drug Treatment Institutions," *Filter*, February 1, 2023. https://filtermag.org/lula-therapeutic-community-support-department/.

Arrigo, Bruce. *Punishing the Mentally Ill: A Critical Analysis of Law and Psychiatry*. Albany: SUNY Press, 2002.

Artaud, Antonin. *Artaud Anthology*. Edited by Jack Hirschman. San Francisco: City Lights, 1965.

Baker, Adelaide Nichols. "The Challenge of The Labyrinth." *Mental Hygiene News* 11, no. 6 (September 1932): 2.

Barraclough, Brian. "In Conversation with Maxwell Jones." *Bulletin of the Royal College of Psychiatrists* 8, no. 9 (September 1984): 166–170.

Basaglia, Franco. "Breaking the Circuit of Control." In *Critical Psychiatry: The Politics of Mental Health*, edited by David Ingleby, 184–192. New York: Pantheon Books, 1980.

———. "The Destruction of the Mental Hospital as a Place of Institutionalization: Thoughts Caused by Personal Experience with the Open Door System and Part Time Service." *PsychoOdyssey* 1. https://web.archive.org/web/20110722062127/http://www.triestesalutementale.it/english/doc/basaglia_1964_destruction-mhh.pdf.

———. *Psychiatry Inside Out: Selected Writings of Franco Basaglia*. Edited by Nancy Scheper-Hughes and Anne M. Lovell. New York: Columbia University Press, 1987.

———. *L'utopia della realtà*. Milan: Piccola Biblioteca Einaudi Ns, 2005.

Basaglia, Franca Ongaro. "The Psychiatric Reform in Italy: Summing Up and Looking Ahead." *International Journal of Social Psychiatry* 35, no. 1 (1989): 90–97.

Basaglia, Franca Ongaro and Franco Basaglia. "Italy's Aborted Psychiatric Reform." *International Journal of Mental Health* 14, no. 1–2 (Spring–Summer 1985): 9–21.

———. "A Problem of Institutional Psychiatry: Exclusion as a Social and Psychiatric Category." *International Review of Psychiatry* 30, no. 2 (2018): 120–128.

Basauri, Victor Aparicio. "Spain: The Critical Movements and the Influence of Franco Basaglia and 'Democratic Psychiatry.'" In *Basaglia's International*

Legacy: from Asylum to Community, edited by Tom Burns and John Foot, 147–160. Oxford: Oxford University Press, 2020.

Bashford, Alison. *Imperial Hygiene: A Critical History of Colonialism, Nationalism and Public Health*. Houndsmills: Palgrave Macmillan, 2004.

Battie, William. *A Treatise on Madness*. London: J. Whiston and B. White, 1758.

Beal, Frances M. *Black Women's Manifesto; Double Jeopardy: To Be Black and Female*. New York: Third World Women's Alliance, 1969.

Beckwith, Ruthie-Marie. *Disability Servitude: From Peonage to Poverty*. New York: Palgrave Macmillan, 2016.

Beers, Clifford Whittingham. *A Mind That Found Itself: An Autobiography*. Project Gutenberg e-book, April 2004/March 1908. https://www.gutenberg.org/files/11962/11962-h/11962-h.htm.

Ben-Moshe, Liat. *Decarcerating Disability: Deinstitutionalization and Prison Abolition*. Minneapolis: University of Minnesota Press, 2020.

Ben Plotkin, Mariano. *Freud in the Pampas: The Emergence and Development of a Psychoanalytic Culture in Argentina*. Stanford: Stanford University Press, 2001.

Benjamin, Walter. *Selected Writings Volume 1: 1913–1926*. Edited by Marcus Bullock and Michael W. Jennings. Cambridge, MA and London: The Belknap Press of Harvard University Press, 1996.

Beresford, Peter and Suzy Croft. "Service Users' Knowledges and the Social Construction of Social Work." *Journal of Social Work* 1, no. 3 (2001): 295–316.

Bigwood, Lyn. "Lyn Bigwood Talk to R.D. Laing—Sanity, Madness and the Psychiatric Profession." *Asylum: The Magazine for Democratic Psychiatry* 1, no. 1 (Spring 1986): 13–21.

Biehl, João. *Vita: Life in a Zone of Social Abandonment*. Berkeley: University of California Press, 2005.

Blanchard, Sessi Kuwabara. "How the Young Lords Took Lincoln Hospital, Left a Health Activism Legacy." *Filter*, October 30, 2018. https://filtermag.org/how-the-young-lords-took-lincoln-hospital-and-left-a-health-activism-legacy/.

Bly, Nellie. *Ten Days in a Madhouse*. New York: Ian L. Monroe, 1887.

Braga, Cláudia. "Arguments for Utopias of Reality and the Brazilian Psychiatric Reform Experience." *Saúde e Sociedade* 29, no. 3 (2020): 1–11. https://www.scielo.br/j/sausoc/a/MZ4V47nnytfHZ9Y9cL3X3dk/?lang=en.

Brink, Cornelia. *Grenzen der Anstalt. Psychiatrie und Gesellschaft in Deutschland 1860–1980*. Göttingen: Wallstein Verlag, 2010.

Brouwers, Evelien P. M. "Social Stigma is an Underestimated Contributing Factor to Unemployment in People with Mental Illness or Mental Health Issues: Position Paper and Future Directions." *BMC Psychology* 8, no. 1 (2020). https://doi.org/10.1186/s40359-020-00399-0.

Browne, W. A. F. *The Asylum as Utopia: W. A. F. Browne and the Mid-Nineteenth Century Consolidation of Psychiatry*. Edited by Andrew Scull. London: Routledge, 2014.

Büchner, Georg. "Danton's Death." In *Complete Works and Letters*, edited by Walter Hinderer and Henry J. Schmidt, 57–123. New York: Continuum, 1986.

Buck v. Bell, 274 U.S. 200 (1927).

Bulhan, Hussein Abdilahi. *Frantz Fanon and the Psychology of Oppression*. New York: Plenum Press, 1985.

Burleigh, Michael. "Psychiatry, German Society, and the Nazi 'Euthanasia' Programme." *Social History of Medicine* 7, no. 2 (August 1994): 213–228.

Burton, Robert. *The Anatomy of Melancholy*. New York: New York Review of Books, 2001.

Bütrer, Hugo. "From the Pleasure Principle to the Wolves' Philosophy." *The German Issue, New Edition*, edited by Sylvère Lotringer, 194–199. Los Angeles: Semiotext(e), 2009/1982.

Cabañas, Kaira M. *Learning from Madness: Brazilian Modernism and Global Contemporary Art*. Chicago: University of Chicago Press, 2018.

Caló, Susana. "Can an Institution be Militant?" *Metabolic Rifts. A Reader*. Lisbon and Berlin: Atlas Projectos, 2019.

———. "The Grid." *Technoscience*, April 23, 2016. https://www.anthropocene-curriculum.org/contribution/the-grid.

———. "Network of Alternatives to Psychiatry # 0 – Project presentation." Chaosmosemedia, May 15, 2021. https://chaosmosemedia.net/en/2021/05/15/network-of-alternatives-to-psychiatry-0-project-presentation/.

Caminero-Santangelo, Marta. *The Madwoman Can't Speak: Or Why Insanity is Not Subversive*. Ithaca: Cornell University Press, 1998.

Canguilhem, Georges. *The Normal and the Pathological*. Translated by Carolyn R. Fawcett. New York: Zone Books, 1991.

Carmichael, Stokely. "Black Power." In Stokely Carmichael, David Cooper, R.D. Laing, and Herbert Marcuse, *The Dialectics of Liberation*, edited by David Cooper. London and New York: Verso, 2015. Epub.

Carrington, Leonora. *Down Below*. New York: New York Review of Books, 1988.

Castel, Robert. *The Regulation of Madness: The Origins of Incarceration in France*. Berkeley: University of California Press, 1988.

Castel, Robert, Françoise Castel, and Anne M. Lovell. *The Psychiatric Society*. New York: Columbia University Press, 1982.

Castel, Robert and Mony Elkaïm. "Excerpts from the Introductory Statement to the Network, Trieste, September 1977." *State and Mind: People Look at Psychology* 6, no. 2 (Winter 1977): 15–16. Courtesy of the Oskar Diethelm Library, DeWitt Institute for the History of Psychiatry, Weill Cornell Medical College.

Castro, Eliane Dias de, and Elizabeth Maria Freire de Araújo Lima. "Resistance, Innovation and Clinical Practice in Nise da Silveira's Thoughts and Actions." Translated by Helena Bononi. *Interface [Botucatu]* 3, no. se (2007). http://socialsciences.scielo.org/pdf/s_icse/v3nse/scs_a22.pdf.

Chamberlin, Judi. *On Our Own: Patient-Controlled Alternatives to the Mental Health System*. New York: Hawthorne Books, 1978.

———. "The Ex-Patients' Movement: Where We've Been and Where We're Going." *The Journal of Mind and Behavior* 11, no. 3 (Summer 1990 – Special Issue, Challenging the Therapeutic State): 323–336.

Chapman, Adrian. "Re-Coopering Anti-psychiatry: David Cooper, Revolutionary Critic of Psychiatry." *Critical Radical Social Work* 4, no. 3 (2016): 421–432.

Cherki, Alice. *Frantz Fanon: A Portrait*. Ithaca: Cornell University Press, 2006.

Chevalier, Michel. *Letters on North America* [1836]. Translated by Steven Rowan. St. Louis: University of Missouri, 2014.

Cohen, B. M. Z. *Psychiatric Hegemony: A Marxist Theory of Mental Illness*. London: Palgrave Macmillan, 2016.

Cixous, Hélène, Keith Cohen; Paula Cohen. "The Laugh of Medusa." *Signs* 1, no. 4 (1976): 875–893.

Clair, Jean. "Parade and Palingenesis: Of the Circus in the Work of Picasso and Others," 21–34. In *The Great Parade: Portrait of the Artist as Clown*. New Haven: Yale University Press, 2004.

Conrad, Peter. *The Medicalization of Society: On the Transformation of Human Conditions into Treatable Disorders*. Baltimore: Johns Hopkins University Press, 2007.

Conreur, Yves-Luc. "A Statement from the Psychiatrized," *State and Mind: People Look at Psychology* 6, no. 2 (Winter 1977): 1. Courtesy of the Oskar Diethelm Library, DeWitt Institute for the History of Psychiatry, Weill Cornell Medical College.

Cooper, David. "The Invention of Non-Psychiatry." *Semiotext(e): Schizo-Culture* 3, no. 2 (1978): 66–74.

———. "Introduction." In Stokely Carmichael, David Cooper, R.D. Laing, Herbert Marcuse, *The Dialectics of Liberation*, edited by David Cooper. London and New York: Verso, 2015. Epub.

———. *The Language of Madness*. London: Penguin Books, 1978.

Costa, Lucy. "Mad Studies – What It Is and Why You Should Care." *madstudies2014*, October 14, 2014. https://madstudies2014.wordpress.com/2014/10/15/mad-studies-what-it-is-and-why-you-should-care-2/#:~:text=Mad%20Studies%20is%20an%20area,inmates%3B%20disabled%20%2Dto%20name%20a.

Costa, Marcela. "Icepick to Paintbrush: Nise da Silveira's Psychiatry." *Synapsis*, February 6, 2018. https://medicalhealthhumanities.com/2018/02/06/icepick-to-paintbrush-nise-da-silveiras-psychiatry/.

Cover, Robert. "Violence and the Word." *The Yale Law Journal* 95 (1986): 1601–1629.

Crossley, Nick. *Contesting Psychiatry: Social Movements in Mental Health*. London: Routledge, 2006.

da Silveira, Nise. *Nise da Silveira—A Revolução Pelo Afeto*. Rio de Janeiro: Studio M'Baraká, 2021. https://www.mbaraka.com.br/nise.

Daston, Lorraine and Peter Galison. *Objectivity*. New York: Zone Books, 2007.

Davis, Peter. "Anatomy of Violence." Villon Films, 1967. Kanopy.

de Almeida, José Miguel Caldas. "The impact in Latin America of Basaglia and Italian psychiatric reform." In *Basaglia's International Legacy: from Asylum to Community*, edited by Tom Burns and John Foot, 95–112. Oxford: Oxford University Press, 2020.

de Assis, Machado. "The Alienist." *26 Short Stories*. Translated by Margaret Jull Costa. New York: Liveright Publishing Corporation, 2018.

de Tocqueville, Alexis. *Democracy in America and Two Essays on America*. London: Penguin Books, 2003.

Deligny, Fernand. *The Arachnean and Other Texts*. Translated by Drew S. Burk and Catherine Porter. Minneapolis: Univocal, 2015.

Dell'Acqua, Peppe. *From the Asylum to Territorial Services for Mental Health*. Trieste: Dipartimento di Salute Mentale, nd. https://www.ideassonline.org/public/pdf/BrochureTriesteENG2.pdf.

———. "Trieste Twenty Years After: From the Criticism of Psychiatric Institutions to Institutions of Mental Health." Trieste Salute Mentale, 1995.

http://www.triestesalutementale.it/english/doc/dellacqua_1995_trieste-20yearsafter.pdf.

Dell'Acqua, Peppe and Silvia D'Autilia. "An Architecture to Set Madness Free. San Giovanni is No Memorial." *FAMagazine* 41 (September 2017): 30–45. http://www.festivalarchitettura.it/public/Articoli/Allegato/h41Og-66fey_224.pdf.

Deleuze, Gilles and Félix Guattari. *Anti-Oedipus: Capitalism and Schizophrenia.* Translated by Robert Hurley, Mark Seem, and Helen R. Lane. Minneapolis: University of Minnesota Press, 1983.

Devers, Lindsey. *Plea and Charge Bargaining: Research Summary.* Bureau of Justice Assistance, US Department of Justice, January 24, 2011. https://bja.ojp.gov/sites/g/files/xyckuh186/files/media/document/PleaBargainingResearchSummary.pdf.

Dhar, Ayurdhi. "Uncomfortable Truths in Survivor Narratives: An Interview with Helen Spandler." *Mad in America,* February 24, 2021. https://www.madinamerica.com/2021/02/uncomfortable-truths-survivor-narratives-interview-helen-spandler/.

Deyres, Martine dir. *Our Lucky Hours.* Alleyras, France: Lightdox, 2019. Vimeo, https://vimeo.com/ondemand/ourluckyhours.

Doerner, Klaus. *Madmen and the Bourgeoisie: A Social History of Insanity and Psychiatry.* Oxford: Basil Blackwell, 1981.

———. "Nationalsozialismus und Lebensvernichtung." *Jahrgang* 15, no. 2 (1967): 121–152.

Dols, Michael. *Majnun: The Madman in Medieval Islamic Society.* Oxford: Clarendon Press, 1992.

Donnelly, Michael. *The Politics of Mental Health in Italy.* London: Tavistock/Routledge, 1992.

Dosse, François. *Gilles Deleuze & Félix Guattari: Intersecting Lives.* New York: Columbia University Press, 2010.

Du Bois, W. E. B. "Strivings of the Negro People." *The Atlantic,* August 1897. https://www.theatlantic.com/magazine/archive/1897/08/strivings-of-the-negro-people/305446/.

Dubow, Saul. *Scientific Racism in Modern South Africa.* Cambridge: Cambridge University Press, 1995.

Duetsch, Albert. *The Mentally Ill in America: A History of Their Care and Treatment from Colonial Times.* New York: Columbia University Press, 1949.

Engels, Friedrich. *The Condition of the Working-Class in England.* Moscow: Progress Publishers, 1980.

English, Charlie. *The Gallery of Miracles and Madness: Insanity, Modernism, and Hitler's War on Art* (New York: Penguin Random House, 2021).

Engstrom, Eric. *Clinical Psychiatry in Imperial Germany: A History of Psychiatric Practice*. Ithaca: Cornell University Press, 2003.

"Evidence for Peer Support." Mental Health America, May 2019. https://www.mhanational.org/sites/default/files/Evidence%20for%20Peer%20Support%20May%202019.pdf.

Fanon, Frantz. *Alienation and Freedom*. Edited and compiled by Jean Khalfa and Robert J.C. Young, translated by Steven Corcoran. London: Bloomsbury Academic, 2018.

———. *Black Skin, White Masks*. Translated by Charles Lam Markmann. London: Pluto Press, 2008.

———. *A Dying Colonialism*. Translated by Haakon Chevalier. New York: Grove Press, 1965.

———. *The Wretched of the Earth*. Translated by Constance Farrington. New York: Grove Press, 1963.

Federici, Silvia. *Wages against Housework*. Bristol and London: Power of Women Collective and Falling Wall Press, April 1975.

Fee, Elizabeth, and Theodore M. Brown. "Freeing the Insane." *American Journal of Public Health* 96, no. 10 (October 2006): 1743–1743. https://ajph.aphapublications.org/doi/10.2105/AJPH.2006.095448.

Felman, Shoshana. "Women and Madness: The Critical Phallacy." *Diacritics* 5, no. 4 (1975): 2–10.

Figueiredo, Gabriel. "Politica de la Salud en Brasil." *Manicomios y prisiones*. Edited by Sylvia Marcos. México: Red Ediciones, 1983.

Foot, John. "Franco Basaglia: A Man, a Movement, Institutions, and Outcomes." *Basaglia's International Legacy: from Asylum to Community*. Edited by Tom Burns and John Foot. Oxford: Oxford University Press, 2020.

———. *The Man Who Closed the Asylums: Franco Basaglia and the Revolution in Mental Health Care*. London and New York: Verso, 2015.

———. "Photography and Radical Psychiatry in Italy in the 1960s. The Case of the Photobook Morire di Classe (1969)." *History of Psychiatry* 26, no. 1 (2015): 19–35.

———. "Television Documentary, History and Memory. An analysis of Sergio Zavoli's *The Gardens of Abel*." *Journal of Modern Italian Studies* 19, no. 5 (2014): 603–624. https://www.ncbi.nlm.nih.gov/pmc/articles/PMC4408445/.

Foucault, Michel. *History of Madness*. Edited and translated by Jean Khalfa. London: Routledge, 2009.

———. *Psychiatric Power: Lectures at the College de France, 1973–74.* Edited by Jacques Lagrange. Translated by Graham Burchell. New York: Palgrave Macmillan, 2006.

Frame Janet. *An Angel at My Table.* London: Virago, 1989.

———. *Faces in the Water.* North Sydney: Vintage Books, 2008.

Frances, Allen. *Saving Normal: An Insider's Revolt Against Out-of-Control Psychiatric Diagnosis, DSM-5, Big Pharma, and the Medicalization of Ordinary Life.* New York: William Morrow, 2013.

Frank, Leonard Roy. "The Journey of Transformation." *Mad in America*, May 7, 2013. https://www.madinamerica.com/2013/05/the-journey-of-transformation/.

Friedlander, Henry. *The Origins of Nazi Genocide: From Euthanasia to the Final Solution.* Chapel Hill: University of North Carolina Press, 1995.

Fusar-Poli, Paolo, D. Bruno, J.P. Machado-De-Sousa, and J. Crippa. "Franco Basaglia (1924–1980): Three Decades (1979–2009) as a Bridge Between the Italian and Brazilian Mental Health Reform." *International Journal of Social Psychiatry* 57, no. 1 (2011): 100–103.

Galt, John M. "The Farm at St. Anne." *The American Journal of Insanity* 11 (1854–55): 352–357.

García, Dora. *The Deviant Majority.* Brazil, Italy: 2013. Vimeo, https://vimeo.com/60874476.

García, Dora and Carmen Roll. "An Interview with Carmen Roll." In Dora García, *Mad Marginal, Cahier #1: From Basaglia to Brazil*, 146–159. Milan: Mousse, 2010.

Garton, Stephen. "Eugenics in Australia and New Zealand: Laboratories of Racial Science." In *The Oxford Handbook of the History of Eugenics*, edited by Alison Bashford and Philippa Levine, 243–257. Oxford: Oxford University Press, 2010.

Gauchet, Marcel and Gladys Swain. *Madness and Democracy: The Modern Psychiatric Universe.* Princeton: Princeton University Press, 1999.

Gelpi, Adriane Hunsberger. "Priority Setting for HIV and Mental Health in Mexico: Historical, Quantitative and Ethical Perspectives." PhD dissertation, Harvard University, 2014. https://dash.harvard.edu/bitstream/handle/1/11744449/Gelpi_gsas.harvard_0084L_11290.pdf.

Genosko, Gary, ed. "The Acceleration of Transversality in the Middle." In *Deleuze and Guattari: Critical Assessments of Leading Philosophers, Volume II: Guattari*, 850–862. London: Routledge, 2001.

———. "Introduction." In *Deleuze and Guattari: Critical Assessments of Leading Philosophers, Volume II: Guattari*, 475–507. London: Routledge, 2001.

Geronimo. *Fire and Flames: A History of the German Autonomist Movement.* Oakland: PM Press, 2012.

Gibson, Nigel C. and Roberto Beneduce. *Frantz Fanon, Psychiatry and Politics.* Lanham: Rowman and Littlefield, 2017.

Gilman, Sander. *Difference and Pathology: Stereotypes of Sexuality, Race, and Madness.* Ithaca: Cornell University Press, 1985.

———. "The Image of the Hysteric." In Sander L. Gilman, Helen King, Roy Porter, G. S. Rousseau, and Elaine Showalter, *Hysteria Beyond Freud*, 345–436. Berkeley: University of California Press, 1993.

Global Evidence for Peer Support: Humanizing Health Care. Peers for Progress and the National Council of La Raza, June 2014. https://www.mhanational.org/sites/default/files/140911-global-evidence-for-peer-support-humanizing-health-care.pdf.

Goffey, Andrew. "Guattari and Transversality: Institutions, Analysis and Experimentation." *Radical Philosophy* 195 (January/February 2016): 38–47. https://www.radicalphilosophy.com/article/guattari-and-transversality.

Goffman, Erving. *Asylums: Essays on the Social Situation of Mental Patients and Other Inmates.* New York: Anchor Books, 1961.

Gomes, Suelen. "Anti-asylum Reform in Brazil: From the Horror to Today." *Fiotec*, February 21,2018. https://www.fiotec.fiocruz.br/en/news/4881-anti-asylum-reform-in-brazil-from-the-horror-to-today.

Gonaver, Wendy. *The Peculiar Institution and the Making of Modern Psychiatry.* Chapel Hill: University of North Carolina Press, 2019.

Goodheart, Lawrence. "'The Glamour of Arabic Numbers': Pliny Earle's Challenge to Nineteenth-Century Psychiatry." *Journal of the History of Medicine and Allied Sciences* 71, no. 2 (2015): 172–196. https://www.ncbi.nlm.nih.gov/pmc/articles/PMC4887602/.

Goodman, Amy and Juan González. "Black Panther Bobby Seale Was Bound and Gagged at His 1968 DNC Protest Trial." *Democracy Now!*, August 28, 2018. https://truthout.org/video/black-panther-party-chair-bobby-seale-describes-his-trial-after-1968-dnc-protest/.

Gorris, Marleen, dir. *A Question of Silence [De stilte rond Christine M.].* The Netherlands: EYE Film Institute Netherlands, 1982. Digital.

Gortázar, Naiara Galarraga. "Barbacena: The Brazilian 'City of Madmen' that Claimed 60,000 Lives." *El País*, September 8, 2021. https://english.elpais.

com/usa/2021-09-08/barbacena-brazils-city-of-madmen-that-claimed-60000-lives.html.

Goulart, Daniel Magalhães. *Subjectivity and Critical Mental Health: Lessons from Brazil.* London: Routledge, 2019.

Griesinger, Wilhelm. *Mental Pathology and Therapeutics.* Translated by C. Lockhart Robertson and James Rutherford. London: The New Sydenham Society, 1867.

Grob, Gerald N. *The Mad among Us: A History of the Care of America's Mentally Ill.* New York: The Free Press, 1994.

———. *From Asylum to Community: Mental Health Policy in Modern America.* Princeton: Princeton University Press, 1991.

Groom, Amelia. "'Eruptions of Silence': The Unheard, the Unsaid, and the Politics of Laughter in Marleen Gorris's *A Question of Silence.*" *Another Screen*, nd. https://www.another-screen.com/silence-laughter.

"Guardianship." Minnesota Judicial Branch, 2020. https://www.mncourts. gov/Help-Topics/Guardianship.aspx.

Guattari, Félix. *Chaosophy: Texts and Interviews 1972–1977.* Edited by Sylvère Lotringer, translated by David L. Sweet, Jarred Becker, and Taylor Adkins. Los Angeles: Semiotext(e), 2009.

———. *Psychoanalysis and Transversality: Texts and Interviews 1955–1971.* Translated by Ames Hodges. Los Angeles: Semiotext(e), 2015.

Guattari, Félix and Suely Rolnik. *Molecular Revolution in Brazil.* Translated by Karel Clapshow and Brian Holmes. Los Angeles: Semiotext(e), 2007.

Ha, Kwiyeon and Linda Sieg. "Japan Confronts Disability Stigma after Silence over Murder Victims' Names." *Reuters*, September 2016. https://www.reuters.com/article/uk-japan-disabled-idUKKCN11M0AK.

Harcourt, Bernard E. "Reducing Mass Incarceration: Lessons from the Deinstitutionalization of Mental Hospitals in the 1960s." *Ohio State Journal of Criminal Law* 9, no. 1 (2011): 53–88. https://chicagounbound.uchicago.edu/cgi/viewcontent.cgi?article=1509&context=journal_articles.

Harrington, Anne. *Mind Fixers: Psychiatry's Troubled Search for the Biology of Mental Illness.* New York: W.W. Norton & Company, 2020.

———. "Psychiatry, Racism, and the Birth of 'Sesame Street.'" *Undark*, May 17, 2019. https://undark.org/2019/05/17/psychiatry-racism-sesame-street/.

Haslam, John. *Observations on Insanity.* London: F. and C. Rivington, 1798.

Head. Bessie. *A Question of Power.* Long Grove: Waveland Press, 2017.

Hegel, G. W. F. *Phenomenology of Spirit.* Translated by A.V. Miller. Oxford: Oxford University Press, 1977.

Hirszman, Leon dir. and Nise da Silveira, writer. *Imagens do inconsciente*. Rio de Janeiro: Embrafilme and Leon Hirszman Produções Cinematográficas, 1986. DVD.

Hoche, Alfred and Karl Binding. *Permitting the Destruction of Life Unworthy of Living* (1920). In *German History in Documents and Images*, Volume 6: The Weimar Republic, 1918/19–1933. https://ghdi.ghi-dc.org/sub_document.cfm?document_id=4496.

Hohendorf, Gerrit. "The Extermination of Mentally Ill and Handicapped People under National Socialist Rule." Case study. Mass Violence and Resistance – Research Network, Sciences Po, November 17, 2016. https://www.sciencespo.fr/mass-violence-war-massacre-resistance/en/document/extermination-mentally-ill-and-handicapped-people-under-national-socialist-rule.html#title1.

Hollander, Nancy. *Love in a Time of Hate: Liberation Psychology in Latin America*. New Brunswick: Rutgers University Press, 1997.

Hudson, Wade. "On Madness." *Madness Network News* 1, no. 4 (1973): 1. https://madnessnetworknews.com/archives-vol-1-accessible-version/archives-vol-1-no-4/.

Human Rights & Mental Health. Washington, DC: Mental Disability Rights International, 2000. https://www.driadvocacy.org/wp-content/uploads/Human-Rights-Mental-Health-English.pdf.

Hutchinson, Phil. "Thirty Years of Democratic Psychiatry Down the Drain or . . . the Struggle Continues?" *Asylum: The Magazine for Democratic Psychiatry* 23, no. 2 (2016): 5–6. https://asylummagazine.org/2016/05/asylum-magazine-volume-23-no-2-summer-2016/.

Illich, Ivan. "To Hell with Good Intentions." Conference on InterAmerican Student Projects (CIASP), Cuernavaca, Mexico, April 20, 1968. https://www.uvm.edu/~jashman/CDAE195_ESCI375/To%20Hell%20with%20Good%20Intentions.pdf.

———. "The Seamy Side of Charity." *America Magazine*, January 21, 1967. https://www.americamagazine.org/issue/100/seamy-side-charity.

"Immigration Restriction Act, 1901." Australian Federal Register of Legislation, Australian Government. https://www.legislation.gov.au/Details/C1901A00017.

"Insistimos." *Manicomios y prisiones*. México: Red Ediciones, 1983.

Jaeggi, Rahel. *Alienation*. New York: Columbia University Press, 2014.

Jane Liebert, Rachel. *Psycurity: Colonialism, Paranoia, and the War on Imagination*. London: Routledge, 2018.

Jervis, Giovanni. "Psychiatry in Crisis: Institutional Contradictions." *International Journal of Mental Health* 14, no. 1–2 (1985): 52–69.

Johnstone, Lucy, and Mary Boyle, with John Cromby, David Harper, Peter Kinderman, David Pilgrim, John Read, Jacqui Dillon and Eleanor Longden. *The Power Threat Meaning Framework: Towards the Identification of Patterns in Emotional Distress, Unusual Experiences and Troubled or Troubling Behavior, as an Alternative to Functional Psychiatric Diagnosis.* Leicester: British Psychological Society, 2018. https://www.bps.org.uk/guideline/power-threat-meaning-framework-full-version.

Jones, Maxwell. *Beyond the Therapeutic Community: Social Learning and Social Psychiatry.* New Haven and London: Yale University Press, 1968.

———. *Social Psychiatry in Practice: The Idea of the Therapeutic Community.* Middlesex: Penguin Books, 1968.

Jones, Nev. *Peer Involvement and Leadership in Early Intervention in Psychosis Services: From Planning to Peer Support and Evaluation.* Substance Abuse and Mental Health Administration (SAMHSA)/CMHS Guidance Manual 2015. https://nasmhpd.org/sites/default/files/Peer-Involvement-Guidance_Manual_Final.pdf.

Joseph, Jay and Norbert A. Wetzel. "Ernst Rüdin: Hitler's Racial Hygiene Mastermind." *Journal of the History of Biology* 46, no. 1 (Spring 2013): 1–30.

Jun Yoo, Theodore. *It's Madness: The Politics of Mental Health in Colonial Korea.* Oakland: University of California Press, 2016.

Kaelber, Lutz. "Eugenics/Eugenic Sterilizations in Indiana." *Eugenics: Compulsory Sterilization in 50 American States.* Online research project, Department of Sociology, University of Vermont, 2009–2012. https://www.uvm.edu/~lkaelber/eugenics/IN/IN.html.

Katsiaficas, George. *The Subversion of Politics: European Autonomous Social Movements and the Decolonization of Everyday Life.* Chico: AK Press, 1997.

Kavan, Anna. *Asylum Piece and Other Stories.* London: Peter Owen, 2001.

———. *Guilty.* London: Peter Owen, 2007.

———. *Machines in the Head.* New York: New York Review of Books, 2019.

Keller, Richard C. "Taking Science to the Colonies: Psychiatric Innovation in France and North Africa." In *Psychiatry and Empire*, edited by Sloan Mahone and Megan Vaughan, 17–40. New York: Palgrave Macmillan, 2007.

Khalfa, Jean. "Fanon, Revolutionary Psychiatrist," 167–202. In Frantz Fanon, *Alienation and Freedom.* Edited and compiled by Jean Khalfa and Robert J.C. Young, translated by Steven Corcoran. London: Bloomsbury Academic, 2018.

King, Colin. "They Called Me a Schizophrenic When I Was Just a Gemini. 'The Other Side of Madness.'" In *Reconceiving Schizophrenia*, edited by Man Cheung Chung, K. W. M. Fulford, Bill Fulford, and George Graham, 11–28. Oxford: Oxford University Press, 2007.

Klee, Ernst. *Dokumente zur Euthanasie*. Frankfurt am Main: Fischer Taschenbuch Verlag, 1995.

———. *Sichten und vernichten – Psychiatrie im Dritten Reich*. Germany: Hessischer Rundfunk, 1995. https://www.youtube.com/watch?v=f9cEbCe-5Mos.

Klein, Anne. "Governing Madness – Transforming Psychiatry: Disability History and the Formation of Cultural Knowledge in West Germany in the 1970s and 1980s." *Moving the Social* 53 (2015): 11–37. https://moving-the-social.ub.rub.de/index.php/MTS/article/view/7471/6643.

Kotowicz, Zbigniew. *R.D. Laing and the Paths of Anti-Psychiatry*. London: Routledge, 1997.

Kovel, Joel. "The American Mental Health Industry." In *Critical Psychiatry: The Politics of Mental Health*, edited by David Ingleby, 72–101. New York: Pantheon Books, 1980.

Kroske, Gerd, dir. *SPK Komplex*. Germany: Realistfilm and Rundfunk Berlin-Brandenburg (RBB) 2018. Vimeo. https://vimeo.com/ondemand/spkkomplex.

Laing, R.D. "The Obvious." In Stokely Carmichael, David Cooper, R.D. Laing, Herbert Marcuse, *The Dialectics of Liberation*. Edited by David Cooper. London and New York: Verso, 2015. Epub.

Lakoff, Andrew. *Pharmaceutical Reason: Knowledge and Value in Global Psychiatry*. Cambridge: Cambridge University Press: 2005.

Langer, Marie. *From Vienna to Managua: Journey of a Psychoanalyst*. Translated by Margaret Hooks. London: Free Association Books, 1989.

———. *Motherhood and Sexuality*. Translated by Nancy Caro Hollander. New York: The Guilford Press, 1992.

"Letter by Man Accused of Mass Stabbings Carried Eerie Warning." *Asahi Shimbun*, July 26, 2016. https://web.archive.org/web/20160726124743/http://www.asahi.com/ajw/articles/AJ201607260083.html.

Levin, Hannah and Mark Seem. "Revolution and Desire: An Interview with Felix Guattari." *State and Mind: People Look at Psychology* 7, no. 1 (Summer/Fall 1978): 53–57. Courtesy of the Oskar Diethelm Library, DeWitt Institute for the History of Psychiatry, Weill Cornell Medical College.

Lewis, Abram J. "'We Are Certain of Our Own Insanity': Antipsychiatry and the Gay Liberation Movement, 1968–1980." *Journal of the History of Sexuality* 25, no. 1 (January 2016): 83–113.

Liberman, Anatoly. "There Are More Ways Than One to Be Mad." *OUPblog*, July 4, 2007. https://blog.oup.com/2007/07/mad/.

Lilly, John. "Madness or 'The History of Religion is the History of Madness.'" *Madness Network News* 1, no 4 (1973): 1. https://madnessnetworknews.com/archives-vol-1-accessible-version/archives-vol-1-no-4/.

Littlewood, Roland, and Maurice Lipsedge. *Aliens and Alienist: Ethnic Minorities and Psychiatry*. London: Routledge, 1997.

Loerzel, Robert. "The Story of Dunning, A 'Tomb for the Living.'" WBEZ Chicago, NPR, April 30, 2013. https://www.wbez.org/stories/the-story-of-dunning-a-tomb-for-the-living/6d71dc74-bb21-4a25-8980-c2d7a5670b06.

Loraux, Nicole. *The Experience of Tiresias: The Feminine and the Greek Man*. Trans. Paula Wissing. Princeton: Princeton University Press, 1995.

Lotringer, Sylvére. *Mad Like Artaud*. Minneapolis: Univocal, 2003.

Lovell, Anne M. "Breaking the Circuit of Control: A Report on the Conference of the European Network: Alternatives to Psychiatry." *State and Mind: People Look at Psychology* 6, no. 2 (Winter 1977): 7–13. Courtesy of the Oskar Diethelm Library, DeWitt Institute for the History of Psychiatry, Weill Cornell Medical College.

———. "From Confinement to Community: The Radical Transformation of an Italian Mental Hospital." *State and Mind: People Look at Psychology* 6, no. 3 (Spring 1978): 7–11; 27. Courtesy of the Oskar Diethelm Library, DeWitt Institute for the History of Psychiatry, Weill Cornell Medical College.

———. "Classification and Its Risks: How Psychiatric Status Contributes to Homelessness Policy." *New England Journal of Public Policy* 8, no. 1 (1992): 247–259.

Lowinger, Paul. "Radicals in Psychiatry." *Canadian Journal of Psychiatry* 17 (1972): 193–196.

Luzio, Cristina Amélia and Solange L'Abbate. "The Brazilian Psychiatric Reform: Historical and Technical-supportive Aspects of Experiences Carried Out in the Cities of São Paulo, Santos and Campinas." *Interface – Comunicação, Saúde, Educação* 10, no. 20 (July/December 2006): 281–298.

MacDonald, Michael. *Mystical Bedlam: Madness, Anxiety, and Healing in Seventeenth-Century England*. Cambridge: Cambridge University Press, 1981.

Madness Network News 4, no. 4 (Fall 1977).

Madness Network News Collective. "Working Draft to Abolish Psychiatry." *Madness Network News* 8, no. 3 (Summer 1986): 3.

Magaldi, Felipe Sales. "Psyche Meets Matter: Body and Personhood in the Medical-Scientific Project of Nise da Silveira." *História, Ciências, Saúde–Manguinhos* 25, no. 1 (2018): 1–20.

Manjeshwar, Sanjana. "America's Forgotten History of Forced Sterilization." *Berkeley Political Review*, November 4, 2020. https://bpr.berkeley.edu/2020/11/04/americas-forgotten-history-of-forced-sterilization/.

Mannix, Andy. "Hennepin Healthcare Workers Demand Hospital Reduce Use of 'Medical Force' on Patients." *Star Tribune*, May 23, 2021. https://www.startribune.com/hennepin-healthcare-workers-demand-hospital-reduce-use-of-medical-force-on-patients/600060524/?refresh=true.

———. "Minneapolis Police Department Still Teaching Controversial 'Excited Delirium' Syndrome—despite Claiming It Had Stopped." *Star Tribune*, February 12, 2022. https://www.startribune.com/minneapolis-police-still-teaching-excited-delirium-syndrome-despite-claiming-it-stopped/600146112/.

———. "Patients Sedated by Ketamine Were Enrolled in Hennepin Healthcare Study." *Star Tribune*, June 23, 2018. https://www.startribune.com/patients-sedated-by-ketamine-were-enrolled-in-hennepin-healthcare-study/486363071/.

Mannoni, Maud. *The Child, His "Illness," and the Others.* London: Maresfield Library, 1967.

Mancilla, Francisco Javier Dosil. "La Locura Como Acción Política. El Movimiento Antipsiquiátrico en México." *Revista Electrónica de Psicología Iztacala* 22, no. 1 (2019): 634–635.

Marazia, Chantal, Heiner Fangerau, Thomas Becker, and Felicitas Söhner. "'Visions of Another World.' Franco Basaglia and German Reform." In *Basaglia's International Legacy: from Asylum to Community*, 227–244. Edited by Tom Burns and John Foot. Oxford: Oxford University Press, 2020.

Marcos, Sylvia. "En Recuerdo a Franco Basaglia." In *Manicomios y prisiones*, edited by Sylvia Marcos, 9–12. México: Red Ediciones, 1983.

———. "Introducción al Primer Encuentro Latinoamericano Alternativas a la Psiquiatría." In *Manicomios y prisiones*, edited by Sylvia Marcos, 13–20. México: Red Ediciones, 1983.

Marks, Sarah. "Dialectics of Liberation." *Hidden Persuaders*, October 25, 2017. http://www7.bbk.ac.uk/hiddenpersuaders/blog/dialectics-of-liberation/#_edn6.

Marx, Karl. *Capital. A Critique of Political Economy. Volume 1. Book One: The Process of Production of Capital.* Translated by Ben Fowkes and David Fernbach. London: Penguin Books, 1990.

———. *Economic and Philosophic Manuscripts of 1844.* Translated by Martin Milligan. Amherst, NY: Prometheus Books, 1988.

———. "The Eighteenth Brumaire of Louis Bonaparte," *Marx & Engels Collected Works, Volume 11: Marx and Engels 1851–53.* London: Lawrence & Wishart, 2010, 99–197.

———. "Theses on Feuerbach," *Marx & Engels Collected Works, Volume 5: Marx and Engels 1845–47.* London: Lawrence & Wishart, 2010, 3–5.

Marx, Karl and Frederick Engels. "The German Ideology," *Marx & Engels Collected Works, Volume 5: Marx and Engels 1845–47.* London: Lawrence & Wishart, 2010, 19–539.

Matos-de-Souza, Rodrigo and Ana Carolina Cerqueira Medrado. "On Bodies as Object: A Postcolonial Reading of the 'Brazilian Holocaust.'" *Saúde Debate* 45, no. 128 (January–March 2021): 164–177.

"*The Maze.* Artist: William Kurelek (1927–1977)." Bethlem Museum of the Mind. https://museumofthemind.org.uk/learning/the-maze/.

Mbembe, Achille. "Frantz Fanon and the Politics of Viscerality." John Hope Franklin Humanities Institute at Duke University, April 27, 2016. https://www.youtube.com/watch?v=lg_BEodNaEA.

———. *Necropolitics.* Durham: Duke University Press, 2018.

McCulloch, Jock. *Colonial Psychiatry and 'the African Mind.'* Cambridge: Cambridge University Press, 1995.

Megaloeconomou, Theodoros. "Franco Basaglia's Influence on the Greek Mental Health System." In *Basaglia's International Legacy: from Asylum to Community*, edited by Tom Burns and John Foot, 161–174. Oxford: Oxford University Press, 2020.

Melitopoulos, Angela. "Ways of Meaning: Machinic Animism and the Revolutionary Practice of Geo-Psychiatry." PhD dissertation, Goldsmiths University of London, 2016. https://research.gold.ac.uk/id/eprint/19684/1/VIS_thesis_MelitopoulosA_2016.pdf.

Mental Hygiene News 11, no. 6 (September 1932).

Mental Patients' Liberation Front. "Mental Health Workers." *Our Journal* (Fall 1977): 28. Courtesy of the Oskar Diethelm Library, DeWitt Institute for the History of Psychiatry, Weill Cornell Medical College.

Metzl, Jonathan. *The Protest Psychosis: How Schizophrenia Became a Black Disease.* Boston: Beacon Press, 2011.

Meyer, Manuella. *Reasoning Against Madness: Psychiatry and the State in Rio de Janeiro, 1830–1944*. Rochester: University of Rochester Press, 2017.

———. "'Work Conquers All': Psychiatry, Agricultural Labor, and the Juliano Moreira Colony in Rio de Janeiro, Brazil (1890–1958)." *Palgrave Communications* 5, no. 99 (2019). https://doi.org/10.1057/s41599-019-0305-y.

Mezzina, Roberto. "Basaglia after Basaglia: Recovery, Human Rights, and Trieste Today." In *Basaglia's International Legacy: from Asylum to Community*, edited by Tom Burns and John Foot, 43–68. Oxford: Oxford University Press, 2020.

Miguel, Marlon. "Psychiatric Power: Exclusion and Segregation in the Brazilian Mental Health System." In *Democracy and Brazil: Collapse and Regression*, edited by Bernardo Bianchi, Jorge Chaloub, Patricia Rangel, and Frieder Otto Wolf, 250–267. London: Routledge, 2020.

Millett, Kate. "The Illusion of Mental Illness." In *Alternatives Beyond Psychiatry*, edited by Peter Stastny and Peter Lehmann, 29–38. Berlin: Peter Lehmann Publishing.

Mills, China. *Decolonizing Global Mental Health: The Psychiatrization of the Majority World*. London: Routledge, 2014.

Mills v. Rogers, 457 U.S. 291 (1982).

Mirza, Mustafa Z. "Are Psychiatric Hospitals in Egypt Hurting Mental Health Care?" *Egyptian Streets*, December 13, 2016. https://egyptianstreets.com/2016/12/13/are-psychiatric-hospitals-in-egypt-hurting-mental-health-care/.

Mitropoulos, Angela. *Contract and Contagion: From Biopolitics to Oikonomia*. Wivenhoe: Minor Compositions, 2012.

Mohaghegh, Jason Bahbak. *Omnicide: Mania, Fatality, and the Future-in-Delirium*. Falmouth: Urbanomic, 2019.

Mora, George. "Vincenzo Chiarugi (1759–1820) and his Psychiatric Reform in Florence in the Late 18th Century." *Journal of the History of Medicine and Allied Sciences* 14, no. 10 (October 1959): 424–433. https://doi.org/10.1093/jhmas/XIV.10.424.

Moreira, María Inês Badaró, André Vinicius Pires Guerrero, and Enrique Araújo Bessoni. "Between Challenges and Possible Openings: Life in Freedom in the Context of the Brazilian Deinstitutionalization." *Saúde Social São Paulo* 28, no. 2 (2019): 6–10. https://www.scielo.br/pdf/sausoc/v28n3/en_1984-0470-sausoc-28-03-6.pdf.

Morrison, Linda. *Talking Back to Psychiatry: The Psychiatric Consumer/Survivor/Ex-Patient Movement*. New York: Routledge, 2005.

Murat, Laure. *The Man Who Thought He Was Napoleon: Toward a Political History of Madness*. Chicago: University of Chicago Press, 2014.

Musto, Marcello. "Revisiting Marx's Concept of Alienation." *Socialism and Democracy* 24, no. 3 (2010): 79–101.

National Institute of Mental Health. "Research Domain Criteria (RdoC)." https://www.nimh.nih.gov/research/research-funded-by-nimh/rdoc.

Ndikung, Bonaventure Soh Bejeng. "Ultrasanity. On Madness, Sanitation, Anti-Psychiatry, and Resistance." In *Ultrasanity: On Madness, Sanitation, Anti-Psychiatry, and Resistance*, edited by Bonaventure Soh Bejeng Ndikung, Elena Agudio, and Kelly Krugman, 18–34. Berlin: Archive Books, 2020.

Nelson, Alondra. *Body and Soul: The Black Panther Party and the Fight against Medical Discrimination*. Minneapolis: University of Minnesota Press, 2011.

Nicholas, Hervey. "Advocacy or Folly: The Alleged Lunatics' Friend Society, 1845–63." *Medical History* 30 (1986): 245–275. https://www.ncbi.nlm.nih.gov/pmc/articles/PMC1139650/pdf/medhist00070-0005.pdf.

O'Brien, Barbara. *Operators and Things: The Inner Life of a Schizophrenic* (Los Angeles: Silver Birch Press, 2011).

O'Connor v. Donaldson, 422 U.S. 563 (1975).

Olmstead v. L.C., 527 U.S. 581 (1999).

Onocko Campos, Rosana T., Mark Costa, Mariana Barbosa Pereira, Ellen Cristina Ricci, Giselli da Silva Tavares Enes, Leidy Janeth, Erazo Chavez, Graziela Reis, and Larry Davidson. "Recovery, Citizenship, and Psychosocial Rehabilitation: A Dialog between Brazilian and American Mental Health Care Approaches." *American Journal of Psychiatric Rehabilitation* 20, no. 3 (2017): 311–326.

The Opal 2, no. 8 (1852). Courtesy of the Oskar Diethelm Library, DeWitt Institute for the History of Psychiatry, Weill Cornell Medical College.

The Opal 4, no. 9 (1854). Courtesy of the Oskar Diethelm Library, DeWitt Institute for the History of Psychiatry, Weill Cornell Medical College.

Osborn, Harold. "'To Make a Difference:' The Lincoln Collective." *Health Pac Bulletin* 23, no. 2 (September 1993): 19–20.

Otsubo, Sumiko and James R. Bartholomew. "Eugenics in Japan: Some Ironies of Modernity, 1883–1945." *Science in Context* 11, no. 3–4 (1998): 547–552.

Otto, Beatrice K. *Fools are Everywhere: The Court Jester around the World*. Chicago: University of Chicago Press, 2001.

Outram, Dorinda. *Four Fools in the Age of Reason: Laugher, Cruelty, and Power in Early Modern Germany*. Charlottesville: University of Virginia Press, 2019.

Owen, Robert. *The Revolution in the Mind and Practice of the Human Race; Or, the Coming Change From Irrationality to Rationality*. London: Effingham Wilson, 1849.

Packard, Elizabeth. *The Prisoner's Hidden Life: Insane Asylums Unveiled*. Chicago: Self-published, 1868.

Pan African Network of People with Psychosocial Disabilities (PANUSP). "The Cape Town Declaration." *Disability and the Global South* 1, no. 2 (2014): 385–386.

Pargeter, William. *Observations on Maniacal Disorders*. Reading: Smart and Cowslade, 1792.

Park, Maureen Patricia. "Art in Madness: Dr. W. A. F. Browne (1805–1885), Moral Treatment and Patient Art at Crichton Royal Institution, Dumfries, with Special Reference to his Medical Superintendence, 1839–1857." Master's thesis, University of Glasgow, 2007.

Parry-Jones, William. *The Trade in Lunacy: A Study of Private Madhouses in England in the Eighteenth and Nineteenth Centuries*. London: Routledge and Kagan Paul, 1972.

Parsons, Anne E. *From Asylum to Prison: Deinstitutionalization and the Rise of Mass Incarceration After 1945*. Chapel Hill: University of North Carolina Press, 2018.

Pierson, Brendan. "D.C. Circuit overturns FDA ban on shock device for disabled students." *Reuters*, July 2021. https://www.reuters.com/legal/litigation/dc-circuit-overturns-fda-ban-shock-device-disabled-students-2021-07-06/.

Pinel, Philippe. *Medico-Philosophical Treatise on Mental Alienation*. Translated by Gordon Hickish, David Healy, and Louis C. Charland. West Sussex: John Wiley & Sons, 2008.

Polack, Jean Claude. "Analysis, between Psycho and Schizo." In *The Guattari Effect*, edited by Eric Alliez and Andrew Goffey, 57–67. London: Continuum, 2011).

Polsky, Samuel. "Present Insanity – From the Common Law to the Mental Health Act and Back." *Villanova Law Review* 2, no. 4 (1957): 504–528.

Pordeus, Vitor. "Nise da Silveira: Brazilian Pioneer in Art and Transcultural Psychiatry." Draft paper, 2017. https://www.academia.edu/34364588/Nise_da_Silveira_Brazilian_Pioneer_in_Art_and_Transcultural_Psychiatry.

Portacolone, Elena, Steven P. Segal, Roberto Mezzina, Nancy Scheper-Hughes, and Robert L. Okin. "A Tale of Two Cities: The Exploration of the Trieste Public Psychiatry Model in San Francisco." *Culture, Medicine, and Psychiatry* 39, no. 4 (December 2015): 684–685.

Porter, Roy and Mark S. Micale, ed. "Introduction: Reflections of Psychiatry and Its History." In *Discovering the History of Psychiatry*, 3–38. New York: Oxford University Press, 1994.

Proctor, Hannah. "Mad World: Radical Psychiatry and 1968." *Verso* [blog], 2018. https://www.versobooks.com/blogs/3888-mad-world-radical-psychiatry-and-1968.

Proctor, Robert N. *Racial Hygiene: Medicine under the Nazis*. Cambridge, MA: Harvard University Press, 1988.

Pross, Christian. "Revolution and Madness – The 'Socialist Patients' Collective of Heidelberg (SPK)': An Episode in the History of Antipsychiatry and the 1960s Student Rebellion in West Germany." Berlin: Christian Pross, 2016. http://christian-pross.de/pross-revolution-and-madness1.pdf.

Reich, Wilhelm. *The Sexual Revolution: Toward a Self-Governing Character Structure*. Translated by Therese Pol. New York: Farrar, Straus, and Giroux, 1969.

Rennie v. Klein, 462 F. Supp. 1131 (D.N.J. 1978).

Reynolds, Emily. "The People Who Want to Get Rid of the Term 'Personality Disorder.'" *Dazed*, May 2018. https://www.dazeddigital.com/life-culture/article/40036/1/bpd-borderline-personality-disorder-diagnosis-label.

Richard, Robert J. "Rhapsodies on a Cat-Piano, or Johann Christian Reil and the Foundations of Romantic Psychiatry." *Critical Inquiry* 24, no. 3 (Spring 1998): 700–736.

Richert, Lucas. *Break on Through: Radical Psychiatry and the American Counter-culture*. Cambridge, MA and London: MIT Press, 2019.

Robcis, Camille. "Disalienation: Philosophy, Politics, and Radical Psychiatry in France." Keynote presented at the workshop *Radical Psychiatry, Psycho-analysis, and 1968*, ICI Berlin, April 23, 2018, video recording, mp4, 48:34. https://doi.org/10.25620/e180423-1.

———. *Disalienation: Politics, Philosophy, and Radical Psychiatry in Postwar France*. Chicago: The University of Chicago Press, 2021.

———. "François Tosquelles and the Psychiatric Revolution in Postwar France." *Constellations* 23, no. 2 (2016): 212–222.

Robertson, Jennifer. "Blood Talks: Eugenic Modernity and the Creation of New Japanese." *History and Anthropology* 13, no. 3 (2002): 194–199.

Rose, Diana and Jayasree Kalathil. "Power, Privilege and Knowledge: The Untenable Promise of Co-production in Mental 'Health.'" *Frontier in Sociology* (July 2019): 1–11. https://doi.org/10.3389/fsoc.2019.00057.

Rose, Nikolas. *Our Psychiatric Future.* Cambridge: Polity, 2019.

Rosen, George. *Madness in Society: Chapters in the Historical Sociology of Mental Illness.* Chicago: University of Chicago Press, 1968.

Rossi, Erika, dir. *Trieste Racconta Basaglia.* Italy: Fantastificio, 2012.

Rothman, David. *Conscience and Convenience: The Asylum and Its Alternatives in Progressive America.* New York: Aldine de Gruyter, 2002.

———. *The Discovery of the Asylum.* New York: Aldine de Gruyter, 1990.

Rubin, Aline. "Collusion with Torture – A Case from Brazil." *Hidden Persuaders*, February 6, 2017. http://www7.bbk.ac.uk/hiddenpersuaders/blog/torture-brazil/.

Rüdin, Ernst. "The Significance of Eugenics and Genetics for Mental Hygiene." *Proceedings of the First International Congress of Mental Hygiene.* New York: International Committee for Mental Hygiene, 1932.

Rush, Benjamin. *Medical Inquiries and Observations, Vol. 1.* Philadelphia: J. Conrad and Co., 1805.

Russel, Marta. *Capitalism and Disability: Selected Writings by Marta Russell.* Chicago: Haymarket Books, 2019.

Russell, Marta, and Jean Stewart. "Disablement, Prison, and Historical Segregation." *Monthly Review*, July 2001. https://monthlyreview.org/2001/07/01/disablement-prison-and-historical-segregation.

Salvini, Francesco. "Caring Ecologies." *transversal texts*, April 2019. https://transversal.at/transversal/0318/salvini/en?hl=basaglia.

———. "Instituting on the Threshold." *transversal texts*, September 2016. https://transversal.at/transversal/0916/salvini/en?hl=basaglia.

Samman, Ghada. *Beirut Nightmares.* Northampton: Interlink, 1999.

The Sayings of the Desert Fathers: The Alphabetical Collection. Kalamazoo: Cistercian Publication, 1975.

Schreber, Daniel Paul. *Memoirs of My Nervous Illness.* New York: New York Review of Books, 2000.

Scheper-Hughes, Nancy, and Anne M. Lovell. "Breaking the Circuit of Social Control: Lessons in Public Psychiatry from Italy and Franco Basaglia." In *Classics of Community Psychiatry: Fifty Years of Public Health Outside the Hospital*, edited by Michael Rowe, Kenneth Thompson, Martha Lawless, and Larry Davidson, 327–359. Oxford: Oxford University Press, 2011.

———. "Deinstitutionalization and Psychiatric Expertise: Reflections on Dangerousness, Deviancy, and Madness." *International Journal of Law and Psychiatry* 9 (1986): 361–381.

Schweik, Susan. *The Ugly Laws: Disability in Public.* New York: New York University Press, 2009.

Scull, Andrew. *Decarceration: Community Treatment and the Deviant – A Radical View.* Englewood Cliffs: Prentice-Hall, 1977.

———. *Madness in Civilization: A Cultural History of Insanity from the Bible to Freud, from the Madhouse to Modern Medicine.* Princeton: Princeton University Press, 2015.

———. *Museums of Madness: The Social Organization of Insanity in Nineteenth-Century England.* New York: St. Martin's Press, 1979.

———. *Psychiatry and Its Discontents.* Oakland: University of California, 2019.

———. *Social Order/Mental Disorder: Anglo-American Psychiatry in Historical Perspective.* Berkeley: University of California Press, 1989.

Sedgwick, Peter. *Psycho Politics.* London: Unkant, 2015.

Segrest, Mab. *Administrations of Lunacy: Racism and the Haunting of American Psychiatry at the Milledgeville Asylum.* New York: The New Press, 2020.

Seldes, Gilbert. *The Stammering Century.* New York: New York Review of Books, 2012.

Stewart Lansley, Joanna Mack, Michael Burleigh, dirs. "Selling Murder: The Killing Films of the Third Reich." London: Domino Films, 1991. https://www.youtube.com/watch?v=c2kV83nPWnM&t=1007s.

Serapioni, Mauro. "Franco Basaglia: biography of a revolutionary." *História, Ciências, Saúde* 26, no. 4 (2019): 1–18. https://www.scielo.br/pdf/hcsm/v26n4/en_0104-5970-hcsm-26-04-1169.pdf.

Shorter, Edward. *A History of Psychiatry: From the Era of the Asylum to the Age of Prozac.* New York: John Wiley & Sons, 1997.

Simone, Antonio S. "Locura y Contencion en Brasil." In *Manicomios y prisiones,* edited by Sylvia Marcos, 93–99. México: Red Ediciones, 1983.

Slater, Howard. "'Comrade Doctor' – On David Cooper and 'Anti-Psychiatry.'" *Datacide,* November 10, 2017. https://datacide-magazine.com/comrade-doctor-on-david-cooper-and-anti-psychiatry/.

———. Practical Overturnings." *Metamute,* December 1, 2016. https://www.metamute.org/editorial/articles/practical-overturnings.

Spinoza, Baruch. *A Spinoza Reader: The Ethics and Other Works.* Edited and translated by Edwin Curley. Princeton: Princeton University Press, 1994.

SPK. *Aus der Krankheit eine Waffe Machen* [*Turn Illness into a Weapon*]. Heidelberg: Trikont-Texte, 1972.

———. "Turn Illness into a Weapon." Translated by K.D. Indybay, 2013. https://www.indybay.org/newsitems/2013/11/14/18746394.php.

Starkman, Mel. "The Movement." *Phoenix Rising* 2, no. 3 (1981): 2A–9A.

"The Statement." *State and Mind: People Look at Psychology* 5, no. 4 (December 1976): 7. Courtesy of the Oskar Diethelm Library, DeWitt Institute for the History of Psychiatry, Weill Cornell Medical College.

Staub, Michael. *Madness Is Civilization: When the Diagnosis Was Social, 1948–1980*. Chicago: University of Chicago Press, 2011.

Steiner, Claude. "Radical Psychiatry: Principles." In *The Radical Therapist*, edited by Jerome Agel, 3–7. New York: Ballantine Books, 1971.

Stepan, Nancy Leys. *"The Hour of Eugenics": Race, Gender, and the Nation in Latin America*. Ithaca: Cornell University Press, 1991.

Stern, Alexandra Minna. "Sterilized in the Name of Public Health: Race, Immigration, and Reproductive Control in Modern California." *American Journal of Public Health* 95, no. 7 (2005 July): 1128–1138. https://www.ncbi.nlm.nih.gov/pmc/articles/PMC1449330/.

Stingelin, Martin. "Paul Emil Flechsig. Die Berechnung Der Menschlichen Seele." In *Wunderblock: Eine Geschichte Der Modernen Seele*, edited by Jean Clair, 297–308. Deisenhofen: KUNSTFORUM International, 1989.

Subiela, Eliseo, dir. *Man Facing Southeast*. Argentina: Cinequanon 1986. DVD.

"Suicide Rising across the US: More than a Mental Health Concern." CDC Vital Signs, November 27, 2018. https://www.cdc.gov/vitalsigns/suicide/index.html.

"Suicide." National Institute of Mental Health, 2020. https://www.nimh.nih.gov/health/statistics/suicide.

Suzuki, Akihito. "The state, family, and the insane in Japan, 1900–1945." *The Confinement of the Insane International Perspectives, 1800–1965*. Cambridge: Cambridge University Press, 2009.

Szasz, Thomas. *Manufacture of Madness*. Syracuse: Syracuse University Press, 1970.

———. *Psychiatric Slavery*. Syracuse: Syracuse University Press, 1977.

Tarabochia, Alvise Sforza. *Psychiatry, Subjectivity, Community: Franco Basaglia and Biopolitics*. Oxford: Peter Lang, 2013.

Telles, Ana Clara, and Gabriela Barros de Luca. "Bolsonaro is Destroying Mental Health Care to Favour Evangelicals." *Aljazeera*, September 1,

2021. https://www.aljazeera.com/opinions/2021/9/1/bolsonaro-is-destroy-ing-mental-health-care-to-favour-evangelicals.

Thiher, Allen. *Revels in Madness: Insanity in Medicine and Literature*. Ann Arbor: University of Michigan Press, 1999.

Tomes, Nancy. *A Generous Confidence: Thomas Story Kirkbride and the Art of Asylum-Keeping, 1840–1883*. Cambridge: Cambridge University Press, 1984.

Topp, Leslie. "Single Rooms, Seclusion and the Non-Restraint Movement in British Asylums, 1838–1844." *Social History of Medicine* 31, no. 4 (November 2018): 754–773.

Troeller, Gordian and Claude Deffarge, dirs. *Im Namen des Fortschritts – Kein Respekt vor heiligen Kühen* [*No Respect for Sacred Cows*]. Germany: ARD, 1976. https://www.youtube.com/watch?v=epD932IBF_Y&t=1397s.

Tromans, Nicholas. "The Psychiatric Sublime." In *The Art of the Sublime*, edited by Nigel Llewellyn and Christine Riding. Tate Research Publication, January 2013. https://www.tate.org.uk/art/research-publications/the-sublime/nicholas-tromans-the-psychiatric-sublime-r1129548.

Tuke, Samuel. *Description of the Retreat, an Institution near York for Insane Persons of the Society of Friends Containing an Account of its Origins and Progress, the Modes of Treatment and a Statement of Cases* (1813). The Retreat Archive, Wellcome Collection. https://wellcomecollection.org/works/dcy3yd8x.

Tuntiya, Nana. "Free-Air Treatment for Mental Patients: The Deinstitutionalization Debate of the Nineteenth Century." *Sociological Perspectives* 50, no. 3 (2007): 469–487.

Turkel, Studs. "Dr. Thomas Szasz discusses his book *The Manufacture of Madness: A Comparative Study of the Inquisition and the Mental Health Movement*." Studs Turkel Radio Archive, 1970. https://studsterkel.wfmt.com/programs/dr-thomas-szasz-discusses-his-book-manufacture-madness-comparative-study-inquisition-and?t=NaN%2CNaN&a=%2C.

Turkle, Sherry. "French Anti-Psychiatry." In *Critical Psychiatry: The Politics of Mental Health*, edited by David Ingelby, 150–183. New York: Pantheon, 1980.

Vandermeersch, Patrick. "'*Les mythes d'origine*' in the History of Psychiatry." In *Discovering the History of Psychiatry*, edited by Mark S. Micale and Roy Porter, 219–231. Oxford: Oxford University Press, 1994.

Venturini, Ernesto, Maria Stella Brandão Goulart, and Paulo Amarante. "The Optimism of Practice: The Impact of Basaglia's Thoughts on Brazil." In *Basaglia's International Legacy: from Asylum to Community*, edited by Tom Burns and John Foot, 113–128. Oxford: Oxford University Press, 2020.

Washington, Harriet A. *Medical Apartheid: The Dark History of Medical Experimentation on Black Americans from Colonial Times to the Present*. New York: Doubleday, 2007.

Walter, B. "Hermann Simon – Psychiatriereformer, Sozialdarwinist, Nationalsozialist?" *Nervenarzt* 73 (2002): 1047–1054.

Watters, Ethan. *Crazy Like Us: The Globalization of the American Psyche*. London: Robinson Publishing, 2011.

Weiner, Dora B. "'*Le geste de Pinel*': The History of a Psychiatric Myth." In *Discovering the History of Psychiatry*, 232–247. New York: Oxford University Press, 1994.

Whitaker, Robert. *Mad in America: Bad Science, Bad Medicine, and the Enduring Mistreatment of the Mentally Ill*. New York: Basic Books, 2002.

Willis, Thomas. *Two Discourses Concerning the Soul of Brutes*. London: Thomas Dring & John Leigh, 1683.

Willse, Craig. *The Value of Homelessness: Managing Surplus Life in the United States*. Minneapolis: University of Minnesota Press, 2015.

Wollstonecraft, Mary. *Mary, A Fiction and Maria: Or, The Wrongs of Woman*. Ontario: Broadview Editions, 2012.

World Health Organization. *Towards a Common Language for Functioning, Disability and Health*. Geneva: World Health Organization, 2002.

"Workshops." hopkins/werkstatt für clownforschung [hopkins/workshop for clown research]. https://www.clownforschung.de/seite/406522/workshops-events.html.

Wright, David. "Getting Out of the Asylum: Understanding the Confinement of the Insane in the Nineteenth Century." *Social History of Medicine* 10, no. 1 (April 1997): 137–155. https://doi.org/10.1093/shm/10.1.137.

Yanni, Carla. *The Architecture of Madness: Insane Asylums in the United States*. Minneapolis: University of Minnesota Press, 2007.

INDEX

B

Basaglia, Franca Ongaro, 89, 91, 93,
95, 104–105, 107, 108–109, 114, 119

Basaglia, Franco, 46, 89–91, 93–95,
97, 99, 102, 104–105, 106, 107,
113–115, 118, 121fn34,
132, 192, 239, 249–250, 262

Biopsychiatry, xiii, 15, 22–23, 27–28,
30, 33, 90, 92, 94, 109, 167, 246;
see also biopsychosocial psychiatry
16; see also clinical psychiatry, 23,
27, 29, 90, 143, 168, 185fn57, 239

Black Panthers, 160

Browne, W.A.F., 20, 34, 36–37, 64–
65, 73, 264

C

Capitalism, xv, 13, 17–19, 21, 35–36,
40, 43, 47, 59, 65, 92–93, 98, 102–
103, 107, 135–139, 145–146, 155–156,
164, 178, 180–181, 184fn31, 210,
216, 218, 239, 241, 252–255, 260–
261, 263

Canguilhem, Georges, 24–26, 63

Castel, Robert, 20, 22, 113, 127, 132,
135, 192, 207, 229fn6

Centros de Atenção Psicossocial
(CAPS), 117, 181

Chamberlin, Judi, 153, 169–174,
187fn97

Charcot, Jean-Martin, 4–5, 269

Chiarugi, Vincenzo, 5, 48fn12, 90

Chronicity, 59, 67, 138, 144–146, 148,
150–151, 176, 181, 184fn31, 236,
239–241, 247, 265

Centro Intercultural de Documentación (CIDOC), 114, 191–192

Civilization, 7, 12–13, 14, 35, 56, 77,
170, 201, 218, 253

Cold War, 14

Colonialism, 16, 102, 149, 202, 210–
216, 219–228, 244, 257, 270, 274;
see also decolonization, xiv, 102,
224, 226–227, 257; see also settler-
colonialism, 13–14, 136, 214–215,
218, 220–222, 224, 227

Communism, 39, 43, 72

Community psychiatry, 3, 99, 109,
174–176, 178, 180, 183fn11, 193

Conolly, John, 9, 54, 97–98

Conreuer, Yves-Luc, 103, 263

Cooper, David, 128–133, 183fn10,
183fn12, 192, 209, 249

COVID-19, 13, 33, 177, 187fn103, 255,
259, 178fn59

Custodialism, 1, 16, 58, 98, 109, 115,
140, 151, 158, 160, 235, 247, 250

D

Deinstitutionalization, 3, 63, 83, 109,
166, 176, 178

Deligny, Fernand, 64, 71–72, 78, 85

Dell'Acqua, Peppe, 100

Degeneration, 6, 15, 23, 74, 77, 146,
149, 156, 215, 239, 240–246

Democratic Psychiatry, xiv, 2, 46, 89,
92, 94, 95–96, 98, 101–106, 109,
114–115, 132, 231fn55

Deutsch, Albert, 7, 48fn16, 157

*Diagnostic and Statistical Manual of
Mental Disorders* (DSM), 166–168

V

W

ABOUT THE AUTHOR

Sasha Durakov Warren is a writer based in Minneapolis. His experiences within the psychiatric system and commitment to radical politics led him to cofound the group Hearing Voices Twin Cities, which provides an alternative social space for individuals to discuss often stigmatized extreme experiences and network with one-another. Following the George Floyd Uprising in 2020, he founded the project *Of Unsound Mind* to trace the histories of psychiatry, social work, and public health's connections to policing, prisons, and various disciplinary and managerial technologies.

ABOUT COMMON NOTIONS

Common Notions is a publishing house and programming platform that fosters new formulations of living autonomy. We aim to circulate timely reflections, clear critiques, and inspiring strategies that amplify movements for social justice.

Our publications trace a constellation of critical and visionary meditations on the organization of freedom. By any media necessary, we seek to nourish the imagination and generalize common notions about the creation of other worlds beyond state and capital. Inspired by various traditions of autonomism and liberation—in the US and internationally, historical and emerging from contemporary movements—our publications provide resources for a collective reading of struggles past, present, and to come.

Common Notions regularly collaborates with political collectives, militant authors, radical presses, and maverick designers around the world. Our political and aesthetic pursuits are dreamed and realized with Antumbra Designs.

www.commonnotions.org
info@commonnotions.org

BECOME A COMMON NOTIONS
MONTHLY SUSTAINER

These are decisive times ripe with challenges and possibility, heartache, and beautiful inspiration. More than ever, we need timely reflections, clear critiques, and inspiring strategies that can help movements for social justice grow and transform society.

Help us amplify those words, deeds, and dreams that our liberation movements, and our worlds, so urgently need.

Movements are sustained by people like you, whose fugitive words, deeds, and dreams bend against the world of domination and exploitation.

For collective imagination, dedicated practices of love and study, and organized acts of freedom.
By any media necessary.
With your love and support.

Monthly sustainers start at $15.

commonnotions.org/sustain

MORE FROM
COMMON NOTIONS

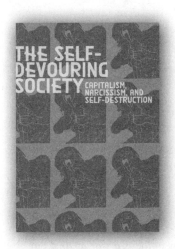

The Self-Devouring Society: Capitalism,
Narcisissm, and Self-Destruction
Anselm Jappe
Translated by Eric-John Russell

ISBN: 978-1-942173-79-3
$22.00
Page count: 256
Subjects: Critical Theory / Capitalism /
Psychology

***Renowned theorist Anselm Jappe explains
how contemporary capitalism has turned everyone into a narcissist.***

In a work that unites the critique of political economy and the psychoanalytic tradition, Anselm Jappe explores the dynamics of contemporary capitalism and explains how internalizing them creates a specific kind of person—a narcissist, someone who can only interact with the world by consuming it and who cannot conceive of limits to this consumption. In conversation with Marx as well as Freud, Erich Fromm, Herbert Marcuse, and Christopher Lasch, Jappe probes the ways in which the churning of the capitalist machine, ceaseless and yet devoid of real purpose, creates an endless hunger that increasingly ends in spectacular violence.

Everyone can feel that the world is getting angrier. *The Self-Devouring Society* provides an original and rigorous explanation of why.

MORE FROM
COMMON NOTIONS

*For Health Autonomy: Horizons of Care
Beyond Austerity—Reflections from Greece*
CareNotes Collective

ISBN: 978-1-942173-14-4
$15.00
Page count: 144
Subjects: Health / Mental Health / Social
Movements

**The present way of life is a war against our
bodies. Can we build the capacity and necessary infrastructure to heal ourselves and
transform the societal conditions that continue to mentally and physically harm us?**

Amidst the perpetual crises of capitalism is a careful resistance—organized
by medical professionals and community members, students and workers,
citizens and migrants. *For Health Autonomy: Horizons of Care Beyond Austerity—Reflections from Greece* explores the landscape of care spaces coordinated
by autonomous collectives in Greece. These projects operate in fierce resistance to austerity, state violence and abandonment, and the neoliberal structure of the healthcare industry that are failing people.

For Health Autonomy is a powerful collection of first-hand accounts of
those who join together to build new possibilities of care and develop concrete
alternatives based on the collective ability of communities and care workers to
replace our dependency on police and prisons.